THE GREEN SPACE

**GLUCKSMAN
IRISH DIASPORA**

IN THE GLUCKSMAN IRISH DIASPORA SERIES

Kevin Kenny, General Editor

Nicholas Wolf, Associate Editor

America and the Making of an Independent Ireland: A History
Francis M. Carroll

The Coffin Ship: Migration and Community during Ireland's Great Famine
Cian T. McMahon

Changing Land: Diaspora Activism and the Irish Land War
Niall Whelehan

The Irish Revolution: A Global History
Edited by Patrick Mannion and Fearghal McGarry

Hereafter: The Telling Life of Ellen O'Hara
Vona Groarke

*Homeward Bound: Return Migration from Ireland and India
at the End of the British Empire*
Niamh Dillon

Young Ireland: A Global Afterlife
Christopher Morash

Aiding Ireland: The Great Famine and the Rise of Transnational Philanthropy
Anelise Hanson Shrout

The Green Space: The Transformation of the Irish Image
Marion R. Casey

The Green Space

The Transformation of the Irish Image

Marion R. Casey

* * *

NEW YORK UNIVERSITY PRESS
New York

NEW YORK UNIVERSITY PRESS
New York www.nyupress.org
© 2024 by New York University

All rights reserved

Library of Congress Cataloging-in-Publication Data
Names: Casey, Marion R., 1962– author.
Title: The green space : the transformation of the Irish image / Marion R. Casey.
Description: New York : New York University Press, [2024] | Series: The Glucksman Irish diaspora series | Includes bibliographical references and index.
Identifiers: LCCN 2023040779 (print) | LCCN 2023040780 (ebook) | ISBN 9781479817450 (hardback) | ISBN 9781479817498 (ebook) | ISBN 9781479817504 (ebook other)
Subjects: LCSH: National characteristics, Irish. | Irish—Ethnic identity. | Irish Americans—History. | Ireland—History—20th century.
Classification: LCC DA925 .C324 2024 (print) | LCC DA925 (ebook) | DDC 941.5082—dc23/eng/20231228
LC record available at https://lccn.loc.gov/2023040779
LC ebook record available at https://lccn.loc.gov/2023040780

This book is printed on acid-free paper, and its binding materials are chosen for strength and durability. We strive to use environmentally responsible suppliers and materials to the greatest extent possible in publishing our books.

Manufactured in the United States of America

10 9 8 7 6 5 4 3 2 1

Also available as an ebook

For Angela and Mel

CONTENTS

List of Figures and Tables ix

Introduction 1

1. Vested Interests 7
2. Media Matters 20
3. Cultural Currency 53
4. Racial Reckoning 87
5. Selling Value 123
6. Emerald Sheen 153
7. Come Back to Erin 189

Conclusion 211

Acknowledgments 217

Abbreviations 219

Notes 221

Bibliography 277

Index 309

About the Author 323

FIGURES AND TABLES

I.1. St. Patrick's Day Parade, Dublin, Ireland, March 17, 2013 . . . 3

1.1. Annual Ball, United Irish Counties Association (UICA), New York, 1942 14

2.1. Advertisement for Coca-Cola, "How Americans make friends in Ireland," 1943 37

3.1. Advertisement for Ireland at the World's Fair, *St. Louis Republic*, 1904 66

3.2. Promotion for the 17th Annual UICA Feis, Central Park, New York City, 1949 80

4.1. "John Bull, Thrown Out of U.S. Front Door, Tries the Rear," *Irish World*, 1926 93

4.2. "The Wearing of the Grin," *Life*, March 1927 109

5.1. Belleek butter dish, fifth mark, 1955 to 1965 133

5.2. Irish Shamrock 300 Recording Tape, 1948 140

Table 1. Sample of Irish words registered as trademarks with the U.S. Patent Office, 1899–1966 141

5.3. Irish coffee demonstration, circa 1964 149

6.1. Postcard, St. Patrick's Day, circa 1907 161

6.2. Sheet music cover, "The Wearing of the Green," 1909 . . . 173

6.3. Advertisement for *Smiling Irish Eyes*, 1929 181

7.1. Postcard, "Kissing the Blarney Stone," circa 1913 194

7.2. Souvenir, Arklow Pottery, circa 1955 205

C.1. Program cover, *The Colleens*, Chautauqua, 1919 214

Introduction

As the twenty-first century opened, Irish was everywhere all at once—on television, the internet, stages, screens, and bestseller lists. Every March, supermarkets sold shamrock-shaped ravioli, and retailers pushed green. New York's Museum of Modern Art named the Aran sweater one of the world's most iconic garments.[1] To explain this phenomenon and unpack its array of images requires a history. Borrowing from math and science, we must recognize a binary system to which Ireland and the United States contribute codes that, together, form a matrix. Since green traditionally signifies Irish and this book is about Irish images, I call that matrix the green space.

How does the green space work? Think of it as a virtual storage unit to which everyone has the key. Open the door and rummage through the artifacts and detritus of high and low culture. Find anything in that mix, from parody to the universal. Pull out whatever you want, and adapt it as needed. There is no one to stop you, as there once was. The green space thus offers a suggestive model for understanding the power dynamics behind any ethnic image and the ramifications of exerting or losing control over time.[2]

Almost every Irish image has a deep connection to the green space. Irish Spring, for example—a famous Colgate-Palmolive brand of soap since the 1970s—has its origins in Schultz and Company's "Great Original and Only Genuine Irish Soap," said to have "national repute" in 1870. Based in Zanesville, Ohio, Schultz claimed that "the cheap green and blue soaps" then flooding the market were poor imitations of their own, which had distinctive packaging: not only the word *Irish* but a couple dancing a jig and the nationalist phrase "Erin go Bragh" (Ireland Forever). Irish washerwomen certainly did enough laundry in the United States to associate ethnicity with industry and cleanliness, although negative images of the Irish were far more current at the time.[3] Irish, like all brands with longevity, acquired meaning in this way.[4] A green pitch could expand almost any consumer market by appealing to heritage or just to the vaguely familiar. Over time, Irish brand personality was so robust that it could sell almost anything: tea in 1901, lemons in the 1930s, cigarettes in the 1950s, breakfast cereal in the 1960s, and Irish coffee derivatives marketed as "Irish Cream" liqueurs from the 1970s. In March 1998, the Gambrinus Company of San Antonio, Texas, promoted Corona Extra—its premium beer, served with a slice of lime—as "All the Green You Need on St. Pat's." Green four-leaf clovers dangled from the sombrero worn by the Mexican man in that ad, which ran in New York's *Irish Voice* newspaper.[5] This kind of consensual commercial application was still effective in the early 2000s, inspiring the Häagen-Dazs flavor "Irish Cream Brownie" as well as a limited-edition Glade air freshener scent called "Marshmallow Irish Cream."[6]

Today, one cannot think or write about the Irish, whether in America or in Ireland, without confronting the limitations imposed by this way of engaging with Irish that has been circulating since the nineteenth century and is being disseminated globally now.[7] Various aspects have been perceptively analyzed as popular culture, but the Irish image has not been addressed from a historical perspective.[8] The scholarship that exists usually begins and ends with contemporary manifestations—like Lucky Charms cereal, Celtic tattoos, and *Riverdance*—that are interpreted as cultural texts to fit into a postmodern literary criticism in which consumption is colonial, kitsch is lowbrow, and ethnicity is overperformed.[9] This approach privileges Ireland as the magnetic north and positions Americans as ignorant and Irish Americans as sentimental. It also obscures their interactions over time as well as the extent of cross-fertilization in the green space.

While Irish permeates popular culture, popular culture is not the sole influence on ways of understanding its meanings. In the 1980 U.S. census, 40.2 million Americans claimed some Irish ancestry, no matter how tenuous in practice. That number increased to 44.4 million in 1990.[10] Thirty years later, however, one in ten (31.5 million) checked the same census box, underscoring that Irish in the United States is a choice, not an obligation. *The Green Space* takes a new approach to understanding this vast Irish America as well as Irish as a multidimensional discourse engaged with by non-Irish and by contemporary Ireland. When the sociologist Andrew Greeley observed in 1971 that "tens of thousands of

Saxons, Africans, Teutons, Semites, Slavs and Latins will march down Fifth Avenue [on St. Patrick's Day] and proclaim the glories of the Emerald Isle," he was pointing to an elasticity that could make anyone Irish for a day. Behind the jumbo green hats and false red beards that signal Irish along modern parade routes is more than a cute leprechaun or a despised stereotype.[11] Green hats and red beards are neither ethnic nor national on their own. Even in combination, they are neither authentically Irish, illegitimately Irish, nor for better or worse, tasteless. But they are ciphers in the green space. Repeated use makes them a powerful and profitable image that is difficult for people to resist, especially for those, in Greeley's words, who "stopped being Irish the day before it became alright to be Irish."[12] That vacuum allowed the unfettered appropriation of Irish as opposed to genuine appreciation for an ethnic heritage and culture for the rest of the twentieth century.

The Green Space follows the transformation of the Irish image from downtrodden and despised ("No Irish Need Apply") to universally claimed and acclaimed ("Kiss Me, I'm Irish"). This book, therefore, is not a traditional history of an ethnic group; nor is it about "Irishness" or

Figure I.1. Dressed for the occasion, this group of spectators attends the 2013 St. Patrick's Day parade in Dublin, Ireland. Photo by Clodagh Kilcoyne © Getty Images.

"hibernophilia." Irish as an image evolved only partly within the history of the Irish in America. Its full dimensions unfolded in a much broader national and international context. Both Ireland and the United States are invested in this evolution, sometimes reciprocally. Michael Roarty, a second-generation Irish American who was chief marketing officer for the German American brewing giant Anheuser-Busch, boosted sales by making a neon shamrock shorthand for Budweiser beer in bars across America during the 1980s. To expand into the European market, Budweiser sponsored the Irish Derby, Ireland's premiere horse race, from 1986 to 2007 and licensed Guinness to brew its pale lager beer in 1987.[13] The reason this worked is because the codes alcohol, shamrock, and sweepstakes were already established in the green space.

Indeed, how to convey or represent Irish in the United States was a protracted struggle between the 1890s and the 1960s. That time frame covers the birth of the modern Irish nation-state, tracks the emergence of markets for mass communication and consumption in America, and follows the steady maturation of Irish America. In other words, it was a dynamic period politically, socially, and culturally for those with a vested interest in the Irish image. Chapter 1 of *The Green Space* offers a brief historical synopsis of Irish immigration to America and of modern Ireland's relationship with the United States to establish the wide array of constituents behind the cultivation, preservation, and dissemination of Irish images in the twentieth century. Then thematic chapters engage with image-making from six related vantage points.

Preconceptions about Irish character and culture routinely colored news reporting during this period. How American print and broadcast journalism reconciled images rooted in the nineteenth century with political developments in Ireland, especially after the creation of the Irish Free State, is essential to understanding what was at stake vis-à-vis image-making. Media mattered, as discussed in chapter 2, and so did efforts to counter negative depictions using the arts and education as cultural currency. This became complicated when older methods that promoted respectability were rejected by those for whom Gaelic culture, as embodied in traditional folk arts, was more Irish. Since Ireland was not a simple peasant country and America was not full of Stage Irishmen, chapter 3 focuses on the tensions that arose over whose image should have primacy.

Ireland (twenty-six of its thirty-two counties) won independence from Great Britain as the United States entered a fraught period in its history. During debates on immigration restriction in the 1920s, Irish Americans intentionally deployed Irish in racial terms by associating nationality with blood. They aggressively opposed the new national origins quotas by using historical arguments to specifically undermine an alternative image, Scotch Irish, that complicated calculations. Since the Irish Free State was indifferent to what Irish Americans believed was Anglo-Saxon bias at the highest levels of American society, chapter 4 reveals how this strategy eventually backfired in the 1960s, with ramifications for image and for immigration from Ireland.

The ways in which this political and cultural history became intertwined with, reinforced by, or altered for profit are the subjects of chapters 5 through 7. Because Ireland was a country not generally known for manufacturing and, indeed, more often stereotyped as incapable of personal or economic industry, it emphasized quality, skill, and artistry when showcasing certain products in the United States. The American marketplace was a critical arena for familiarizing consumers with a material concept of Irish, but chapter 5 argues that it was also where imitations undercut Irish commercial progress as well as image. This is most clearly seen in legal battles over trademarks.

Likewise, as St. Patrick's Day emerged as the first ethnic holiday in the American calendar, March 17 changed from a civic and religious celebration of ethnicity into a secular and commercial opportunity. The holiday's popularity rose in direct proportion to its trivialization by business interests, including motion picture producers, exhibitors, and promoters. The American spin—an emerald sheen—put on St. Patrick's Day became so pervasive that it was widely accepted in the United States as Irish. Ultimately, Ireland itself became a commodity packaged and sold to Americans using specific images and places long associated with Irish. To be successful as a tourist destination, it had to be transformed from a troubled country of successive famines and political unrest into an idealized pastoral land that rivaled any for its breathtaking scenery and friendly people. Only by reaching deep into the green space could any appeal to "come back to Erin" be accomplished.

Throughout this book, I suggest that the power of the ethnic image in the United States is separate and distinct from the processes of acculturation and assimilation, even more so when the homeland adopts and uses codes familiar to Americans.¹⁴ *The Green Space* demonstrates that debates over authenticity are now moot. In 1996, the Republic of Ireland inaugurated the St. Patrick's Festival, a four-day extravaganza of public performances that includes a parade with thousands of participants, many from overseas. This intentionally wrests the public's focus on March 17 celebrations away from Irish America and fixes it on Ireland. As festival promotional material frames it, Dublin is now "the epicentre of celebrations of all things Irish—a true representation of the ever-expanding spectrum of Irish identity and culture."¹⁵ Miriam Lord observed in 2007, "There is no shame in silly hats . . . sartorial decorum on St. Patrick's Day is a thing of the past." The twenty-first century Irish took that baggage, she explained to readers of the *Irish Times*, and stitched "it into cheesy leprechaun suits."¹⁶ Whether we like it or not, the green space enables cultural gymnastics like this.

The Green Space is a history of contested Irish image-making that examines who the stakeholders were and why; the media, cultural, commercial, and political forces that shaped their debates; and how certain representations became enduring. Why do people think the way they do about Irish? How did that happen? From this perspective, *The Green Space* is also relevant to the ways in which any immigrant or ethnic group in the United States is represented by itself as well as by others.

1

Vested Interests

For hundreds of years, Ireland and North America have been intertwined. Conditions of empire dictated the westward movement of people from one to the other so that throughout the seventeenth and eighteenth centuries, the Irish found their way across the Atlantic through various colonial avenues. As did most from the British Isles, the Irish came as paying passengers, indentured servants, administrators, merchants, transported convicts, sailors, or soldiers, with an estimated 350,000 to 500,000 arriving between 1700 and 1820.[1] With so many local variables in both the sending and receiving countries, Irish as a descriptive word was far more expansive than it would be later. Ireland's people were culturally, socially, and religiously mixed as well as geographically scattered. Presbyterians farming on the American frontier like Andrew Jackson's parents; the New York City merchants trading with the enemy during the French and Indian War; the thieves caught and hung in Burlington, New Jersey, in 1765; and the Carroll cousins of Maryland, who worked on the Declaration of Independence and the U.S. Constitution—all defied ethnic homogeneity. Thus, the Irish were loved and loathed in about equal measure throughout the colonies of the New World.[2]

At the end of the eighteenth century, perceptions about the Irish quickly altered. Now they were called wild—seen as dangerously independent, prone to excess—and their support for the French and American Revolutions as well as the 1798 rebellion in Ireland appeared to prove it.[3] As Catholic emigration became more regular and more intense, any memories of Irish republicanism and patriotism during the American War of Independence were replaced by suspicions of radicalism and foreign allegiance. In the nineteenth century, Irish Americans kept General Richard Montgomery, who died at the siege of Quebec in 1775, and John Barry, a captain in the Continental navy, as their heroes for these very reasons. Anti-Irish prejudice flourished as the public identification of Irish with Catholicism grew closer and as an expanding American Catholic Church, with an Irish patina, provoked a nativist backlash.[4] For a variety of historically rooted rationalizations, all connected to image, Irish Protestants in the United States increasingly preferred Scotch Irish as their ethnic designation. It neatly set apart those with Ulster roots at the same time that it made them racially and religiously more akin to the perceived American norm, one that did not include Blacks, Indians, or Catholics.[5]

During a critical period from the 1830s to the 1870s, 2.7 million Irish were propelled westward by economic conditions and a multiyear famine.[6] Their arrival coincided with key geographic and metropolitan expansion in the United States. An enormous demand for workers created livelihoods for the Irish, but it also raised their visibility as housing, health care, and religious and ethnic tolerance strained to adapt. The Irish were "the most corrupt, the most debased, and the most brutally ignorant portion of the population of our large cities," declared the *New England Review* in 1834.[7] Such attitudes made the Irish image even more vulnerable. By midcentury, negative connotations frequently outweighed positive ones so that "ignorant, turbulent, and brutal," "lip Republicans," "Jesuits in disguise," and "drunkards and criminals" meant Irish in American popular discourse.[8] Even widely known songs about emigration and exile—like "Kathleen Mavourneen," which was published in America in 1840—associated Ireland and the Irish with raw emotion and melancholy rather than reason.[9]

Immigration from Ireland continued almost unabated for the rest of the nineteenth century. Another 1.5 million Irish left for the United States between 1881 and 1920.[10] There were no actual legal barriers erected to prevent their entry and settlement, thus emigration quickly became an accepted and expected part of Irish life, particularly as rural inheritance patterns changed in the aftermath of the Great Famine. An informal but effective system of integrating these newcomers evolved. Relatives and remittances directed the migratory flow from specific areas in Ireland to specific areas of the United States.[11] Fully 89 percent of the four million who identified themselves as first- and second-generation Irish Americans in the 1890 U.S. census lived in a broad swath of territory from the northeastern seaboard to the north central states. Within that, New York dominated settlement patterns, followed by Massachusetts and Pennsylvania, then Illinois.[12] Fueled by thousands of letters extolling the tangible benefits in America, chain-migration from Ireland funneled men and women primarily to Boston, Philadelphia, Chicago, and the New York metropolitan area, then on to smaller industrial cities and towns in their immediate hinterland.[13] There, Irish America was built upon social, religious, political, and economic networks that had been sustaining vibrant communities for at least fifty years.[14]

When the dust finally settled on this great movement of the Irish across the Atlantic, the contours of Irish America were clearly visible and fully matured. The quiet and steady integration of the second, third, and fourth generations gradually redeemed the Irish image, while self-help initiatives, Civil War pensions, high rates of naturalization, education, and political participation all accrued to a better impression of the Irish. Still, as the twentieth century opened, that impression was narrow: even though farmers, Protestants, and Canada were all part of the story of Irish immigration to North America, the phrase Irish America usually described a Catholic people living in the urban United States.[15]

The very existence of substantial communities of friends and relations abroad—reinforced by a continually refreshed first generation and rising numbers of American-born children and grandchildren as well as social mobility over time—was a powerful incentive to those who were restless or disillusioned at home. With nonfarm work scarce in fin-de-siècle Ireland, the lure of good wages, youthful adventure, and marriage in the United States proved an irresistible force: "Children learn from their childhood that their destiny is America; and as they grow up, the thought is set before them as a thing to hope for," observed Michael O'Riordan in 1905.[16] "We always talked and dreamed of going to America. . . . My love for America was strong before I ever arrived," recalled Jimmy Lucey, who was born in 1897 near Macroom, County Cork, and emigrated to the States in 1923.[17] Martin Ó Cadhain perhaps expressed it best in his short story "The Year of 1912": "Life and her ideas of it had been shaped and defined by the fame of America, the wealth of America, the amusements of America, the agonised longing to go to America."[18]

By 1920, there were 203,450 Irish-born living in New York City's five boroughs (without counting significant numbers in neighboring

Jersey City, Newark, and Yonkers), followed in population by Philadelphia (64,590), Boston (57,011), and Chicago (56,786).[19] The children of Irish immigrants made such concentrations even larger. They all had a recognizable Irish subculture based on neighborhood, parish, political clubhouse, social and benevolent organizations, and local sports that helped hundreds of thousands make the adjustment to life in the United States.[20] Overlapping associational relationships and high rates of English literacy often translated into municipal influence via civil service jobs and union membership, thereby privileging the Irish working class and providing a reliable path for upward social mobility.[21]

This great urban base, with its multiple, variously assimilated generations, ensured that Irish Americans remained significant politically, economically, and culturally even as their share of the total population was dwarfed by the numbers of southern and eastern Europeans settling in cities across the United States as well as African Americans migrating from the rural South. When Jewish immigrants needed a model, they didn't have to look far: "We identified the Irishman not only with the English language but also with the image of what an American looked like."[22] In New York, where most American Jews encountered the Irish, Irish America was incredibly diverse, though proportionally more middle class than elsewhere in the country.[23] There, in the first few decades of the twentieth century, George M. Cohan, the grandson of Famine-era immigrants, built a musical theater legacy, while construction magnate John D. Crimmins and communications pioneer Clarence Mackay (both also substantial patrons of the arts) became second-generation success stories. At the same time, nascent labor leader Mike Quill (a transit clerk) and future mayor William O'Dwyer (a policeman) were immigrant legends in the making. Boxing and baseball made sports heroes of Jack Dempsey and John McGraw, and Olympic champions—like marathoner John J. Hayes, the grandson of Tipperary immigrants, as well as track-and-field star Martin Sheridan, who left County Mayo for New York when he was nineteen—inspired pride well beyond Irish America.[24]

With promises of opportunity such as these, the Irish continued to leave for America in numbers that represented a significant loss of population for Ireland. Another half-million or more arrived between 1921 and the end of the twentieth century despite a series of American federal immigration restrictions that made emigrating a more expensive and involved process than moving to neighboring England.[25] Emigration was sensitive in the Irish context, especially after Ireland achieved political independence in 1921. There had been an implicit expectation that once free of British rule, no one would need to leave; instead, the country hemorrhaged at regular intervals. Entrenched social and economic policies delayed inheritance, postponed marriage, and stunted rewarding employment, while Ireland's standard of living continued to lag behind that of the United States, especially for modern essentials like running water and electricity.[26] The *Cork Weekly Examiner* concluded, "It is hard to blame such persons for seeking to better themselves abroad" when commenting on the "increasing tide of immigration" in 1925.[27] The *Irish Echo*, which debuted in New York in 1928, was quickly filled with advertisements for reunion dances pitched at "boys and girls" newly arrived from various counties.[28] A ticket to America enabled siblings to reconstitute their families, and despite a significant fare increase between 1892 and 1939 (from $19 to $140 for steerage and $40 to $184 for second class), passage money was often the most welcomed gift for relatives and friends in Ireland.[29]

The 1941 census revealed that Ireland's population was 2.9 million down from a high of 8.5 million a century earlier. As overseas possibilities glittered, some wondered if the Irish in Ireland were headed for extinction, since "more than one out of every three persons born" in Ireland seemed destined to leave it.[30] The New York publisher McGraw Hill was more sensational, publishing *The Vanishing Irish* in 1953, in which writers like Seán Ó Faoláin and Paul Vincent Carroll anticipated a 1956 Irish government report that blamed depopulation on "the cinema and the radio, and above all by direct experience either personal or through relatives" for highlighting the attractions of urban life abroad. By and large, these women and men reinforced the constants of traditional Irish emigration—that is, they tended to be underwritten by remittances, follow chain-migration networks, settle in cities, enter the American workforce through ethnic niche employment, and have very low rates of return.[31]

As Ireland struggled to come to terms with continuing emigration that pushed the population on the island even lower—more than eighty-four thousand left for the United States in the 1940s and 1950s, while five hundred thousand more went to Great Britain[32]—Irish America attained a popularity quite unimaginable only a hundred years earlier: "Ireland lives and flourishes in the United States," crowed the *Chicago Daily Tribune* in 1949, "and its strain is one of our greatest."[33] Although only 10 percent of Irish emigrants were choosing the United States as their destination by the 1960s, there they also had the company of some twenty million Americans who claimed Irish birth or descent and for whom Irish heritage had been transformed by wartime patriotism "into a major asset."[34] By that time, the Irish image in America had ostensibly made a full 180-degree turn, symbolized by the 1960 election of John Fitzgerald Kennedy as president of the United States.[35]

* * *

In the early twentieth century, political developments in Ireland caused some fluctuation in perceptions about the Irish. The Gaelic Revival movement, the Easter rebellion and its suppression in 1916, the subsequent war for independence with England, the Anglo-Irish Treaty that created the Irish Free State in 1921, and then a bitter civil war seared issues of national self-identity on the Irish.[36] In 1937, Ireland took the name Éire; twelve years later, it became the Republic of Ireland. "Irish Ireland" was the identity proclaimed by the government, a policy that exalted the position of agriculture in the nation's economy and Gaelic as its official language, thereby enhancing the already enormous significance of the rugged western half of the country as the standard for authenticity.[37] The harp was chosen as Ireland's symbol, and new coins were struck that reproduced images of native birds, livestock, and fish. This definition of Irish was then exported to the United States through diplomacy, the promotion of trade goods, and the development of tourism. Unofficially, Ireland's image of itself as a society outside of time, unaffected by the modern world, reached sophisticated American audiences through the 1934 fictional documentary *Man of Aran* by filmmaker Robert Flaherty and the Harvard-funded fieldwork of the anthropologists Conrad Arensberg and Solon Kimball, who published *The Irish Countryman* in 1937.[38]

Those who left Ireland for the United States during this period came of age in turbulent times; they were, to a greater extent than any previous generation of Irish immigrants, men and women who were often personally politicized by events they had witnessed.[39] In addition, they had a greater sense of pride because the cultural ideology of "Irish Ireland" had been nurtured in tandem with revolutionary nationalism for at least a generation.[40] As it had so often in the past, the fertile soil provided by Irish American networks of associations, friends, and family now began to incubate a new way of articulating Irish that was intended to help Ireland buttress and fully extend its new political legitimacy. A distinct Irish identity became so closely equated with traditional music, for example, that in 1925, Columbia Records began to cross-list jigs and reels in its foreign catalog. Foreign meant a new ethnic market, whereas previously this kind of music had simply been one of many strands in American popular music.[41]

In this milieu, Irish was culturally and structurally more insular. The New York, Boston, Philadelphia, and Chicago Irish communities were soon directed by leaders who emerged from among the new immigrants, and when the United States received another wave of emigrants from Ireland between 1945 and 1965, they integrated seamlessly into communities that sustained societies based on place of origin in Ireland as well as language, music, dance, drama, glee, and sports clubs, many of which continued to flourish for decades.[42] These all fostered a strong sense of identity. "The South Bronx was such an Irish neighborhood," recalled James O'Beirne, the son of immigrant parents who grew up in New York City in the early 1950s, "that until I was seven or eight years old I actually thought everybody in America was Irish."[43] The small farms of western Ireland were still an emigrant nursery; therefore, the young people arriving in America after World War II had much in common with their aunts and uncles who had emigrated in the 1920s. Connections to home were reinforced and became even tighter as air travel and telephones began to collapse the Atlantic divide.

There were four main weekly newspapers circulated nationally to serve this community: Patrick Ford's *Irish World* (1870–1984), John O'Connor's *Irish Advocate* (1893–1988), John Devoy's *Gaelic American* (1903–51, then merged with the *Irish World*), and Charles Connolly's *Irish Echo* (1928–). Together they were the voice of a twentieth-century Irish subculture within Irish America.[44] New York emerged as its epicenter. The percentage of the Irish-born living in New York City doubled from 17 percent in

1900 to 34 percent in 1960.⁴⁵ Before suburbanization accelerated thereafter, they consistently averaged about two hundred thousand there, and with approximately four hundred thousand second-generation Irish, New York's Irish stock population was greater than that of Dublin or Belfast.⁴⁶

Figure 1.1. The 1942 ball of the United Irish Counties Association (UICA) at the Hotel Commodore on East Forty-Second Street in New York City gathered together a crowd of first-generation Irish, many of whom had emigrated from Ireland in the 1920s. Formal evening wear (or service uniforms during the war years) projected an image of personal respectability and patriotism, while collectively they promoted "Irish Ireland" through the work of the UICA. Credit: Kathleen Kearney Walsh Papers (AIA.029), box 4, folder 6, Archives of Irish America, Special Collections, Bobst Library, New York University.

Of course, things were much more complicated because this newest Irish America was also part of a much larger, much older Catholic America. One of every two American Catholics had Irish-born parents in 1890, and from that time Irish men and women dominated the clergy and religious of the American church, serving in parishes but also as teachers, social workers, and administrators throughout big city dioceses. Despite intellectually and politically divisive issues among them, the Irish shared their faith with Germans, Poles, and Italians. For many, Catholicism, broadly defined, offered a worldview with a greater call for them than ethnicity, especially when recurrent nativism made the appearance of unity an imperative.[47] As successive classes of Irish American alumni from Catholic colleges like Fordham (1841), Villanova (1842), Boston College (1863), and Loyola (1870) entered the professions in New York, Philadelphia, Boston, and Chicago, they were joined by high school graduates who made their careers in accounting, insurance, real estate, education, health professions, and sports, swelling the ranks of Catholic fraternal societies like the Knights of Columbus. Comfortable, even wealthy, Irish Americans like these supported an extensive network of Catholic institutions and charities that were critical to the effectiveness of urban social work at this time.

Nevertheless, Catholics continued to shoulder "otherness" and the related problems of negative perceptions—as when Alfred E. Smith was defeated in his bid for the presidency of the United States in 1928. Anti-Catholicism was partially challenged by a large body of journalism in newspapers and magazines frequently edited by Irish Americans. The *Boston Pilot*, the *Freeman's Journal*, the *Catholic World*, the *Catholic News*, and the *Catholic Herald* were among the newspapers with influence on the Irish American middle class, first and second cousins of the new immigrants from Ireland, who were straddling ethnic and religious worlds in transition in the decades immediately preceding Irish independence.[48]

* * *

Ireland may have declared that the harp, not the shamrock, officially signified Irish, but American popular culture, not to mention Irish America, was not so easily persuaded.[49] For many generations of Irish in America, an older understanding retained a powerful nostalgic appeal and an immediacy of recognition. The sentimental symbolism of the color green, shamrocks, and St. Patrick's Day attenuated a folk culture based on Ireland's long tradition of emigration to the United States since the eighteenth century. Indeed, that symbolism was embedded in Thomas Moore's *Irish Melodies*, which by 1841 were already so ubiquitous in America that to criticize them was akin to "venturing a new ode to the Moon, or endeavouring after a new praise of the Rose."[50] It was this image—in print and broadcast media, on commercial goods, in the theater and the classroom—that pervaded America as Irish while simultaneously eclipsing knowledge of contemporary Ireland.

American mass culture was itself an emerging national phenomenon undergoing rapid transformation at precisely the time Ireland was working toward independence.[51] While a common shopping and entertainment experience had the potential to speed acculturation to a recognizable American standard by erasing Irishness, it was an equally powerful means of condensing a very long and complicated Irish American experience for the mainstream. This binary relationship between ethnic image and reality is reflected in a 1905 *New York Daily Tribune* news headline on emigration: "Race of Hibernian Cooks and Housemaids Will Soon Be Extinct."[52] Readers would have immediately understood this as a reference to Bridget, one of the stock Irish characters that were then current in America whose blunders and bluster in the kitchen provided comic relief on the stage and in jokes. But the headline also sums up contemporary American impressions of the Irish as a separate people and as America's white serving class. This was an image reinforced by employers who depended on the Irish every day.

In addition to Bridgets, American audiences were familiar with characterizations of Irish policemen, politicians, priests, laborers, widows, and rogues whose speech was peppered with peculiar expressions like "begorra," "darlin'," "divil," and "faith."[53] From the immensely popular plays of Dion Boucicault and Edward Harrigan to the syndicated Mr. Dooley columns by Finley Peter Dunne—each a different representational tradition than the sober and moralizing Catholic fiction of novelists like Mary Anne Sadlier—such depictions entered the green space, where they coexisted until freely reinterpreted by journalists, advertisers, and businessmen for their commercial and nostalgic possibilities. By then, the Irish were a convenient source of raw material for American consumption in general as well as an emerging market for late-generation Irish Americans.[54]

Within living memory, the Irish in America had been the focus of antiforeign, anti-Catholic nativism; now, significantly more educated and white collar by 1900 than it had been in 1850, Irish America actively cultivated respectability.[55] Appeals to memory that turned a blind eye to reality and overlooked painful episodes were potentially lucrative under these circumstances. Tin Pan Alley—the center of the American popular music publishing world and an engine of mass culture from the 1880s to the 1920s—churned out sheet music for parlor pianos about Killarney and Tipperary, Irish eyes, and dear old mothers. Technology helped these songs remain in circulation. The Irish-born tenor John McCormack recorded the definitive version of "Mother Machree" for Victor in 1911; it sold so well that it was reissued in 1927, inspiring the young director John Ford (the son of County Galway immigrants to Portland, Maine) to adapt the song as a screenplay for the 1928 silent film of the same name distributed by Fox.

Consumers of such sheet music, 78 rpm records, and movies were not exclusively Irish by birth or ancestry, but in time, these songs and the images they projected were absorbed by Irish America, where, beyond the third generation especially, little or no distinction was made between them and any Irish folk songs that might have been heard from the lips of grandparents. "All was 'bliss and blarney,'" concluded Daniel Patrick Moynihan in 1963 about such sanitized nostalgia.[56] Radio gave Irish Americans even greater access to this seductive new image of themselves, full of sweet colleens and sentiment for the Old Country. It was an image with no serious challenger, particularly when immigration from Ireland was reduced by national origins legislation in the 1920s, then the Depression and World War II.[57] Bing Crosby had top-ten hits in 1944 with "Too-Ra-Loo-Ra-Loo-Ral (That's an Irish Lullaby)," in 1946 with "McNamara's Band," and in 1949 with "Galway Bay," confirming that these kinds of American songs could still define Irish in popular culture.[58] But even old nineteenth-century favorites, like Moore's "The Minstrel Boy" and "The Harp That Once through Tara's Halls" or Boucicault's "The Wearing of the Green," were given new currency by the new media, anchoring American and Irish American perceptions of Ireland and the Irish to specific romantic notions that were, in fact, alien to modern Ireland and the Irish.

Irish immigrants arriving in Boston, Chicago, Philadelphia, and New York in the 1920s, and even more so in the 1950s, encountered a hybrid image—a sometimes dim, sometimes garish reflection—of themselves on radio, records, the stage, newsreels, and television; in moving pictures; on greeting cards, sheet music, and novelty items; as well as in newspapers, magazines, and books—all of which were targeted to consumers who were removed from Ireland by either the distance of generations or non-Irish ancestry. Unbounded by time or place, that image was endlessly recycled. For example, the Irish immigrant couple Maggie and Jiggs, who debuted in George McManus's 1913 comic strip *Bringing Up Father*, had a long career in a variety of media and material formats for more than eighty years. Their humor hinged on the incongruity of Jiggs's rough, working-class ways and Maggie's social ambitions—on an image of the Old World fumbling to make its way in the New World. The implications of this particular Irish image in American popular culture just as Ireland was becoming a nation are almost incalculable: thirty-one senators and ninety-one congressional representatives were among the Washington glitterati who toasted the twentieth anniversary of Maggie and Jiggs in 1932.[59]

The new vision of Irish that independent Ireland promoted, and that Irish immigrants in the twentieth century tried hard to support, never really posed a threat to a well-established American paradigm about Irish. Within a very short time, the Irish themselves had to reassess their strategy vis-à-vis their image in the United States. Ireland began to appropriate familiar symbols and stereotypes for official use, only partially to lend dignity to the hackneyed; as American popular culture regularly demonstrated, an ethnic gloss was profitable, and Ireland itself could no longer ignore the economic potential of its American commercial image. At the 1939–40 New York World's Fair, the government of Ireland's much-anticipated trade promotion pavilion was built in the shape of a shamrock. When Aer Lingus, Ireland's national airline, inaugurated transatlantic flights in the 1950s, the three-leafed clover was emblazoned on the tails of its aircraft, and Shamrock Thriftflite was the name of its most affordable airfare.[60] Thereafter, as

Ireland validated Irish in the language Americans had long been conditioned to understand, the economic possibilities were endless.

When President John F. Kennedy visited Ireland in June of 1963, Ireland and Irish America were closer than at any previous time in history, a portent of the future. The day after he laid a wreath in Wexford Town, the birthplace of U.S. naval commodore John Barry, President Kennedy presented a gift to the Irish nation: a Civil War battlefield flag of the Irish Brigade's Fighting 69th Regiment.[61] By referencing a key turning point in the evolution of the Irish image in America, it was intended to symbolize both their patriotism and resilience. In concluding his address to the Irish Parliament in Dublin, Kennedy said, "My friends: Ireland's hour has come. You have something to give to the world—and that is a future of peace with freedom."[62] But in a *Time* magazine cover story on modern Ireland the following month, Irish playwright Seán O'Casey lamented, "What do we send out to the world now but woeful things—young lads and lassies, porther [Guinness], greyhounds, sweep tickets, and the shamrock green? We've scattered ourselves over the wide world, and left our own sweet land thin."[63]

The dissonance between Kennedy and O'Casey is not just the difference between an American perspective and an Irish one. It is the result of how and why various iterations of Irish were deployed over time, whether as a straightforward noun about a specific people or a loose adjective that was endlessly malleable and only tangentially connected to actual national or ethnic identity. As we will see, America and Ireland had diverged by 1963, but they eventually converged thereafter. The reason was the green space.

2

Media Matters

Between 1890 and 1960, Ireland was transformed from a member of the United Kingdom and of the British Empire into a free and independent republic with membership in the United Nations. In the United States, Ireland's efforts to modernize as well as gain political sovereignty regularly made headlines. Even though current events in the 1910s and 1920s revealed that the Irish were as capable of political intrigue and military strategy as the next in Europe, many American reporters and commentators nevertheless persisted in painting a different portrait. "Glowing accounts of life in the 'wee whitewashed thatched cabin' at the end of a long 'boreen,' where the four-footed beasties mooed a morning welcome through the open windows . . . was all grand grist for the mill of American journalism," observed Muriel Sperry, the Irish-born wife of the dean of the Harvard Divinity School, in the *Atlantic Monthly* in 1934. From her Cambridge, Massachusetts, perspective, she concluded that "many a stay-at-home read it entranced and thrilled vicariously to these flights from reality and the sentimental symbolism of the Celtic Twilight as interpreted by the USA."[1]

Transformations in journalism and the demand for knowledge among the better educated increased public interest in foreign affairs. In newspapers and magazines, as well as in new media such as the radio and newsreels, greater emphasis was placed on interpretive reporting.[2] When it came to the dissemination of information, no place in America compared with New York City. The publishing industry there printed seventy-five million books annually by the 1930s as well as forty-three daily newspapers, "close to" six hundred weekly or monthly periodicals, and 80 percent of all magazines with a national circulation. It handled 65 percent of the total American advertising business. The city also had twenty-two moving picture palaces and 669 movie houses.[3] Book publishing giants like Macmillan & Company; magazines varying in point of view from *Collier's* to *Commonweal*; newsreels distributed by Paramount, Universal, and Time, Inc.; and newspapers like the *New York Times* all helped form American opinions on literature, culture, and current events. During the 1930s, broadcasting news and commentary expanded the popularity of radio, and as technology improved, New York also took the lead in producing material for seventeen million receiving sets on nationally syndicated networks like CBS (with 97 stations) and NBC (with 127).[4]

Americans had access to information on Ireland through such media outlets, but even in ostensibly objective mainstream forums, a disjunction between fact and fiction permeated everything about Ireland and the Irish. Audience point of view was directly influenced by the choice of subjects and the selection of specific writers or commentators as well as by certain vocabulary and the degree of rhetoric used. By the middle of the twentieth century, Americans tended to separate the island of Ireland from Ireland as a nation and, still further, from the Irish as a diaspora people in their midst. This prepared fertile ground for preconceptions that contributed to the transformation of the Irish image.

* * *

British-Irish relations were an important interest in Irish America but never more so than in the last decades of the nineteenth century, when Ireland's agitation for political independence was closely followed. By then, the revolutionary nationalism of the Fenians and the Clan na Gael had yielded to the constitutional nationalism of the Land League and Home Rule movements.[5] Progress on "the Irish Question" was watched by an American media interested in nation-building generally and Anglo-Irish diplomacy specifically. In cities with large Irish American populations, competition for circulation often paid attention to Ireland whether the editors or publishers were "of Irish ways of thinking or not." William Randolph Hearst's papers were particularly vocal.[6] In addition, Irish American journalists with nationalist sympathies worked for some of the major American newspapers so that the subject of Ireland was never far from the news pages. As Paula Blair points out, the escalation of political events on the island from World War I through the 1920s meant an "increase in available material" for newsreels, in particular, but Irish content for all media in general.[7]

The pace and results of constitutional nationalism were slow, causing widespread dissatisfaction in Ireland as well as among Irish people living in the United States. Westminster was still legislating Irish affairs at the start of the First World War. Combined with John Redmond's support for Irish enlistments in the British Army and President Woodrow Wilson's rhetoric about the right to self-determination for small nations, Irish American efforts to achieve self-government in Ireland accelerated. Militant nationalists seized the opportunity to make an armed bid for independence at Easter in 1916 with assistance from the Clan na Gael and their compatriots in America who had long distrusted Redmond's motives.[8] They proclaimed an Irish Republic. In the midst of an international military conflict, the Easter Rising and its suppression by the British focused American journalists' attention on Irish affairs even further.[9]

Éamon de Valera, the highest-ranking leader to escape execution, became head of the political party Sinn Féin in 1917. With Irish independence and withdrawal from the British Parliament as its election platform, Sinn Féin won seventy-three seats in late 1918. This was essentially a public mandate to establish an extralegal parliament, Dáil Éireann, in Dublin with de Valera as its president. Sinn Féin was soon at war for independence with England, and de Valera was touring the United States to raise funds and gain American recognition for the fledgling Irish Republic. Pleas for the latter fell on deaf ears in the White House and at the Paris peace conference, although the U.S. Congress did pass a resolution in favor of Irish self-determination after much lobbying by a new American group, the Friends of Irish Freedom (FOIF).[10] De Valera also used mass media to disseminate his message. He made at least three radio broadcasts over CBS; one assured Americans that the Irish did not hate England and desired peace; another offered a eulogy for Terence MacSwiney, the Lord Mayor of Cork, who died in an English prison after seventy-four days on hunger strike just before de Valera returned to Ireland in December 1920.[11] His frequent visits to the New York office of the *Nation* not only made that weekly journal of opinion a forum for discussion of the Irish republican cause in 1919 and 1920 but resulted in the formation of the American Commission on Conditions in Ireland and, indirectly, the American Committee for Relief in Ireland. "No paper that could command respect would dare take the lead" in pressuring England to change its policy toward Ireland "except *The Nation*," recalled Lewis Gannett two decades later.[12] Reports issued by both commissions focused attention on the excessive use of force during the Anglo-Irish War, increasing American pressure on England to resolve the conflict.[13]

The struggle ended in January 1922 when Dáil Éireann accepted the Anglo-Irish Treaty of December 1921, creating the Irish Free State out of twenty-six of Ireland's thirty-two counties (six counties in Ulster remained part of Great Britain). Ireland now had dominion status within the British Commonwealth. Henry Bayard Swopes, editor of the *New York World*, immediately asked Francis Hackett to write a popular history of Ireland as quickly as possible. Hackett was the Irish-born editor of the *New Republic* and a special correspondent for the *New York World* from 1920 to 1923.[14] In February 1922, the *Washington Post* sold out Hackett's "The Story of the Irish Nation" in a four-part Sunday magazine supplement, and that spring the Century Company published it in book form.[15] The rapid way in which these American publishers were able to capitalize on recent headlines hints at the level of interest in Ireland that existed among readers of the mainstream press. It also indicates the centrality of Irish-born freelance writers like Hackett who were already working in the United States and who were conveniently available to step into roles as Irish spokesmen for the American media.

Hackett positioned the Irish Free State as the triumph over a seven-hundred-year history of trials and oppression. But soon after *The Story of the Irish Nation* was in circulation, Ireland split into supporters of the original concept of an all-Ireland republic (as proclaimed in 1916), led by de Valera, and those who accepted the Treaty and the Irish Free State. De Valera refused to recognize the new constitution that was drafted, objecting to the oath of allegiance to the Crown taken by members of the Dáil and to British retention of certain naval bases in Irish ports. A bitterly fought civil war followed for the remainder of 1922. In New York, Joseph Connolly, the consul general of the (pre–Free State) Irish Republic to the United States, anxiously followed the aftermath of the divisive Treaty debates in the Dáil: "Reports of events in Ireland in the American papers became more and more depressing," he recalled, noting "the definitely hostile attitude of a certain section of the press." He publicly pleaded for unity: "The dignity of Ireland and more particularly the dignity of the Irish race in America demands that unity in the name of our common Motherland." In an ambiguous diplomatic position, Connolly resigned from his post in late November.[16]

The senior Irish journalist in America chronicling subsequent developments was the revolutionary nationalist John Devoy, publisher of the *Gaelic American*, then age seventy-four.[17] He was not at all surprised by the Irish Civil War because he believed de Valera had sown seeds of discord among the Irish in America too, causing an embarrassing organizational rift that robbed Ireland of momentum and financial support at a critical juncture. Keenly aware that American opinion frequently viewed "the Irish as disorderly and prone to rows," Devoy opted to report on American politics in the *Gaelic American* rather than the Irish Civil War.[18] Devoy, in a departure from the expected, backed the Irish Free State as the first step toward a republic and, until his death in 1928, had no reason at all to redeem de Valera's reputation in the American press.[19] De Valera suspected as much as early as 1920, when concerns about his image prompted him to assure his friends in Dublin that his behavior was no different in America than in Ireland: "That will enable you to judge whether anything I may by newspapers be reported to have said is true or false. Never forget that the Press is the instrument used by the enemy—garbled statements, misleading headlines, etc."[20]

Using emergency powers, including internment and executions, the Irish Free State government forced de Valera and his republicans to end hostilities in the spring of 1923. "Back of Irish Revolt Broken," read the headline over Irish prime minister William T. Cosgrave's byline in the *Chicago Daily Tribune* on February 26, 1923. This was one of Ireland's first post–civil war proactive efforts at public relations, probably placed with aid from Devoy and his close associate Judge Daniel F. Cohalan. "Looking at Ireland from the outside, one might imagine that a normal life is non-existent," Cosgrave wrote, pointing to American journalism's preference for the sensational. He continued, "From its nature the press records all abnormal occurrences and ignores the humdrum lives of the average industrious Irish citizens."[21]

News of Ireland was largely filtered through three American press associations: the Associated Press (AP), United Press Associations (UP), and International News Service (INS). Combining new communications technology with journalism that aspired to impartiality, these services reported stories that were disseminated rapidly around the world.[22] The AP, UP, and INS all exchanged news with their three European equivalents based in England, France, and Germany. But impartiality about Ireland was questionable at best, since news of it came either via Reuters of Great Britain or through a foreign correspondent or bureau usually based in London. From at least 1920, it was the policy of the British Foreign Office to propagandize its position on Ireland "through friendly American press correspondents assigned to London."[23] Both the *New York Times* and the *Chicago Daily Tribune* had foreign-based reporters who filed stories on Ireland; the latter's London bureau chief, John Steele, was said to have brokered the initial 1921 negotiations between the Irish republicans and Lloyd George for a scoop during the Anglo-Irish War.[24] Other journalists were not so objective, indulging "in racist stereotyping and deliberate propaganda using a mixture of half-truths, fantasies and lies" or falling "victim to a variety of practical jokes, deceptions and exaggerations" by Irish-based sources "who regarded the picture of Ireland which was presented in the foreign press far less seriously" than the Irish government.[25] By 1930 in New York City, there were no less than twelve English-language daily newspapers serving as media outlets for press association reports on Ireland. These ranged in average circulation from the 36,532 of the *Telegraph* to the 1,319,654 of the *Daily News*.[26] Figures for the *Chicago Tribune* surpassed 650,000 in 1925 and rose to a million thereafter.[27]

The main news stories reported in the United States about Ireland after 1923 were the tasks associated with establishing democratic government—that is, the creation of systems for finance, justice, commerce, elections, and diplomatic representation in the United States as well as the selection of a distinctive currency, flag, and national anthem. The internal political feuds that lingered as a result of the Irish Civil War continued to make headlines, as when the Free State's vice president, Kevin O'Higgins, was assassinated in 1927. But media attention also focused on the scheme to harness the Shannon River as a major source of electricity supply; persisting emigration from Ireland; and a series of Irish Free State legislative acts that restricted divorce, introduced censorship of films and publications, and set up a military tribunal for political crimes. Momentous topics were covered multiple times and had implications for the Irish image.

One of the earliest news sensations of the period was the report of a famine in Ireland in 1925. Famine rang alarm bells in the United States, especially among Irish Americans descended from nineteenth-century famine refugees and survivors, but to non-Irish readers—who had just spent 1922 reading about the Irish Civil War in their newspapers—it added to the impression that Ireland was incapable of handling independence. The Irish government acknowledged that there was distress in parts of the west of the country but declared that talk of famine was "unjustified." The *New York Times* quoted de Valera as saying it was nothing but an English press scare, even though he was opposed to Cosgrave's government and might have been expected to make political capital out of the suggestion of famine in American newspapers. The *Times* used the news to print an editorial, "Irish Difficulties," highlighting political discontent with the Irish Free State among former Home Rule Party members.[28] Throughout February there were more denials (including reports of accusations in the Dáil that special press correspondents with an anti-Irish agenda were exaggerating conditions without evidence), but in New York, relief efforts were organized by Tammany Hall and the New York Kerrymen's Association.[29] Cosgrave's plea for American aid was published in the *Chicago Tribune* on February 2, two days after a report that fifteen thousand Irish children needed to be fed.[30]

A local story consistently covered by the *New York Times* was the case *Irish Free State v. Guaranty Safe Deposit Company*, which was argued in New York courts between 1922 and 1933. As president of the declared Irish Republic, de Valera had spoken to audiences across the United States from 1919 to 1920 and, through a bond-certificate drive, had succeeded in raising $5.8 million as an external loan to Dáil Éireann. The bonds were redeemable, with 5 percent interest, after the withdrawal of British troops. When he returned to Ireland in late 1920, de Valera left nearly half of the money on deposit in New York City banks, which became a point of contention once the Irish Civil War broke out. The money had been raised in the name of the Irish Republic by de Valera, but now he opposed the Irish government recognized by the Anglo-Irish Treaty of 1921.[31]

During the bond-certificate drive, de Valera was at the center of a personality clash and ideological conflict that caused a rift between the

FOIF (anti–de Valera), an Irish American organization headquartered in New York City that advanced $100,000 to get the Irish Bond Drive underway, and a new organization, the American Association for the Recognition of the Irish Republic (AARIR, pro–de Valera), which carried out the actual fundraising.³² The FOIF now aligned on the pro-Treaty side and supported the Free State's lawsuit to gain control over the bond monies in New York. The suit was designed to prevent de Valera, who was anti-Treaty, from gaining access to the money with which he could then finance an insurgency to subvert the Irish Free State. Funds remained tied up in court from August 1922 until the New York State Supreme Court ordered the money returned to subscribers in 1927. Various plans for the distribution of the funds were described on page 1 of the *New York Times* into the 1930s, including a claim by the FOIF to recoup its seed money.³³ The good faith and enthusiasm with which many Irish Americans had contributed to financing the Irish Republic bond drive were dispelled by the subsequent court fight. To compound matters, Ireland's dirty laundry was publicly aired in the pages of the American press, adding to the impression of bitter dissension that was already attached to reports of the Irish Civil War.³⁴ It was another embarrassing contribution to the American image of the Irish as petty faction fighters, and it helped create a media atmosphere in which de Valera's motivations were regarded with suspicion by Americans.

One of the most enduring nonpolitical stories during the 1930s was the Irish Hospitals' Sweepstake. This was a lottery organized by Joseph McGrath and R. J. Duggan, with the permission of the Irish Free State government, for the benefit of hospitals in Ireland and run in connection with three English horse races. It was a lucrative business for its promoters. The bulk of tickets sold—at ten shillings each, in books of twelve with two free to the seller—were among expatriate Irish women and men in Great Britain and the United States. A *Harper's* magazine feature story observed,

> The natural, voluntary, and large-scale ticket-distributing facilities provided by the resident Irish among their millions of relatives abroad, with their traditionally prolific families and their innate Hibernian ability to make multitudes of friends wherever they happen to settle, have helped tremendously

to make the Sweeps so successful.... The keynote of the Sweeps' advertising [is] a glamorous get-rich-quick offer [that] is more forceful than a charity plea to everybody, everywhere, every time."[35]

Ticket sales quickly surpassed those of similar lotteries in India and Canada. Augmenting its annual value as a news item in the pages of *Newsweek*, the *New York Times*, and newspapers across the country was the fact that lotteries were illegal in the United States. During the Depression years and on the heels of America's disastrous stock market crash, the sweepstakes lottery seemed too good to be true. The 1931 draw had a turnover of nearly £3 million, "the biggest lottery in the world."[36]

American fascination with the Irish sweepstakes phenomenon—which overrode even the news of political dissension in Ireland—was evident: in the "Irish Sweepstakes Party" that *Good Housekeeping* suggested for St. Patrick's Day in 1934; in a 1937 CBS broadcast of a radio play tracing the lives of four fictional Irish sweepstakes winners; in a 1938 NBC variety program that interviewed Irish sweepstakes losers; in a *New York World-Telegram* series of profiles on local winners in 1939; and in a Fred Allen comedy sketch for radio, which aired as late as 1947. It provided the plot for several British and American films, such as "Sweepstakes Annie," "Sweepstakes Winner," and "In Ireland's Garden."[37] Mainstream media coverage gave the impression that in Ireland, one really could find the proverbial pot of gold. At the same time, like the bond-certificate case, there was a sense that this money, in effect the profits of gambling, was somehow tainted.[38] With a thin veneer of respectability provided by pretty Dublin nurses who drew winning tickets from a huge drum on Dublin's O'Connell Street, the Irish Hospitals' Sweepstake nevertheless contributed to an image of the Irish as not being completely honest.[39]

In 1932, de Valera gained enough political support to form a government and become Ireland's *taoiseach* or prime minister. He had spent the previous five years building toward that moment: he broke with Sinn Féin, stood for election as the head of a new party (Fianna Fáil), declared that the oath of allegiance to the Crown in the Irish constitution was hollow, and took his seat in the Dáil. Thereafter, Ireland's relationship with Britain was tenser. American media scrutinized de Valera's willingness to push on issues related to the monarchy; although integral to Britain's imperial image, their removal was essential to Ireland's definition of a republic. Developments in Ireland during this critical transition from empire to commonwealth were newsworthy because of their potential to alter the status of all British overseas colonies, particularly much larger countries like Canada, Australia, and India.

Sixteen front-page headlines and two feature articles in the *New York Times*, plus five page-one stories in the *Chicago Tribune*, during March and April 1932 followed the uproar that ensued when de Valera announced his new administration's policy, including plans to revoke the oath of allegiance to the Crown.[40] During June and July, as reports on the threats of a tariff war and Irish secession from Great Britain escalated, there were also three stories on the alleged landing of arms, especially Russian weapons, for the Irish Republican Army (IRA). The implication was that Ireland was once again on the verge of settling its diplomatic problems by force of arms and that its judgment in choosing partners was faulty.

Americans watched uneasily as de Valera played chess with Westminster, incrementally loosening Ireland's official ties to Great Britain. If de Valera's persona was most directly associated by the media with Ireland, the impression he often gave was that Irish meant stubborn and intransigent. A major news story throughout 1937 was Ireland's new constitution, which de Valera intended to replace the one drawn up in 1922 at the creation of the Irish Free State. It removed all references and subservience to the British Crown, thus making Ireland a de jure republic. There had been indications that Ireland was moving in this direction in *New York Times* reports late the preceding year. The Free State did not send a representative to King George V's funeral in January 1936 and in July refused to participate in the coronation ceremonies for King Edward VIII. The American mass media, preoccupied with the lead-up to Edward's abdication of the throne and seduced by the pomp of another coronation, was shocked by the speed with which de Valera seized the political advantage to remove the king from the Free State constitution and abolish the British office of the governor-general of Ireland.[41]

In some quarters there were fears that de Valera would be another European dictator. Fear of communism led the *New York Times* to give extensive coverage (including five feature articles) during the 1930s to his dissolution of the Irish Senate and to subversive influences in the IRA, in the Blueshirts (a short-lived fascist organization), and in the Irish Christian Front.[42] There were scores of stories on the IRA's 1939 bombing campaign in England, fulfilling its mission to generate publicity in America.[43] The outlawing of the IRA in June of 1939 was a page-three story in the *New York Times*, and thereafter news of internment for treason, hunger strikes, and the executions of republican prisoners filled its pages as de Valera's official crackdown began. The irony was not lost on American readers: the very man who was implementing the harsh "Offences against the State Act" (1939) had once denied the legitimacy of that state himself.[44] It wasn't difficult for America to see Irish parallels with political developments in Germany and Italy.

In this intense environment, the Irish Free State felt it necessary to formally protest the negative depiction of the Irish revolutionaries of 1798 in a historical play for radio, Conal O'Riordan's "The Piper," that was broadcast by NBC in 1939. J. P. Walshe, secretary of the Department of External Affairs, observed, "The chief purpose of State representation in America at the present time and for a great many years to come must be propaganda against the old British caricature of Ireland and the Irish."[45] Indeed, Ireland would have to engage on multiple fronts to try to change that Irish image.

* * *

An important distinction must be made about this juncture in the evolution of Irish America. Many older first-generation immigrants who had worked for Irish independence through the United Irish League, the FOIF, and the AARIR were either satisfied with the achievement of the Irish Free State; disillusioned by the Irish Civil War and its aftermath, drifting away from nationalism altogether; or increasingly more concerned with English influences on the United States. Others, as well as those who were of second-generation or later Irish ancestry, followed current events with a detachment that did not necessarily translate into active political nationalism. Many more were simply listing toward the American part of their Irish American identity following the patriotic experiences of World War I military service and the sobering anti-immigrant/anti-Catholic nativism of the 1920s. In contrast, even those new immigrants who did not join Irish republican clubs still gravitated toward a cultural nationalism (traditional music, dance, language) to express their support for politically independent Ireland at the same time that they were assimilating into older Irish communities in established ways (work, housing, religion).

This wide variation of experiences and political sympathies in Irish America was either too complicated for the media or not expedient, especially when Ireland did not follow Great Britain into the Second World War.[46] The decision by Éire to remain neutral limited Great Britain to Northern Ireland for defense of its western flank, to the chagrin of Winston Churchill. When the United States entered the war, there was concern that Irish neutrality was an espionage vulnerability that could compromise Anglo-American efforts.[47] It became the major Irish news story covered in the New York and Chicago papers through the early 1940s, particularly when de Valera made a highly controversial decision to pay condolences at the German Legation in Dublin on the death of Hitler in May 1945.[48] The level of editorial hostility to Irish neutrality varied in degree. The U.S. Office of War Information's Bureau of Special Services compiled media summaries for President Roosevelt's daily intelligence reports based on editorials and influential columns in more than three dozen major newspapers and nearly twenty news magazines, plus commentary from thirty-five radio journalists.[49] At a White House lunch in January 1941, Roosevelt surprised the young actress Maureen O'Hara by stating that Ireland was communist. "I've never heard such rubbish in my life," she retorted, "I don't know where you get your information, Mr. President."[50] While reputable newspapers like the *New York Times* and the *New York Herald Tribune* were more objective in their use of language about Ireland, popular daily papers frequently chose adjectives like "unfortunate," "fascist-like," and "savage" to describe the Irish.[51] Much of the negative publicity was generated through the influence of David Gray, the U.S. ambassador to Ireland, who was openly hostile to de Valera and to Irish neutrality. To discredit the man and his politics with Irish Americans, Gray was responsible for the media frenzy that ensued from allegations that Dublin was a base for German and Japanese spies.[52]

To counteract the antineutrality propaganda that was flooding the media,[53] as well as to educate Americans about why Ireland was neutral, the American Friends of Irish Neutrality (AFIN) spun off from the AARIR in November 1940, hard on the heels of Churchill's condemnation of Ireland's position, especially with regard to the closure of Irish ports to the British Navy. Paul O'Dwyer—who had arrived from County Mayo in 1925—soon became its chairman. From headquarters in New York City, the group hired a former Hearst reporter to write press releases but initially had trouble getting them into print. O'Dwyer seized every opportunity for publicity. When a group of 129 prominent Irish Americans including academics, writers, union leaders, and politicians cabled de Valera in March 1941 with a request to open Irish ports to the Allies, O'Dwyer gave a statement to the press that exposed a new generation gap in Irish America. He said the cable signers did "not represent Irish-American thought in the United States" and that "Irish American societies" (i.e., those run by first-generation immigrants) were against interfering with Irish neutrality.[54] This distinction was lost on most Americans, for whom Irish was homogeneous.

There were five Gallup polls specifically about Irish neutrality between 1941 and 1944.[55] The first two attempted to sound "Irish American" as well as American sentiment on the issue, drawing a sample of the former from among Irish immigrants and their children in large metropolitan centers across the country.[56] In response to the question "Would you like to see the Irish give up their neutrality and let the English use war bases along the Irish coast?" 63 percent of Americans said yes. Among the first- and second-generation Irish Americans polled, only 40 percent responded yes, 52 percent said no, and 8 percent had "no opinion."[57] The second poll was taken in February 1942 and *seemed* to indicate a dramatic rise in Irish Americans who responded positively.[58] But the question substituted "Allies" for "English," and in the intervening thirteen months, several things had happened to influence popular opinion in the United States.

In March 1941, de Valera sent his minister for the coordination of defensive measures, Frank Aiken, to the United States. Aiken toured the country for thirteen weeks under the auspices of the AFIN, speaking in the major Irish American centers where immigration from Ireland during the 1920s had been strongest. He found important nonethnic platforms too, such as a CBS radio broadcast in June and a signed article in *American Magazine* (circulation in excess of two million) in August.[59] When Churchill announced plans to extend conscription to Northern Ireland in May 1941, objections by the AFIN got extensive American coverage even in influential papers like the *New York Times*.[60] The result was a deluge of propaganda in the mainstream American press that was either unabashedly pro–Irish neutrality or a pro-British U.S. State Department countermeasure.[61] In addition, both the *Gaelic American* and the *Irish World*, with combined circulations of about 150,000, were volubly in agreement about the integrity of Ireland's neutrality and the importance of America remaining isolated from European conflicts too.[62]

The first question the February 1942 Gallup poll asked was designed to winnow the pool of respondents to just those already familiar with Ireland's neutral status among first- and second-generation Irish Americans. But incredibly, 82 percent were reported to have answered "Yes, it has," to the question "Do you happen to know whether the Irish Free State (Éire) has gone to war against Germany?" This level of ignorance demands further interpretation, since only 50 percent of Americans had responded yes to the same question. The *Gaelic American*, well-schooled in the art of propaganda, labeled anyone who believed the February 1942 poll "a 'Gallup stooge.'"[63] Gallup asked the subsequent two questions only to the subset of the "Irish American" sample—those 18 percent who correctly answered no—thereby artificially inflating the percentage of those Irish Americans who approved of Éire allowing the Allies to use its coastal ports (72 percent) and who thought Ireland should declare war on Germany (56 percent).

Given the work of organizations like the AFIN and the generous coverage of the neutrality issue in both the ethnic and mainstream press during 1941, it seems likely that the poll was designed to prove that the image Frank Aiken had portrayed of universal Irish American support for neutrality was all wrong. A scientific demonstration of Irish American sympathy with the Allied war effort—such as the jump from 40 percent in January 1941 to 72 percent in February 1942 with regard to Irish ports—was politically expedient in the wake of the December 1941 attack on Pearl Harbor. Perhaps more significantly, the second Gallup poll was taken within weeks of the arrival of the first American troops to be stationed in Ulster at the end of January 1942, and soon millions of cinema-going Americans saw Paramount's newsreel about American troops drilling in Northern Ireland.⁶⁴ This very strong image of an Irish war effort, in which Ulster was merely a detail for most in the audience, quickly blurred Irish political reality: How could Ireland be neutral if Allied soldiers were there? After all, the American media had been using four different names—"Ireland," "Irish Free State," "Éire," and "North Ireland"—for the same geographic island in recent years, and some popular conflation was only natural.⁶⁵

* * *

To further complicate matters, *Life* magazine ran an unsigned seven-page photographic essay in the summer of 1939 called "Ireland: A New Flag Brings Hope to an Old and Pious Land." On accomplishments since 1921, the editorial comment was as follows:

> All this has been given in eighteen years to a people of great charm but little efficiency who inwardly believe that the dead go West, that a curse kills crops and cattle and men, that a woman must not do a man's work or a man a woman's, that it is dangerous to see a woman on the way to the fair, that there's "great power in a hazel stick to keep the dead away," that the wren is the king of birds, that "the good people" (fairies) are a regular part of the population and that the *banshee* cries for death.⁶⁶

Two of its seven pages were devoted to de Valera, although the essay's subtitle, "Makes Ireland Work and Forget Its Past," was undercut by secondhand observations like "[He] has giggling fits and is probably crazy" and "The history of Ireland is to a great extent the story of the incompetence and venality of its leaders." More than one million copies of this issue were circulated across the United States; with actress Ann Sheridan as the magazine's cover girl, this story on contemporary Ireland, which was reportedly "very hospitable to Nazis," slipped into American hands as fact. There were three letters to the editor objecting to the bias of the essay in a subsequent issue of *Life*. Among these was one from twenty-year-old Eithne Golden, daughter of the late Irish nationalist Peter Golden, who complained that readers would misinterpret *Life*'s statement on Irish reunification, that "the Ulstermen want to join Ireland about as much as the Czechs wanted to join Germany." She suggested a better parallel: "England has about as much right to Ulster as Germany has to the Sudetenland."⁶⁷

The American media's ability to manipulate the Irish image at precisely this time must take account of how specific print or visual repetitions reinforced damaging perceptions. A sobering example is the twelve-page report from Ireland published in the December 1941 issue of the intellectual magazine *American Mercury*. It was penned by William Bayles, who had just concluded a four-year stint as *Time* magazine's London-based correspondent, spending "several weeks in Ireland while preparing this report on the Emerald Isle."⁶⁸ Ostensibly writing about the subject of Irish neutrality but without any objectivity, Bayles attempted to strike fear in American readers' hearts. He described how the German and Italian flags were flown in Dublin and how the "scar-faced, silent Reichswehr officer" who was head of the German Legation could be found at Gaelic League events where Irish "nationalist hotheads congregate." After a visit to de Valera, Bayles concluded that the *taoiseach* was naïve: "Éire is perhaps the last country in the world where grown men have seen banshees, and where fairies on moonlit toadstools are seriously discussed."⁶⁹ *American Mercury* had a small subscription base of approximately 55,000, but Bayles's report was condensed for the March 1942 issue of *Reader's Digest*, a general interest magazine whose circulation was soaring and would reach nine million in 1946. It is possible that Bayles's article originated with *Reader's Digest*, since it had a policy of paying small magazines, like *American Mercury*, a subsidy for a "planted" story that would be "reprinted" later.⁷⁰

Against these media images must be weighed the now famous 1943 St. Patrick's Day radio address to the United States by de Valera, then Ireland's prime minister:

> The ideal Ireland that we would have, the Ireland that we dreamed of, would be the home of a people who valued material wealth only as a basis for right living, of a people who, satisfied with frugal comfort, devoted their leisure to the things of the spirit—a land whose countryside would be bright with cosy homesteads, whose fields and villages would be joyous with the sounds of industry, with the romping of sturdy children, the contest of athletic youths and the laughter of happy maidens, whose firesides would be forums for the wisdom of serene old age.

Essentially echoing the popular sentiment about the "wee whitewashed thatched cottage" identified by Muriel Sperry nearly a decade earlier, de Valera referenced a conception of the motherland that was already fully developed, one that he had certainly encountered firsthand on several visits to the United States, especially in the 1920s. In addition, as he toured its entire length and breadth, he had the opportunity to speak before ordinary Irish Americans in hundreds of audiences and to witness the ways in which many of them were living an urban version of "the ideal Ireland that we would have." Irish America was not mired in poverty and slums in the 1920s; in general, frugal comfort, cozy homes, ardent Catholicism, and bright prospects for the next generation were everywhere evident. In this respect, de Valera was only wishing for Ireland what Irish Americans had achieved for themselves. Of course, de Valera had also been exposed to the sophistication of American public relations and the media while in the United States, and that experience surely informed his decision to broadcast this particular speech in 1943, when he was under pressure for refusing to yield Ireland's neutrality during World War II.[71] By referencing a conventional American view of Ireland—a harmless land of little white cottages and happy people, a view that also resonated with Irish American nostalgia—some of the negative propaganda then circulating in the news media about Ireland might be defused enough to sway American popular opinion.

In the run-up to St. Patrick's Day in 1944, Ireland was front-page news because de Valera refused to comply with a U.S. State Department request to expel the German and Japanese representatives from Dublin on charges of espionage. During the next three weeks, the *New York Times* published nineteen articles (five of them on page 1), two commentaries, an editorial, and a magazine feature story ("De Valera's Inflexible Creed") on the situation. *Time* and *Newsweek* ran several articles with headlines like "Irish Spies Are Smiling."[72] With the exception of *Commonweal*, the Catholic magazine, which presented "Éire's case" in their March 24 issue, the media coverage generally painted de Valera as a "German dupe" who was wantonly tempting a Nazi invasion. The *New York Times* editorial pictured "men and women fleeing from their burning towns . . . all along the lovely roads where the jaunting cars used to go."[73] But de Valera took the broadcasting opportunity of his

Figure 2.1. This late 1943 advertisement for Coca-Cola obscured the contentious fact of Irish neutrality by juxtaposing de Valera's premodern image of Ireland with the reality of American servicemen stationed in Northern Ireland during the Second World War. Norman Price's painting also taps into the rural iconography and rhetoric of hospitality that pervaded prewar Irish tourism campaigns. Credit: Mick Moloney Irish-American Music and Popular Culture Irish Americana Collection (AIA 031.004), box 54, folder 20, Archives of Irish America, Special Collections, Bobst Library, New York University. Image © The Coca-Cola Company.

March 1944 address to the American people to defend his decision not to deport the Axis legates from Ireland. The advantage of this powerful medium was that de Valera's comments were broadcast directly and not filtered through a reporter, as were the summaries of these broadcasts published, usually the next day, in the pages of the *New York Times*.[74]

The result of all this publicity was that three out of every five persons surveyed by two 1944 Gallup polls taken one week apart had heard or read about the State Department's request. During the week of March 17, Americans were told, "Ireland has said that because she is neutral in this war she will not send the German and Japanese representatives home. Do you think the United States should do anything further about this?" Sixty-six percent said yes, 30 percent said no, and 4 percent had no opinion. Beginning March 31, the pollsters introduced the idea of economic sanctions by asking, "Do you think we should stop all trade with the Irish Free State if it doesn't send home the German and Japanese representatives?" This time, 69 percent said yes, 19 percent said no, and 12 percent had no opinion.[75] Without supplying hard numbers, Gallup reported that first- and second-generation Irish Americans felt the same way, "although the majority is somewhat smaller than is the case for all voters."[76] Since only the *Washington Post* published the results of these polls, their impact is questionable. They did convey a popular image of a "stern attitude towards Éire" among Americans that probably reached President Roosevelt and his advisers, but it was an image that in all likelihood was quite meaningless in the Irish subculture of the biggest American metropolitan centers. In New York City, for example, in addition to the ethnic newspapers available, issues of de Valera's *Irish Press*, a Dublin paper, were "snapped up" by Irish immigrants "within hours" of reaching newsstands even though typically six weeks old.[77]

On the other hand, more than 108 million Americans were exposed to newsreel programming before feature films on thousands of motion picture screens across the country. The five companies that produced newsreels in the 1930s and 1940s operated "exactly like newspapers, with a news desk and an editor who assign[ed] stories." Foreign news was gathered by local cameramen whose negatives were then shipped to New York for cutting, music editing, and voice-over commentary. Contemporaries considered the newsreels to be "an amazing and ingenious system of world news coverage which dwarfs everything of its kind except the great press associations."[78] Among those that featured Ireland during this period were "Éire Cut Off by Allies" (1944), de Valera greeting New York's Cardinal Spellman (1946), and Irish citizens casting ballots (1948). *The March of Time* ventured from radio into theaters with filmed dramatizations of current events such as 1938's "Ulster" on the controversy over partition (the 1921 political division of Ireland into North and South) and 1944's "The Irish Question," a nineteen-minute piece on Ireland's neutrality.[79] According to Brian P. Kennedy, the Irish government commissioned these *March of Time* segments.[80]

There was one longtime *New York Times* correspondent for Ireland whose reporting was more balanced. Anne O'Hare McCormick, a Catholic and Pulitzer Prize–winning member of the newspaper's powerful editorial board, submitted signed commentaries between 1937 and 1947 that covered the new constitution, IRA terrorism, a wartime election, charges of abetting Axis espionage, and economic and political conditions. During these years, the *New York Times* had a daily circulation of 474,277 and 788,997 on Sunday, and it was "the newspaper" read first thing by the U.S. State Department.[81] On de Valera, one of many European leaders McCormick profiled for the *Times*, she concluded, "He may be a dictator by temperament, but by philosophy he is a passionate democrat."[82] As 1947 came to an end, McCormick filed three reports on Ireland for the *Times* editorial page, calling Ireland "a fascinating and important news story," especially as a participant nation in the Marshall Plan, a U.S. economic initiative to help postwar Europe recover.[83] McCormick was honored with the gold medal of the American Irish Historical Society (AIHS) in the spring of 1949.[84]

With the war over, partition rather than neutrality was the way in which first-generation Irish immigrant nationalists in the United States kept Ireland in the media spotlight. The main objectives of the AFIN and its successors—the United Irish Counties Association's Anti-Partition Committee (1945), the American League for an Undivided Ireland (1947), and the American Irish Minute Men (1949)—were to educate Americans about the existence of a border in Ireland and to lobby for U.S. intervention toward its removal.[85] When Ireland (then called Éire) declared itself a republic, effective April 1949, the British Government passed the Ireland Act to reaffirm that the six counties partitioned in 1921 as Northern Ireland remained part of His Majesty's Dominions, a status that could only be changed by the Parliament of Northern Ireland. The American Irish Minute Men disagreed; based in New York City, the new home of the United Nations (UN), they advocated instead for a UN plebiscite that would allow the people of Northern Ireland to decide whether or not to join the Republic of Ireland. On March 30, 1950, the *New York Times* reported that Northern Ireland prime minister Basil Brooke, an avowed anti-Catholic member of the Ulster Unionist Party, objected to any U.S. mediation on partition and denied that his forthcoming American tour was at the behest of the British Foreign Office to "counteract a strong anti-partition feeling in the United States."[86]

The timing was auspicious. In Washington, DC, the U.S. House of Representatives was considering a vote on the suspension of Marshall aid to Britain unless the Irish partition issue was resolved because anti-partitionists had argued that American money was being used to support British troops in Northern Ireland.[87] In New York City, William O'Dwyer, who used many public occasions to speak out on the need to end partition in Ireland, was mayor. He said he would not welcome Brooke to city hall and, to make sure of it, planned a Florida vacation to coincide with the visit.[88] The latter announcement alone resulted in thirteen articles, an editorial, and commentary in the pages of the *New York Times* plus two articles and an editorial in the *Chicago Tribune*, far more media coverage than two years earlier when O'Dwyer had lunched with de Valera at Gracie Mansion.[89] Brooke's visit especially aroused the ire of the New York Irish, hundreds of whom turned out to picket him under the auspices of the American Irish Minute Men.[90] On April 6, when Brooke changed planes at New York International Airport (Idlewild) en route to a speaking engagement at the National Press Club in Washington, DC, he was on the ground for less than an hour, but a large, orderly Irish picket was there to welcome him. Men and women carried signs that included sentiments like "If Brooke is an Irishman, Benedict Arnold was a great American" and "The British Gestapo Chief Sir Basil Brooke is here."[91]

Brooke claimed the picket made no impression, but it was covered in the pages of the *New York Times*, the *Chicago Tribune*, the *Washington Post*, and the *Christian Science Monitor*.[92] More importantly, the Brooke protests indicate a significant maturation of the 1920s generation. Paul

O'Dwyer, the mayor's brother, recalled that the American League for an Undivided Ireland supplied the American press with uncomfortable questions to put to Brooke through a paid spokesman with journalism experience.[93] Combined with the guerrilla protest tactics of the American Irish Minute Men, this generation of Irish immigrants was beginning to understand not only that print and broadcast media were critical to how Americans understood political affairs in Ireland but that the media was a field on which it was imperative to contest false British and American images.[94]

* * *

Magazines and books supplemented newspapers, newsreels, and radio in disseminating news about Ireland and the Irish in the United States. Between 1890 and 1963, there were 3,500 feature articles on Ireland in American periodicals—48 percent published between 1916 and 1949—an extraordinary amount of coverage about a country that, for a general American audience, was only a small island on the periphery of Europe. Ireland appeared in the pages of large (million plus) circulation magazines like *Collier's*, the *Literary Digest*, *American Magazine*, *National Geographic*, and *Life* as well as in smaller, special interest journals like the *Nation*, *American Mercury*, *Foreign Affairs*, *Commonweal*, and the *New Yorker*. While articles on Irish antiquities, the Irish language, Irish writers and literature, and descriptions of Ireland and Irish travel were perennial favorites, there was a sustained interest in Irish current events as well. The *Literary Digest*, for example, published 188 pieces on Ireland between the rising and the republic.[95] The debuts of *Time* (1923) and *Newsweek* (1933) coincided with Ireland's major political developments, prompting forty-three stories in *Time* and thirty-nine in *Newsweek* through 1949.[96]

De Valera's tour of the United States in March 1948, while he was out of power for the first time in sixteen years, prompted a major article in *Harper's* by Herbert L. Matthews, head of the *New York Times*'s London bureau and author of *The Fruits of Fascism* (1943). It is representative of insidious perceptions of Ireland and the Irish at the highest levels of American journalism that lingered in the aftermath of the war. Calling de Valera a "demagogue of the first order," Matthews told over 100,000 *Harper's* readers that partition was a dead issue; Ulster would not budge,

Ireland had no power, and "the world, and especially Great Britain, does not really care enough."⁹⁷ He rejected Éire's description of Northern Ireland as an "occupied part of our country . . . upheld by force of British arms" in favor of his own reductive conclusion that "religion is, indeed, the basic reason for Partition, just as it is in India." Stereotyping was sprinkled throughout: "The granite-faced Ulsterman is steadier, harder . . . his conversation is practical [while] down in Dublin the talk is abstract, brilliant, argumentative for the sake of argument . . . there is no blarney stone in Ulster—more's the pity!"⁹⁸

De Valera's visit provided material for more than just *Harper's*. On the ninth of March, an estimated fifteen thousand people saw de Valera parade through ticker tape in an open car from New York's Battery to city hall, and then thousands more heard the radio broadcast of the ceremony that made him an honorary citizen. The *New York Times* reported that the sidewalks on lower Broadway were packed and the office windows above the street were full. Shouts of "'Hi'ya Dev,' mingled with more restrained hand-clapping and cheers."⁹⁹ Within days Fred Allen, considered one of the funniest comedians of his day, immortalized the excitement in a radio sketch heard by as many as twenty million American listeners coast-to-coast.¹⁰⁰ A year later, when Ireland seceded from the commonwealth and declared itself a republic, Allen broadcast another sketch that once again assumed a degree of familiarity with Irish current events:

> FRED ALLEN: Ajax Cassidy! What is that green flag with the gold harp on it?
> PETE DONALD: Erin go Bragh!
> ALLEN: What's the celebration?
> DONALD: Haven't you heard the news, you heathen infidel? Ireland is free!
> ALLEN: Have you been celebrating all week?
> DONALD: As soon as word reached Kerrigan's we all drank a toast to the Republic.
> ALLEN: Uh-huh.
> DONALD: Then we drank a toast to Éamon de Valera.
> ALLEN: Uh-huh.
> DONALD: Next a toast to King George.

ALLEN: Uh-huh.
DONALD: Then a toast to Morton Downey.[101]
ALLEN: Uh-huh.
DONALD: Then a voice said—"This drink is on the house."
ALLEN: On the house?
DONALD: How we all got up there—nobody knew.
ALLEN: The new Republic is off to a great start.
DONALD: Now we can concentrate.
ALLEN: How?
DONALD: With the English out of Ireland—
ALLEN: Yeah?
DONALD: We can keep fightin' among ourselves.
ALLEN: Now that Ireland is free a great injustice has been remedied.
DONALD: Only one injustice remains.
ALLEN: What is that?
DONALD: The greatest injustice of the world is that money is green and the Irish have so little of it. Me especially.[102]

Allen cleverly melded a number of codes the media had introduced to the green space to prepare this sketch. "De Valera" and "the Republic" were convenient shorthand that made the Irish just familiar enough for mass consumption. Even those listeners who didn't recognize the context would still get the old jokes about drinking and fighting Irishmen, thereby extending the incongruity of incompetence and political independence. Similarly, when *Time* called Ireland that "weird, neutral land," it drew on the green space. In reporting on the hanging of an IRA member in Belfast in 1942, the story began, "In the wild glens of Antrim and in the villages, those who listened hard into the wind swore they heard the banshees wailing."[103] The very first column of Robert Shaplen's long 1952 "Letter from Dublin" in the *New Yorker* also freely mixed current events with fantasy: "From their dogged and frequently maddening isolation and neutrality, and from the air of unreality that beclouds so much of their unresolved domestic debate, political and otherwise, one gets the impression that the Irish are a troupe of carnival performers who both leap like leprechauns and lumber like giants."[104]

There were a handful of quite regular Irish commentators in the first five decades of the twentieth century who were heard in the United

States as authentic voices speaking with authority on current affairs in Ireland. They were often the first spokesmen many media outlets approached for comment because many were recognized authors of novels or short stories, prefiguring what would become a long-lived relationship between journalism and Irish literary culture in America. For example, in 1925, when New York's Macmillan & Company acquired the distribution rights for *Ireland* (252 pages), it advised its author Stephen Gwynn to add a short chapter "bringing the history of Ireland down to practically the present date" for publication as *The Student's History of Ireland*.[105] Within twelve months, this was being used as a reference text in some American universities, even though Gwynn described the book as "essentially a popularisation, not a scientific work of research."[106] He had already published several books of travel literature about Ireland, including *Highways and By-Ways in Donegal and Antrim* (1903), as well as prewar political propaganda for Irish Home Rule and a long piece for the *New York Times* in 1923 on Ireland's general election, a critical milestone in the wake of the country's recent civil war.[107] *The Student's History of Ireland* was going into the hands of American college students when Gwynn commented on the tenth anniversary of the Easter Rising for the *Living Age*: "Possibly [Padraig] Pearse and his colleagues who launched this train of consequences would, if they were living now, approve of Mr. de Valera. . . . Ireland has gained much, but has no pride of her victory. Her experience has left her dejected, bitter, and without gratitude to the handful of men who with set teeth have restored order, though not yet prosperity. We have no heroes living; and even those who died in 1916 are besmirched by the ugliness that followed."[108] Blurring the lines between facts, fiction, and opinion like this was yet another way in which the Irish image was confused by the media.

The Irish writers Seumas MacManus, Padraic Colum, and Seán Ó Faoláin all made their living by the pen and were paid well by the American press and periodicals. Despite a wide range in terms of background, education, class, and political persuasion, these men were privileged over others to interpret contemporary Irish politics, history, neutrality, and economics for Americans because of their literary reputations. Their actual ability to effect widespread opinion formation in the freewheeling media environment of the United States, however, is difficult to measure, yet it is also suggestive.[109]

Seumas MacManus was from County Donegal farming stock and wrote short stories and plays based on the folk culture he knew firsthand while growing up. He had ten stories published in the *Washington Post* in the summer of 1900, ten in the Sunday magazine section of the *New York Tribune* between 1905 and 1907, and five poems in the *New York Times* in 1909 and 1910. By 1911, he could command between $400 and $600 a story from American magazines.[110] MacManus was also booked by the Redpath Chautauqua agency for the American lecture circuit, with a number of one-hour talks such as "Stories of Irish Fairy and Folk-Lore," "Irish Life and Character—Its Humor, Pathos, and Beauty," and "The New Ireland of Today."[111] Outside of the big cities with their daily newspapers, lectures were one of the key means by which the average American learned about Ireland's revolution and postcolonial efforts at governing. MacManus made at least six tours of the breadth of the country, from Bangor to New Orleans and New York City to Los Angeles with more than forty other stops in between. In 1912 and 1913 alone he gave over eighty lectures to audiences as diverse as the Daughters of the American Revolution (Meridian, MS), the YMCA (Bellingham, WA), the Knights of Columbus (Minot, ND), the Episcopalian Church (Faribault, MN), and Normal Schools (where teachers trained) such as those in Oshkosh, Wisconsin, and North Adams, Massachusetts.[112]

Indeed, Seumas MacManus had been heard by so many audiences across the United States that he was guaranteed a forum in the press whenever he offered commentary on Irish current events, such as "Erin in Uproar against Britain" (1915): "It will be news to many to hear that every day women as well as men are arrested and imprisoned for patriotic propaganda; that raids by the British authorities are made sometimes in the middle of the night upon the houses of people suspected of loving Ireland better than good stepmother England, their papers ransacked and stolen, themselves arrested or ordered to depart."[113] In 1917, MacManus argued for independence in the book *Ireland's Case*; in 1919, his essay "The Birth of Sinn Féin by One Who Was There" had a two-page spread in the *New York Times*; and in October 1921, he published a popular and affordable history of Ireland from its pagan days to the present. Based on his lectures, *The Story of the Irish Race—from the Tuatha Dé Danann to the treaty—*was in its third edition by 1922 and remained affordable and in print into the twenty-first century.[114]

The impact of a speaker like MacManus in America's heartland should not be underestimated. When the poet William Butler Yeats, one of the architects of the Irish literary revival, toured the United States in 1903 and 1904, he spoke almost entirely at prestigious universities in the orbit of Boston, New York, Chicago, and San Francisco. His subsequent tours in 1911, 1914, 1920, and 1932 were also booked in private clubs and colleges.[115] Not for him the small-town tent circuit of lyceums and chautauquas, where there were guaranteed audiences who craved passionate oratory that doubled as mass entertainment, especially in the summertime.[116] The differences are palpable on many levels. Yeats preached about Irish heroic literature and the intellectual revival to elite audiences; MacManus brought folktales and contemporary Irish political developments to venues that William Jennings Bryan declared were the "potent human factor in molding the mind of the nation."[117] It was 1932 before Yeats's official American lecture topic was "The New Ireland"—by then he had served in the Irish Senate—but his main audiences were still at Dartmouth, Columbia, Bryn Mawr, and Wellesley.[118]

Padraic Colum—who is remembered for his published poetry, folktales, short stories, and children's literature as well as a travelogue—supplemented his literary income with magazine work for *American Mercury*, *Commonweal*, *Catholic World*, *Forum and Century*, and the *Saturday Review of Literature* among others. Like MacManus, he also lectured after arriving in the United States in late 1914.[119] When the press came to him with questions after news of the Easter Rising reached New York, Colum quickly began calling himself an Irish publicist as the demand to explain Ireland to Americans escalated. He adapted a commentary published on April 30 in the *Washington Post* for a full-page essay called "The Trouble with Ireland" that appeared in the *National Sunday Magazine* on June 25, 1916. It began by addressing perceived ignorance: "An American unconsciously assumes that the relations between England, Scotland, Ireland and Wales are federal in some way. That assumption is wholly wrong."[120] This periodical had a circulation of 2,046,935 and was distributed as inserts in newspapers like the *Boston Sunday Globe*, *Chicago Sunday Tribune*, *Cincinnati Enquirer*, *Pittsburgh*

Dispatch, and *San Francisco Call*. That September, prior to a lecture tour of the American West, an extensive quote from Colum on conditions in Ireland was followed by a paragraph promoting two literary collections by him to be published in October.[121] Political commentary did not hurt the pocketbook.

Thereafter, developments in Ireland kept Colum's name in the public eye.[122] In letters to the editors of the *New York Times* he commented on the 1925 "famine," the boundary issue and Irish debt, partition, Ireland's new constitution in 1937, and Sir Basil Brooke's 1950 visit to the United States.[123] On Irish neutrality, Colum focused on the positive, pointing out what American newspapers overlooked, such as Ireland's gift of $1 million for famine relief to India in 1944.[124] In his biography of Arthur Griffith for Macmillan & Company, Colum chronicled modern Ireland's formative years. Reviewing the manuscript in 1953, B. W. Maxwell confirmed the American market appeal of recent Irish history, although he didn't think "this manuscript should be judged from the standpoint of historiography but rather from a literary and impressionistic point of view. As such, with the necessary revisions, it should be accepted favorably by many readers, especially those who have a physical and emotional relationship to Ireland." Among these he included "those who like Mr. Colum's poetry, dramas and prose, and many do."[125]

By the 1950s, Seán Ó Faoláin had emerged to claim the mantle of Irish spokesman in the United States. Unlike MacManus and Colum, he returned to live in Ireland after some time at Harvard and Boston College in the late 1920s. Ó Faoláin's fiction began to be read in the United States in the 1930s. Both the short story collection *Midsummer Night Madness* (1932) and the novel *A Nest of Simple Folk* (1934) were published by New York's Viking Press and drew upon Ó Faoláin's firsthand experience of the Irish War of Independence and Civil War.[126] A *Washington Post* reviewer remarked that "his diffuse realism throbs with genuine dramatic power and glows with latent poesy," while the *New York Times* headline declared "Fine Tales of the Irish Rebellion."[127] This early success endeared him to American universities and the media: his subsequent books, some of which were banned in Ireland, got many column inches in the press and created a demand for him on lecture tours. Both gave him a platform to comment on the literary scene and new books in Ireland, to reminisce about Yeats and Æ (George Russell), to reflect on St. Patrick, Roger Casement, and "how to acquire a brogue."[128]

It was Ó Faoláin's voice, more than any others, that interpreted post–World War II Ireland to Americans, complete with his own unresolved tension about modernization and nationalism as well as a vendetta against the "puritanism and chauvinism which came up like a jungle of weeds on the first founding of the Irish Free State."[129] This disillusionment with circumstances in Ireland greatly interested American publishers and added a new vein of negativity to the Irish image. His 1949 "psychological history" *The Irish: A Character Study*, which garnered review headlines such as "Spanks the Irish with Olive Branch" (*Boston Globe*) and "Dream and Actuality in a Green Land" (*Christian Science Monitor*), classified Ireland's population into five types: The New Peasantry, The Anglo-Irish, The Rebels, The Priests, and The Writers. "There is a sixth type which I have barely hinted at," Ó Faoláin wrote: "the new middle-classes, or native bourgeoisie: they are the peasant in process of development or final decay, it is too soon to say which."[130] The *New York Times* labeled this the perspective of a "professional Irishman" and wondered—as was to be expected about seemingly perennial problems—why he did not discuss the effect on the national character of political and economic events in Ireland since 1922, neutrality, emigration, potatoes, and the weather.[131]

The American perception of Ireland at this time is confirmed by the selection of Ó Faoláin to write the script for a propaganda film produced by Washington's Economic Cooperation Administration as part of the Marshall Plan. Ireland, only recently an intransigent backwater on the fringe of Europe in U.S. diplomatic circles, became a mutually convenient anti-communist bulwark in the North Atlantic. As such, it qualified for an infusion of funds—$146.2 million, mainly in the form of loans and technical assistance—and Ó Faoláin's *The Promise of Barty O'Brien* (1951) showcased just how American concepts could "fix" Ireland. Centering on the conflict between a traditional Irish farmer and his son who craves improvements, especially electricity, the film (a mix of drama and documentary) follows Barty O'Brien's efforts to acquire the technical knowledge he needs to power local industry as well as light dark farmhouses. It emphasized how American generosity through assistance from the European Recovery Program achieved both his personal dreams and Irish security through the promotion of modernity and prosperity.[132] At one stroke, Ó Faoláin also vindicated a correspondent for the *Nation* who, in 1929, had condemned Irish censorship with this prediction: "When electricity hums through the air, driving the wheels of Irish industry, when the new schools which are being built are filled with eager scholars, then Ireland will be linked with the life, the thought, and the industry of the world."[133] As the harbinger of the future for Ireland, electricity was undercut by reporters who struggled to balance Irish government ambitions with the paucity of economic results on the ground for American readers; as Milton Marmar wrote for the Associated Press in 1954, "Ireland's new electricity for the farm has merely meant more amenities for housewives . . . to make life more worthwhile at home and to keep the Irish in Ireland."[134]

On the heels of *Barty O'Brien*, Ó Faoláin submitted a controversial piece to *Life*, "Love among the Irish," that pointed to what he considered a more profound challenge. The essay was commented on at length in *The Spectator* and then republished as part of the 1953 McGraw Hill collection of essays *The Vanishing Irish: The Enigma of the Modern World*. Catholicism, celibacy, and censorship, Ó Faoláin declared, were to blame for "fostering racial decay in his country."[135] *Life*'s editors continued this theme of hopelessness when they chose twenty-one images taken by American photographer Dorothea Lange in the west of Ireland in 1954 for the magazine's 1955 St. Patrick's week issue. These included an Irish sheep farmer straight out of a Thomas Nast cartoon and emphasis on the fifty-two pubs for the six thousand people of Ennis, County Clare, to help them cope with endless rain. No surprise, then, that Ó Faoláin was tapped for commentary on Ireland as a "small country with big problems" when CBS produced "Ireland: The Tear and the Smile" for its television documentary series *The Twentieth Century*. It was broadcast in two installments, on January 29 and February 5, 1961, and seen by more than eleven million Americans, heralding yet another medium with the potential to distort the image of Ireland and the Irish. Ó Faoláin's influence, combined with that of his fellow Irish novelist Elizabeth Bowen, who wrote the script, is reflected in the complaint of the Irish Embassy in Washington, DC that Ireland had been portrayed with "a general air of fatalism and decay" and as "a poverty-stricken country riddled with backwardness, unemployment and emigration."

CBS, via the program's producer, responded, "We covered the main points of the story of Ireland today.... For us to pretend that these situations did not exist would be journalistically dishonest as well as unconstructive."[136]

The Irish government's outrage at the CBS documentary reveals what was at stake: the small and incremental but significant shifts in image-making that Ireland had been cultivating throughout the preceding decade. Unlike "Ireland: The Tear and the Smile" (a title that referenced a favorite Thomas Moore melody), the Irish image was quite positive in American headlines when the focus was on how foreign capital could stimulate the Irish economy. The U.S. Treaty of Friendship, Commerce, and Navigation with Ireland in 1950 provided "a legal framework for general economic relationships between the two countries." The roots of what would be later called outsourcing are evident in the incentives Ireland offered: grants to cover costs of construction, multiyear exemptions on income tax and profits, and "complete freedom to repatriate capital and transfer profits in dollars." Political stability was an additional attraction; "the country is free of Marxian taint," the *San Diego Union* reported in 1951.[137] Ireland posed no threat of "military, political, social or economic upheavals," and American investors and industrialists gained "an abundant supply of stable labor at wage rates good by Irish standards but moderate by comparison with American rates."[138] In 1959, after spending six months in Ireland, Padraic Colum told a journalist for the *Evening Star* in Washington, DC, "If Ireland could create a chain of small factories in the next twenty years, the tide [of unemployment and emigration] could be turned."[139] Nevertheless, this was an Ireland virtually imperceptible to most Americans for whom the word Irish had, for so long, been equated with poverty and political dysfunction in the media.

* * *

In 1959, United Artists released *Shake Hands with the Devil* for summertime moviegoers. The *Washington Post* called the film "as clear-eyed an account of 'The Troubles' as you're ever likely to see on the screen . . . offered without any brogue-ish malarkey."[140] Based on the 1934 best-selling first novel by Rearden Conner that had been a popular Literary Guild selection in the United States, the production was filmed on location in Ireland with actors from the Abbey Theatre in secondary roles.[141] It starred James Cagney as an Irish university professor who is also a soulless leader of the underground republican movement in 1921 Dublin and Don Murray as the Irish American medical student who reluctantly gets caught up in the Irish War of Independence. Both, by pursuing violence as the means to an end, metaphorically "shake hands with the devil." Most of the major American newspaper reviews were fairly balanced with regard to that dramatic theme and relatively objective as far as the image of revolutionary Ireland that was projected, albeit in a manner reminiscent of earlier book reviews ("How the headlines in the newspapers flash back to mind!"). Many could not resist a comment on what the *Christian Science Monitor* called the "ultrarealism" of the film's cinematography, particularly in capturing the Irish landscape: "Fine photography creates a low-keyed, moody atmosphere for a grim and unrelenting melodrama and the shots of Dublin, the coast and a village hideaway are arresting," the *Richmond Times Dispatch* concluded.[142]

This film reminds us of just how porous the green space had become over the first half of the twentieth century and of the number of different stakeholders contributing to the construction of what each felt was a genuine image of Ireland and the Irish. *Shake Hands with the Devil* was the first major production of an infant Irish film industry based at Ardmore Studios south of Dublin, and for that reason, it "received unprecedented cooperation from government authorities" who saw such filmmaking not as a "positive cultural activity, but in the same manner of any manufacturing industry."[143] Profit was ultimately the bottom line but no less so than for United Artists—which, in an advance press release calculated to pique interest and sell tickets, insinuated that Ireland had banned the novel on which the film was based.[144] When producer George Glass told the New Orleans *Times-Picayune* that he went to Ireland "to not only get authenticity of background but also to get people in the cast who look different," he was undoubtedly oblivious to such a statement as a potential national insult because, in the United States, the media was saturated with long-established preconceptions that were understood as fact.

The negative image of Ireland that had served British foreign policy best and was especially virulent during World War II, when Ireland stayed neutral and Anglo-American relations were close, was compounded when New York publishers flooded the consumer market with dubious interpretations of the modern Irish experience. Simultaneously, nonpolitical media coverage of Ireland in magazines and on radio perpetuated a romanticized view or cleverly dressed up old stereotypes for mass consumption. As we shall see in the next chapter, all of this did not go unchallenged; there were cultural elements in the green space that could be drawn on to create yet another iteration of Irish.

3

Cultural Currency

Even as Irish Americans began to achieve more financial, educational, and religious security at the turn of the twentieth century, the need to rehabilitate the Irish image continued to be a pressing concern. It was no longer acceptable, for example, to name monkeys and baboons "Mike," "Paddy," or "Biddy," as New York City's Central Park Zoo learned in 1893.[1] While some objections made little impact and others were scoffed at by the media, an effective way to counter negative depictions emerged that invoked Irish heroes and a precolonial golden age in Ireland. This approach stressed Irish America's relationship with the United States, which dates back to the colonial and revolutionary periods (evidence of American patriotism), as well as a distinctive heritage that had contributed to Western civilization (evidence of Ireland's antiquity and right to self-determination). The image that was defined and refined by these two criteria served to enhance the social profile of the Irish in the United States while simultaneously reflecting positively on Ireland and its people.

However, as explored in chapter 2, political developments in Ireland led to transatlantic tensions over who had the authority to speak for her. Likewise, questions about what constituted Irish made cultural representations deployed to elevate the Irish image in the United States problematic too. This chapter demonstrates how, over time, self-perceptions and conceptualizations shifted. Gaelic culture as embodied in traditional folk arts (evidence of Ireland as a distinct nation) became more authentic than older cultural markers that had long been embraced by second- and late-generation Irish Americans, something modern Ireland struggled to see as legitimate. The proximity of both perspectives in the green space influenced new articulations of Irish that were increasingly influential for Ireland and the United States as the twentieth century progressed.

* * *

The ground for an Irish cultural image in the United States was well seeded by Irish songs for a century before the advent of the Irish Free State in late 1921. Music lovers were familiar with *Moore's Melodies*, a piano arrangement of more than a hundred very old Irish airs with English lyrics by the poet-composer Thomas Moore, which was published in ten volumes between 1808 and 1834. Thereafter, it remained in print on both sides of the Atlantic in a variety of formats for decades.[2] Affordability and critical acceptance spurred circulation. In 1854, Oliver Ditson of Boston pitched his edition of *Moore's Celebrated Irish Melodies* to consumers with encomiums from the American press, like that of the respected periodical *Dwight's Journal of Music*: "Great favorites they have been, sweet spiritual visitants in many a household, and perhaps the first revelation of the power of melody to many of us."[3] In sophisticated social circles, Moore's music was valued as a high art form in its own right, but more significantly for the Irish image, *Moore's Melodies* introduced a visual and literary vocabulary for Ireland to Americans. His themes were inspired by the Romantic canon's affinity for classical allusions and its emphasis on the natural world as well as by the aspirations of the United Irishmen, a nationalist movement whose hopes Moore personally witnessed the British crush between 1798 and 1803. His lyrics were highly attuned to the power of imagery; they emphasized "Erin as the female persona of Ireland, the cause of liberty, the longing for home and for childhood, the mixture of joy and sadness, the harp and the shamrock as important national symbols, the beauty of the Irish landscape, and the exile's ineradicable love of the native land."[4]

Moore's Melodies became one of the earliest modern iterations of Irish to spread in the United States, and because Moore's music was played in comfortable homes as well as affluent drawing rooms and concert halls, its influence on a sentimental Irish image was enormous. In an 1850 feature on Moore, the *Irish American* newspaper declared that Ireland was indebted to him "for at least the beginning of the association of her name with elegant literature . . . inseparably connected with all that is graceful in music and song."[5] At the time, famine was raging in Ireland and anti-Irish, nativist sentiment was roiling American politics. In other words, Moore's benign Irish image coexisted with more malignant ones, like brutish stereotypes and "No Irish Need Apply" advertisements, because art and politics occupied different rhetorical realms that reached widely diverse audiences. When a new edition orchestrated by Michael Balfe was published in 1859, not long after Moore's death, the *Musical Times and Singing Class Circular* declared, "The *Melodies* breathe in every line the true spirit of patriotism and liberty . . . a more genuine Irishman, in the strictest sense of the word, never existed, nor one more deeply imbued with the love of country."[6] Because Moore's image of Ireland and the Irish was respectable on an intellectual plane far above the social backlash to rising immigration and its attendant challenges for the United States, he had enormous utility for subsequent generations of Irish Americans who sought through art to challenge the narrow racial or political depictions of them that American audiences were familiar with from print media.[7]

The centennial of Thomas Moore's birth in 1879 presented Irish Americans with a unique cultural opportunity. There were public celebrations in St. John (New Brunswick), Boston, New York, Brooklyn, Newark, Philadelphia, Baltimore, and Washington, DC. Thousands packed New York's Academy of Music for a concert of Moore's music by a choir of three hundred singers and a large orchestra conducted by Patrick Sarsfield Gilmore. The St. Patrick Society of the City of Brooklyn presented a bronze bust of Moore by John G. Draddy to the Concert Grove in Prospect Park. It was raised on an eleven-foot-high granite pedestal whose cost would be the modern equivalent of six figures. Among the orators at the unveiling ceremony was the criminal lawyer Charles W. Brooke, who declared that "Moore appealed, through the medium of his poetry and his prose, to the sentiment and justice of the educated and well-informed of his day, not in Ireland alone but wherever his genius was admired and his works read."[8] A second bronze bust of Moore, this one by D. B. Sheahan, was presented to the city of New York and unveiled by the Friendly Sons of St. Patrick near the Fifty-Ninth Street and Fifth Avenue entrance to Central Park on May 28, 1880, before a crowd of a thousand.[9] The use of public sculpture in this way was an intentional expression of Irish cultivation that was only possible because Moore already represented all that was accepted as dignified.[10]

Behind these efforts was a group of influential individuals—Democrats and Republicans, Catholics and Protestants—linked together socially by their Irish heritage, who consciously projected an image of urbanity in the civic, business, and cultural circles where such things mattered. Whereas in living memory social consideration had been accorded to the Irish only grudgingly, now new avenues for ethnic advancement were opening up. Structural changes in the American economy affected the composition of the urban upper classes in the second half of the nineteenth century.[11] Those with capital were increasingly from trade, manufacturing, and finance sectors rather than the old mercantile elite, and alliances between these two wealth sectors were made through marriage. In addition, as the professions were institutionalized, doctors, lawyers, and judges formed yet another class that "made their way into the circles of the socially elect." The glue that held a monied metropolis and its expanded bourgeoisie together was cultural identification.[12]

John D. Crimmins epitomizes this. He was born in New York in 1844 and made his fortune in the family contracting firm, one of the city's largest employers responsible for the construction of the Croton Aqueduct, the extended waterfront, sewers, gas mains, electric duct lines, and street and elevated railways. Crimmins belonged to the Metropolitan Club, Manhattan Club, and New York Yacht, Turf & Field, Riding, and Grolier clubs. His listing in the *Social Register* indisputably indicated that he had broken through barriers previously used to exclude Irish Catholics. In 1910 he lived on Manhattan's Upper East Side at 40 East Sixty-Eighth Street, where his household included eleven servants, nine of whom had been born in Ireland. His large family summered in their fourteen-bedroom, nine-bath house on eighteen acres in Darien, Connecticut.[13]

Crimmins was in a stratosphere reached by only a select few Americans, never mind Irish Americans. As expected in that world, his son, Cyril, graduated from Harvard; his daughters wed strategically; and he cultivated the same antiquarian interests as other monied gentlemen by collecting art, rare maps, and books—except that he did it in association with the American Irish Historical Society (AIHS, est. 1897) instead of with the New York Historical Society (est. 1804). In Irish circles, the Crimmins pedigree was equally sterling and linked through his father, Thomas, to the Reidys and Barrys of Buttevant, County Cork—old Gaelic families who were also United Irishmen.[14] The Friendly Sons of St. Patrick, an important incubator of respectability, also claimed Crimmins. The overlapping membership in these two ethnic fraternal associations operated as a social network for wealthy Irish Americans that simultaneously helped integrate them into the city's upper classes. The annual dinners of both societies were lavish affairs attended by influential politicians (including President Theodore Roosevelt in 1905), with toasts and menus that reflected the gestures and language of cultural and social elites. The music played on these occasions always included selections from *Moore's Melodies*, such as "The Minstrel Boy" or "Let Erin Remember the Days of Old."[15]

The maturity and increased visibility of the American Catholic Church were also embodied in such Irish laymen, their wives, and their families, who were active in philanthropy and equally concerned with appearances, reared as they had been on Catholic literature that equated religion with ethnic identity by providing "images of beautiful, handsome, intelligent, and moral Irish American men and women."[16] Crimmins was a member of the Catholic Club, which operated for an Irish American rising elite like the exclusive Protestant clubs in the city. Founded in 1871, the Catholic Club entered the twentieth century with a new five-story headquarters on Central Park South, a fifty-thousand-volume library, and a resident membership roll of more than a thousand who comprised some of the wealthiest men in the city. Several, including Crimmins, were also Knights of St. Gregory, an elite papal order that recognized Catholic philanthropists.[17] The centennial of the Archdiocese of New York in 1908 was followed by the 1910 consecration of St. Patrick's Cathedral and the 1912 elevation of Archbishop John Farley to Cardinal (only New York's second); all three occasions were marked with highly elaborate public ceremonies that were dignified civic as well as religious events covered in the press of the day.

Efforts at self-representation were not limited to ethnic or religious events for the Irish. In 1909, when John D. Crimmins was treasurer of the Friendly Sons and on the Executive Council of the AIHS, both societies jointly coordinated representation for eighty Irish organizations in the city's enormous, weeklong commemoration of Henry Hudson's 1609 voyage and Robert Fulton's 1807 successful steam engine experiment on the Hudson River. Both were historical events that New Yorkers viewed in terms not only of American patriotism but of civic pride. The Irish were invited to participate by the Hudson-Fulton Celebration Committee's presiding vice president Herman Ridder, a German

American publisher who was also a member of the Catholic Club. The invitation signaled an unprecedented level of social acceptance because Ridder gave the "right of the line" to the Irish for the September 28 historical parade that was intended to represent the forty nationalities then contributing to New York's population. According to reports, following the mayor and his police escort "came a line of green, Irish flags with crownless harps of gold." In all, five thousand Irish marched and had the additional honor of escorting three of the fifty memorial floats in the parade, including the prestigious Governor Thomas Dongan one that reminded spectators that an Irishman was responsible for New York's 1683 Charter of Liberties and Privileges.[18] The Irish also offered to produce a grand concert of Irish music. It was given an official spot in the week's program of events and took place on Sunday, September 26, 1909, at Carnegie Hall under the direction of the distinguished Irish composer-conductor Victor Herbert. According to the newspapers, Archbishop Farley presided over "a large and fashionable audience, comprising the elite of the music lovers of the City of New York, and many . . . distinguished visitors," including Crimmins and his daughters but also Governor Hughes of New York State, officers of the naval fleet anchored in the Hudson for the week, and Seth Low, former mayor and past president of Columbia University. The response of the latter is indicative of the way this select approach to changing popular perceptions of the Irish was succeeding. Low wrote, "I think that those who have labored so hard for so many years to awaken interest in Gaelic culture have not only done a service for the members of the Irish race in this country, but, as illustrated by this really beautiful concert, they have rendered a valuable service to the whole country."[19]

The AIHS and the Friendly Sons of St. Patrick led the way with this kind of ethno-cultural diplomacy in public discourse as did similar groups in Philadelphia, Boston, and Charleston. Significantly, and with motivations of respectability not unlike those behind the earlier Thomas Moore monuments, the man they chose to symbolize Irish American patriotism was Commodore John Barry (1745–1803), a native of County Wexford who was regarded as the father of the American Navy. Like Moore, Barry had already been memorialized in stone as part of the Catholic Total Abstinence Union Centennial Fountain in Philadelphia's Fairmount Park, dedicated in the summer of 1876.[20]

Then he was the face of Catholic contributions to the republic; now he was more useful as an ethnic icon. In 1902 Archbishop John Ireland of St. Paul, Minnesota, was one of the first to advocate for a Barry monument to "be placed in a public square in Washington, D.C."[21] Ultimately, there were two new Barry statues erected, one in the nation's capital and the other in the nation's cradle of independence, Philadelphia. Their locations were as intentional as their designs.

A Barry statue was presented to the city of Philadelphia by its Friendly Sons of St. Patrick in March 1907. The dedication ceremony was attended by U.S. naval and military officials as well as political leaders. Thomas J. Stewart, adjutant general of the Pennsylvania National Guard and president of the Philadelphia Friendly Sons, underscored the importance of the statue's situation at the very center of Independence Square. "It is the fitting place," he said, "to rear this tribute to one of that galaxy of great men who made way for liberty, and who steadied the steps of the infant republic that today stands enthroned among the nations of the earth." Mayor John Weaver articulated the implicit purpose of the statue when he said, "God is good to America because He has given to America so many of the brave sons of Ireland; and of all these sons, none was braver than the man we honor today." In other words, Barry enabled the Irish to be easily framed as Americans. Sculpted by Samuel Murray, the son of Irish immigrants, Barry is depicted as a dashing young man braced in action atop a fifteen-foot granite base. The Friendly Sons underwrote the entire $10,000 cost and suggested Murray as the artist for a second Barry statue.[22]

Four years earlier, in 1903, the New York Friendly Sons had initiated the National Commodore John Barry Statue Association. Its chairman was New York State Supreme Court justice Morgan J. O'Brien, whose brother-in-law, John D. Crimmins, was its treasurer.[23] This group both fundraised for the cost of a bronze likeness of Barry and lobbied for a public site in Washington, DC. In June 1906, the U.S. Congress appropriated $50,000 for the initiative as "the expression of the grateful tribute of a nation."[24] In 1908, a competition for the commission was opened and Irish American sculptors were encouraged to submit designs. Andrew O'Connor Jr. was selected by the prize committee, only to then have his concept opposed by the Ancient Order of Hibernians (AOH), a Catholic fraternal association established in the United States in 1836, and other Irish organizations. O'Connor's design included a frieze illustrating "the suffering of Ireland and the resultant emigration of her people," connecting two freestanding groups representing "Exile from Ireland" and "The Genius of Ireland," the latter a seated figure of the motherland surrounded by her sons.[25] Its realism—especially "tormented nudes looking west across the ocean to a new life"—was rejected "mainly on the ground that it was too Irish in theme and execution for an American patriot."[26] O'Connor argued that to ignore the consequences of colonization in Barry's native land was to repudiate his support for the American Revolution "against the same oppressors for the same object—liberty," but he ultimately failed to persuade the Irish.[27] O'Connor's vision of the past was too raw a memory only sixty years after the Famine and undercut the patriotic criteria that was its emotional cover. Irish Americans wanted something more heroic, in keeping with the depictions of great men in the nearly forty statues that had been or were soon to be placed in the capital city.[28] John J. Boyle, a member of the Friendly Sons who had not entered the competition, was ultimately awarded the commission. Boyle's more traditional Commodore John Barry was modeled between 1911 and 1912, then cast in bronze in 1913. It depicts the mature naval hero wearing "his military uniform, a long cloak, and a three-cornered hat" with his right hand resting on an unsheathed sword.[29] Located in Franklin Park (Fourteenth Street side, between I and K Streets), the twenty-six-and-a-half-foot monument was dedicated before thousands, including men and women from Irish organizations all across the country, who gathered on May 16, 1914. That ceremony generated news headlines in a wide range of states because it was attended by President Woodrow Wilson and other dignitaries. The statue's unveiling was preceded by an impressive military parade that subsumed Irish with American patriotism.[30]

Overlapping with these Barry projects was the establishment of the Emmet Statue Committee, chaired by Judge Victor J. Dowling of the New York State Supreme Court's Appellate Division.[31] Its forty-eight members included influential Irish Americans like Boston's mayor James Michael Curley and President Wilson's secretary Joseph P. Tumulty. The name and memory of the United Irish patriot Robert Emmet had deep roots in Irish America, "invoked and exploited for a range of . . . aims and agendas."³² When the committee commissioned a statue of him as a gift to the American people in 1912, Ireland was pressuring Great Britain for Home Rule, and the Emmet name was shorthand for democratic republicanism. The sculptor Jerome Connor, who had just unveiled his bronze of Archbishop John Carroll on the campus of Georgetown University in May of that year, was chosen as the artist. According to Connor's biographer, the sculptor "selected his model so as to make the historical Emmet act the part expected of him in the Irish, or Irish-American, public mind." Dr. Thomas Addis Emmet made his granduncle's death mask available to Connor, who also asked the actor Brandon Tynan to model for the statue.³³ Tynan was the author and star of the dramatic play *Robert Emmet*, which ran in New York City for eighty performances in 1902 and another twenty-four in late 1904 through early 1905. The result was a six-foot-eight-inch bronze portrait of Emmet giving his famous oration before his execution in 1803. Its granite base bore a quote from that speech from the dock, "I wished to procure for my country the guarantee which Washington procured for America." This Emmet statue was placed in the main rotunda of the Smithsonian's National Museum of Natural History, in the presence of President Wilson, on June 28, 1917, just over one year after the Easter 1916 Rising.³⁴ News of its unveiling was printed in papers from Vermont to Colorado and Louisiana. The program included two of Thomas Moore's melodies— "Oh, Breathe Not His Name" and "She Is Far from the Land," sung by the popular operatic tenor John McCormack. Following remarks by Senator James D. Phelan of California, Judge Dowling made a political statement: "It is peculiarly appropriate that this statue should be unveiled when the land from which Emmet took his inspiration and in whose freedom he gloried, has taken up arms to vindicate the rights of all nations and to make the world safe for democracy."³⁵ Copies of Connor's Emmet statue were subsequently commissioned for the city of Emmetsburg, Iowa, and for Golden Gate Park in San Francisco, the latter unveiled by Éamon de Valera during his 1919 tour of the United States.³⁶

Yet another Irish memorial was presented to the United States by the Ladies' Auxiliary of the AOH in 1924, after a decade of planning. Honoring the role of Catholic women religious who had served as nurses during the Civil War, this was the brainchild of the organization's president, Ellen Ryan Jolly of Pawtucket, Rhode Island. It was approved at the group's national annual meeting in 1914. Jolly was inspired by the motto of the AIHS, "That the World May Know," to emphasize Irish contributions to American history.[37] Cardinal James Gibbons of Baltimore summarized the need for such a monument: "By the lips of many thousand veterans they [nuns] have won for the Catholic religion the praise and recognition of grateful hearts in every section of the United States, regardless of creed or race or sectional strife." Jolly succeeded in getting congressional support, then federal authorization in March 1918, with the intention of placing Jerome Connor's "The Nuns of the Battlefield" in Arlington National Cemetery.[38] This was an extraordinary achievement for the Irish; unlike the Barry and Emmet statues, this monument would officially recognize the Irish contribution to the United States in a public space of more national significance than a small capital park or a science museum. Jolly had been among those who opposed Andrew O'Connor's design for the Barry statue in 1908, but now she actively promoted the selection of Jerome Connor's design: two bronze allegorical figures, the angels of Patriotism and Peace, seated opposite each other to support a frieze depicting twelve nuns, each representing a different congregation of Catholic women.[39] The trouble with the artist's concept this time came from the Commission of Fine Arts rather than from the Irish; between 1918 and 1924, there were repeated objections to the angels in particular. Likewise, the aspiration for a place in Arlington met with sustained procrastination from the War Department and some members of Congress. While the official reason for refusing the national cemetery site was that no nuns were buried there, Jolly concluded that this carried the whiff of anti-Catholic and anti-Irish bigotry. In the end, the twelve-by-twenty-foot memorial was dedicated on September 20, 1924, in the presence of Cardinal William O'Connell, directly opposite St. Matthew's Roman Catholic Cathedral at Rhode Island Avenue and M Street in Washington, DC.[40]

As these examples suggest, ethnic leadership was critical to promoting a specific and elevated Irish image. The Irish Americans who conceived, financed, and executed these public displays were able to draw together a diverse range of class and political perspectives to support a discourse of patriotism. This was also clear at the 1904 World's Fair in St. Louis, where a replica of the County Antrim ancestral cottage of the late President William McKinley could be toured before viewing "The Irish American Historic Loan Collection," 174 items that emphasized the Irish role in the formation of the United States. The executive committee behind this display included Chairman William Bourke Cockran, Treasurer John D. Crimmins, Honorary Secretary John Quinn, and Assistant Secretary Thomas H. Murray. Crimmins has already been introduced; Cockran and Quinn were also New Yorkers, the former a popular Democratic congressman, the latter a wealthy attorney and art collector; Murray, a New England–based journalist, was the secretary-general of the AIHS and editor of its annual journal.[41] With the exception of Cockran, who emigrated from Ireland when he was seventeen, the others were second-generation Irish Americans, suggesting that social mobility worked in tandem with their motivation to redeem the Irish image.[42]

The items shared with the public through this effort ranged chronologically from the colonial period to the end of the nineteenth century to demonstrate the longevity of the Irish experience in the United States, such as flags belonging to the Twenty-Eighth Massachusetts and the Sixty-Ninth New York regiments that had seen battlefield action during the Civil War. The letter accompanying the New York flag described it as priceless: "It has always been our unswerving custom never to allow these flags out of our custody, but when we read the names of the gentlemen that make up your organization, and the worthiness of the project contemplated, we felt that we could safely trust these sacred relics in your hands."[43] Forty percent of the Irish American Historic Loan Collection came from the personal library of Crimmins, including letters written by Governor Dongan and Commodore Barry. While these so-called relics were only a small part of the whole Irish effort at the fair, they reportedly attracted "good crowds" and reactions. One of the organizers observed, "It is quite a reward for the trouble to have some old farmer from Minnesota or somewhere come up and tell one his mind about it and to see his pride in the display we have made. It gives Americans or even Irish visitors quite a new conception of Ireland."[44]

* * *

The fair in St. Louis was also an opportunity to showcase the arts that had been revived in recent decades as a form of cultural nationalism that could distinguish Irish from English. Its alignment with political nationalism (specifically, the Land League and Home Rule movements from the 1880s) was a means of elevating the image of the Irish at home and abroad.[45] The United States, therefore, became a significant early vector for the spread of this form of ethno-national self-respect in a transatlantic movement that became known as the Gaelic Revival. By 1904, the Irish Village at the Louisiana Purchase Exposition in St. Louis was thus not only able but obliged to feature music and drama as part of its cultural offerings in its 1,809-seat theater.[46] The opening ceremonies included a parade of two thousand performers, among whom were those who would portray Irish manners and customs to American fairgoers; as the *St. Louis Republic* described them, "Real Celtic people will ride in the jaunting cars, and Irish pipers will play. Celtic beauties will be seen on several gorgeously decorated floats."[47]

In reality, the experience, of course, was subjective. There was an admission fee for the Irish Village to help underwrite its costs and therefore an implicit awareness of the audience. The promoters, on the Irish end (the Department of Agriculture and Technical Instruction for Ireland, DATI) as well as on the American end (the Irish Exhibit Company), sought to impress and surprise their visitors. The cultural delegation sent from Ireland included the respected operatic singers Marie Narelle and John McCormack, who spent seven months performing at the World's Fair.[48] Three boy pipers, the brothers Harrison, were also among those who traveled from Ireland; their ranks were expanded when the Irish Village hired two of the most highly skilled traditional uilleann (or Union) pipers then based in the United States: Patsy Touhey (né Patrick Touhey), who emigrated from Ireland as a child and performed at New York Gaelic Society concerts in 1901, 1903, and 1904; and Charles Mack (né Charles McNurney), the son of an Irish immigrant who had impressed the Gaelic League of Ireland when he performed in Belfast in 1897. Both Touhey and Mack also successfully earned a living as musicians on the vaudeville circuit.[49]

County Cavan native Michael Muldoon, a well-traveled sculptor and prominent businessman based in Louisville, serves as a barometer of audience reaction: "The Irish Theater and the Irish exhibits generally are more liberally patronized than any of the other attractions at the Exposition," he told the *Kentucky Irish American*. "I thought at first that my partiality toward Irish exhibits might prejudice me in their favor, but I have heard from attendants generally that the Irish section was the most attractive to them. These expressions came from Germans, French and Americans. . . . I was amazed and agreeably surprised at the Irish exhibit . . . it is always crowded." After several days at the fair, Muldoon concluded that nothing else compared with it. "They have high class attractions. I have heard many good singers, but I have never heard better than some of these in this theater. I certainly never heard 'The Wearing of the Green' sung with such pathetic feeling as it was by a young woman at this theater. She had a pure soprano voice, and did her part well." He singled out Myles Murphy, the manager of the Irish Village, for praise.[50] Muldoon's impressions are corroborated by T. W. Rolleston, an Irish journalist and critic who was employed by DATI: "Murphy is far the best man they've got," he wrote to John Quinn in New York, "and is indeed a treasure. He is doing about three men's work, and if any good comes out of the show, it will be . . . due to him."[51]

Nevertheless, Irish Village organizers and local St. Louis Irish community leaders were forced to defend their programming choices against accusations that some representations in the theater were caricatures. As early as June, they issued a statement denying that the theater performances were anything other than "refined and attractive."[52] The accusations were not from the American or Irish American audiences but from the Dublin actors who had been recruited by Murphy to present some of the new dramatic interpretations of Irish legends that had emerged from the Gaelic Revival in Ireland, including George Russell's three-act play *Deirdre*.[53] The actors claimed that they were offended by Touhey's stage routine and that they "wouldn't take part in performances where the Irish race is burlesqued."[54] Their principal objections were reported to be two then-popular Tin Pan Alley songs, one about St. Patrick's Day that inferred a lingering holiday hangover and "It Takes the Irish to Beat the Dutch."[55] From the promoters' perspective, these were merely sour grapes, as attendance for *Deirdre* was low, audiences were unenthusiastic about the play, and the actors were uninterested in substituting a comedy instead. Murphy told Rolleston that their "performance was wretched."[56] In the end, Irish Village management prevailed, and the Irish actors were barred from the theater—"properly sacked," in Rolleston's opinion. "We are

Figure 3.1. Advertisement for Irish amusements at the 1904 World's Fair, *St. Louis Republic*, October 2, 1904, Part II, 6. Credit: *Chronicling America: Historic American Newspapers*, Library of Congress.

exiles from the only Irish soil in America," the actress Mary T. Quinn declared.⁵⁷

The influential voice of Seumas MacManus interpreted what happened in St. Louis through a distinctly different Irish lens: "The Irish at home right heartily applaud the plucky action of the players forfeiting their position, rather than countenance the disgusting caricature that was believed had long since been banished from, at least, the Irish stage in America. . . . They have won the gratitude of the Irish people at home, who, in turn, are highly incensed with the management of the Irish exhibit."⁵⁸ In objecting to Touhey, whom they called the "Bowery" Irishman, the Dublin actors actually used him as an excuse to break their contract for reasons that remain unclear, since the other members of the Irish cultural delegation do not appear to have made similar protests. In some quarters, they were accused of posing as "indignant patriots" who simply wanted control of the Irish Village theater in what was reminiscent of an earlier power struggle the same actors had had in Dublin with William Butler Yeats.⁵⁹

This contretemps foreshadowed questions about artistic authenticity that bedeviled Irish / Irish American relations thereafter. But it did not occur in a vacuum. The AOH, in concert with members of the Gaelic League and the Clan na Gael, had an established record of protests against demeaning depictions of the Irish, using a form of "practical censorship" that M. Alison Kibler calls both "a show of force and a political platform." In 1902 and 1903, they complained about a burlesque, *McFadden's Row of Flats*, during productions at Denver, New York, and Philadelphia theaters because it characterized the Irish as "low, drunken, ignorant and brutal."⁶⁰ Significantly, 1904 was the same year that the AOH and its Ladies' Auxiliary undertook a national campaign to eradicate the "Stage Irishman" in all media, a position vocally supported by the *Gaelic American* and the *Irish World* newspapers.⁶¹ The Stage Irishman was a "creature with baboon face, wild whiskers and lowering brow—dressed up in the garb of ignorance and buffoonery and poverty," presented "to the American public as a type." The campaign also targeted "vile newspaper cartoons, the deliberate misrepresentation of Irish action and sentiment, [and] the suppression of Irish news."⁶² *McFadden's Row of Flats* was accused of giving people "incorrect impressions of Irish home life from seeing distorted and libelous misrepresentations." At the time, *The Gael*, a monthly magazine originally published as *An Gaodhal* in New York City, wrote that "Irishmen do not object to honest caricature. . . . The play would not worry them were it not for the evil and misleading effect it is having on the American people and others who have not had opportunity to know the Irish at close range." The *Cleveland Leader* asserted, "We enjoy a good Irishman. The public finds a charm in the wit and humor of the comedian in any reputable playhouse. The better playhouses have done away with the exaggerated national stage character."[63]

Thus, when hundreds of delegates to the AOH national convention attended Irish Day at the St. Louis fairgrounds on July 21, 1904, the Hibernians engaged with the Irish Village exhibits and the entertainment after having just passed a resolution condemning the Stage Irishman that was well publicized in a syndicated news story.[64] If they saw Touhey's act on the stage of the Irish Theater, they must have received it in much the same way that two hundred members of the International Association of Chiefs of Police did: "[They] encored his playing repeatedly, and wanted him to continue his wonderful music indefinitely, but four encores were all the stage manager would allow. Neither sentiment nor early associations had much to do with this acclaim, for the majority of those present were of other than Irish ancestry, and of the latter less than half were of Irish birth."[65] This corroborates Murphy's statement to the *Gaelic American*: "As for the 'stage' Irishman, I am as much opposed to any gross travesty on the race as anybody. Tuohy's [sic] performance was within bounds at all times, and whatever objectionable points it may have had at first were promptly cut out. Only a supersensitive individual could take offence."[66] There is ambiguity about what the Wisconsin AOH state president, John T. Kelly, was referring to when he declared in early August that "we were also enabled to remove some objectionable shows from the Irish village at the St. Louis fair. We are proud of such actors as Joe Murphy, W. J. Scanlon, and Chauncey Olcott, but we do not propose to countenance the insulting and indecent burlesques which are perpetrated by fellows from the Bowery."[67] Patsy Touhey was still on the entertainment bill for the Irish Village in mid-August 1904.[68] Indeed, his approval by audiences at the World's Fair derived not only from his prized skills on the pipes but from his reputation as a recording artist; thus, his talents more than aligned with the exhibit's goal of showcasing Irish arts. Touhey's version of the "Shaskeen Reel" had been issued the previous year for purchase as an Edison wax cylinder.[69]

As Ireland began to engage with image-making, there was disparity about why (motive) and how (content) to represent Ireland and the Irish in the United States in new ways. After 1904, the tensions between Irish cultural brokers in Ireland (largely Anglo-Irish Protestant elites) and those in the United States grew, coming to a head in 1911. Those very earnest advocates of the Gaelic Revival in Ireland did not fully comprehend the reach of an important strand in the green space and its relationship to the evolving Irish image. An avant-garde drama like *Deirdre*—set in pre-Christian Ireland, with actors behind a gauze screen backlit in green and amber, performed in 1904 St. Louis rather than 1902 Dublin[70]—paled against popular melodramatic star vehicles like Brandon Tynan's *Robert Emmet*, set during the rebellion in late eighteenth-century Ireland, and Chauncey Olcott's *Barry of Ballymore*, which introduced "Mother Machree" (1910) and generated sheet music and recording sales thereafter. When Dublin's Abbey Theatre toured the United States with a production of John Millington Synge's *The Playboy of the Western World* in 1911, it ran headlong into this well-established genre of presenting Irish on the American stage. In the historiography of transatlantic Irish cultural currency in the twentieth century, most arguments champion Ireland's prerogative without any serious regard for Irish America's contributions.[71] *The Playboy of the Western World* was written by an Irish-born playwright and performed by a company of Irish actors, yet it caused trouble in Dublin at its premiere in 1907 because of long-simmering tensions between cultural nationalists who were jockeying for supremacy there.[72] Trouble over *The Playboy* in the United States in 1911 was useful in, once and for all, anointing a victor in that battle. But it also became the moment when all the hard work of cultural representation by Irish America for close to a century—including the successful 1907 campaign against the Russell Brothers' Irish servant girl vaudeville routine[73]—was hijacked.

Most accounts of the *Playboy* "riots" in Boston, New York, and Philadelphia paint a portrait of reactionary Irish American narrow-mindedness, of an obsessive aversion to profanity, even glibly claiming that "two generations in the slums of New York killed" Irish ability to appreciate the new literature.[74] But there was a more subtle and important issue at stake—namely, that the company chose to project from the stage of major theaters, in the hearts of principal American cities and to mainly non-Irish audiences, an image of the Irish that purported to be "soberly documentary." The Abbey Theatre performed in the United States as the Irish Players, a public relations move calculated to maximize recognition of the word Irish. As such, they attracted mainstream media attention while claiming that the dramas in their repertoire "contain a large proportion of essential truth and are actually characteristic of the race which they profess to illustrate."[75] The *Gaelic American* was opposed to *The Playboy* on the grounds that it was not a true account of the people of Ireland but in fact an "artistic" interpretation.[76] Irish American objections were thus inevitable.

The *New York Times* reviewer described *The Playboy*'s subject matter as "disillusionment, the breaking of idols, the rending of a veil of misconception."[77] It was a contemporary drama, set in a supposedly realistic depiction of rural Ireland, about a young man who becomes a local hero by boasting that he has killed his father. The Central Council of Irish County Associations in Boston "condemned the play 'as bearing false witness and the foulest level that has ever been perpetrated on the Irish character.'"[78] Opening night in New York City, November 27, 1911, brought strenuous protests only five minutes into the performance, complete with hissing, vegetables, eggs, and asafetida bombs. "Son of a bitch, that's not Irish," the *Gaelic American*'s fiery editor John Devoy is said to have shouted from the audience.[79] Police ejected over fifty persons from the theater and arrested ten men. Lady Gregory, as chief spokesperson for the dramatic troupe, later disdainfully listed the occupations of those arraigned: "Two of them were bartenders; one a liquor dealer; two clerks; one a harness-maker; one an instructor; one a mason; one a carpenter; and one an electrician."[80] But other accounts noted that the audience also included "a group of women in fashionable evening gowns" who were insulted. Standing on their orchestra chairs they screamed that the play's "presentation was a part of the oppression that England had always imposed on the Irish, that that downtrodden race was entitled to fair play and it was expected that these United States would furnish the battleground whereon that fair play was to be won."[81]

Devoy, who had been advocating for Irish independence for fifty years at that point, was particularly aggravated: "The worst is that Yeats has managed to fill every American editor with the idea that his theatre company is a product of the Gaelic League," he wrote to a fellow Clan na Gael leader. "It is repeated almost every day, as in a *Times* editorial today, and we are lectured as being 'out of touch' with Ireland by people who never knew Ireland."[82] And yet, also in the audience that night was Rosina Emmet, the great-grandniece of the patriot Robert Emmet, who declared, "I say give them [the Abbey players] a chance" after turning in one of the egg throwers to the police.[83] These contrasting perspectives are reminiscent of the internal divisions about image that had surfaced only a couple of years earlier over the Barry statue for Franklin Park.

Where there was common ground for Ireland and Irish America was on the importance of the American imprimatur. As Lucy McDiarmid persuasively argues, protests over *The Playboy* were not really about its content but about who had the power to generate the most controversy and thus the most publicity: "Boston responded to Dublin, Providence responded to Boston, New York responded to all the previous cities, and Philadelphia to Dublin, New York, etc. Each separate controversy was inspired not by what was happening on stage but by the dynamics of the whole sequence." Lady Gregory was a masterful publicist who had used the threat of British censorship to good effect in Ireland; now she had the ear of Anglo-Saxon Protestant elites in the United States who would naturally object to any attempt to control artistic expression.[84] But she underestimated the legacy of Irish American cultural currency as well as the extent to which those invested in it knew their way around American law.

The Abbey Theatre presented *The Playboy* in east coast cities whose Irish populations, full of immigrants with deep loyalties to their native counties, were heavily drawn from the west of Ireland, including Mayo, the setting of the play.[85] The Mayo Men's Patriotic and Benevolent Association in New York City, for example, was over thirty years old in 1911, and it was a county with a genuine hero: Martin Sheridan, a New York policeman born in Bohola, County Mayo, who held national and world records in discus and javelin throws, pole vault, and standing broad jump, among others. In 1906, Sheridan had been named "the greatest track and field athlete of all time" by New York City sports writers before fulfilling that promise at the 1908 Olympics; the following year he was tapped to play Robert Fulton on the *Clermont* float for the Hudson-Fulton Celebration.[86] Although Yeats could claim that Synge's play was realistic and truthful,[87] he was naïve about the extent to which such claims would open *The Playboy* to scrutiny in the United States. The County Tyrone Society of New York considered it "a challenge that could not be ignored," and it picketed Maxine Elliott's Theatre nightly.[88]

The Playboy was presented in the autumn of 1911, a year that had opened with complaints by the AOH about offensive St. Patrick's Day postcards. Significantly, it was also the year that the St. Patrick's Day Parade Committee promulgated a new dress code—sober, dark clothes—for all participants in the annual March 17 parade in New York City. This was intended to eliminate the most obvious sartorial features that the press had been fond of using to caricature and ridicule the Irish.[89] Even though Christy Mahon, Synge's playboy, did not wear the typical Stage Irishman costume of knee breeches and a tall felt hat or carry the usual Stage Irishman symbols of a clay pipe and shillelagh, his "swagger, his boisterousness and his pugnacity" bore the very hallmarks of the "psychology of the Stage Irishman" that were so offensive in the American context.[90]

For nearly a decade, *The Gael* had warned that "stamping Ireland as the land of fools and menials, militates against the honor of the country in America and everywhere else."[91] The Abbey Theatre's depiction of Irish people as so ignorant that they could condone parricide as a heroic deed was insidious in such an environment. When *The Playboy* projected an image of a degenerate country full of liars and murderers, it was completely at odds with Irish America's critical need to portray Ireland as a modern society inherently worthy of political autonomy. It also undermined the Catholic Church's insistence that the Irish were capable of being loyal, law-abiding citizens of the United States, in spite of nativist suspicions to the contrary.[92] Nevertheless, in a statement to the *New York Times*, Yeats persisted, warning Irish Americans to be "very careful how they criticise the drama of the Irish players . . . they should not form hasty judgements about things upon which the Irish of Ireland had already given favorable opinion."[93] The Gaelic League replied that "the hero worship of murderers and the exposure of young girls to the mercies of villains and the breaking of plighted faith to court the smiles of scoundrels is not now and never was a characteristic of the Irish, and that said play put forward as typical of Irish life and manners is a gross falsehood." The AOH, "ever alert and zealous at all time to promote the best interests of our people, both at home and abroad from insult," agreed, calling Synge's poetic drama "a thin veneer" in which "every line leads to or conveys an insult."[94]

At first glance, the decision to protest *The Playboy* through physical means seemed to support the stereotype of the Irish as an unruly people. It was all "delightful Hibernianism," the first of two *New York Times* editorials remarked: "Synge's *Playboy* may or may not misrepresent the character of the Western Irish peasantry, but it is quite clear that the howlers and egg-throwers have grossly misrepresented the great law-abiding American citizens of Irish birth and descent."[95] In reality, the protests were a calculated attempt to work within the American legal system to shut down a play that public opinion kept insisting was Irish simply because the image was being projected by the Irish from Ireland. Irish Americans knew better. Joseph McGarrity, the Philadelphia Clan na Gael leader, felt that "there was nothing in the play that would cause anyone who would witness it to have love or admiration for the people and the country represented in it."[96] Since the offense was clearly a subjective one, the only recourse was to carefully choose words and phrases like *blasphemous* and *obscene*, which placed Irish American objections to *The Playboy* in a legal realm where decency was covered by public statutes. Municipal authorities were approached in Boston, Providence, and New York to little effect, but in Philadelphia, there was a 1911 law that forbade "lascivious, obscene, indecent, sacrilegious or immoral" productions.[97] Lady Gregory, who insisted on referring to McGarrity only as "the liquor dealer," was apparently oblivious to his transatlantic work on behalf of Irish nationalism that was no less committed than her own.[98] Because of his efforts, the company was arrested and the case was brought to trial in Philadelphia.[99]

Although the judge later dismissed the charges, the point was clearly made: the Irish in Ireland, just like the producers of *McFadden's Row of Flats*, would not be permitted to upset the image that was being so carefully constructed by the Irish in the United States. The Abbey Theatre's "insolence in presuming to stand for Irish literature and in drama anywhere" was summed up in an *Irish American Weekly* editorial: "A few more douches of cold water will enable these people to realize how absurd it is for an arrogant and bigoted coterie to attempt to misrepresent a nation."[100] Lady Gregory's defense was not only tone-deaf; it revealed what was at stake. She declared, "The plays have been taught in the dramatic classes of the University of Pennsylvania, that the President of Bryn Mawr had invited the players to the College for the day, and had sent a large party of students to the last matinée of *The Playboy*."[101]

To counter *The Playboy*, Irish New Yorkers took over the Sixty-Ninth Regiment Armory in Manhattan on April 24 and 25, 1913, for the premiere of *An Dhord Fhiann* (*The Fenian Rallying Cry*), a pageant of Irish history written and directed by Anna Throop Craig. This dramatic format was internationally popular at the time, including in Ireland between 1908 and 1914, where it served a nationalist agenda by presenting a heroic historical narrative about the Irish past.[102] The New York pageant was in this same vein, but it also implicitly echoed the aspirations regarding the Irish image that lay behind the historic exhibits and some of the cultural programming at the World's Fair in St. Louis just a few years earlier. Presented under the auspices of the Gaelic League in New York, this use of entertainment for public education was coordinated by Judge Victor J. Dowling (a veteran of the Emmet Statue Committee), New York City Tenement House commissioner John J. Murphy (chairman of the American Committee of the Gaelic League), and two prominent women physicians, Dr. Gertrude B. Kelly and Dr. Madge C. L. McGuinness.[103] By this time, New York City was the headquarters for dozens of organizations devoted to the promotion of Irish music, dance, and language through local chapters all across the country. The Irish Historic Pageant was a direct reflection of this activity: its hundreds of participants were drawn from "members of the Irish-American societies here and abroad and were assisted by a corps of professional actors and actresses" who rehearsed for weeks.[104]

The pageant depicted Ireland's conversion from pagan to Christian in two parts. In the dramatized story of the ancient hero Fionn mac Cumhaill, a Gaelic nation of skilled warriors is ruled by one High King, Conn. Then through the influence of St. Colmcille, Ireland becomes the safe keeper of Western civilization and learning during the dark sixth century. These major points could be read as a metaphor for contemporary Ireland. In 1913, there was still rosy optimism that the Irish Parliamentary Party would successfully shepherd a Home Rule bill through the British Parliament, thereby making Ireland "a nation once again," a phrase popular among Irish nationalists. In addition, more than a dozen members of the renowned Irish American Athletic Club (including its 1908 Olympic medalists such as hammer thrower Matthew McGrath) performed stone throwing and jumping contests on the "Field of Sports" as part of the first segment of the pageant. The circular that the Gaelic League sent to the press intentionally evoked a mystical Ireland. "The past [will] live again," it declared, promising "groups of Clerics and old-time Bards . . . Irish wolfhounds introduced in the tableaux . . . the ancient Hill of Tara, seat of the Irish Kings . . . fairy-like music, sonorous choruses, beautiful lighting effects, with sunrise, moonlight, and the mists ascending from bogs and fens, where ancient spirits and goblins float, specter-like, through the haunted valley." The effect, according to the critic of *The Outlook*, "was very beautiful."[105] It was all set to old Irish airs, orchestrated by Alfred Robyn. The sophistication of the men and women who produced the pageant was clear from this romantic hook to get the attention of the press and public because, for them, the pageant's true purpose was "to show folk who have listened to the writings of detractors that Erin even back in the dim ages was not a land of unthinking savages."[106] Significantly, this characterization of Irish culture in terms of high art—with references to a classical heritage centered on Tara and the singing of Thomas Moore's "The Harp That Once through Tara's Halls" (which the *New York Times* called an "ancient lyric" even though it was no more than a century old!)—lifted Irish into that gray area where antiquity legitimizes culture.[107]

An Dhord Fhiann has long been forgotten, while the plays of the Abbey Theatre were quickly accepted as canonical in Ireland as well as among educated non-Irish elites in the United States.[108] The entry of the Abbey's Irish image into the green space in this way had so much longevity and influence that it created "a stereotypical view of an Irish play, which was invariably rural and rich in brogues and trademark antics," an image that John Harrington argues "was especially artificial" in places like New York.[109]

* * *

After the establishment of the Irish Free State, circumstances became more complicated for Irish cultural representation in America. There was a short-lived effort to introduce New Yorkers to visual art that would be "a necessary corollary to the new political state of affairs in Ireland." The Helen Hackett Gallery and the Irish Art Rooms (later briefly known as the Museum of Irish Art) functioned as salons where the city's cultural literati could see "post-Treaty" art that reflected "distinct national character," or new "Irishness," while being introduced to Irish consular officials. But some of the challenges of media representation discussed in chapter 2 surfaced in this cultural realm too; the *Charleston News and Courier* ran a review of the first group show under the headline "Irish Exhibition Hits Modernism: Stormy History of Land Put on Canvas—Characteristic Melancholy Shown" and then described the art as "almost undisturbed by modernism."[110]

The artist who helped translate Irish best was the realist painter Seán Keating, said to be "unfettered by any worn out tradition or convention." In March 1929, he made his American debut with the *Tipperary Hurler*, which was pictured in the New York Times being viewed in the Hackett Gallery by the new Irish Free State minister to the United States.[111] The press noted that it was the painting "visitors continually return[ed] to and discuss[ed] most." When it was subsequently included in a show of contemporary Irish artists in Boston that May, the press called it Keating's "masterpiece."[112] It depicted a strong, young Gaelic athlete, a portrait that easily resonated with Irish immigrants in the United States, where physical prowess in sports like baseball, boxing, basketball, and track and field had long been integral to improving the Irish image.[113] Indeed, this was evident two years before Keating's painting was shown when the actual Tipperary team, the 1926 All-Ireland Hurling Champions, toured America. Fifteen thousand saw the Irish defeat a California all-star team in June, "one of the largest crowds ever to witness an athletic event" in San Francisco.[114] That Tipperary won every match against teams of Irish and Irish Americans in every city it visited also telegraphed the vitality of independent Ireland. In the crowd were men and women who had personally lived the Gaelic Revival and/or had emigrated in the wake of internecine disagreements over the direction of Ireland's political future between 1922 and 1923. Keating's *Tipperary Hurler*, in this respect, was as iconic for them as John Barry and Robert Emmet had been for Irish Americans only twenty years earlier. Éimear O'Connor even calls the painting's title "evocative of ancient Irish history and myth."[115]

These same new immigrants were eager to preserve the Irish part of their identity, so in 1933, they revived the Gaelic League's feis model and made folk traditions the bedrock of Irish cultural self-respect.[116] Under the auspices of the United Irish Counties Association (UICA), founded in 1904 as a central administrative body to guide and coordinate the nonsporting activities of New York's thirty-four county organizations, this all-day event—in essence, a deconstructed pageant—offered dozens of competitions for amateurs. Its organization was a year-round pursuit for as many as eighty-six committees, involving the preparation of syllabi, logistical arrangements, and fundraising for or soliciting the donation of medals and prize cups.[117] The *Irish World* concluded, "It is certainly a credit to the Irish race that in cosmopolitan New York men and women may be found who are willing to devote their time and energy to the preservation of our ancient Feiseanna."[118]

Within ten years of its inception, the UICA Feis had national press coverage with headlines that annually noted a record attendance, often in excess of ten thousand. By 1942, it was drawing fifteen thousand spectators for 975 participants in seventy-five competitive events.[119] Three things made the UICA Feis unique: it was almost invariably a large outdoor, public event held on a summer Sunday, for many years on the grounds of Fordham University or Hunter (later Lehman) College in the Bronx (which had the secondary effect of exposing young people to the possibilities of higher education); it went to great lengths to demonstrate the positive benefits of Irish culture; and it provided a model for similar activities in other cities across the country. Paul O'Dwyer, who was destined for a long legal career as an advocate for Ireland in America, told the Federal Writers Project in 1939 that "in preserving and reviving such customs, the Irish in America believe that they are giving to their nation and to the world at large the most graphic as well as the only authentic method of studying the Irish people."[120] An *Irish Echo* editorial in 1942 supported the feis ethos with rhetoric reminiscent of that used by the turn-of-the-century second-generation Irish elites discussed earlier: "We would be doing ourselves, and incidentally the country of our adoption, a serious wrong if we were to allow the fine traditions, the simple and lovely arts, the graceful dances, the incomparable melodies, which we brought here and which are not the least of our contributions to America, to die out because of disuse and neglect."[121] James J. Comerford, a native of County Kilkenny who was a UICA president and a Manhattan assistant district attorney, concluded that because the feis was highly visible, it projected "the name of the UICA out among the other Irish Societies in America with great force and create[d] an image of success."[122]

Efforts to organize the feis also coincided with annual festivals in the United States organized by the National Council for the Traditional Arts, a "multicultural celebration" established in 1933, which soon included an Irish component.[123] After the Second World War, the feis ascended in the United States even as it declined in Ireland, where it was seen as having served out its "political" function—that is, as "an assertion of the distinctiveness of Irish separatism.... Some ill-defined idea lay embodied in the Feis of the pure, noble, upright, hard-working and Irish-speaking peasant as the chosen custodian of this old and better way of life."[124] Despite such negative, antimodern associations in Ireland and the irony of Irish America's earlier aversion to the peasant image, the feis was still a useful concept in the United States because it could undergird Irish self-respect just as statues of Moore, Barry, and Emmet and the 1913 historic pageant had decades earlier. This was reflected in the elaborate syllabi of the UICA Feis, an amalgamation of folk art and high art as well as history that was the antithesis of the Stage Irishman or of a demeaned peasantry.[125] In 1940, for example, girls under twelve in the vocal section were required to sing two pieces: the Gaelic nursery rhyme "Óró Bog Liom Í" and "My Bonny Cuckoo," an Irish air. The juvenile violin solo competition (under age nine) required a sight-reading test as well as the ability to play Thomas Moore's "Rich and Rare Were the Gems She Wore" plus a dance tune of their choice. Nonnative speakers in the Irish language competition had to be able to recite the Lord's Prayer in addition to discussing such things as the time, weather, and salutations. The essay contest for grammar school students that year was six hundred to eight hundred words on "the Irish part in the building of New York City," while the journalism competition required a four-hundred-word "news report of a happening in Ireland in 1940, showing accuracy and newspaper style." One year, the recitation competition might be a dramatic presentation of an Irish epic poem; another, it could be an excerpt from a political speech by an Irish nationalist like John Mitchel, Thomas Francis Meagher, or Henry Joy McCracken. Clearly, the newest immigrants from the Irish Free State had a vested interest in elevating the meaning of Irish in the United States through culture, especially during the years when Ireland's neutrality was being demonized in the American press.[126]

This generation also raised the profile of traditional Irish folk music in the United States when they purchased commercial recordings by renowned masters, many of whom were also preparing the children of immigrants for the feis. Indeed, the market was so robust that by World War II, thousands of sides had been recorded by hundreds of American-based Irish instrumentalists.[127] Irish music flourished on the radio too. As early as 1928, the *Irish World* recognized its potential vis-à-vis the Irish image: "Realizing that the radio is now the most powerful weapon of spreading the truth about Ireland . . . Irish radio owners are asked to write the various stations when the programs offend or when they please, and thus make their influence felt for bringing this great medium to their side in enlightening America about their race and its culture and combatting anti-Irish propaganda." Programming was regularly undercut, however, by superficial descriptions of Irish radio content. "The ether will be tinted green and the air thick with brogue," the *Kentucky Post* wrote to introduce its March 1929 "shamrock-laden program."[128]

Defining Irish music was also highly fluid because a market for older classics still existed. Records enabled John McCormack, a native of County Westmeath and a veteran of the 1904 Irish Village, to reach audiences beyond opera lovers; he made over 580 records, most on Victor's Red Seal label during the 1920s and 1930s, including Irish songs. It was his interpretation of Thomas Moore's melodies—like "The Minstrel Boy," "Believe Me If All Those Endearing Young Charms," and "The Harp That Once through Tara's Halls"—that became definitive. "The Last Rose of Summer," for example, sold "more than one and a half million copies in America alone."[129] Just as *Moore's Melodies* had done a hundred years earlier, these recordings elevated the link between Irish and the arts as they infiltrated American homes, whether the purchasers had roots in Ireland or not. Radio extended their reach

Figure 3.2. D. B. Sheahan's bust of Thomas Moore in New York's Central Park was the location for a demonstration of Irish traditional music and dance to promote the 1949 feis of the UICA. The harpist is Josephine Patricia Smith, whose radio program *Rambles in Erin* featured Irish music, history, and language broadcast on 126 networks between 1926 and 1942. Credit: United Irish Counties Association Collection (AIA.056), box 10, folder 2, Archives of Irish America, Special Collections, Bobst Library, New York University.

and cemented connections between Irish and a male voice in American popular culture, leading to careers for tenors in the McCormack vein like Morton Downey and John Feeney, who introduced new songs to the nostalgic repertoire with such hit recordings as "That's How I Spell I-R-E-L-A-N-D" (1931) and "When It's Moonlight in Mayo" (1934), respectively.[130] They were soon eclipsed by the baritone Bing Crosby who, after his first Irish single, "Did Your Mother Come from Ireland?" (1941), released four Irish-themed albums, contributing a critical infusion to the green space: *St. Patrick's Day* (1947), *When Irish Eyes Are Smiling* (1952), *Shillelaghs and Shamrocks* (1956), and *A Little Bit of Irish* (1966).[131]

All the while, the Friendly Sons of St. Patrick carried on their tradition of annual dinners; instead of advocating for statues in the public square, it was now easier to demonstrate ethnic self-respect simply by attracting distinguished speakers who could garner positive press coverage, making generous charitable contributions to social welfare (usually Catholic) organizations, and providing a professional network for its members who were largely drawn from lawyers and judges by the mid-twentieth century.[132] The music of McCormack and Herbert, both members, remained favorites especially on March 17 programs. The AIHS continued its mandate ("That the World May Know") by publishing an annual journal, edited by Michael J. O'Brien, that preserved in more detail the Irish contribution to colonial America. Both societies were no less Irish in their motivation but, by independent Ireland's definition, they were really more American than Irish.

* * *

After the Irish Free State agreed to contribute to the 1933–34 Century of Progress Exposition in Chicago, the Irish consul in New York, Bill Macaulay, observed that "at former expositions, Ireland reproduced its typical peasant life." Now it intended to "show the development of our industries since 1922" by ensuring that Americans saw how Ireland had "transformed the River Shannon from a subject of sentimental songs to a great new [electric] power development." This dichotomy between old and new images was exacerbated by American expectations that the Chicago Fair would include not just the Irish Free State exhibition in the Travel and Transport Building but an Irish Village as there had been in 1893 and 1904. Ireland was leery about any entertainment and souvenir concessions that it could not control, fearing they would "reflect adversely on the Irish people." The new Irish consul general in Chicago, Dan McGrath, tasked with making arrangements for the official Free State displays, was adamant that the very concept of an Irish Village conveyed "something of the type that is wholly out-moded in Irish life and perhaps of a character derogatory to our people."[133] Exposition organizers were sensitive to Irish Free State objections throughout 1933 when evaluating several requests to set up an Irish Village. In 1934, they settled on the Irish Village Corporation, a group of investors who initially seemed to have a copacetic vision that emphasized Ireland's golden age; the village would "turn back the pages of time a thousand or more years and show what Erin was like in days of old," its promotional literature declared.[134]

In practice, as Charles Fanning sums it up, "the result was a rip-roaring saga of embarrassments, bankruptcies, and tangles with authority."[135] Without an endorsement from the Irish Free State, the attractions at the Irish Village quickly ran into strenuous objections from Irish Americans. These were somewhat allayed during the summer when the respected dancing master Pat Roche, a native of County Clare only four years in Chicago, was hired to lead a troupe of forty-nine students to perform at the Irish Village. He also assembled the Harp and Shamrock Orchestra, drawn from the wealth of talent available among local Irish musicians, who played every day on the "Emerald Green" and got postfair recording contracts with Decca Records. But in Fanning's words, "the infusion of traditional culture was too little, too late."[136]

The Irish Free State kept its distance, taking pride in entertainment that conveyed a different image, such as the achievement of its army jumpers at the fair's horse show and the promise of its boxers in a Golden Gloves match, both in 1933.[137] Despite rainy weather, Irish Day on August 15, 1934, attracted 82,769 for a three-hour program in the fair's Court of States. But the challenge of negotiating what was Irish helps explain how a 1912 Tin Pan Alley tune, "There's Only One Ireland," slipped into an otherwise elevated and official agenda.[138] The song preceded the Reverend Ambrose M. Griffin's "Address on the Educational, Cultural, Political and Economic Evolution of Ireland" and the day's keynote speech, "The Irish, the Gulf Stream of Civilization" by

Quin O'Brien, Chicago's assistant corporation counsel. "Most believe that the origin of the Irish is uncertain," O'Brien said, in the presence of Consul General McGrath, "that before the coming of St. Patrick they were a barbarous, benighted people. Such has been the Anglo-Saxon teaching and perversion of history. Modern research fully demonstrates their ancient genesis and glories."[139] This theme foreshadowed *The Pageant of the Celt*, held over two days a couple of weeks later. Reminiscent of *An Dhord Fhiann*, it traced Irish history from pre-Christian to Easter 1916, dramatized by a cast of thousands, and seen by as many as twenty thousand people. The audience was encouraged to "join in mass singing of the Irish National Anthem," whose words were printed in the pageant program along with short essays on "Recognition of Celtic Culture in Our Universities," "Trail of the Irish Pioneers in America," and "Éire, Monastery of Europe."[140] The grip of green space influence was tightening.

Ireland's engagement with the subsequent 1939 World's Fair in New York was far more direct. It had two pavilions for international audiences, one devoted to culture and history in the Hall of Nations and another focusing on trade promotion. Now with Éamon de Valera in place as *taoiseach* and a new name, Éire, the government of Ireland commissioned Dublin architect Michael Scott to "project both a distinct national identity and a modern, progressive image for the country."[141] His glass and steel trade pavilion was a futuristic elevation on a shamrock-shaped plan. Since the association of Ireland and Irish with the shamrock was well known in America, as chapter 6 demonstrates, the building met established expectations at first glance. However, dominating the space inside was Seán Keating's massive (80′ × 35′) mural to industrializing Ireland, which emphasized water-powered electrification and Shannon Airport.[142] Keating's *Tipperary Hurler* was exhibited nearby, a juxtaposition that reassured Irish immigrants that modernity was not displacing Gaelic tradition.[143]

The Irish section of the Hall of Nations embodied themes more familiar to Americans, both Irish and non-Irish, as nurtured for decades in the green space. Maurice MacGonigal's mural (32′ × 20′) depicted George Washington with allegorical figures representing America and Liberty, flanked by Commodore John Barry among "thirty or forty of the famous Irishmen who helped America win and hold her independence." The *New York Times* described it as "one of the most striking of the murals at the fair."[144] It formed a backdrop to exhibit cases that displayed reproductions of George Washington's order to his army "making 'St. Patrick' the password for March 17th" and of the naval commission issued to Barry.[145] On panels of green marble from Connemara, a familiar timeline of Irish history and culture began with the Bronze Age and proceeded to the present day via "the Missionary Age" and the period of "Invasion and Resistance." Ireland's avowed purpose was to associate its image with "love of liberty and love of learning," twin strands that had proven cultural currency for the Irish in the United States.[146]

Students from Columbia University's Irish Society presented Irish Day at the fair complete with dancers, pipers, a harpist, and a poet; lectures and papers about early Irish influence on, and immigration to, America; and Rita McLoughlin's rendition of Thomas Moore's "The Last Rose of Summer," which "was roundly applauded."[147] The following spring, at Ireland Day in 1940, the Gaelic Society of New York arranged the program of music and dancing at the fair, and Julia Lennon sang Moore's "Let Erin Remember the Days of Old."[148] In contrast, a commercial concession called "Giant's Causeway" was objected to by the Irish government. Although it was completely separate from the Irish pavilions, it was too easy for visitors to be confused when its amusements included a Blarney Stone and promotional headlines that promised "Faithful Replicas of Ireland's most famous sites, together with a Complete and Authentic Old Irish Village." Ireland's official representative to the 1939 World's Fair, its New York consul general Leo McCauley, found the "growling fifty-foot giant" at the entrance who was meant to be the warrior hero Fionn mac Cumhaill particularly offensive: "I asked the promoters whether if they had a Greek exhibit they would portray Achilles in this fashion. They answered that they would not, but that the Greeks of those days were more advanced than the Irish. This is the typical opinion of an Englishman and a Scotsman, springing from a complete ignorance of Irish cultural history."[149]

In 1955, the Irish government sponsored a tour by the Irish Festival Singers, who were "widely known in Dublin and throughout the British Isles because of concert, television, and radio appearances."[150] Among the featured artists in the group were mezzo-soprano Veronica Dunne and contralto Sylvia O'Brien; tenors Liam DeVally, Joseph McNally, and Dermot Troy; and baritone Austin Gaffney, with Miss Terry O'Connor on harp and violin. All were accomplished professionals who could represent Irish as high art at major venues like New York's Carnegie Hall and on recordings they made for the Angel Records label.[151] In addition to some Moore favorites and ballads in the Irish language in their repertoire, audiences were introduced to new folk songs such as "The Foggy Dew" and "The West's Awake." Popular culture's influence on the Irish sound was reflected in the Irish Festival Singers' decision to include "Danny Boy."[152] This 1913 composition, set to an old Irish air, had already been recorded by American celebrity artists Judy Garland (1940), Glen Miller (1940), and Bing Crosby (1941). A review of their 1956 concert in San Francisco admired the troupe's talent but not their "tasteless" material: "They are all eminently capable of doing something magnificent with and for the music of their country. Perhaps they will when they can convince their managers that the American audience is not exclusively interested in light entertainment."[153]

The Irish American version of this cultural effort was Dorothy Hayden's Irish Memories Stage Revue, which played festivals, church concerts, and dancehalls from the late 1940s. More Americans saw their seven appearances on the nationally broadcast television program *The Ed Sullivan Show* in the 1950s than ever heard the Irish Festival Singers. Hayden, a second-generation New Yorker, assembled her performers mainly from the ranks of UICA Feis winners, imbued with pride in their Irish heritage as well as in American patriotism. Her dancers, led by champion Timmy Cronin, wore tap shoes; although strictly forbidden in traditional Irish step dancing, the taps were a concession made for an American audience.[154] Likewise, her accommodations to changing musical tastes meant offering more "American arrangements, textures, and rhythms" to the "popular Irish repertoire."[155] By 1959, Ed Sullivan, whose paternal grandparents were born in Ireland, unconsciously demonstrated how much green space cross-fertilization had taken place for Irish since his own birth in 1901.[156] He filmed on location in Ireland for a St. Patrick's Day special that was interspersed with live entertainment during the television broadcast. Lily Comerford's Dublin students demonstrated step dancing; Liam DeVally of the Irish Festival Singers performed "The Gentle Maiden," a nineteenth-century ballad; and a "trio of young harmonica players" gave a rendition of "Danny Boy." Éamon de Valera was interviewed; so too was the delightful "caretaker of Blarney Castle" as Sullivan kissed the fabled stone. These images shared American living room screens with the Irish American septuagenarian Pat Rooney, who showcased his famous vaudeville clog dancing. Jewish comic Myron Cohen told some Irish stories, and the Glee Club of the Friendly Sons of St. Patrick sang a medley of Irish ballads.[157]

This hybrid image was soon directly challenged by the Clancy Brothers and Tommy Makem, a folk group of recent Irish immigrants who, through television and multicultural folk festival appearances, reached American audiences that numbered in the millions. Their recordings, especially 1963's *In Person at Carnegie Hall*, were often best sellers. Makem recalled that American audiences in the late 1950s wanted popular rather than traditional songs: "When we started out, we refused to sing for Irish audiences because they would all be into Bing Crosby, 'Danny Boy,' things like that. That's what they were being fed by the radio programs at the time. . . . They figured this was all there was to it. They had left Ireland and sort of looked down on Irish music. You were a peasant if you sang that kind of thing. These people were trying to drag themselves up by their boot straps and you know, be ultra-respectable. It wasn't what we were about." According to Liam Clancy, they also gave young Irish Americans tacit permission to reject American sentiment and nostalgia for what they perceived as more "artistically advanced" and authentic Irish music.[158]

What, in fact, was authentic by then? Ireland's perspective couldn't prevail over Irish America's simply because it had political legitimacy. Ireland couldn't simply say it was right and Irish America was wrong. Too much had been invested by so many for so long. After the Clancy Brothers and Tommy Makem made their first appearance on *The Ed Sullivan Show* in 1961, the Irish Export Board estimated that there was a 700 percent increase in American sales of the Aran sweater, an essential heavy woolen knit article of clothing characteristic of fishermen in Ireland's west. It was the group's signature look, chosen by their Brooklyn-born manager Marty Erlichman. This cream-colored patterned sweater made the old peasant stigma palatable and profitable, once again setting Irish off as distinctive while adding yet another Irish code to the green space.[159]

4

Racial Reckoning

White, Protestant Americans generally viewed Irish contributions to the United States, both historical and contemporary, from the polar-opposite perspective to that promoted by the American Irish Historical Society (AIHS), the Friendly Sons of St. Patrick, the Ancient Order of Hibernians (AOH), or even the Irish Free State. Anglo-Saxon Americans were just as "hyphenated" as Irish Americans, according to Edward Cuddy. They viewed their own patriotism through "a narrow prism of ethnic consciousness" that privileged "Anglo-Saxon culture and institutions" as "the core of real Americanism."[1] They also supported a new version of American colonial history that emphasized the advantages the United States inherited from the British (like language, literature, law) while diminishing "non-British achievements."[2]

In an echo of nineteenth-century anti-Irish discrimination, this context fostered the rise of a strong anti-Irish element in the nativism and xenophobia of 1920s America. "Every man in this country who seeks to stir up enmity between Great Britain and America, is committing a crime against civilization, and ought to be deported," complained one citizen to a United States senator.[3] The Irish were traitors with a vote and, to make matters worse, were taking over urban life: "Three fourths of the political rottenness and corruption in our country is due to the Irish," an Illinois lawyer opined. "Every large city in our section of the country (north and east), is congested with them, where they furnish the policemen, the politicians, the ball players, the prize fighters, the race horse fraternity, the saloon keepers, the bootleggers, the idlers and criminals, in much the largest proportion."[4]

Such perceptions and prejudices, compounded by the historic identification of Irish with Catholic, had major implications when, in May 1921, the United States Congress passed the Emergency Quota Act. While not primarily directed at the Irish, it included the first quantitative restriction ever imposed on immigration from Ireland. This was soon further complicated by the emergence of the Irish Free State at the end of 1921 and by revisions to the quota laws over the course of the next decade. Concurrently, heated public debate on America's ethnic origins spilled over from "history wars" about textbook content into the arguments for and against restricting the entry of the foreign-born. The Irish got entangled in both these highly charged political battles. The tactics that had served Irish Americans best in the realm of cultural currency—that is, the emphasis on Irish colonial and revolutionary contributions to America described in chapter 3—were now challenged on the basis of blood and race under the supposedly scientific guise of national origins.[5] Irish Americans opposed quota restrictions and revisionist histories because both undermined their carefully crafted aura of patriotism and respectability; instead, they emphasized racial distinctiveness as a political strategy. The government of Ireland, on the other hand, remained politically ambiguous and culturally sensitive about enduring emigration and partition. As a result, Irish as a racial code ricocheted in the green space, subject to developments both in the United States and on the island of Ireland from the early 1920s through the late 1960s. The Irish image appeared to be improving with regard to Anglo-Saxonism until it took a major hit. Just as the Clancy Brothers' rebel songs and the outbreak of the Troubles in Northern Ireland began to contribute new elements to the matrix, America closed its doors to Irish immigrants.

* * *

"If They Don't Want the Irish in Ireland, Let's Bring Them over Here," a Tin Pan Alley tune published in 1920, aptly reflected the welcome nearly nine hundred thousand Irish had experienced on arriving in the United States since 1891.[6] For the vast majority, the technicalities of federal immigration laws were little more than an inconvenience. American policies designed to restrict the entry of the foreign-born by selectively measuring physical fitness, intelligence, and industriousness (like the infamous inspections at Ellis Island and the literacy test introduced in 1917) had a limited impact on the Irish.[7] Most of them traveled on second-class tickets sent by relatives in what was, by then, a well-worn chain migration path that also ensured a cursory examination on board ships and disembarkation directly at transatlantic ocean liner piers such as those on the New York and New Jersey sides of the Hudson River.[8] The biggest challenge facing Irish immigrants was tuberculosis (TB); in 1906, the disease was responsible for "nearly 16% of all Irish deaths," and the U.S. Immigration Act of 1907 excluded "consumptives." TB cases in Ireland remained high into the 1950s.[9] An obligatory head tax, which was first implemented at fifty cents under the Act of 1882, rose from $2 in 1903 to $4 in 1907 and doubled again to $8 in 1917, increases that Irish immigrants had to absorb in the price of their passenger tickets.[10] Under the Passport Act of 1918, a visa was required before traveling, and by 1921, the fee for that was $10; soon thereafter, two copies of the immigrant's birth certificate and a photograph were required before an American visa was issued.[11] When Paul O'Dwyer emigrated in 1925 from County Mayo, in the rural far west of Ireland, he also needed "the approval of the American consul and references from any three of the following: a banker, solicitor, parish priest and sergeant of the new police force."[12] This was not always easy in the wake of a bitterly fought civil war.

Taken altogether, these requirements made leaving Ireland for America an increasingly involved and expensive undertaking, while Irish emigration fees generated considerable income for the U.S. government; the $119,436 collected in 1924 grew to $244,459 by 1926.[13] The achievement of dominion status for the Irish Free State, moreover, did not reduce emigration as had been expected. Instead, there was a significant surge that sent 220,591 to the United States between 1921 and 1930, in a resumption of historical migration patterns.[14] "The newly independent Irish state," as Enda Delaney observes, "was one of the few countries in the world to have experienced a declining population from the 1850s until the 1960s, wholly as a result of emigration."[15]

Handling this volume of emigration required uncoupling the American consular service for Ireland from Great Britain in early 1924, which made Dublin and Cobh (formerly Queenstown, County Cork) the "two largest U.S. visa offices in the world."[16] In addition, under an experimental preimmigration screening system set up by American public health officials in those ports, Irish immigrants were examined prior to departure rather than in their ports of arrival in the United States.[17] When the first sixty-five, all of whom traveled on third-class tickets that previously had required examination on

Ellis Island, were landed by the *Carmania* directly at Cunard's West Fourteenth Street pier in New York in the summer of 1925, they were headline news. The *Gaelic American* directly quoted the *New York Times*'s report: "The immigration inspectors who saw them on the way from Quarantine to the pier, said they were as fine a type of immigrant as they had ever seen enter the United States."[18] This conclusion, however, did not square with contemporary rhetoric about the dangers of an increasingly foreign-born population. In the aftermath of World War I, the fear of foreign radicalism, labor unrest, and a declining native birth rate had become key arguments for proponents of immigration restriction.[19]

The Emergency Quota (or Johnson) Act in 1921 set a limit on the number of immigrants who could enter the United States from each European country in any given year, based on 3 percent of that country's foreign-born who had been recorded in the 1910 census. Three percent of the 1,352,251 Irish-born in America that year would have essentially mirrored the annual rate of emigration from Ireland to America, which averaged about 34,000 between 1901 and 1910.[20] However, there was no Irish quota because Ireland was subsumed under the United Kingdom's quota of 77,342.[21] The new law's numerical limitations were not especially onerous for the Irish; in 1922, only 42,670 from Great Britain and Ireland emigrated to the United States under the quota.[22] The act permitted additional foreign-born to enter through categories exempt from the quota, such as family reunification (for those with relatives who were American citizens) and employment preferences (for example, nurses and domestic servants).[23] Although it was intended as a temporary, one-year stopgap measure while Congress considered more effective means of restricting total immigration, the 1921 law was extended twice. But it was not tracked by an ethnic press totally distracted between 1921 and 1923 by the extreme political developments in Ireland—that is, the Anglo-Irish War and the Civil War.[24]

The 1924 Johnson-Reed Immigration Act refined the law by reducing the numerical quota for each nation from 3 to 2 percent of the foreign-born population present in the United States in the base year and, significantly, pushed that year back from 1910 to 1890, when the so-called new immigration from eastern and southern Europe was just getting underway. Fully 86 percent (141,000) of the quota slots thereby went to immigrants from northern and western Europe, with the new political entities of Northern Ireland and the Irish Free State still considered part of the British allotment. It was impossible, of course, to determine from the 1890 U.S. census how many of the recorded 1,871,509 Irish-born had emigrated from the north or the south of Ireland. The 1924 law therefore set aside 28,567 quota slots for the Irish Free State, a generous 37 percent of Britain's 77,342.[25] The quotas were absent from the headlines in the Irish American press that spring, although the *Irish Times* did report the deportation of an eligible Irish woman just because her newborn infant was "in excess of the British and Irish quota for 1923–1924."[26]

While the 1921 law had attempted to preserve the foreign-born white composition of the United States, the 1924 law was directed at curtailing immigration.[27] The Irish Free State quota remained at 28,567 through 1927 while experts presented testimony to Congress to determine whether new quota numbers should be based on a percentage of the foreign-born, as in the past, or on a new approach called national origins. The latter amendment to the Johnson-Reed Act, ultimately accepted but not fully implemented until 1930, introduced a system that had an annual, all-nation cap of 150,000; it also shifted the basis for the quotas from birth lands to national origins, a classification that included the foreign-born as well as those of foreign ancestry. This was problematic from the beginning because there was no reliable method of calculating such a population; inevitably, "social values and political judgements" constructed how people were classified. "At one level, the new immigration law differentiated Europeans according to nationality and ranked them in a hierarchy of desirability," Mai Ngai observes. "At another level, the law constructed a white American race, in which persons of European descent shared a common whiteness that made them distinct from those deemed to be not white."[28] From this perspective, the Irish would benefit from the new law because they ticked the right racial and ethnic boxes. However, as details about the pending change filtered into the press in the spring of 1926, the *Gaelic American* cried foul about the "National Origins Joker."[29]

Under this new approach to immigration, the Irish were restricted to a percentage that was equivalent to those who had claimed Irish birth or descent in the 1920 U.S. census. Descent was especially challenging because the 1920 census combined "English and Celtic" together in the tabulation of foreign white stock, based on mother tongue. Thus, English-speakers from Ireland, Scotland, and Wales were considered Celtic.[30] The restriction lobbyist John B. Trevor circumvented this by devising a formula based on a surname analysis of the 1790 U.S. census that had been prepared under Congressional order and published by the Bureau of the Census in 1909 as *A Century of Population Growth* "because no other data existed."[31] Using that document's ethnic classification system, adjusted statistically to account for natural increase, the annual Irish Free State quota was to be reduced by over 70 percent to 8,330, to take effect in 1927.[32] It is worth noting that Trevor's experience dated to his time in 1920 as "associate counsel for the U.S. Senate Subcommittee on Foreign Relations [chaired by Senator David Reed (R-PA)] and . . . as counsel of the New York State Legislative Committee Investigating Subversive Activities."[33] His potential for pro-British bias was high given the extent of, and controversies around, Irish American nationalism during the First World War and then during Ireland's War of Independence.

The Irish suspected a political motivation behind the national origins clause because in practice, as the *Irish Times* reported, Trevor's calculations would mean that "three out of every five immigrants who will be allowed to enter the United States" fell under the British quota.[34] Marion Bennett points to a special consular report, *Immigration into the United States*, prepared in 1909 by the British Embassy in Washington, DC, for presentation to Parliament, the same year that *A Century of Population Growth* was published. While the former described the shift toward, and presented statistics related to, southern and eastern Europeans in American immigration, it also "admitted that in pauperism, crime and insanity the Irish immigrants outranked all of the rest."[35] Such characterization was a not unsurprising remnant of nineteenth-century prejudices, but it was quite a different story when the calculations of twentieth-century statisticians, responsible for compiling the U.S. census, were infected by deterministic thinking. The inference was, Margo Anderson concludes in her 1984 study of power and the census, that "the racial pollution of the American white population" would only progress if immigrants had such defects and "American democratic institutions" would be threatened. This was "bad social science and bad

Figure 4.1. The *Irish World*, May 15, 1926, published this editorial cartoon, probably by Frank Fleming, during the national origins debates when the Irish protested against a perceived Anglo-Saxon bias in new immigration restrictions as well as in the teaching of American colonial history. Credit: author's collection.

politics"; nevertheless, it percolated just beneath the surface of the immigration quotas.[36] A 1924 *New York Times* editorial in favor of restriction cloaked its argument in the racial terminology of the period: "There is no question of 'superior' or 'inferior' races or of 'Nordics' or of prejudice, or of racial egotism. Certain groups not only do not fuse easily, but consistently endeavor to keep alive their racial distinctions when they settle among us. They perpetuate the 'hyphen' which is but another way of saying that they seek to create foreign blocs in our midst."[37]

The AIHS passed a resolution at its spring 1926 meeting deploring "the shifting of the method of computation from the comparatively certain basis of birth lands to the nebulous hypothesis of national origin, which is calculated to create dissension among the various national elements composing our citizenship and to widen the regrettable schisms caused by the World War."[38] It argued that the proposed amendment to the 1924 law was based on "unstable and hypothetical" grounds.[39] In June, the National Council of the FOIF resolved that the law had no "basis in truth" and was "unnecessary and not in accord with tradition or history." It was neither restriction nor regulation "but gross discrimination, and in the interests of justice we demand that it be changed to conform to the facts of history and to the standards set by Washington, Jefferson and the other illustrious founders of the Republic."[40]

A month later, members of the AOH across the country received a circular letter from Michael Donohue, their national president and a former congressman from Pennsylvania: "The other European nations, with one exception, are given still smaller quotas than the Irish," Donohue wrote, "so that Great Britain may send annually almost 60% of all the quota immigrants that shall be permitted to enter the United States."[41] It was this dimension of the national origins formula, far more than its reductive impact on any Irish quota, that galvanized anti-restriction activism among Irish Americans. Dr. Edward F. McSweeney, former assistant commissioner of immigration in New York, told New York State Supreme Court justice Daniel F. Cohalan that "the Immigration Act of 1924 would not have been possible in 1920. In other ways we are being exploited by people who five years ago would not dare to assume their present attitude."[42] McSweeney feared that Irish America was fast "losing racial leadership, politically as well as morally."[43] His concern was about their "vulnerability of status," a legacy of nineteenth-century discrimination in Ireland and the United States that helps explain the position Irish Americans took in 1927.[44] The Irish experience with race in the United States had conferred privilege on them, but in the specific context of the restriction debates, fair skin did not guarantee quota equality.[45]

During congressional hearings early in 1927, Joseph Carey, an insurance man from Detroit and president of the American-Irish Republican League, summed up the Irish position. "I believe it is generally thought that the Irish Free State quota under the present law is quite liberal," he replied to a question from William Perry Holaday (R-IL). "Our complaint is that the national origins method of computation would cause one country to contribute one-half of our immigration and the rest of the world subject to the quota restriction contribute the other half."[46]

The Irish argument against national origins recognized that the new system favored the British while being prejudiced against future emigration from other European countries.[47] Writing for the *Boston Pilot*, John Bantry noted how "other races are shoved in the background" not only by quotas—Germany's numbers were cut by more than half, for example—but by classifying "Italians, Jews and South Irish" as "inferior." He declared, "The act is based on racial and religious bigotry. It depends on fraudulent statistics which have no existence in fact"; and he rejected any "expert" findings that the "English, Scotch and Scotch Irish" exceeded "all the Germans, Swedes, Norwegians, Poles, Russians together, in fact every other race in America including the Irish (as of 1920)."[48] In a letter to Congress in March 1928, John S. Murphy of the AIHS was even more forthright: "Our opposition to the quotas announced does not proceed from any desire to encourage or increase future immigration from the Irish Free State," he wrote. "No such determination of national origins can be based on other than a more or less unscientific hypothesis which is susceptible of distortion in prejudiced hands."[49]

In making these very specific arguments—that the national origins quotas were unfairly biased in favor of one country, Great Britain (composed of England, Scotland, Wales, and Northern Ireland), and that the basis for the national origins calculations was inaccurate[50]—the Irish pointed to what they saw as pro-British meddling in American domestic policymaking and to the flawed logic and methodology being used to determine the ethnic composition of the United States. Irish opposition was twofold. First, they challenged the conventional wisdom about the Anglo-Saxon underpinnings of American colonial history by refusing to accept that only a "small percentage" of Irish blood contributed to "American stock."[51] Second, by emphasizing that the Irish were racially distinct from the English, they asserted Ireland's new status in the immediate aftermath of its hard-won independence. Both approaches drew from Irish cultural content in the green space.

* * *

Irish nationalism ran counter to many ideas about white racial superiority driving the forces of immigration restriction in the United States after 1900. The Irish Free State had disturbing implications for Anglo-Saxon theorists. As chapter 3 demonstrated, achieving self-government was predicated on convincing a generation at home and abroad of the ability of the Irish by associating nationality with culture.[52] When Congress began to limit the entry of the European foreign-born, the spurious concept of national origins was a real threat to the Irish. "The Johnson-Reed Act of 1924," as Matthew Frye Jacobson contextualizes it, "was founded upon a racial logic borrowed from biology and eugenics; and, consequently, the civic story of assimilation . . . is inseparable from the cultural story of racial alchemy." He describes this as a dual process by which the Irish became American at the same time that the Celt became Caucasian.[53] However, the Irish were not able to jettison being Irish that easily, especially as Ireland took its place among the nations of the world in 1922.

According to *A Century of Population Growth*, the 1790 U.S. census recorded 61,534 Irish people, comprising 1.9 percent of the white population, whereas the Scots (then designated as Scotch) accounted for 7 percent and the English for 82.1 percent.[54] When this report appeared in 1909, Michael J. O'Brien, the historiographer of the AIHS, undertook a massive factual refutation. The result was *A Hidden Phase of American History: Ireland's Part in America's Struggle for Liberty*, published in 1919 and then republished by Dodd, Mead, and Company in 1920, the latter with an introduction by the society's president, Joseph

I. C. Clarke. He called chapter 23 of the book a "remorseless exposure of the erroneous figures relating to the Irish in America in 1790, as set forth in a certain United States Government publication."⁵⁵ The *Gaelic American* claimed that O'Brien's work "must convince any open mind that the enumeration of inhabitants of Irish blood, as constituting less than 2% of the white population of the United States in 1790, is such a grotesque understatement as to render conclusions drawn from the Census of 1790 utterly unreliable as regards 'national origins.'" It was historical fraud, plain and simple.⁵⁶

O'Brien compared the 1790 census with other contemporary sources and found major discrepancies. Instead of "only 2,525 persons of Irish descent" in New York State, for example, he found several thousand more Irish names "listed in the marriage, land, military, and court records, and in other Colonial records published by the New-York Historical Society and the New York Biographical and Genealogical Society [*sic*]."⁵⁷ He also showed that the analysis of nomenclature in *A Century of Population Growth* was faulty: "The name of Donnelly is a striking illustration of this. Of the persons of this name of both sexes there are said to have been a total of one hundred and eighty-seven in the United States in 1790, yet there were one hundred and fifty-five Revolutionary soldiers so named. . . . It is perfectly plain that all of the Donnellys were not counted."⁵⁸

The original motivation for writing *A Hidden Phase of American History* was clearly stated in Clarke's introduction: "In boldly traversing the statements of such historians as George Bancroft and Henry Cabot Lodge, [O'Brien] has in all cases quoted their own words on the related points, and proceeded therefrom to the utter demolition of their premises and conclusions with a crushing weight of evidence, marshalled with care, argued with acumen, and presented in admirable order."⁵⁹ Bancroft and Lodge were among a cadre of influential historians at the turn of the century whose interpretations of the American past were heavily influenced by theories on the superiority of English culture and by the works of British colleagues like James Bryce, Edward Freeman, and George Trevelyan.⁶⁰ They questioned the country's ability to assimilate all stocks and urged "the end of America's traditional welcome to European immigrants."⁶¹ They wrote revisionist histories like Lodge's *The Story of the Revolution* (1898) and *A Short History of the*

English Colonies in America (1881 with new editions in 1909 and 1923) that altered American perceptions of the colonial period. The English were no longer tyrants whom the colonists had to overthrow but now benefactors of democratic institutions and American culture. "She is, after all, the Mother Country," Charles Altschul wrote of England in 1917, "from whom we have acquired what really counts in the long run: language, customs, political liberty, tradition."[62] This rationalization was anathema to Irish nationalists.[63]

The Irish had particular problems with Henry Cabot Lodge, "whose political career prevented him from repeating on the platform what he wrote disparagingly about the Irish Celts as an historian" and who supported the idea of national origins when it was introduced in the Senate.[64] Back in 1896, Lodge had analyzed entries in *Appleton's Encyclopedia of American Biography* and determined that less than 1 percent of all eminent Americans were of Irish origin, prompting James Jeffrey Roche, editor of the *Boston Pilot*, to point out "such an astounding percentage of errors that Lodge's article was proved to be not merely unreliable but worthless."[65] Lodge's influence, however, was barely challenged by books that offered alternative, albeit strained, accounts such as James Haltigan's *The Irish in the American Revolution and Their Early Influence in the Colonies* (1908) and Thomas Hobbs Maginniss Jr.'s *The Irish Contribution to America's Independence* (1913). "One of the faults chargeable against the Irish people, and particularly Americans of Irish descent, is that they are ignorant of the achievements of their race in the past," Maginniss claimed. As for "the gospel of 'Anglo-Saxon superiority,'" it was "perhaps the most pernicious falsehood promulgated by pro-English writers."[66]

The FOIF and the Irish National Bureau, both advocates for Irish independence, countered with public relations materials that pointed to the numbers of Irish who signed the American Declaration of Independence and were members of the Constitutional Convention or the Continental Army.[67] Pamphlets like *De-Americanizing Young America: Poisoning the Sources of Our National History and Traditions* (1920) rejected attempts by academics to downplay the courage, patriotism, and republicanism of the revolutionary generation. The Knights of Columbus created a Historical Commission in 1921, chaired by Edward McSweeney, that intended "to investigate the facts of history, to correct historical errors and omissions, to amplify and preserve our national history, to exalt and perpetuate American ideals, and to combat anti-American propaganda by means of pamphlets, each to be complete and authoritative in itself."[68] These groups all recognized that the "Anglo-Saxon myth" only fed the forces of immigration restriction.

Until the national origins debates, efforts to counter this myth never reached much further than Irish American audiences. Then almost improbably, Michael O'Brien's *A Hidden Phase of American History* became a racial manifesto against the dubious restriction math.[69] As part of the Irish campaign to repeal national origins that was undertaken beginning in 1926, chapter 23 of O'Brien's book was reprinted in a special pamphlet under the title *The Unreliability of the First Census of the United States*. The AIHS and a coalition of other organizations sent this pamphlet to the president, to all members of Congress (including the House and Senate committees on immigration), to a thousand members of the press across the country, and to all the Catholic bishops in the United States as well as about 11,000 priests with Irish last names.[70] This coalition argued, on the basis of O'Brien's work, that it was impossible to analyze "the racial composition of the present population of the United States with even approximate accuracy."[71] In January 1927, the *Gaelic American* (with a circulation of approximately 33,000) carried chapter 23 in its pages, and Michael O'Brien, James McGurrin, and John J. Murphy went to Washington, DC, to interview Senators Walsh, Shipstead, Nye, Copeland, and Johnson. "They were impressed with O'Brien's data," McGurrin reported to McSweeney on January 10. "It is this *definite* data, *confirmed* by State documents, that appealed to them with so much force. As soon as O'Brien has his material in typed shape they will use it. This will of course serve to blow sky high the 'national origins' figures."[72]

A week later O'Brien's pamphlet came up in a congressional hearing chaired by Albert Johnson (R-WA). Adolph Sabath (D-IL), a Czech American, pointed out that O'Brien's work was written long before anyone ever thought Congress would adopt Trevor's national origins scheme. John J. Douglass (D-MA) concurred, "Yes, before the national-origin scheme came up, indicating these figures were not made up with reference to this hearing. This book was something that already existed and the facts and figures contained in it were discussed for some time."⁷³ Johnson's questioning, which tried to tar the pamphlet by association with Irish nationalist organizations, indicates that the Irish image was still vulnerable to subtle but effective challenges about the loyalty of Irish Americans by people in positions of power.⁷⁴ Trevor, who had worked in military intelligence in New York City during and after the First World War, did the same thing when, the following day, he suggested to the House Committee that there were segments of the foreign-born Irish who were conducting treasonous activity. He related the story of a man who he said had plotted to blow up one of the Panama Canal locks during the war. According to Trevor, this man was "the head of one of the subsidiary groups of a well-known Irish organization. I have forgotten which one." Rather than have him arrested, Trevor testified that he spoke privately with the man and convinced him that destroying the lock would, in a chain reaction, affect Irish Americans then fighting with the Sixty-Ninth Regiment: "He said, 'I never thought of that.' . . . The fellow was quite upset and he swore he would not continue these activities, but, I, of course, by virtue of my position, took occasion to observe what he was doing thereafter, and I believe he actually tried to stop some of his enthusiastic fellow-members from overt acts against the United States."⁷⁵

Whether or not this account is true, it was not difficult for Trevor, a lawyer who represented a coalition of nonethnic patriotic societies, to plant a seed of doubt in the minds of the House Committee because some members of the Irish community, particularly John Devoy and the Clan na Gael, had indeed received high-profile media attention for their active pursuit of German support for the Irish rebellion in the period leading up to America's entry into World War I.⁷⁶ In 1918, issues of the *Gaelic American* and the *Irish World* had been suppressed under the Espionage and Sedition Acts, and Jeremiah O'Leary, publisher of an anti-British satirical journal, was charged with obstructing the draft.⁷⁷ Later that same month, Joseph Carey, the Detroit insurance man, testified on behalf of the American-Irish Republican League and was subjected to a suggestive line of questioning:

> MR. HOLADAY: When the agitation and movement for the freedom of Ireland was under way a few years ago, were you connected with any organization that was interested in it?

MR. CAREY: I am afraid you are using up valuable time [at the immigration hearing].
MR. SABATH: I think we can spend a little time in listening to the gentleman's answer to that question.
MR. CAREY: As an American citizen I am glad to see another country establish itself independently.
CHAIRMAN [ALBERT JOHNSON]: The question is whether you were connected with any societies or organizations interested in the movement for the freedom of Ireland at that time.
MR. CAREY: No; I was not.
MR. HOLADAY: Are you connected with any society in this country that has been interested in a movement looking to freedom for Ireland?
MR. CAREY: Yes; the society with which I am connected now.
MR. HOLADAY: What action did your organization take in the movement looking to Irish freedom?
MR. CAREY: That is a rather difficult question to answer. The organization did hold [a] mass meeting, and did other such work.
MR. HOLADAY: Did your organization raise any money for that purpose?
MR. CAREY: We aided in any way we could within the law, just as France and other countries have aided the United States in her struggle for independence.
MR. HOLADAY: Here is my purpose in asking that question: By descent I sympathize with you, but do you think it is a good situation, having in mind the best welfare of America, when you have a group of American citizens, either foreign born or native born, banding themselves into an organization and by propaganda and financial means undertaking to play a part in the internal politics of foreign countries?
MR. CAREY: I do not think we undertook to play any part in the internal affairs of any other country. The United States aided Cuba not so many years ago when she was putting herself on her own feet as a Republic. Other countries have aided the United States, and I do not believe we should be accused of having done something unwise or that would act adversely to the welfare of our native land.[78]

This tactic—implying widespread disloyalty among Irish Americans—was one of two gaslighting positions taken to rebut Irish protests during the congressional hearings on repeal of the national origins clause. The second took a leaf from an influential 1891 essay published by Henry Cabot Lodge in *Century Magazine* called "The Distribution of Ability in the United States," which popularized the idea that the Scotch Irish were a racial stock unrelated to the Irish. Given the nature of Presbyterian emigration from Ireland's northern province of Ulster, mainly an eighteenth-century phenomenon, this argument was inextricably associated with America's colonial origins.[79] The concept of two separate races on the island of Ireland was then used to discredit O'Brien's *A Hidden Phase of American History*, as "Celtic-Irish" became a surrogate for "Irish Catholics" and "Ulster-Scots" for "Irish Protestants"; by extension, then, all Catholic emigration occurred in the nineteenth century and was from counties now within the political borders of the Irish Free State.[80]

The Scotch-Irish Society of America (established in 1889) had already advanced the belief that Presbyterians from Ulster counted for one-third of the colonial population and the rhetoric of their annual congresses began to surface in history books published after the turn of the century. Charles Knowles Bolton wrote in *Scotch Irish Pioneers in Ulster and America* (1910), "[Historians] have so pictured the Scotch traits developed under Irish skies, that Scotch Irish blood, once a reproach, is now cause for pride." The political scientist Henry Jones Ford made the case in *The Scotch-Irish in America* (1915) that the majority of the "Irish" in the United States in 1790 were actually "Scotch-Irish."[81] He declared, "In that plantation [of Ulster] was formed the breed known as Scotch-Irish, which was prominent in the struggle for American independence and which supplied to the American population an ingredient that has deeply affected the development of the nation."[82]

But Michael O'Brien "believed that if a person was born in Scotland he/she was Scottish, but if born in Ireland the person was Irish." A native of Fermoy, County Cork who emigrated to New York in 1889, he "criticized those who tried 'to rob Ireland of the credit that accrues to her simply because some of her sons were' the descendants of Scotch planters of the early seventeenth century."[83] Chapter 16 of *A Hidden Phase of American History* was devoted to "The 'Scotch-Irish' Myth": "What possible justification can there be for the persistent claim that Irish immigration to America, outside of the 'Scotch-Irish,' was an unimportant and negligible factor? Of course, the real fact of the matter is that every Irish immigrant whose name began with 'Mac,' or whose name apparently was not of Irish origin, or who was not of the Catholic faith, was placed in the 'Scotch-Irish' category."[84] While nomenclature in the British Isles can be distinctive (O'Connor is a Gaelic name, Llewellyn is a Welsh name), there were just too many examples of names that were common (like Brown or Carter), had similar prefixes (McDonald, MacDonald), or had been anglicized (Mac Gabhann, MacGowan, Smith). The Irish were indignant, for example, when steamboat inventor Robert Fulton—whose Scottish surname was associated with County Antrim from the seventeenth century and who had been claimed publicly by the Irish in New York's 1909 Hudson-Fulton Celebration—was appropriated for the Scottish "honor role [sic] of one hundred names from American history."[85]

This "filiopietist acrimony" had been evolving for at least thirty years. Trevor also introduced the divisive Scotch-Irish theory into testimony before the House Committee in 1927: "It so happened, whether for good or ill is not the question, the laws regarding entry of Catholics . . . into the American Colonies were very stringent, and there is very little evidence to show that the Irish immigration from southern Ireland, or what is now the Free State, amounted to a very serious figure because of this fact," he declared. "Conclusive proof" that the colonial population was of British, Scotch, Welsh, and Scotch-Irish origin in overwhelming proportions was "the character of the Government they established, the like of which did not exist in any nation of the world outside of the land of their origin."[86]

Behind this ahistorical conflation lay the specter of both anti-Catholicism and racial nativism. The AIHS, the FOIF, the Clan na Gael, and the AOH went on record that they had "no desire to see Ireland further depopulated by emigration. We do protest against the alleged reason for their practical exclusion, namely, that the Catholic Irish are 'inferior.'"[87] The same day as Trevor's testimony, January 19, 1927, the *New York Times* published a letter from the historian Benedict Fitzpatrick that began, "One of the worst features of the national origin section of the new Immigration law, the fate of which now hangs in the balance, is the injury it inflicts on the Irish people by representing 'Northern Ireland' as nationally different from the rest of the country."[88] The Irish artist Seán Keating visualized this troubling sentiment in a

1928 painting he ironically titled *Race of the Gael* that was exhibited in Pittsburgh and New York the following year. It depicts two serious men, shoulder to shoulder, who had fought in Ireland's War of Independence. The dark-haired figure on the left wears a red tartan shirt beneath his coat, with a mountain covered by a granite-like cloud as his backdrop. His fair-haired companion on the right pensively gazes on a patchwork of rolling fields. They each reference northern and southern Irish images, respectively, yet are bound together for a common purpose. As Keating explained it, "The meaning to me is that I have made fun of that venerable myth [of racial difference] by setting two extremely different human types (either typically Irish, or western European) and juxtaposing them. Both, however, are Irish and nothing else by religion, outlook, temperament, etc., and this to me is the interest and the joke." *Race of the Gael* was subsequently featured in the IBM Gallery of Science and Art at the 1939 New York World's Fair, where it was seen by millions and won first prize in an international competition of artwork.[89] In the green space, Scotch Irish could be as potent as Irish when needed.

* * *

From its beginning, the AIHS confronted Anglo-Saxonism by correcting "erroneous, distorted, and false views of history in relation to the Irish race in America."[90] In 1899, Edward A. Moseley, its president-general, wrote, "We assert that all European nationalities have contributed to our advancement and magnificent citizenship. The purpose of our Society is not to attribute all our splendid traits and achievements alone to the Irish element in our composition. Unlike our Anglomaniac brethren, who contend that everything great and good must be Anglo-Saxon, we merely claim credit for a just share in the upbuilding of the nation."[91]

Irish claims to the "upbuilding of the nation" were challenged by the racial hierarchy of Europeans that had been tossed around among theorists from the turn of the twentieth century. Scientists divided Europeans into halves, making racial distinctions between northern and southern peoples at precisely the historical moment when immigration to the United States was shifting in its composition from "Old" to "New." W. Z. Ripley, Madison Grant, and John W. Burgess classified three dominant types of Europeans (the Nordic, the Alpine, and the Mediterranean), each with distinctive physical and political characteristics. The Nordic was blond and long-headed, of a race of "rulers, organizers and aristocrats," while the Alpine was brunet and round-headed, of "a race of peasants." The Mediterranean, although long-headed, was very dark and had less physical stamina, and his intellectual attainments were a thing of the past.[92] The Nordic peoples were said to be the most superior of the European races, and these included the Anglo-Saxons, who were related to the Teutons and descended, like them, from the racially pure Aryans. The Irish defied this tripartite division because they were traditionally defined as Celts, an anthropologically mixed European type that, since the 1840s, had made it "conventional to treat the Irish as a distinctive 'race.'"[93] In studies that were coated with the veneer of science, such as phrenology, craniology, physiognomy, anthropometrics, and eugenics, the Irish were historically the inferior white prototype. As late as 1897, the head measurements of Irish and Irish Americans in a Brooklyn prison were the subject of a scientific treatise by a professor at New York University's medical school.[94]

This association of the Irish with racial difference lingered. In a 1922 lecture at the Boston University School of Theology, for example, Dr. Martin Edwards declared that the differences in characteristics between the English and the Irish could be explained by diet. The Irish were Irish, so his theory went, because of a lack of protein caused by the export of meat and eggs to England: "Too much Irish stew, with a preponderance of vegetables over meat, and buttermilk, are responsible for the fighting Irish nature."[95] This was a page-one story in the *New York Times*, as was Julius Pokorny's 1925 theory that the Irish were related to Indigenous peoples: "In isolated parts of Ireland and Scotland are to be found types with Mongol features, oblique eyes, straight black hair and thin lips. Anthropologically these types could only be connected with the Eskimos," suggested the respected German philologist and Celtic scholar on the occasion of receiving an honorary doctorate from the National University of Ireland.[96] Despite the fact that no one in Ireland took his conjecture seriously, the story was distributed by the Associated Press to an American readership in which "eugenic outlooks on immigration and other social questions were in ascendance."[97] The *New York Times* editorial page predictably resorted to stereotype: the Inuit were "an unwarlike tribe," while the Irish did not have "the temperamental characteristics of a people who preferred running away to fighting."[98]

A similar racial discourse appeared in England during the 1920s that essentially argued that "the Irish were living fossils, representatives of an atavistic or primitive human strain that the more intense struggle for existence elsewhere in Europe had rendered extinct."[99] There was even a concerted effort to link the Irish to the Attacotti, "an obscure Eastern Mediterranean tribe," that was propagated in 1921 by Lord Alfred Douglas in his short-lived political weekly *Plain Speech*. In an example that makes clear the potential ramifications if such a fanciful pedigree had gained any traction in the United States during the restriction debates, the Irish-Attacotti were described as follows: "Along with their beady eyes, low foreheads, dark, coarse, and often kinky hair, a strain of negro blood, and an abnormal fondness for destruction, the Attacotti have inherited skins which are not sensitive to dust or dirt, and not irritated or inflamed by it."[100] The Reverend W. R. Inge, dean of St. Paul's Cathedral, applauded the American Immigration Act of 1924 as a model effort to halt the leeching of white vitality by the Irish: "These immigrants," Inge wrote in 1926, "are more dangerous to the solidarity of the American type than the negroes"; he called for the British to adopt a similar "Irish Exclusion Act."[101]

Obviously, the Irish were a problem for any restriction calculus that made distinctions between European immigrants using physical, cultural, and linguistic deviations from the English standard. Anglo-Saxonism permeated the national origins hearings on Capitol Hill; John B. Trevor, who had made the original ancestry calculations and whom the Irish accused of being on the payroll of the pro-British Carnegie Foundation, told the House Committee on Immigration and Naturalization that "in spite of what some of these people have said about me, I really like the Irish. I employ practically nothing else in my house, because I like them."[102] Francis H. Kinnicutt, of the Immigration Restriction League and Allied Patriotic Society of New York City, in testimony before the Senate Committee on Immigration in 1929, opposed revisions to the national origins figures because "in 10 years we should get . . . 450,000 more Germans and Irish than immigrants from Great Britain and Northern Ireland. This excess, moreover, as already pointed out, would represent further dilution of the Anglo-Saxon element in our population."[103]

The Irish opposed interpretations of American history that claimed Anglo-Saxons formed "the great mass of the citizens of this republic" with broadsides like *The Anglo-Saxon Humbug*, *About the Pilgrims*, and *Playing Up the Puritans* that argued such a claim was "an extravagant conceit."[104] They had their work cut out for them because the decade of the 1920s was accompanied by an avalanche of hagiography at the same time that Britain's share of the total immigration allotment was artificially boosted from 21 percent to 57 percent.[105] The tercentennial of the Pilgrims' arrival on the Mayflower in 1920, the sesquicentennial of the United States' founding in 1926, and the bicentennial of George Washington's birth in 1927 initially prompted the Irish to fight for a place in the pantheon of American history rather than for quota slots. Distrusting Anglophiles, the Irish took every opportunity to remind their fellow citizens of the role they had played in the creation of America and to protest the forging of any "hands-across-the-sea" links between the United States and Great Britain. "The promotion of English influence in the United States is the aim of . . . people who regard England as their mother country and who are willing at all times to place English interests before those of their own country," the *Gaelic American* concluded in 1927. "They long for a re-union of the United States and the British empire under the English flag. They are not 100% Americans."[106] Anglo-Saxonism "is reappearing in newspaper articles and headlines," the Irish weekly newspaper charged, "and in the outgivings of Carnegie's hired College Professors, and the Know-nothing Immigration Laws seek to make it a reality."[107]

This was not idle rhetoric because pro-restriction had strong support from the Ku Klux Klan (KKK) as well as the American Legion, an organization of World War I veterans, who concluded that the proverbial melting pot was impotent and a barrier to "true democracy."[108] Their advocacy was often fueled by both Anglo-Saxonism and anti-Catholicism directed at white foreigners.[109] In 1924, the *Illinois Fiery Cross*, published in Chicago, ran the page-one headline "Irish-Catholic Claim to Valor in Revolutionary War Is Refuted by Figures of U.S. Census Bureau" over an article riddled with Catholic conspiracy claims that mocked *A Hidden Phase of American History* as "A Corned Beef and Cabbage Propaganda

Plant, Unlimited."[110] That same year, the Wisconsin Klan campaigned to ban "The Star-Spangled Banner" from state public schools as "alien propaganda" because it was "a song of the Irish to show their hatred of Protestant England."[111] The *American Standard* went even further in decrying Irish "hatred against America's partner in Protestantism" and Irish support for the adoption of the Francis Scott Key song as the national anthem: "The Jesuits have cleverly taken advantage of America's patriotic spirit, by striving to associate that spirit with an unworthy and impossible medium for its expression. . . . Anglo-Saxon Protestantism cannot be split into hostile factions by Roman trickery; neither shall America's school children be brought up, under Irish influence, to hate Britain."[112]

Life, then (pre-1936) a fifteen-cent humor magazine published monthly, visualized such racial attitudes. Its illustrations reflected the Irish image in that particular genre while also demonstrating how easily the green space absorbed the sociopolitical issues of the day and then influenced American popular culture. In 1924, for example, two Black musicians were depicted leading a lone Irishman through an avenue of hooded Klan members in a cartoon called "St. Patrick's Day in Atlanta, GA," an unambiguous equation of race and religion.[113] The following year, *Life*'s March cover depicted an Italian pushcart vendor bewildered by Irish flags—the old green banner with the golden harp, not the new tricolor of the Irish Free State—flying from Casey's Grocery at the fictitious intersection of Kenmare Street and Sullivan Avenue. This bore the provocative title "The Dare-Devil," suggesting that the poor Italian was taking his life in his hands by entering an Irish neighborhood.[114] In 1926, the cover for *Life*'s "Saint Patrick's Number" depicted a brawl as a circular jumble of clenched fists, boots, and angry faces under the title "It Seems There Were Two Irishmen—," a reference to hackneyed ethnic jokes.[115] By 1927, when the Irish were seriously pushing back against quota restrictions, the magazine cover for St. Patrick's Day depicted eighteen racially exaggerated heads all wearing the same smile under the rubric "The Wearing of the Grin." In this image, the Irish were not only *not* Anglo-Saxon, but they were equated with groups then considered far from the Anglo-Saxon standard, like Italians, Native Americans, Chinese, Mexicans, Japanese, Blacks, Turks, and Indians.[116] This particular issue of *Life* had a circulation of 160,439, five times that of the *Gaelic American*, with the largest distribution in the states of Massachusetts,

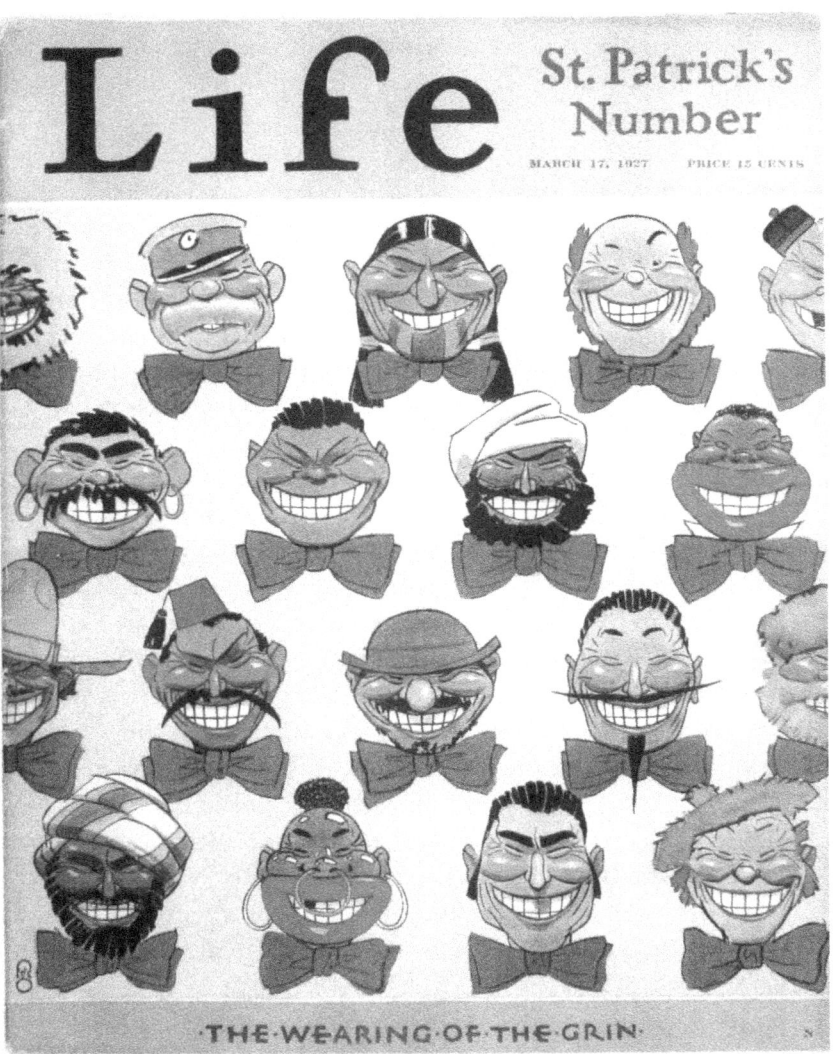

Figure 4.2. The St. Patrick's Day 1927 issue of *Life* magazine, with its red-bearded Irishman and parody of the old song "The Wearing of the Green," did not include the English among the many men with stereotyped racial features on its cover. Credit: From the John and Selma Appel Collection of Ethnic Images (7572.1095), Michigan State University Museum.

New York, and California, where debates about immigration restriction were topical.[117] Consumption of such images was damaging for the Irish, not unlike the Anglo-Saxon magniloquence on display in the national origins debates.

* * *

It is important to distinguish this kind of spurious representation from the racial separatism intentionally deployed by Irish nationalists.[118] If race was useful in establishing Irish contributions in the American colonial period, it was also beneficial in proving "Ireland's status as an independent state."[119] This dovetailed with restrictionist thinking in which national origins was a euphemism for "fitness for self-government" and quotas were simply the political expression of such a philosophy.[120]

Between 1921 and 1924, the emergency quota laws in effect did not have a provision for changes to the British Empire such as the creation of self-governing dominions after 1890. This meant that the entire island of Ireland was part of the large quota (77,342) for the United Kingdom of Great Britain and Ireland. During hearings on the Johnson-Reed Act of 1924, the U.S. secretary of state, Charles Evans Hughes, recommended that the Irish Free State, New Zealand, and South Africa be separated from under the British quota for ease in administering the law going forward.[121] A separate quota for the Irish Free State became paramount for another (political) reason when that June, following months of negotiations between the British and the Irish, Timothy Smiddy was appointed as the Irish Free State representative in Washington, DC. This was, in practice, tacit approval of Ireland's new status by the State Department.[122] Smiddy asked Judge Cohalan, one of the Irish American activists connected with the AIHS and the Clan na Gael, to use his influence to get the national origins legislation amended "to suit Irish interests." Through Cohalan's friend Senator Hiram Johnson (R-CA), a proposal was floated that would create "separate quotas for the self-governing dominions within the British empire."[123] When this was accepted by the House Committee on Immigration and Naturalization, the next challenge was to lobby to increase the Irish Free State quota from the 8,330 that had been determined by Trevor and was scheduled to take effect in 1927.

Doubts raised during Congressional testimony about Trevor's formula for the quotas led to a review of the Irish, Scottish, and English elements of the 1790 population by the American Council of Learned Societies (ACLS), subsequently published by the American Historical Association.[124] The conclusion acknowledged that, in the 1909 analysis of colonial last names, there had been "a tendency to place too high a percentage of the population in the English category."[125] The new percentages put forward increased the Irish element of the colonial population to 9.5 percent, 5.9 percent of whom were said to have originated within the modern political boundaries of Northern Ireland and 3.6 percent in the Irish Free State.[126] The Free State was officially content with any ACLS revisions that increased its quota—up to 13,862 in 1927, then to 17,427 in 1928, and finally settled at 17,853 in 1930.[127] Indeed, even the loss of nearly eleven thousand visas from its portion of the 1924 British quota suited Irish nationalist rhetoric. In *Old Castle Garden*, the magazine of New York's Mission of Our Lady of the Rosary for the Protection of Irish Immigrant Girls, Patrick J. Temple wrote in 1938, "We should all be in favor of continuing the ban on Irish immigration in this country that has been applied the last eight years. . . . Surely none of us would like to see the catastrophic collapse that would take place in Ireland if once more the flow of her people to the Western hemisphere were to begin on a large scale. It would be the end of the Irish nation."[128]

However, because emigration from Ireland had been steadily normalized since the nineteenth century's Great Famine, it was only truly sensitive to major global deterrents like the Great Depression and the Second World War rather than to any sense of duty to a nation-state.[129] This made numbers irrelevant too. American consular officials in Ireland, without regard to the established quotas, had the discretion to discourage emigrants by stricter enforcement of "Likely to Become a Public Charge" screenings in response to the reduced economic circumstances in the United States.[130] Emigration from Ireland to the United States steadily began to fall so that, by 1933 and 1934, only 2 percent of the Irish Free State quota (338 out of 17,853) was being filled.[131] After World War II, emigration surged back up again to levels not seen since the 1920s, with destinations in England or Scotland rather than in America increasingly more attractive for the Irish. Nevertheless, between 1941 and 1961, the United States was the destination for 68,151 Irish women and men, "mostly single and under the age of thirty-five," as the Irish economy struggled to diversify or grow.[132] The departure of a cohort of young people significantly relieved Ireland's unemployment distress, "rid the electorate of its most malcontent members," and injected cash into an otherwise weak economy through remittances. As Linda Dowling Almeida notes, the Irish government's study of emigration and other population problems refused to label this spike in emigration as a brain-drain or loss of talent, preferring to describe it as "an individual's choice."[133] Northern Ireland also experienced elevated levels of emigration in the 1950s and, likewise, had no official policy to deal with it.[134]

This hemorrhaging of the first generation to come of age on the partitioned island conveniently coincided with America's 1952 McCarran-Walter Act, which, providentially for the Free State, made no change to the Irish quota of 17,853 or to the national origins system for northern Europeans generally. Even with the 1950s spike in emigrants, Ireland's quota continued to be annually undersubscribed. Since "unused quota visas were not transferable" to other countries where demand for visas was higher, pressure mounted once again for major immigration reform with President Truman calling out national origins legislation on the grounds that "the idea behind this discriminatory policy was, to put it boldly, that Americans with English or Irish names were better people or better citizens than Americans with Italian or Greek or Polish names." It was, he added, "utterly unworthy of our traditions and our ideals."[135] In an ironic reversal of the pro-restriction arguments made in the 1920s, the Irish were now perceived as superior rather than inferior immigrants.

It was only a matter of time before Ireland's tendency to officially disassociate itself from the perpetual social, cultural, and economic challenges of emigration, as well as its policy of "cordial diplomacy" with the United States, became its Achilles' heel in the context of American immigration reform debates. According to the community activist Adrian Flannelly, "After JFK visited Ireland in [June] 1963, the word was about that de Valera had complained that the U.S. was creating a brain-drain."[136] President Kennedy had long believed that the American system was inequitable, and in July 1963, he asked Congress to phase out the national origins system over five years as part of more extensive reform legislation. For Ireland, this would mean an annual cut of 20 percent from its generous quota—that is, a reduction from 17,853 to 5,300 by the end of the decade.[137] Still, the Irish government remained unconcerned, even when Kennedy's assassination removed the highest potential leverage it might have had. Ireland was in a period of modernization during the 1960s that included positive improvements in education and social services, foreign direct investment for economic growth, and return migration from the United States, including pensioned retirees.[138] As its ambassador to Washington, DC, Thomas J. Kiernan, told the State Department in 1964, "Emigration has finished."[139] When de Valera, then president of Ireland, visited President Johnson and gave a speech before a joint session of Congress in May 1964, no "substantive issues" were raised. Indeed, the *Washington Post* saw the visit as purely "symbolic and sentimental."[140]

Edward M. Kennedy, as acting chairman of the Senate Judiciary Committee, persisted in fulfilling his late brother's legacy. The 1965 congressional hearings on immigration reform were in striking contrast to those of the 1920s. In the spirit of the times, abolishing the national origins quotas was akin to achieving civil rights reform for many, a cause that played well with a liberal American electorate.[141] Many Irish Americans, like the labor union executive James B. Carey, took this progressive view, while the unexpected champion of preserving the Irish quota was Senator Sam Ervin (R-NC), a notorious Southern segregationist:

SENATOR ERVIN: Under the McCarran-Walter Act, the quota of each nation is determined by a mathematical formula, is it not?
MR. CAREY: It is a discriminatory formula.
SENATOR ERVIN: But it is a mathematical formula.
MR. CAREY: It is based on the superiority of the Anglo-Saxon group of which I am a member and it is unfair; it is undemocratic and it is an insult to people throughout the rest of the world.
SENATOR ERVIN: Yes. I understand that, Mr. Carey, but still it is a mathematical formula, is that not so, whether it is the most outrageous one in the world or not?
MR. CAREY: There are a lot of things that can be done, Senator, in the name of mathematics.[142]

Carey's grandparents had emigrated from Ireland to Philadelphia earlier in the century, long before any legal restrictions. His understanding of the appellation *Anglo-Saxon* in this exchange appears to have been more geographical than racial, in itself an indication of a significant transformation of Irish by the 1960s. As Ray O'Hanlon notes, "While many [first-generation] Irish would have winced at being lumped in with Anglo-Saxons," their late-generation Irish American cousins did not.[143] With the passage of time, the Celt was apparently equal to the Anglo-Saxon, at least when it came to immigration. Over in the House of Representatives, the statement of Dr. James H. Sheldon, from the Council for Christian Social Action of the United Church of Christ, was similarly free of old prejudices: "My wife is of Irish descent. Years ago, when I lived in Massachusetts there would have been quite a little irritation in the Commonwealth, as well as in New York, if we had a local statute giving an Englishman a four times better chance than an Irishman. Irritation is too moderate a word."[144] Senator Ervin also equated the Irish with the English, arguing that they both made better Americans than people from other parts of the world. His exchange with Carey on March 15, 1965, was typical of his approach:

> SENATOR ERVIN: I don't think the McCarran-Walter Act states anywhere that a person of Irish Catholic descent or a Scotch Protestant is better than anybody else. I think the McCarran-Walter Act says we shall give to Ireland an immigration quota equal to one-sixth of 1 percent of the number of Americans who trace their national origins to Ireland and I think that the McCarran-Walter Act does that because it assumes that a person from Ireland is more readily assimilated into the American life than people from any other area of the world which have not contributed anywhere near the same amount to our population. . . . Do you have an opinion as to whether or not it is reasonable to believe that an immigrant from Ireland can be more readily assimilated into the United States than an immigrant from Indonesia?
>
> MR. CAREY: At the moment, yes, I would say the standard of living in Ireland is so much lower than the United States that there will be problems [for] a person from Ireland with qualifications that could make a contribution here, getting adjusted to a better life and even to a greater extent with regards to Indonesia. But the purpose of S. 500 is, as

the American labor movement understands it, is to get away from the national origin quota basis . . . to get away from this inadequate concept that no longer has application in a democracy; that because people are white or come from one area that they are superior to some other people of a different race or a different nationality.[145]

The Republic of Ireland's attitude was duly noted too. When Ervin asked Norbert Schlei, the assistant attorney general, whether the governments of England, Germany, and Ireland had been consulted about cuts to their quotas, he replied that the Department of State had had general discussions "with all those countries, and they all feel that it is a fair proposal, that they certainly would have no desire to ask us to change. . . . They do not claim any right to, of course." The U.S. secretary of state, Dean Rusk, told Ervin, "We have not had any protest from Ireland on this matter, Senator." Even the national chairman of the American Committee on Italian Migration noted that Ireland had been discouraging emigration "for some years."[146] The final vote in the Senate was 76–18, with Democrats making up 46 percent of the majority in favor of reform, including the six senators representing states with the heaviest Irish American populations (Illinois, Massachusetts, and New York).[147]

A news blackout because of a ten-week printing strike in Ireland in the summer of 1965 meant that those thinking about emigrating to America were totally unaware of the impact the new legislation would have on them after June 1968.[148] Under the Immigration and Nationality Act of 1965 (Hart-Celler), nuclear family reunification was prioritized. This closed off the United States as a legal destination for Irish women and men who did not have a parent or sibling already living there; the law essentially "created a paper divide between American aunts and uncles and their Irish nieces and nephews" where none had existed before.[149] However, it also coincided with the firstfruits of Ireland's 1958 program of economic expansion that, over the course of time, led "to a period of in-migration through the seventies, rising marriage and birth rates, and an increase in population."[150] As O'Hanlon astutely chronicles, both changes produced unintended consequences for Ireland.[151] Its government simply shrugged.

In contrast to that willful blindness, some Irish Americans viewed legislative changes with alarm. The historical patterns of Irish immigration could not meet the requirements of the new law (sponsorship by immediate family members or skill preferences), putting the Irish at a disadvantage. Initially, there had been some hope because, so the thinking went, the Irish "were a superior breed with strong political connections and strong work ethic [that] would garner an exception."[152] A new organization founded in 1967, the American Irish Immigration Committee, while recognizing "that the former U.S. immigration policy discriminated against some nationalities," wanted "to protect the interests of those members of the Irish race who desire to immigrate to the U.S."[153] Words like *breed* and *race* were still surprisingly effective political rhetoric for the Irish at the time. Some thought this was a legacy of recent Irish American anti-communism, including approval of Senator Joseph McCarthy's attacks on the white Anglo-Saxon Protestant establishment and institutions of higher education like Harvard.[154] But it was just as much part of the linguistic continuum of the Irish anti-restriction position.

More than five thousand Irish settled in America in 1965; although certainly not the only factor, the new law thereafter contributed to the reduction in that annual number to about a thousand.[155] But those men and women were absolutely critical to the survival of the ethnic subculture described in chapter 3, especially in the New York metropolitan area, the mid-twentieth-century epicenter of Irish America.[156] One of the founders of the American Irish Immigration Committee, Father Donald O'Callaghan, made this point as he tried to raise awareness. He "told his hearers that if the 1965 law was not changed, the GAA organization (composed of many new immigrants) would be the first to go, followed by the UICA and then lastly the AOH." Another founder, Judge John P. Collins of New York's Criminal Court, concluded that the "Irish were being hurt as a result of a Kennedy administration proposal," a charge that naturalized Irish immigrants who had voted for John F. Kennedy did not particularly want to hear.[157] Their Irish American cousins, many of whom had been drifting toward the Republican party and the suburbs since the 1950s, were indifferent; continuous immigration from Ireland was not the lifeblood of their communities.[158]

When the U.S. Congress opened in January 1969, fifty-four representatives from eleven states introduced H.R. 165 (the Ryan bill) to the Committee on the Judiciary in an effort to allocate additional visas for "immigrants from certain foreign countries." Judge Collins's committee hoped it would "allow a reasonable number of Irish to again enter the U.S."[159] On December 10, 1969, near the end of hearings on amendments to the 1965 Act, Congressman William T. Murphy (D-IL) reviewed the provisions of several previous bills that had been unsuccessful in addressing visa inequities. He also submitted letters of support from the AOH as well as a statement from Rep. William T. Cahill (R-NJ), the governor-elect of New Jersey and a cosponsor with Rep. Peter Rodino (D-NJ) of H.R. 10618, which was "designed to take care of these short run temporary dislocations in the pattern of immigration." This would create a pool of all unused 1968 visas to be made available on a first-come, first-served basis to countries like Ireland for two years. Cahill wrote, "I am strongly in favor of a temporary measure to give the Irish and other disadvantaged intending immigrants the opportunity to catch up and to recover their rightful place of equality under the law. This is a temporary problem and we feel a temporary solution is necessary."[160]

Father O'Callaghan and Judge Collins traveled to Washington, DC, for this hearing. Judge Collins testified as national chairman of the American Irish Immigration Committee and disagreed with Cahill, advocating for a permanent solution instead. He began with the tried-and-true appeal to conscience, noting Irish contributions during the American Revolution and Civil War to law and infrastructure: "If the handiwork of the Irish were painted green, the average American city would be splashed in all sides with emerald hues. Yet there are few who are aware of this." He declared that the 1965 act, "in its effect on Ireland," did "not demonstrate the thanks of a grateful Nation." He submitted letters of support from a number of labor unions that made similar arguments to buttress his case for H.R. 165, which would include a formula to create a permanent floor of 75 percent for each country based on its immigration over the decade prior to 1965, essentially permitting approximately five thousand Irish to emigrate to America every year. Collins then addressed specifics, such as the way in which the skilled visa preference categories of the 1965 legislation had only benefited 122 qualified Irish in 1969. He also noted that, while the majority of Irish who had traditionally emigrated were unskilled, they "came here to better their lives economically and in turn hopefully they bettered the Nation. We know that they contributed heavily to the independence and security of this Nation down to this very day in Vietnam. . . . They are similar to my father and mother and to the fathers and mothers of many members of my Committee and of this Congress."[161]

This specific construction of Irish contributions to the United States is implicit in the origins of the model minority concept Ellen Wu and Madeline Yuan-yin Hsu describe, in which "a series of intersecting political, social, and cultural imperatives—ethnic and mainstream, domestic and global"—triggered a new understanding of race and ethnicity in post–World War II America.[162] The Irish in America had actually been trying to make this case about themselves for decades from the perspective that being Irish and Catholic was a minority position in an overwhelmingly Anglo-Saxon Protestant country. It was part of their traditional rationale opposing immigration restriction: Ireland sent good immigrants and the Irish made patriotic Americans. However, times had changed. The Judiciary Subcommittee chairman, Michael Feighan (D-OH), felt that H.R. 165 was too much like a "vestige of the national origins quota system" to be enacted.[163] When Rep. Rodino questioned Collins's steadfast commitment to that proposed legislation rather than to some other alternatives being discussed, he replied, "You stated that the Ryan bill is a return to national origins and I am afraid I must disagree with that. We all know that national origins was a racial theory. In reality it says that some races were morally and genetically superior to others. . . . We again categorically reject national origins. . . . We want to see it dead."

National origins might be rhetorically and legally moribund by the late 1960s, but issues of race and Irish nationalism were set on a collision course.

**

Michael J. O'Brien, the historian of the AIHS, died in 1960, discouraged by the "popular indifference" to "the Irish American historical consciousness he had done so much to serve" during the original national origins debates.[164] In his last years, he witnessed a new generation of historians approach the Irish American experience as a problem rather than a contribution. Filiopietism was banished in the 1940s and 1950s by Marcus Lee Hansen, Oscar Handlin, Robert Ernst, Carl Wittke, and Arnold Schrier, who were all more clear-eyed than O'Brien about the social and economic challenges that immigration had caused for the Irish and for the United States.[165]

By the time of the 1965 congressional hearings, George Potter's *To the Golden Door: The Story of the Irish in Ireland and America* (1960), *The American Irish* by William V. Shannon (1963), and a chapter on "The Irish" in *Beyond the Melting Pot*, edited by Nathan Glazer and Daniel Patrick Moynihan (1963), were advancing yet another iteration of the ethnic experience. A January 1964 *New York Times* review of Shannon's book, for example, stressed that it was neither hagiography nor "even sociology": "As the Irish become less Irish in the pejorative sense, they acquire an acceptable 'image' in a land where the image counts for so much. The brogue is giving way to the Harvard accent. Significantly, the late President Kennedy was educated for politics by the Establishment, which can afford ideals as well as privileges, and in some ways he was more Yankee than Irish."[166]

This understanding of Kennedy framed him with the same equivalencies about Anglo-Saxons and Celts that were made in the immigration debates the following year. Clearly, it was a concept already circulating widely in the wake of his assassination. "The Irish political culture that groomed him for the White House," observed Joe Lee, was thereby rendered invisible.[167] The journalist Pete Hamill pointed to the president's violent death as the "turning point" in how "other Americans perceived Irish Americans: there was a sense of dues paid, of finality. Many glib assumptions were shot away with that Mannlicher Carcano rifle. Among them were the assumptions of the larger society, expressed in the shorthand of stereotypes."[168] This was only partially true.

A tremendous racial reckoning had taken place for the Irish in the decades after 1921. National origins (birth or descent) was not only obsolete after 1965, but thereafter Irish was integrated into a white catchall box in the racial self-identification section of the U.S. census. Being white, as the Irish obviously were, was an advantage, while being Black continued to disadvantage millions. This did not mean that ethnic identity was no longer relevant, but it was quantitatively and qualitatively disassociated from race as color. On the other hand, civil rights, part of the rationale for abolishing national origins, were more volatile in a transnational context. In America, they were defined by polarized Black-white relations and the challenges of dismantling legal segregation. In the 1960s, there were Irish Americans who followed institutional Democratic and Catholic policies on integration and tolerance to support efforts toward racial equality and postwar liberalism, including President Kennedy's brother Robert.[169] There were also conservative Irish Americans for whom solidarity with other white ethnics took precedence over helping African Americans. The spectrum of Irish opinion on race was wide. Irish Americans were also confronted during this period with civil rights in Northern Ireland, an emerging cause that, while not racially based, modeled its activism on the American movement. The Northern Ireland Civil Rights Association, founded in 1967, garnered the sympathy of the National Association for the Advancement of Colored People.[170] Its demonstrations, marches, and sit-ins were used in the same way to advocate for change in the unequal white-white relations that had resulted from the partition of Ireland and disadvantaged Catholics under British rule. But these tactics were "a form of resistance alien to Irish-republican tradition," which historically had seen dispossession in terms of the loss of status and power rather than as racial discrimination.[171]

In the immediate aftermath of sectarian rioting in Derry in August 1969, Bernadette Devlin, a young member of Parliament for Mid Ulster, was invited to tour the United States for a week to raise awareness and funds. Her visit was facilitated by the progressive lawyer Paul O'Dwyer, an immigrant who left County Mayo in 1925, a founder of the American League for an Undivided Ireland in 1947, and a Democratic candidate for the U.S. Senate in 1968—an Irish American political trifecta as far as credentials. She was also sponsored by the National Association for Irish Justice, a brand-new American support organization that politically leaned left.[172] Devlin's seriousness rattled expectations. The *San Francisco Chronicle*, for example, described her "tone":

> A television interviewer thrust the inevitable microphone in her face as Miss Devlin walked down an airport corridor and asked her to "sing an Irish song." Regarding him with pale grey eyes that have none of that storied Irish twinkle, Miss Devlin coldly replied: "Forget it." She was here as part of her nationwide tour to raise $1 million for the relief of the people in Northern Ireland left homeless and jobless by the bloody conflicts there.

And she made it starkly plain there was to be no blarney or laughter, no flashes of Gallic [sic] wit, no jigs. Not this time.[173]

The British politicians who trailed Devlin across the United States used a different strategy. They tapped into a political discourse in which Irish Americans were super patriotic and anti-communist—then deliberately undercut it.[174] Robin Bailie, a member of the Ulster Parliament in Belfast, told the *New York Times* that Devlin wanted "a worker's republic similar to that in Cuba" and that she was "mixed up in the international socialist movement." W. Stratton Mills, member of Parliament for North Belfast, was described as "looking solemn but sounding determined." There were no stereotypes used about either man by the media.[175]

According to an *Irish Times* journalist writing at the time, Devlin's embrace of socialism as a practical solution for economic disparity "shocked, surprised, and horrified" Irish Americans, although readers of the *Irish Echo*, typically members of several overlapping ethnic organizations, were much more likely to be confused.[176] For them, the issue had been and remained partition: "The ultimate objective is not to make our oppressed brethren in northeast Ireland more comfortable British subjects," wrote *Echo* columnist Seán Maxwell. "The final solution is not social demands and reforms but a unified nation."[177] As Matthew O'Brien's research demonstrates, "several generations of Irish-American ethnics had reduced the situation in Northern Ireland to one that could be clearly, if somewhat superficially, understood and explained in the context of American political independence."[178] Here, again, media mattered for those with vested interests.

For the Irish image, characterizations of Devlin as a "female Castro in a Mini-skirt," "the mini-skirted militant," "a miniskirted Marxist," and a "Joan of Moscow" inflicted serious damage, especially when the origins of the insinuations for communist influence were made by the Bailie-Mills "'truth squad' from Northern Ireland": "Miss Devlin's associates" were "a weird mélange of Communists, Trotskyites, Socialists, Maoists, Castroites, and assorted leftists and revolutionaries."[179] So too with stories like that in the *Chicago Daily News*, picked up from its foreign news service in Belfast, that described how "the Joan of Arc with Feet of Clay" was "making violence seem like a patriotic duty, and this appeals to the youngsters of today who have a streak of violence anyway."[180] Non-Irish readers in the American heartland naturally wondered how the Irish could claim to be loyal Americans when they were supporting someone like Devlin. After nearly fifty years of carefully curating their image against Anglo-Saxon propaganda, these kinds of accusations made it almost impossible for Irish Americans to thread their once historically reliable needle to stitch together American patriotism and Irish self-determination.

Then Devlin created a quandary when, through an intermediary who "castigated Irish Americans as 'hypocrites,'" her golden key to New York City was presented to the Black Panthers in a gesture of solidarity.[181] The Federal Bureau of Investigation had labeled the controversial Black Power group as a domestic terrorist organization in 1969. Devlin's decision was criticized in a nationally syndicated column designed to be picked up as the Irish story for St. Patrick's week in 1970: "Apparently nobody told the Mayor that Bernadette besides being a humanitarian (we can give her that credit), was, by her own account, 'a militant socialist aiming at the creation of an Irish Workers Republic,'" the conservative journalist John R. Chamberlain informed American readers. "No crime in being that, of course, provided you don't advocate violence.... [Devlin isn't] interested in civil rights save as a means to promote 'revolution.' Nor are the Black Panthers in the United States interested in normal democratic policies.... To give any of them the keys to our cities is to invite our own destruction."[182]

The main political issues taken up by Irish Americans on behalf of Ireland in the twentieth century—self-determination, partition, and immigration—had never intersected with race in this way. Now boxed in by slick public relations moves that associated them not only with African American unrest in the United States but also with support for communism in Northern Ireland, Irish America stepped away from Bernadette Devlin, their "petite Irish crusader in blue jeans," as well as from trying to pry open America's golden door for immigrants.[183] The sea change their own racial consciousness had undergone, from fierce Celt to generic Caucasian, still was not enough to shield the Irish when they encountered dangerous waters like this. There was a path of least resistance available. For decades, consumer culture had also steadily contributed to the green space. Irish didn't have to be racial or partisan; it could just be immensely profitable.

---------------------------------- 5 ----------------------------------

Selling Value

If the Irish image was contested, negotiated, and transformed by the winds of political, cultural, and racial change in both Ireland and the United States, the power of certain products and descriptive language to influence market expectations on both sides of the Atlantic also jockeyed for supremacy in the green space. Products identified with Ireland, or labeled in some manner as Irish, positioned legitimate exports against imitations that did not originate in Ireland at all. Despite taking many forms, the potential to generate revenue linked them all together. As historic Irish brands became consubstantial with American ones, the material and psychological definitions of Irish were stretched in unexpected ways.

Ireland had a history of commodifying the nation to foster economic growth, and it introduced its products through international exhibitions. In the American context, this was most critical in Chicago (1893) and St. Louis (1904). Irish exports deliberately equated with quality, like linen, lace, and whiskey, struggled thereafter with competition and trademark violations, especially as American consumption and advertising rapidly expanded.[1] By the 1960s, Ireland had unwittingly prepared the ground for a narrow visual and linguistic Irish sales spectrum in the United States. The result was tension between image and reality in the marketplace, between Ireland's need to be economically pragmatic and American popular culture's appropriation of the familiar for profit. Consumer expectations were further complicated when the appearance of the leprechaun, for example, redirected Irish from a mark of quality to a dubious ethnic signifier. Simultaneously, the selling value of Irish was reinforced by tourism, motion pictures, and the celebration of St. Patrick's Day, all important commercial arenas for the Irish image that will be discussed in subsequent chapters.

* * *

Salted fish and linen, part of North American trade since the eighteenth century, set a precedent for market longevity and the association of Ireland with quality consumer goods. The United States still imported 4.4 million and 1.9 million pounds, respectively, of cured Irish herring and mackerel in 1911.[2] Processed foods such as preserved fruit, breadstuffs, meat, and dairy products also found gourmet markets in the United States. One New York City dealer claimed that "the costliest of all smoked meats are the fine hams and bacon that come from Limerick, Ireland"; indeed, on the eve of the First World War, more than one hundred thousand pounds of Irish bacon and hams were shipped to the United States.[3] As H. D. Gribbon points out, "For Ireland, selling the products of her industry meant competing in a world market where success required an industry to be either very large or highly specialized or to be favoured with some particular cost or technical advantage."[4] The survival of certain industries like linen depended on the continued cultivation of an American market where its association with Ireland and its reputation for quality had deep roots. Seventy percent of that trade was crossing the Atlantic as the twentieth century opened; the United States—where Irish linen was still largely perceived as a luxury item—imported over forty-three million square yards (worth $7.1 million) in 1914.[5]

The 1893 World's Columbian Exposition in Chicago showcased some other high-end Irish products, especially lace, crochet, and embroidery. As part of Ireland's ongoing nationalist efforts, rural crafts with consumer appeal were revived to demonstrate the level of quality, skill, and artistry that was possible in a country too often stereotyped as incapable of helping itself. Donegal Industries, under the auspices of Mrs. Ernest Hart (née Alice Rowland), and the Irish Industries Association, the brainchild of Lady Aberdeen (née Ishbel Hamilton-Gordon), championed craftwork as a means of alleviating generational poverty in Ireland and halting emigration. The former preferred to work alone, while the latter had the support of Sir Horace Plunkett and the Irish Agricultural Organisations Society; this explains the origin of two similar but separate Irish initiatives at the fair, both so-called Irish Villages located on the Midway Plaisance.[6]

Chicago's *Daily Inter Ocean* dedicated a full page to a description of Mrs. Hart's "charming" village in August 1893, praising it as "the effort of a single-souled philanthropy in the midst of money-making enterprises" and "the evident intense earnestness to represent with fidelity, dignity, and sympathy a misrepresented country." After passing through a recreation of St. Laurence's Gate (a thirteenth-century barbican in Drogheda, County Louth), there was an open green space surrounded by seven cottages in which eighteen Irish women demonstrated their crafts for visitors. In addition, a handful of men executed woodcarving, stone masonry, and iron and silver smithing. Mr. McSweeney, age seventy-nine, danced and played the uilleann pipes for entertainment. Souvenirs such as lace curtains, replicas of the Book of Kells (a ninth-century illuminated copy of the Gospels), and "portraits of great Irishmen" were for sale in a scale reproduction of Donegal Castle. There, visitors could also enjoy "well-served meals," including "Irish stew," in a restaurant at the base of a hundred-foot-tall round tower.[7] Asked by a reporter how their village compared with Lady Aberdeen's, one of Mrs. Hart's girls replied, "The difference is the devilish poor imitation they are of us."[8]

Although Mrs. Hart's Irish Village was the original concession granted by fair organizers, Lady Aberdeen's Irish Industries Village had the advantage not only of being the first Irish experience encountered by visitors entering the Plaisance but of being a much larger and more elaborate reproduction of Ireland.[9] Its centerpiece was another castle, this one a facsimile of Blarney that was famous for granting eloquence to those who kissed one particular stone. The public's pathway through this village also gave visitors a behind-the-scenes glimpse of the skilled hands that made specific luxury goods. Among these were young women carefully selected to embody Ireland, and dressed accordingly in custom-made costumes, whom the *Irish World* referred to as "The Handsome Irish Girls and Their Handiwork."[10] It took care to name them as well as their specialties:

> Ellen Aher trained at the Presentation Convent at Youghal County [*sic*, County Cork], makes the beautiful needle-point lace which is so highly prized by those who are its happy possessors; Kate Kennedy illustrates the making of *appliqué* lace as it is done in the cottage homes of Carrickmacross, and Mary Flynn does the same for the much admired fine crochet work made by the poor women around Clones, in County Monaghan, and

which is already much appreciated in America; Ellen Murphy shows how the pretty light Limerick lace is made, which is gaining in popularity. . . . Bridget McGinley works at her old-fashioned wheel in the next cottage, preparing the wool for Patrick Fagan from Donegal to weave into those delightful homespuns whose merits have been found out of late years by the fashionable world, as well as by the sportsman and athlete; Maggie Dennehy, who talks real Irish, also sits nearby and shows how . . . the women of Valencia Island, County Kerry . . . earn their livelihood by knitting.[11]

Perhaps the most surprising additions to this repertoire of Irish crafts were the applied arts. The display of ornaments carved from bog oak or Connemara (green) marble was supervised by Miss Goggin of the Dublin firm that dominated the trade, while the Dublin art jeweler Edmond Johnson showcased silver brooches, bracelets, charms, and spoons. Visitors could also purchase bog oak souvenirs, blackthorn sticks, and jewelry that reproduced antiquities like the Tara Brooch—an ornate, circular metal clothing fastener dating from Ireland's early medieval period—which was "celebrated," according to Johnson's full-page advertisement in the *Guide to the Irish Industrial Village*. He also sold replicas of the Brian Boru Harp, St. Patrick's Bell, and initial letters from the Book of Kells, all "in good taste, and copied from the antique." These served to introduce Americans to a new visual vocabulary, part of the Celtic revival that had been rising in popularity in Ireland and England since the 1850s.[12]

As one of the hosts on opening day at the Irish Village, Lord Aberdeen asked Irish Americans to help raise Ireland's profile. "We want them to go among their American friends and induce them to patronize the beautiful products of the Irish cottages."[13] Writing about the village in the *North American Review*, Lady Aberdeen pointed to the importance of establishing Ireland in the niche market for handmade rather than machine-made items: "The newest shapes, the best designs, the most modern colors must all be studied and carried out by these peasants in the wilds of Ireland if our modern hand-workers are to secure and maintain their hold on the market."[14] She was confident that "the excellence of Irish goods" was being recognized; indeed, A. Shuman & Company of Boston was among the first American manufacturers to use the World's Fair to promote its line of woolen overcoats for men made from Irish frieze, "imported directly by us from the mills in Ireland."[15] By 1900, *The Gael* reported that "American women are developing a great enthusiasm for Irish lace, and, of course, the demand will lead to its being greatly used in Paris and Vienna."[16] Two years later, *The Gael* noted that Irish poplin, a fabric woven of silk and wool and "thought to go well with Irish guipure [lace]," was prized by European royalty and patronized "notably by American visitors."[17] About this time, fashion trends in London and New York also began to incorporate Irish homespuns into contemporary costumes; in 1902, a delegate to the First International Woman Suffrage Conference in Washington, DC, modeled her Donegal-made blue and brown tweed gown for a reporter.[18] Consequently, the volume of woolen goods exported from Ireland doubled between 1904 and 1914, with the value in 1909 at over half a million pounds and with sales "mostly to a high-class market."[19]

In addition to *The Gael*, the Irish Industrial League of America, an organization established in New York in 1903, encouraged the sale of Irish-made goods in the United States.[20] The men on the league's board of directors, who aimed to support the work of the Irish Agricultural Organisations Society, included some of the same cultural brokers discussed in chapter 3 (Morgan J. O'Brien, John D. Crimmins, and John Quinn). The purchase of Irish products, critical to self-help in Ireland, also had the potential to reflect well on the Irish image in the United States. The World's Fair in 1904, therefore, was an opportunity not to be missed. The team that sent the Irish-American Historic Loan Collection to St. Louis also sent an Irish Historic Loan Collection to prove "in visible form . . . the art, industry and social life of the country for a period of 4,000 years." The catalog declared, "It will be seen that Irish artists and craftsmen of the present day are working largely in the spirit of a traditional national art which flourished in prehistoric times long before the civilization of the European continent and of the East entered with Christianity into Ireland. Not many nations can claim so long and continuous a record of national life."[21] This was an important corollary to claims simultaneously being made about Irish American patriotism and respectability.

The Irish industrial exhibit in St. Louis was financed by a local, wealthy Irish American contractor, Thomas F. Hanley, and organized by the new Department of Agricultural and Technical Instruction for Ireland (DATI, established 1900).[22] Because Ireland was not an independent country, it could not be represented by a national pavilion; instead, under the designation of a concession, DATI grouped Ireland's industrial efforts together rather than scattering them throughout the fair as part of other British exhibits.[23] Myles J. Murphy, the general manager of the Irish Village, promised that it would "be the most dignified and praiseworthy representation that Ireland has ever been given at any international exposition. . . . National ideals will not be sacrificed on the altar of catchpenny commercialism. The life of Ireland is at stake. Industries can save it. . . . No stone will be left unturned to show the world what the old land is capable of doing. . . . There will be no ridiculous blarney stone to catch the foolish coin, nor is it an Irish village, the keynote of which is poverty."[24]

To that end, there were demonstrations on how to make a variety of products, from ordinary soap and candles to the extraordinary hand-tufted wool carpets from County Donegal, in what Homer Potterton describes as "a combination of an art exhibition and a trade show."[25] "This striking representation . . . will give many Americans quite a new conception of Ireland," wrote T. W. Rolleston in *Harper's Weekly*. "Ireland was coming to be known too much, like a heroine of modern drama, as a country 'with a past' . . . but it is breaking fresh ground in the direction of the artistic handicrafts. . . . St. Louis should have the effect of turning the mind of American or American-Irish captains of industry to the unworked field for business enterprise lying in readiness for exploitation in Ireland."[26] As Lady Aberdeen had anticipated less than a decade earlier, the abundance of machine-made consumer goods in the United States created a "great fancy for hand-manufactured articles," a luxury market in which Ireland already had a claim.[27] Once again, visitors encountered Irish jewelry, lace, crochet, and other lesser-known Irish goods, including fifteen types of marble and a claddagh jewelry exhibit by Faller of Galway.[28] In a long narrative description, the *Dallas Morning News* was "astonished" by the large Linen Manufacturers' Joint Exhibition, "even though much was expected." It also noted that "many visitors to 'Ireland' [at the fair] linger long before the laces, linens and woolens who never notice other exhibits equally as artistic and unusually interesting because they are happy surprises. The wood carving, metal work, enameling, leather work, book plates and illuminations are delightfully artistic."[29]

Many of the St. Louis displays were brought to New York in September 1905 to obtain maximum exposure for this wide range of Irish-made goods. The AOH sponsored this effort, funded by private contributions totaling $50,000.[30] The Irish Industrial Exposition and Amusement Company (whose financial officer, state judge Victor J. Dowling, would chair the Emmet Statue Committee discussed in chapter 3 within the decade) oversaw its business management. Organizers hoped that a broad range of "intelligent persons of all nationalities," especially "merchants and importers," would "be favorably impressed and influenced."[31] Irish-speaking weavers and spinners from Connemara as well as lace makers from Sligo were recruited to demonstrate their skills in the vast halls of Madison Square Garden, and John Quinn "bullied and persuaded his friends to buy" Dun Emer textiles like tapestries and embroidered church vestments.[32] Because "the famous linens of Ireland are scarcely represented," the definition of Irish seemed unconventional to the *New York Times*. "It would not do to suppose that this exposition shows what Irish industries really are. There are finely appointed jaunting cars; a showing of cane furniture of no special importance; vast stacks of shillelaghs and blackthorn cudgels; and minor objects in jewelry which have nothing specifically Irish in appearance."[33]

Nevertheless, exhibits like these—in Chicago, St. Louis, and New York—continued to be an important means for Ireland to connect production and consumption, as American buyers literally saw the Irish hands that made Irish goods or saw Irish products in the context of Irish export promotion. Demand for Irish woolens, linen, herring, and mackerel as well as Irish-cured bacon remained steady, as did the association with quality and specific niche markets.[34] Such word-of-mouth advertising contributed to a positive Irish image. A large New York City department store described "Irish Homespuns," for example, as "hand-loomed, Ireland's best. Woolens woven in the old-fashioned way have lots of old-fashioned wear in them, and a distinctive appearance all their own."[35] Framing Irish industrial development as untainted by "the evils of capitalism, materialism, and urbanization" also contributed to the idealized image favored by Irish nationalists.[36]

The big American World's Fairs, as well as the 1905 New York exposition, schooled a significant segment of the foreign-born Irish in America and their children in how individual purchasing power could affect economic change in Ireland. Subsequent "Buy Irish" campaigns had the potential to target millions of ethnic consumers in the United States.[37] Irish import shops—such as the Irish Industries Depot, run by the New York Gaelic League on premises donated by John D. Crimmins in 1915—reinforced this kind of consumerism. So too did rhetoric like that declared at the fifty-fourth national convention of the AOH in Atlantic City, New Jersey, in 1925: "The growth of an Irish economic system would draw forth the latent genius of the Irish people and [the AOH] urges all members of the race in this country to buy Irish-made goods whenever possible."[38] Eileen Phillips also noted the sales power of nostalgia and of specific products to conjure a visual image of Ireland: "To many an exile in a far-off colony the possession of some specimen of Belleek [pottery] becomes doubly precious, not only for its own intrinsic value, but for the memories it recalls—memories of the tang of the heather, of blue turf smoke rising from some whitewashed homestead, of the sound of rushing waters, where the salmon leap."[39] Writing in 1922 on behalf of the Irish Women's Co-operative League of America, in the same spirit as Lady Aberdeen in 1893, trade union organizer Leonora O'Reilly believed that "by bands of devoted salespeople in every State in the United States we can get Irish goods known and asked for everywhere. The goods need only an introduction; they will sell on their own merit after."[40]

To that end, seeking a market beyond its diaspora, the Irish Free State appointed Lindsay Crawford as its Irish trade representative in New York that December; in his opinion, the average American needed to be convinced that there was more to Ireland than "famines and distress."[41] A government board, Córas Tráchtála Teoranta, assisted Irish manufacturers in boosting their export trade with North America.[42] Large public displays of Irish goods were again exhibited in Cleveland at the All-Nations Exposition in March 1929 and in New York City at the 1939–40 World's Fair as well as during a two-week "Salute to Ireland" promotion at Gimbels department store in November 1949, a merchandising partnership with a high-end American retailer that would be replicated by Bloomingdale's and Neiman

Marcus in the 1970s.[43] In Chicago, at the 1933–34 Century of Progress Exposition, the Irish Free State showcased many of the same items it had forty years earlier at the Columbian Exposition, although there was some acknowledgment in the *Irish Trade Journal* that American tastes were changing. Woolen steamer rugs were now pushed as an export for the "vast untouched market" opened by "the universal motoring habit," while upholstery made from linen, tweed, and poplin was a "novelty" that "American manufacturers, if properly approached, would probably welcome [as an] innovation and apply it." The *Irish Trade Journal*, published by the Irish Free State's Department of Industry and Commerce, was adamant in 1934 that the development of the American market hinged on advertising: "Spasmodic efforts are not sufficient and constant stimulation and education are needed.... The generation that knew Irish quality is passing away and newcomers know nothing of the quality of Irish goods. Incidentally, the stoppage of immigration from Ireland is having an adverse influence on the sale of Irish goods by reducing the potential market and potential source of favourable propaganda."[44]

* * *

These Irish efforts came during a period when the American market for manufactured goods vastly expanded, aided by a variety of advertising techniques designed to facilitate sales. Jennifer Black points to a climate that developed in the decades before and after the turn of the twentieth century "where it could be profitable to copy someone else's goods and sell them as one's own.... For counterfeiting to be worthwhile to the criminal, the brand itself (not necessarily the product) needed to have enough cultural value to present a likely case for copying.... There has to be enough of an existing reputation built up to make it worth stealing."[45] A prime example of Ireland's efforts to negotiate this new terrain is Belleek, a specific type of porcelain that imitated carved Parian marble, produced in a small County Fermanagh village beginning in 1857.

At the 1904 World's Fair in St. Louis, Belleek had a specially commissioned exhibition of its finest "breakfast, tea and dessert ware; vases, flowerpots, card and cake baskets, biscuit and tobacco jars, bonbonnieres and ware suitable for cabinet decoration."[46] Indeed, its reputation preceded it; Belleek's eggshell thinness, creamy color, iridescent glaze, and embellishments of delicate hand-painted shamrocks and flowers were qualities not easily mass-produced. In addition, its design lines were unique; "Neptune," for example, was inspired by seashells.[47] Each piece had the Belleek crest stamped on its bottom, a group of iconic elements associated with Ireland's nineteenth-century Celtic revival.[48] Writing in *Antiques* magazine in 1922, Eileen Buckley concluded that "Belleek has been reasonably well known in America since the close of the Civil War, and . . . has never been inexpensive. . . . The harp, the round tower, and the wolf hound, united in the potter's mark, express a rare appreciation of harmonious symbolism. Indeed, so peculiarly associated in Ireland's history are these objects that any one of them might well stand as an emblem of the country."[49]

In the 1880s, a series of management and ownership crises at Belleek Pottery caused many of its skilled potters to emigrate. Among them were William Bromley and John Gavigan, who began working for Ott and Brewer in Trenton, New Jersey, a pottery that soon produced porcelain that, according to some accounts, was "'fully equal' to Irish Belleek."[50] The *Trenton Evening Times* described Gavigan as "a skilled mechanic" and "one of the best informed men in the country on matters pertaining to the pottery industry" when he died in 1911.[51] By then, almost twenty American companies had produced a "Belleek"-type porcelain. Although only five of these remained in business for any significant length of time, each used the Irish place name.[52]

From 1906, real Belleek was stamped with the Irish Trade Mark, a distinctive design: "an old Celtic Fibula or Collar" with the words *Déanta I nÉirinn* (Made in Ireland) "in the crescent-shaped space between the two circles of the mark."[53] The Irish Industrial Development Association (IIDA), founded in Cork City in 1906, created the Irish Trade Mark to prevent the use abroad of any trademark that falsely suggested a product originated in Ireland; Belleek was quick to adopt it so that "those who know little or nothing of the markings on china can have no doubt as to the genuineness of what they are buying."[54] Since Ireland was still part of the United Kingdom at the time, the IIDA registered the mark under Section 62 of the 1905 British Trade Marks Act as an added measure of protection. The IIDA then licensed it to producers of goods made in Ireland; there were 495 firms using it by 1911 and about 700 by 1920 on approximately "400 distinct industrial commodities."[55]

Although the IIDA notified Belleek that American-made imitations were being sold in New York as early as 1915, no action was taken until 1925 when new owners took over the pottery.[56] In September, Francis Dolan wrote to the secretary of the IIDA that Perlee, Inc. of Trenton, New Jersey, had been using the name "Lenox Belleek" on its pottery and "selling this American made Belleek as Irish Belleek to unsuspecting persons, much to the annoyance of our best customers in the USA."[57] In fact, Lenox Belleek sold all across the United States at the time, with newspaper advertisements that targeted brides in cities like Boston, Dallas, New Orleans, Cleveland, and Omaha.[58] The IIDA was concerned about whether restraining such a rival would legally succeed in America; Belleek had acquired a secondary meaning

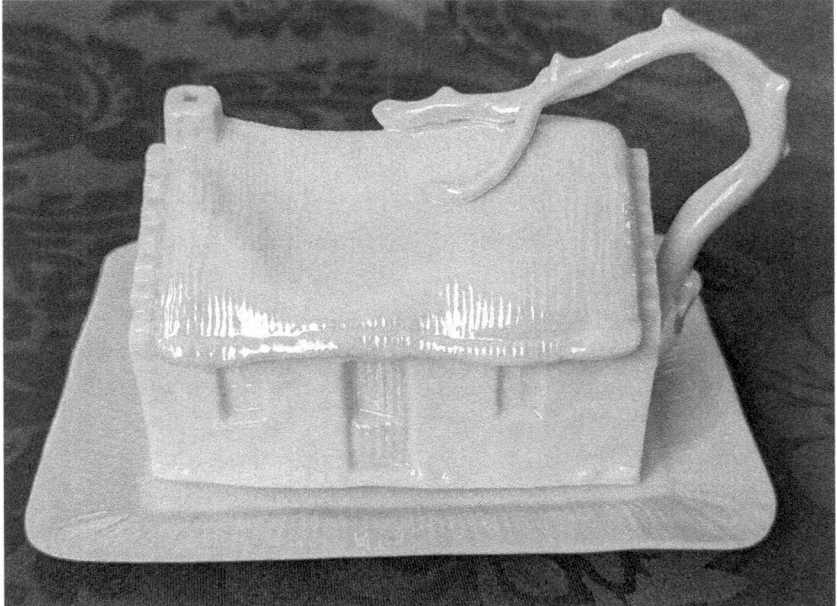

Figure 5.1. A delicate thatched cottage butter dish made by Belleek, the County Fermanagh pottery (fifth mark, 1955 to 1965), embodied both luxury and nostalgia for the twentieth-century consumer. This type of simple house represents an Irish vernacular building tradition that used local materials and blended into the landscape even when whitewashed. In the west of Ireland, where it was ubiquitous in the nineteenth century, this nursery of so many emigrants to America was usually only one room deep on either side of the half door. Credit: author's collection.

there that conveyed a particular finish, but it was also clearly a geographic name.⁵⁹

Macy's department store in New York City was one of the outlets selling the Trenton china. Belleek and the IIDA brought the matter before the Irish Free State's Department of Industries and Commerce, and after protests by the Irish commercial representative in New York, both Macy's and the Perlee company agreed to "discontinue the use of the word 'Belleek.'"⁶⁰ Four years later, Belleek won an important victory in litigation against the Morgan Belleek China Company of Canton, Ohio. The American courts upheld Belleek's "exclusive right to the name" and made it "illegal to mark ware with the word 'Belleek' as had been done in the past in America."⁶¹ In the interim, however, the White House had acquired a 1,700-piece dinner set of Lenox's "high-grade china, known as Beleek [sic]" for state dinners, demonstrating how easy it had become to blur the lines about what was genuinely Irish even in the most sophisticated American foreign policy circles.⁶²

In one of its longest battles before the Belleek case, the IIDA fought to protect the Irish Trade Mark itself in an opposition brought against Dennis D. Barrett, an enterprising thirty-five-year-old Irish-immigrant merchant tailor in Terre Haute, Indiana. Barrett first sent a letter to the IIDA in December 1909 in which he praised the concept of the Irish Trade Mark and claimed to have the endorsement of the AOH to promote Irish products in the United States: "I have been before three of the Division[s] of the A.O.H., and related the many points of encouragement as to the necessity of encouraging Irish product[s]," Barrett wrote, "and particularly of calling for the Irish Trade Mark know[n] as the celtic collar Brand and In each of those Divisions they hailed the good work and pledged themselves to do their utmost along this line."⁶³ He asked for power of attorney so that he could represent the IIDA in the United States, suggesting that his contacts would facilitate the recognition of the Irish Trade Mark.⁶⁴ At the same time, he wrote to the editor of the *Contract Gazette*, "I must if possible get the name of this Symbol or the Name of the Design. Now Please can you get this for us as it is important."⁶⁵

Barrett applied to the U.S. Patent Office in June 1910 to register the Irish Trade Mark in his name, essentially pirating it for use on wool or cotton collars, coats, trousers, and vests made in America. The IIDA filed oppositions with the Trade Mark Department and with the Commissioner of Patents, spending £1,000 in legal fees over the next three years to prove, through depositions from importers and customers, that its symbol had been known and recognized as the Irish national trademark in the United States since 1906. "I remember one of the words to be 'erin' which was stamped on the mark," Michael Fahey, a young lawyer from Charlestown, MA, testified. "The design was rather unique. . . . [It instantly conveyed] the fact to me that they were of Irish manufacture, and therefore guaranteed to be what I consider the best linen obtainable."[66] At the time, the Senate and House Committees on Patents were considering bills to amend the statutes relating to trademarks, especially a potential act of Congress to extend the British privileges of the Irish Trade Mark to the United States.[67] In 1912, the Patent Office rendered its decision, finding that Barrett's use constituted "a fraud upon the public." Barrett took the case to the Court of Appeals in Washington, DC, where, in November 1913, Chief Justice Seth Shepard found in favor of the IIDA.[68] The IIDA believed it was necessary to "safeguard the Irish Trade Mark" because Barrett—"in a daring letter he has sent to the Association since the decision in this case has been issued," as the IIDA reported—had stated, "'We can get millions of dollars out of the power of the registration of the Irish Trade Mark in America.'"[69] Indeed, by the end of its first decade, the IIDA could "produce definite evidence that the Irish Trade Mark branded on an article has proved to be a good selling point in most other countries—at home and abroad—as well as in the United States of America."[70]

Protecting the reputation of the Irish Trade Mark and Belleek in American courts, by extension, protected all other Irish exports.[71] By the 1920s, the selling value of the word Irish equaled that of Quaker, which sold oatmeal (among other items) by implying honesty.[72] The Irish Free State interpreted this as a marketing advantage: "In a wealthy population of 110 millions it is natural to find a considerable section of consumers to whom quality and repute are quite as important as price."[73] Nevertheless, the prized historical reputation of certain Irish exports could also lead to assumptions about products that used words like *linen* and *poplin*.[74] Marcus Ward, Inc., a subsidiary of Marcus Ward & Co. of Belfast, made high-grade stationery, including "Royal Irish Linen," at its factory and main office in Long Island City, New

York. The company advertised this as "the standard of quality for half a century," stating, "Its reputation is world-wide." Because "Royal Irish Linen" was an original Irish trademark for finished fabric, it was not a stretch for a Belfast firm to use it as a sales pitch for paper in the United States. The company also promoted "Irish Poplin" writing paper as "substantial and elegant in appearance and moderate in price."[75] But when an American company, Elam Paper of Marion, Indiana, sought women's custom for their popular "Irish Lawn" with the slogan "Aristocratic Stationery at a Democratic Price," it was purely to compete with Marcus Ward's share of the market. Elam told stationery dealers, "Man, if you want to get your hands on something live, just order an $8.46 assortment (24 boxes) of Elam's Irish Lawn from your wholesaler. It will bring you $14.10 or 66 2/3 per cent profit—and that's just your start!"[76] Although lawn was typically made from cotton, not linen, it was a textile; in conjunction with the word Irish, it was a clever gloss that made conflation easy for the average American consumer.

In this respect, Irish as a brand was vulnerable, as the IIDA knew from experience with "ambiguous titles" on non-Irish products in England, Scotland, France, Australia, South Africa, and Ireland itself. The association successfully intervened in those countries to stop words like Irish, Colleen, Killarney, Galway, Erin, Hibernian, and Gaelic from being used as brand names on ordinary household products such as stoves and incandescent mantles; brushes, combs, and hairpins; cloth, sewing cotton, sheets, and pillowcases; flour, cornmeal, chocolate, tea, salt, and baking powder; boots and boot laces; and tobacco, paint, toilet perfume, wax candles, and bicycle repair kits.[77] As a result, the IIDA lacked the resources to prevent the use of Irish words or symbols in advertising, in trademarks, and on non-Irish goods in the United States other than in the Belleek and Irish Trade Mark cases. Even though it forced Burton Brothers & Co. of New York, a wholesale dry goods merchant, into printing "Manufactured in the USA" on the selvage of its poplin cloth in 1916,[78] a decade later American companies were in litigation with one another over Irish words. Burton Brothers sued Jacobs Brothers, Inc. of Baltimore in 1927 for allegedly selling "an inferior grade of poplin" and "for alleged infringement of the trademark 'Burton's Irish Poplin.'" The trademark covered both those words and the image of a shamrock, which the company claimed they had used since 1895. Jacobs, a manufacturer of nurses' and maids' uniforms, countersued for libel and sought $750,000 for damage to the company's reputation.[79] As the distance between Ireland and the consumers of products like these expanded, "the problem of counterfeits and legitimacy" flourished in the United States.[80]

Global competition also greatly exacerbated imitations.[81] Irish lace and crochet, the pride of the world fairs in Chicago and St. Louis with their distinctive designs, are a case in point. They were nearly impossible to physically stamp with the Irish Trade Mark. Both quickly encountered foreign competitors, starting with government-sponsored Austrian crochet that included Irish motifs. France, Switzerland, Italy, China, Japan, and the Philippines also cut into Irish crochet exports, quickly followed by what the *Irish Industrial Journal* called "cheap oriental work." In 1913, the *Irish American Weekly* reported that "Syrian crochet" had "flooded the American market to the serious detriment of the Irish industry" and that, in New York, "many Italian emigrants" were "chiefly employed in producing 'Irish crochet.'"[82] Adding the word *Real* to any print advertising initially made Irish handcrafted lace less susceptible to competition from German and Swiss machine-made imitations.[83] The IIDA retained a firm of solicitors in New York City, Rosenbaum and Stockbridge at 41 Park Row, to investigate reports of advertising and sales of spurious Irish goods in the United States (some labeled "Real Irish Article of English Make"), and it encouraged Irish manufacturers whose exports were being affected by "this dishonest form of trading" to take direct action to stop it.[84]

In 1926, Crawford, the Irish Free State's trade representative in New York, lodged protests with the U.S. Federal Trade Commission (FTC) that several American firms were importing lace from China and then advertising, labeling, and selling it as Irish for a third of the price the genuine article could demand.[85] Targeting the New York City firm of Bardwil Brothers in particular, the FTC ordered the practice stopped in a landmark decision that established "for the first time in the United States the exclusive right of all products originating in Ireland to the trade designation 'Irish.'"[86] The *Gaelic American* applauded the May 1926 ruling, noting that it would also accrue to the benefit of imported Irish bacon, ham, mackerel, and herring. "Every nation deserves the exclusive enjoyment of the fruits of its own industry and capacity," it editorialized.[87] In commenting on the Bardwil case, the *Irish Trade Journal* blamed disruptions caused by World War I for creating circumstances ripe for exploitation that were seized by "a class of European traders, chiefly from the Balkans." Using Chinese labor and "persistent advertising in trade journals and by aggressive salesmanship," they "sought to establish in the minds of American retailers and public the idea that these Oriental laces were identical in pattern and quality with those made in Ireland, and were similar in all respects to laces, made in other countries, that were alleged to be known in the trade as 'Irish' lace."[88] The FTC's Irish ruling applied to Nanyang Brothers, Inc. of New York and, in November 1928, to the Lian and Mabarek firms, who were labeling lace with the words "Chinese Irish," "Shanghai Irish," and "Swataw Irish."[89]

Bulk sales of Irish lace destined for the United States compounded the problem for the Irish Free State. These were made in London and Paris, shipped under export invoices prepared by American consular officials in England and France, and thus lace often "lost its Irish identity in American statistics." The Bardwil Brothers tried to use those official statistics "to prove that comparatively little Irish-made lace is sold in America."[90] They also argued that Irish crochet was too "stiff and starchy."[91] Moreover, as offshore clothing factories were opened in the Philippines and Puerto Rico, both exempt from American customs duties, New York importers ("chiefly Syrian") shipped Chinese lace there for insertion into dresses and underwear, then reshipping the finished products to the United States where they were advertised as being trimmed with 'Irish lace.' The Philippine and Puerto Rican free markets also encouraged the development of local embroidery and lace industries to eventually supplant even the Chinese product. "The market for Irish-made laces has been virtually lost to the Syrian importers," lamented the *Irish Trade Journal*, "[who] look for quantity [rather than quality] production in countries where labour is cheap."[92]

Sweeney and Johnson—an importer and distributor of lace and other merchandise with offices in Cincinnati, Chicago, and New York—tried to withstand such global forces. Patrick M. Sweeney, a native of County Donegal, emigrated in 1883 and went into business with his son and nephew.[93] From the late 1930s, the company worked with the manufacturing firm of McKinneys, Ltd. in Belfast. Its Irish line included "The O'Donnell," "The O'Neil," "The O'Reilly," "Blarney," "Emerald," and "The Shamrock," mainly to meet an American consumer vogue for lace medallions to decorate furniture.[94] By referencing historical Irish chieftains or familiar word cues for Irish, the pattern names suggest the market value of such linguistic permutations. But by 1949 and 1950, the cost of importing two hundred hand-stitched and machine-embroidered tablecloths and napkins from Ireland, with an 18 percent markup, severely cut into the company's previous profits.[95] Sweeney and Johnson was eventually squeezed into importing less-expensive hand-embroidered linen and cotton cut-work sets from Hong Kong and Shanghai. With even more distinctive pattern names like "Innis Carra" and "Cruiskeen Laun" (both misspelled phrases from the Irish language), the true point of origin of this lace was cleverly obscured.[96]

The registration of word trademarks, including Irish expressions, accelerated in the United States in the twentieth century.[97] Over the course of sixty years, as the selling value of Irish was extended geographically well beyond the traditional northeastern urban enclaves of Irish immigrants, the freewheeling and unchecked American culture of consumption soon usurped any of the exclusivity that Ireland had for its exports. The word Irish sold a new diversity of products like American tobacco, shoe thread, and magnetic recording tape while shamrock, as both a label and a visual cue, appeared on fruit juices and window shades.[98] A wide range of American companies, including Armour in Illinois, Goodyear in Ohio, and Red Wing in Minnesota, used such ethnic shorthand to sell non-Irish-made goods. Liggett & Myers of Durham, North Carolina, sold Chesterfields with creativity by capitalizing on a song that had been popular for two decades; in its 1936 ad, a young woman looks directly at the consumer as she cradles her smoking cigarette while the association creates a chain of ideas: "When Irish Eyes are Smiling . . . They Satisfy . . . All You Could Ask For."[99]

As Irish became something that could be commercialized without much effort, it became increasingly abused. Two court cases in New York City during the 1940s tested the limit of this commercial value. The plaintiff in both was Leland Holzer. As a used car dealer in Manhattan doing a brisk wartime trade under the sobriquet of the "Smiling Irishman," he sued two competitors for infringement of its tradename.

Figure 5.2. John Herbert Orr—the founder of Orradio Industries in Opelika, Alabama, and one of the pioneers of magnetic recording tape—trademarked "Irish" as his brand name in 1948. Orradio Irish is one of the earliest American commercial alignments of Irish with the leprechaun, the shamrock, and a reputation for quality. David Morton suggests this was probably to compete with 3M's Scotch Brand, but it may also have been a nod to either the musical *Finian's Rainbow* (1947) or the film *The Luck of the Irish* (1948), both of which feature a leprechaun. Credit: author's collection.

Smiling Irishman, Inc. used shamrock and clay pipe cues printed in green on its stationery, business cards, checks, advertisements, and outdoor signs; in the ten months prior to the first trial, the business also spent approximately $50,000 on radio advertising. A witness testified that the name "Smiling Irishman" was "a very valuable asset," had "established good will," and was "a feeding source for its business." The

TABLE 1. Sample of Irish words registered as trademarks
with the U.S. Patent Office, 1899–1966

Date of first use	Name	Product	Registrant
1899	Irish	hams and bacon	Armour & Company Corporation, Chicago, Illinois
1906	Shamrock	fresh citrus fruits	Placentia Mutual Orange Association California; Blue Banner Company, Inc.
July 15, 1916	O'Shannon Irish	whiskey	Park & Tilford, 529 W. 42nd Street, New York, New York
December 1925	Ireland	tea	Ireland Coffee-Tea, Inc., Pleasantville, New Jersey
1927	Shamrock	fruit juices & fruit-flavored drinks	Shamrock Foods Company, Phoenix, Arizona
1927	Emerald	paper bags	Southern Advance Bag & Paper Co. Inc., Bangor, Maine
October 15, 1928	Emerald Cord	hose of all kinds	Goodyear Tire & Rubber Company, Akron, Ohio
June 1, 1929	Shamrock	corned & smoked meats	Roberts Turkey Brand Corned Meats, San Francisco, California
December 18, 1931	Erin Maid	hosiery	Massachusetts Knitting Mills Corporation, Jamaica Plain, Massachusetts
May 12, 1933	Irish	smoking and chewing tobacco	R. R. Tobin Tobacco Co., Detroit, Michigan
June 1935	Barbour's Best Irish Flax	shoe thread	The Linen Thread Co., 60 E. 42nd Street, New York, New York
March 1935	Shamrock	window shades	G. C. Murphy Company, McKeesport, Pennsylvania
1935	Shamrock	travel agency services	Shamrock Tours, Tacoma, Washington
November 23, 1936	Colleen	cigarettes	Axton-Fisher Tobacco Company, Louisville, Kentucky
September 1, 1938	Erin Go Bragh	whiskey	John Gross & Co., Baltimore, Maryland
April 19, 1939	Tobin's Irish	smoking tobacco	Larus & Brother Company, Tucker, Georgia
September 29, 1939	Irish Moss	rock and rye	Leroux & Company, Philadelphia; Joseph E. Seagram & Sons
August 31, 1940	Irish Maid	fresh potatoes	Michael T. O'Brien, Bryant, Wisconsin

TABLE 1. Sample of Irish words registered as trademarks with the U.S. Patent Office, 1899–1966 (*continued*)

Date of first use	Name	Product	Registrant
September 1940	Irish Brand	cream ale	Beverwyck Breweries, Inc., Albany, New York
1942	Ireland's	canned meat products	Ireland's Chili Company, Wichita Falls, Texas
July 1948	Irish Brand	magnetic recording tape	Orradio Industries, Inc., Opelika, Alabama; Ampex Corp.
March 1, 1950	Irish Setter	hunting boots	Red Wing Shoe Company, Red Wing, Minnesota
1950	Fightin' Irish	drinking glasses and ceramic steins; paper napkins and decals; watches and charms; cigarette lighters; belt buckles; embroidery kits; T-shirts, sweatshirts, and jerseys; pennants and flags	University of Notre Dame, South Bend, Indiana
January 1, 1951	Irish Pride	baler twine	Davis Cordage Company Partnership, Portland, Oregon
January 1, 1951	Emerald Isle	baler twine	Davis Cordage Company Partnership, Portland, Oregon
February 25, 1952	Irish Brand	cream ale	F. & M. Schaefer Brewing Company, Brooklyn, New York
May 16, 1955	Wild Irish Rose	wines	Canandaigua Industries Co., Buffalo, New York
1957	Dunphy's Original Irish	whiskey	American Distilling Co., 150 E. 42nd Street, New York, New York
March 27, 1957	Golden Leprechaun Light Beer	beer	Reiter's Beer Distributors, Brooklyn, New York
October 5, 1959	Emerald Dry	wine	Paul Masson, Inc., Saratoga, California
April 11, 1961	Blarney	fresh vegetables	Kelly Vegetable Farms, Oxnard, California
February 2, 1962	Emerald	shampoo	John H. Breck, Inc., Springfield, Massachusetts
June 1962	Blarney the Leprechaun	greeting cards	Norcross, Inc., 244 Madison Avenue, New York, New York
May 18, 1966	Irish Hearth Recipe	orange marmalade	Louis Sherry, Inc., Long Island City, New York

Source: *Trademark Electronic Search System (TESS)*, United States Patent and Trademark Office, accessed January 15, 2022, https://www.uspto.gov/trademarks.

name had "become so popular" that it was "practically synonymous with the automobile business."[100]

The defendants, John Murphy of Red Hook, Brooklyn (the "Laughing Irishman"), and John J. McDonald of Manhattan (the "Happy Irishman"), both charged that Holzer had no monopoly on the descriptive word Irish and that his use of it constituted a fraud upon the public, especially since he was not Irish or of Irish extraction himself. "They are attempting to capitalize on the well-known virtues of the Irish by pretending either the individual or his corporation is a 'Smiling Irishman.'" Justice Ernest E. L. Hammer, who heard arguments for the first case at the end of 1943, considered each word alone and in combination in order to reach a verdict. After cataloging the characteristics that supposedly distinguished the Irish from other ethnic groups as well as Holzer's advertising semantics, Hammer declared, "Plaintiff makes no claim that he is Irish. What led him to apply such a descriptive phrase to himself is not explained, nor is it discernible. As those words have no relationship to second-hand automobiles, and do not seem suggestive of the origin of the proprietor, or his wares, in the absence of plausible explanation such use might easily be suspected to have been concocted with the intent of misrepresentation." He reminded Holzer that, since the Irish had succeeded in banishing caricature "from stage, press and picture . . . the words 'smiling' or 'laughing' descriptively used of an Irishman may have some special significance such as has often been expressed by bard or minstrel. . . . They do not appear to be definitive of anything in plaintiff's business."[101]

Nevertheless, on legal technicalities on both occasions, Holzer convinced the judge that "Laughing Irishman" and "Happy Irishman" constituted unfair competition. His success was short-lived; Holzer was sued by his former business partner, Walter R. Wellman of Los Angeles, who had been using the "Smiling Irishman" to sell used cars since 1937. Wellman's newspaper advertisements reinforced the hospitable Irish image with copy like "Sell Your Car to the Smiling, Friendly, Happy, Irishman." In July 1945, the New York State Supreme Court ruled in Wellman's favor not only on the grounds of precedent but because he was "Irish on both sides of his family."[102] The American press found these legal wranglings amusing; in Beaumont, Texas, for example, the headline read "Squabbling 'Irishmen' Evidently Talk with Accents Old

Erin Never Heard."[103] The New York case prompted another used car dealer, John J. Kennedy of Cleveland, to sue Sol Comp for unfair competition in 1948. Comp, who was not Irish and also in the used car business only a block away, used billboards and print advertisements with the same ethnic associations, including shamrocks, as Kennedy, who was bringing in $400,000 a year under the trade name "The Smiling Irishman." Cognizant of the publicity advantage of the calendar and the large Irish community in Cleveland, Comp told the *Plain Dealer* on March 11, "The Smiling Irishman hasn't got a corner on all the Irishmen. My attorney says he's crazy. I'll fight him to the Supreme Court. Lawsuit or no, we're planning to open on St. Patrick's Day." This time the headline was "'Smilin' Irishman' Scowls in Court, Auto Dealer Sues Rival for Gaelic 'Infringement.'"[104]

* * *

By the middle of the twentieth century, Irish had become less the mark of origin or quality that the IIDA had intended and more a generic, even ambivalent, word—at once devoid of ethnic meaning and yet loaded with cognitive associations for the American consumer. There was, however, one important exception: "The Fighting Irish," the slogan of the University of Notre Dame in South Bend, Indiana.

Chartered as a college in 1844, Notre Dame expanded rapidly at the turn of the twentieth century. According to Brendan O'Shaughnessy, "The press often referred to Notre Dame teams as the Catholics—or worse, the Papists or Dirty Irish—because the school was largely populated by ethnic Catholic immigrants, many of them Irish."[105] Following tense confrontations with the local Ku Klux Klan in 1924, the university's president, Rev. Matthew Walsh, approved the nickname "The Fighting Irish" in 1927.[106] Around the same time, under two legendary coaches, the Notre Dame football team garnered national press attention. Alumni and athletic fans provided a revenue stream by purchasing drinking glasses and ceramic steins; paper napkins and decals; watches and charms; cigarette lighters; belt buckles; embroidery kits; T-shirts, sweatshirts, and jerseys; and pennants and flags, all trademarked as "Fightin' Irish" with the U.S. Patent Office in 1950.[107] The registration of this slogan made no claim to the exclusive use of the word Irish, just to the unique pairing of it with the adjective *fighting*. Notre Dame added a new logo to its wordmark in 1964: a stylized leprechaun with upraised, clenched fists to exemplify "the Irish qualities of determination and perseverance." He wore a green suit and a bowler hat. Like the "Fightin' Irish" phrase, Notre Dame used the leprechaun—a figure from Irish folklore—on merchandise from 1966 and eventually also registered it as a trademark.[108] In conjunction, both quickly became an internationally recognized symbol for the university that generated a million dollars in annual revenue.[109] Cementing the image in popular culture, a student embodying the leprechaun replaced the traditional Irish terrier as the football team's mascot from the late 1960s, with advice from Hollywood's Warner Bros. regarding makeup, wardrobe, beard, and props.[110]

Indelibly tying a pugnacious expression to a specific ethnicity—an American development—disconnected Irish from the contemporary Republic of Ireland and its concerns about the word as a quality brand for exports. Once again, Ireland had a pavilion at the 1964 New York World's Fair through which it urged, "Buy Irish Goods to Help Employment in Ireland."[111] While Irish citizens saw the Notre Dame leprechaun as an offensive stereotype, he represented success—in sports or as acculturated and assimilated Catholics—for Americans, whether of Irish ancestry or not.[112] In the green space, multiple images and interpretations of Irish were, by then, not necessarily mutually exclusive after decades of intercourse. The history of brewed and distilled exports from Ireland in the American market, which also used a combination of words and symbols to indicate origin, demonstrates how Irish-made products adapted to this kind of consumer expectation in the United States.

Among the principal exports from Dublin destined for the American market for the year ending June 30, 1904, were $494,000 worth of stout, $95,000 worth of ale, and $43,000 worth of whiskey.[113] At the World's Fair in St. Louis that year, the "Joint Whiskey Exhibit" showcased the products of thirteen Irish distilleries, and in New York the following year, "a twenty foot minaret" of whiskey bottles formed the centerpiece at the Madison Square Garden exposition.[114] Among Irish brewers, only Guinness had established name recognition in the American market. As early as 1851, Guinness's XX Brown Stout, a strong porter or high-quality dark malt beer, was sold in New York City in quarts or pints as a "superior brand." It was for sale in Virginia and Louisiana before the Civil War and by 1871 the "large increase" in the brewery's

"American trade" led its sole agent in the United States, E. & J. Burke, to open a branch office on Beaver Street in New York City.[115]

After the passage of the British Trade Marks Act in 1875, Guinness quickly registered its distinctive brown label with a harp device, the signature of Arthur Guinness, and the address of the brewery, "James's Gate, Dublin." Likewise, John Jameson & Son, one of Ireland's first whiskey exporters, became a word trademark in 1881, followed by Old Bushmills in 1882.[116] These three giants of Ireland's nineteenth-century industrial economy did not need to use the word Irish to confirm origin or quality in Ireland or in the United Kingdom. However, as Belleek discovered, the United States presented a challenge; there, Irish brewers and distillers not only encountered fraudulent labeling on inferior stout and whiskey but found themselves in the path of social and political movements against the consumption of alcohol.

At the end of the nineteenth century, estimates noted "that more than ten percent of the so-called Guinness sold in the United States was other beer" because forgery of its label was "widespread." Even E. & J. Burke sold "Burke's Guinness Stout"![117] Brewery policy that relied on local bottlers for its American promotion and sales enabled imitations. In 1899, Guinness hired A. T. Shand to assess the situation. His recommendations included increased advertising to promote brand recognition; the introduction of Guinness Extra Stout on draft in New York, where the brewery should also open an office; more aggressive prosecution of trademark infringements; and the promotion of bottling in the United States to reduce the price of imported Guinness over domestic imitations. Guinness went into partnership with vetted and reputable bottlers such as Hudson Distributing, which only used the Guinness label, and then opened its own bottling plant in New York in 1910. By 1914, it had more than doubled the number of hogsheads shipped for the American trade, accounting for at least 40 percent of all Guinness sales worldwide.[118] In the process, Guinness became a brand even more clearly associated with Ireland and in a highly specialized market. Its label also evolved distinctively and was trademarked in the United States in 1907; it included a word mark ("Guinness's Extra Stout James's Gate Dublin Bottled by Arth Guinness Son & Co. Limited") and a design-with-words mark (a harp and the signature of Arthur Guinness). In 1935, the brewery registered the sole word "Guinness" too.[119]

Likewise, "John Jameson & Son. Dublin Irish Whiskey Established A.D. 1780" used a label on its bottles that incorporated those words, three stars, the initials "JJ&S," as well as John Jameson's signature for its American trademark from 1908.[120] The distillery registered the initials alone as a word mark in 1948, followed by the signature alone in 1950 and "Jameson" in 1969.[121] Bushmills, an even older Irish distillery in County Antrim, also protected its reputation through similar trademarks in the United States.[122] Exports of Irish whiskey were robust at the turn of the twentieth century; between seven and eight million gallons a year supplied "about ninety percent of the world whiskey market." Then decades of temperance advocacy culminated in the Eighteenth Amendment to the U.S. Constitution and closed Ireland off from American sales from 1920 to 1933.[123]

During the Prohibition era, consumers already confused by a host of fake Irish products were disconnected from the historic brewing and distilling industries that were most valuable to Ireland in terms of top-shelf brand-name association. Inferior quality bootleg whiskey in bottles, "often using the real distilleries' labels," significantly undercut the taste for and reputation of Irish whiskey. The Irish Consul in Chicago advised the Irish Department of External Affairs that distillers like Jameson should "appeal to the more discriminating drinkers" to make up for lost ground.[124] William Jameson—identified on its label as "Dublin I.F.S. since 1752," an incongruous conflation of Irish history, since the Irish Free State only dated to 1921—distributed "Old Dublin Whiskey" in the United States in 1934 with a shamrock on the neck of the bottle, something totally unnecessary in the previous century. The company pitch emphasized a decade of aging in sherry casks that made its flavor "different than any whiskey you've ever tasted." Four years later, it partnered with a Cincinnati firm called National Distillers to introduce "Irish American Whiskey," a blend of twenty-year-old pot still Irish (25 percent) and twelve-month-old straight Kentucky (75 percent) advertised as "especially created for modern living—especially recommended for civilized drinking" and for a "discriminating American public."[125] But neither iteration achieved the ambassadorial status of Irish like the original Jameson.

Despite spending over a million dollars on American advertising between 1933 and 1940, Irish whiskey also faced intense competition in North America from blended Scotch exports. When the Irish government prioritized the production of Guinness over whiskey for its domestic market during the Second World War, there were tight restrictions on malting barley and exports. In contrast, British support for Scotch led to its entrenchment "in the United States without any great promotional expense while the Irish, after twelve years of drastic reductions were, to a large extent, starting afresh in 1953."[126] Guinness also had difficulty in the United States after the Prohibition years. Although recognized by "so many people in all walks of life," the name meant little in practice because it had been "twenty years since any of them had actually drunk Foreign Stout, and apparently the new generation did not like it. Advertising was of no avail, and sales dwindled."[127]

Irish coffee stepped into this breach. Made from black coffee, laced with sugar and whiskey, then topped with a floating layer of cream, it looked like Guinness but tasted nothing like it. Vague familiarity like this gave the novel hot beverage important traction. Created with "eye-appeal" in mind by chef Joe Sheridan for Ireland's strategic Foynes seaplane air base restaurant in 1944, it was sold at the country's new economic initiative, Shannon Airport, where transatlantic flights began in October 1945. Not only did Irish coffee serve to reintroduce American visitors to Irish whiskey in a palatable way, but Brendan O'Regan began selling bottles of whiskey for $1.50 in the summer of 1950; the next year, he opened the world's first duty-free shop at Shannon, where Irish whiskey sold below retail cost.[128]

By 1958, New York City served up Irish coffee to theater folks in Downey's Steak House on Eighth Avenue. Jim Downey, an emigrant from Ballinasloe, County Galway, and his hostess Rosaleen Cahill, from nearby Ahascragh, added an Irish coffee bar to the restaurant in April 1961 that reportedly served 1,200 glasses of it a day.[129] In May, the *Beverage Retailer Weekly* pictured the pair with Brian MacMahon of the Irish Export Board on its cover. Eight months later, Jameson's ran a full-page color advertisement with the recipe in the *New Yorker*, under a photograph that situated an Irish coffee in an elegant, stemmed glass between a Belleek teapot and a bottle of its trademarked three-star JJ&S.[130] This cleverly inserted the new into the pantheon of older, quality Irish product associations in American popular culture while appealing to a sophisticated magazine readership. It also underscored that what made the

Figure 5.3. Rosaleen Cahill demonstrates how to make Irish coffee using Irish whiskey, circa 1964. Rosaleen Cahill Fitzgibbon Papers (AIA.007), box 7, folder 12, Archives of Irish America, Special Collections, New York University.

coffee Irish was the whiskey in it. When Downey got a catering concession at the 1964–65 World's Fair, this kind of synergy solidified.

As manager of the Irish coffee bar at the fair, Cahill strove to present a "true and dignified image of a people with traditions extending deep into the past, who are facing the challenge of modern times with resourcefulness and industry."[131] As in previous international exhibitions, visitors encountered Irish-born women attired in Irish fabrics; in New York, Cahill's staff wore a stylishly modern, narrow sheath dress in pastel shades by Dublin designer Evelyn Gaughan, whose hallmark was "sophistication plus elegance."[132] In another echo of Chicago and St. Louis, the Book of Kells inspired Cahill's logo.[133] The centerpiece of the Pavilion of Ireland, which housed the Irish coffee bar, was a stylized round tower designed by Dublin architect Andrew Devane. Although it was a modern riff on past Irish Villages, the interior featured the same Irish arts and crafts, such as textiles and pottery. Even the inclusion of Waterford cut-glass crystal, an eighteenth-century industry only revived in 1947, was in the tradition of associating luxury products with Ireland. Waterford glass had been steadily gaining prestige in the United States since 1960 through the marketing efforts of John Miller, the chief buyer for B. Altman's department store in New York City, who subsequently ran Waterford Glass Incorporated on Fifth Avenue. Miller insisted on a distinct trademark label and "a written quality assurance that the product was mouth-blown and hand-cut in the Republic of Ireland." He also urged the development of a larger whiskey glass, since Americans drank theirs on the rocks, typically with three cubes of ice. Waterford's redesign soon "achieved great recognition in the United States" and was prominent in Old Bushmills advertisements too.[134]

A spokesman for the Irish Pavilion told the *New York Times*, "We are aware that there are certain and laudable notions about Ireland as a land of romance and perhaps a bit of mystery, but we also want our friends to know that we are a growing industrial nation with facilities and know-how, capable of taking our place in the world's business and industrial complex." Lady Aberdeen would have approved. And yet, America had been changed by the alchemy in the green space between 1893 and 1964. Non-Irish visitors to Flushing Meadows asked for leprechauns and shillelaghs to the frustration of the Irish government, even though seventy-proof Leprechaun Irish Whiskey was for sale in the duty-free shop at Shannon Airport by 1967, the year after Notre Dame's new mascot debuted.[135]

The surviving Irish whiskey firms combined as United Distillers of Ireland Limited in 1966, and they commissioned a study of their image. Among the conclusions were two key points. First, negative perceptions of Irish whiskey were influenced by nonproduct prejudices about the Irish; feedback from a study group of foreigners included, "Of course, the reputation of the Irish is that you'd be taking a glass of Irish whiskey and be fighting in no time. There's a lot of people think that, you know"; and that "sales of Irish [whiskey] may be accelerated abroad, Irish being advanced in effect, as a novelty. But longer term, the acceptance of Irish as a whiskey is likely to be a different story. In any event, the image of Irish is indivisible, as between the home and export market; it will come to the same thing, for better or worse."[136]

Concerns about the American market prompted United Distillers to hire Ernest Dichter, the inventor of the focus group, to undertake a motivational research study in 1969. He proposed five main questions:

Q. Have there been any changes taking place over the last few years in American attitudes toward Ireland—which might be beneficial or harmful to the acceptance of Irish whiskies?
Q. What is the role of genuine Irish origin?
Q. What is the prestige value of Irish whiskies?
Q. Is there a different attitude toward Irish whiskey among people of Irish descent? Among people who have been in Ireland? Among people who have traveled abroad? Are these types of Americans different from other Americans?
Q. Are there any good or bad connotations regarding Irish whiskey? Is it thought to be made from potatoes, for example?[137]

Dichter's 131-page report in 1970 expanded these to twenty-three questions to be as comprehensive as possible. The results—based on engagement with 375 men and women in major metropolitan areas across the country that accounted for age and degrees of affluence—shed significant light on the green space after seventy-plus years of selling Irish in the United States.[138] Leaving aside attitudes it documented toward drinking alcohol in general and perceptions of Irish whiskey brands more specifically, the Dichter study concluded once again that "advertising equals legitimacy" for Americans: "Advertising serves to make a product 'familiar' and in becoming familiar it becomes psychologically legitimate." Central to this premise was the ability to "'trigger' positive responses and induce 'mental rehearsal'—the actual 'living out' in the imagination of the experience." Among several practical applications Dichter suggested, "'talk their language' and not your own" stands out. "More imaginative descriptive language is required," he wrote. "Language that appeals to the senses, stimulates them, makes the consumer experience the product vicariously will be most successful." He also made the case that positioning Irish whiskey in the market as the "creative liquor" would appeal to the young and affluent: "Irish whiskey has soul. It comes from the people—it is part of Irish folklore, folk music, folk-rock."[139]

As it approached its two hundredth anniversary as a distiller, the staid and respectable Jameson brand tentatively experimented with these Dichter approaches. "Scotch without smoke," read the tagline for an *Esquire* magazine ad, while a shamrock affixed to the phrase "New Jameson: The spirit of uncommon gentleness" appeared in Canada. To trigger consumer curiosity about Irish whiskey, the company also tried the familiar. A little green-clad cartoon man appeared on Jameson promotional materials, declaring in speech balloons, "Top o' the mornin', afternoon or evenin' to yez!" "'Tis many a rare surprise you'll be in for Begorrah!" and "Sure it's Jameson, the taste of the Irish, I'd be toastin'!"[140] This was America talking, not Ireland. Notre Dame would have approved; after all, it had already shown how to "succinctly and legally [subsume] a nationality."[141] The despised burlesque, the offensive Stage Irishman, was reincarnated as the more acceptable leprechaun in the process. Now St. Patrick's Day in the green space must be considered as yet another powerful influence on the Irish image.

6

Emerald Sheen

Harry Truman was the first U.S. president to review New York City's St. Patrick's Day parade. "Sporting a green carnation in his lapel and a green tie with white dots," America's chief executive was among the million and a half who watched the annual March 17 tradition from the sidelines of Fifth Avenue in 1948. Parading, by then, was a familiar Irish point of reference in American popular culture.[1] Five years earlier, the *Texaco Star Theatre with Fred Allen* had poked fun at marching in March for an estimated 16.5 million radio listeners:

> FRED ALLEN: Jimmy, don't you enjoy Spring in New York. The birds, the trees, green things shooting up.
> JIMMY: Green things? Name me one green thing you've seen in New York.
> ALLEN: Did you see the St. Patrick's Day Parade last Wednesday? That was greener than a grapevine and twice as long.
> JIMMY: Say, that was some parade. I couldn't get across Fifth Avenue for six hours.
> ALLEN: You should have done what I did, Jimmy.
> JIMMY: How did you get across Fifth Avenue?
> ALLEN: I joined the Ancient Order of Hibernians, marched four blocks in the parade, at an angle, and then stepped out on the other side of the street.
> JIMMY: Say, how come every March 17th they let 50,000 Irishmen stop traffic and parade down Fifth Avenue?
> ALLEN: Do you know anyone who can stop 50,000 Irishmen?[2]

Truman and Allen demonstrate an extraordinary level of national visibility for the Irish in the 1940s when, as we have seen, their image was still evolving. The holiday was a potent accelerant wherever, and whenever, March 17 encountered competing Irish, Irish American, and American political, media, cultural, and commercial interpretations of Irish. The result was a powerful emerald sheen that transformed a minor religious feast day into a major secular business opportunity.

"Only Christmas Day is more widely observed than the Seventeenth of March," *The Gael* told readers in 1900, a time when St. Patrick's Day was not even a national holiday in Ireland.[3] Thirty years later, the American women's magazine *Good Housekeeping* stated with assurance that "the celebration of St. Patrick's Day has become a universal custom."[4] Truman's tie and boutonniere—which the *New York Times*, the *Chicago Daily Tribune*, and the *Los Angeles Times* all noted in their coverage of the 1948 parade—reflect only the sparest style for March 17.[5] American retailers drew on so many imaginative means to convey Irish that, increasingly, anyone could celebrate St. Patrick's Day regardless of ancestry. The holiday was commercialized by florists, greeting card designers, and novelty manufacturers, thereby enabling it to metastasize in children's classrooms and through the pages of their mothers' magazines. Indeed, such a robust repertoire for March 17 merchandising emerged that it also provided a convenient arsenal for promoting certain motion pictures. During Hollywood's golden age, the ballyhoo extended shallow Irishness beyond the month of March and far beyond immigrant cities like New York. This diffusion of the emerald sheen, seeping unchecked from the porous green space, was blithely accepted even by American Catholics of Irish descent. For independent Ireland, however, this was an awkward reality. It could reject the shamrock as a hackneyed symbol with "no dignity of age behind it," but it eventually had to acknowledge that America had, yet again, defined what constituted Irish without regard to Ireland.[6]

* * *

To understand the roots of America's embrace of St. Patrick's Day and its subsequent commercialization, one needs to look back to the 1840s, when a wave of nostalgia for holiday celebrations in the United States coincided with the rapid growth of markets for consumer goods and the rise of a leisure-time economy. Attractive shorthand like Santa Claus, eggs, and cornucopias on all sorts of consumer products lured people to celebrate Christmas, Easter, and Thanksgiving.[7] Because St. Patrick's Day conveniently came with an adaptable symbol, the shamrock, its potential for profit was obvious, and the holiday put the Irish on American popular culture's radar quite early. St. Patrick's Day became the only ethnic celebration in the American holiday calendar, as fundamental to March as Valentine's Day would soon be to February. Its observances on the seventeenth day of March could not even be displaced by St. Joseph on the nineteenth when Italian immigrants arrived in the United States later in the century.

Patrick, Ireland's patron saint, was a Romano-British Christian who converted the Irish in the fifth century. In 1631, Pope Urban VIII added the feast of St. Patrick to the Roman Catholic Church's calendar, and in 1687, Pope Innocent XI elevated March 17 further by prescribing prayers for its celebration during Mass.[8] The seventeenth century was a volatile period in colonial Ireland, marked by political sectarianism; thus, recognition of St. Patrick by the Vatican was a boon to beleaguered Irish Catholics. Patrick as a personal name also gained favor from this time.[9] However, the saint's connection with the shamrock, a three-leafed plant that the Irish believed he used to teach the doctrine of the Holy Trinity, is an eighteenth-century legend. This religious gloss countered the increasing secularization of March 17: St. Patrick's Day was popular among the Irish rural poor because it carried a dispensation from Lenten restrictions on eating and drinking. A cult of St. Patrick soon developed in Ireland. As Alannah Hopkin observes, "Saint Patrick as national hero, a grey-bearded man in green bishop's robes with the expelled serpents [another legend] writhing at his feet and a border of shamrocks," then crossed the Atlantic, annually inspiring "a boisterous and showy celebration on 17 March."[10]

Affinity for St. Patrick was only one factor in the increasing association of the shamrock with Irish. Shamrocks appeared as elements in the political iconography used by those opposed to the Act of Union, which dissolved the Irish Parliament and made Ireland part of the United Kingdom at the beginning of the nineteenth century.[11] As early as 1810, *The Shamrock, or Hibernian Chronicle*, the first newspaper published by and for the Irish in New York, made this identification of the trefoil with Irish nationalism explicit in its masthead.[12] Likewise, the Shamrock Friendly Association, an early emigrant welfare organization, telegraphed its ethnic persuasion by the adoption of the little leaf in its name; it marked St. Patrick's Day as early as 1817 with toasts like "May the recollections of this day remain as fresh on your memories as your own emblem—the evergreen Shamrock."[13]

As explored in chapter 3, Thomas Moore was key to Irish American claims of dignity and self-respect. His *Irish Melodies* promoted a particular romantic conception of Irish, in which shamrocks, harps, and the color green were essential elements; by making Irish fungible, Moore's music also provided an appealing bridge for Americans to engage with St. Patrick's Day.[14] In 1852, the *Salem Observer* reported that Ireland's emblem was "symbolical of love, valor, and wit," demonstrating the extent to which Moore's song "Oh the Shamrock" displaced the Holy Trinity as it permeated American popular culture even during a period of heightened nativism:

> Through Erin's Isle
> To sport awhile
> As Love and Valour wander'd
> With Wit, the sprite
> Whose quiver bright
> A thousand arrows squander'd
> Where'er they pass
> A triple grass
> Shoots up with dew-drops streaming
> As softly green
> As emeralds seen
> Thro' purest crystal gleaming
> Oh the Shamrock, the green immortal Shamrock!
> Chosen leaf
> Of Bard and Chief
> Old Erin's native Shamrock![15]

This lay construction of an Irish Catholic symbol made the subsequent embrace of St. Patrick's Day much easier for a majority Protestant country like the United States. It also enabled American merchants to make March 17 a commercial holiday, as did the vogue for green that accompanied the success of *Arrah-na-Pogue*, an Irish melodrama produced in New York in 1864. One of its popular songs declared:

O Paddy dear and did ye hear the news that's going round?
The shamrock is by law forbid to grow on Irish ground;
St. Patrick's Day no more we'll keep, his colors can't be seen,
For there's a bloody law against the wearing of the green.[16]

Such a figurative idea quickly monetized March 17 in the United States, by then home to the largest Irish diaspora on earth.

Over the next twenty years, as the New York City parade grew larger and larger, "Every Irishman that could get a day off took his wife and children into the open air and joined the great congregation that was proudly 'wearing of the green.'"[17] This took the form of inexpensive bows, scarves, ribbons, neckties, veils, and umbrellas, a phenomenon distinct from any organizational regalia (rosettes, medals, sashes, badges, uniforms, etc.) seen in the parade. Soon, even the horses pulling the city's street cars were "decorated with miniature green emblems."[18] Holiday sartorial style rose to new heights when Mayor A. Oakey Hall, who won election in 1868 largely with the support of New York's Irish Democrats, wore a custom-made green suit with a "fancy green cravat" to review the parade. In Chicago, Bridget Barry's appearance "fantastically attired in green and gold, with ribbons and decorations," was a feature of that city's parade in the 1870s.[19]

In Philadelphia, Duval & Hunter published a chromolithograph in 1872 called *St. Patrick's Day in America*, capitalizing on the sentiments of Irish nationalism behind the phrase "the wearing of the green." This print bore the subtitle "Commemorative of Ireland's unswerving fidelity to her ancient religion and the devotion of her exiled children to the sacred principles of her freedom and redemption as a nation." Its depiction of an Irish family on March 17, however, is also evidence of the extent to which Irish America had embraced the material culture of the holiday: a mother pins a shamrock on her son's lapel while her daughter waves a green "God save Ireland" flag from the window of their home. Blessing this strikingly prosperous domestic scene, a framed color lithograph of St. Patrick hangs on the wall.[20]

Traditional Irish exports like the linens and laces described in chapter 5 were not widely connected with the celebration of St. Patrick's Day; instead, demand for holiday paraphernalia sparked sales innovations, such as the window of a clothing merchant described by J. H.

Wilson Marriott in 1888: "The entire background, sides and dressing of the window was in green, while on the suits of clothes the prices were displayed on cards cut in the shape of a shamrock, the color of the card being green."[21] Over time, in order to grab consumer attention, such simple signifiers were extended to the actual articles for sale. In 1927, the *New York Times* noted that "shops where gowns and other feminine apparel are sold offered their best green frocks, men's stores were giddy in green scarfs and handkerchiefs."[22] That year, New York governor Al Smith "kept faith with the old tradition and delighted the friends of Erin." He wore an outfit complete with "green socks, green handkerchief, green striped shirt and tie and a shamrock in his lapel" that make Truman's 1948 attire tame by comparison.[23]

Consumption and a measure of disposable income steadily increased for America's first- and second-generation Irish population—which numbered over four million nationally by 1890—thereby driving the popularity of St. Patrick's Day and the development of an emerging holiday market. There was a corresponding demand for real shamrock. According to the *Irish World*, New York City postal clerks were assigned to handle the volume of shamrock arriving by mail from Ireland in 1898: "One little box, which was destined for a member of the AOH whose name is well known in Brooklyn, had this injunction written on the back: 'Wear what you find inside With noble Irish pride On the glorious 17th of Ireland.'"[24] But live plants were often in a sorry state after the Atlantic crossing, necessitating alternatives. Fresh shamrock, grown from seeds imported from Ireland in the greenhouses of Charles Hunt's Sons in Port Richmond on Staten Island, supplied the New York metropolitan market each March from at least 1882.[25] Poehlman Bros., an enormous floral operation in Morton Grove, Illinois, was the source for Chicago buyers; it offered retailers a hundred plants for three dollars and a thousand for twenty-five dollars in 1915, the same year that *Good Housekeeping* reported, "Shamrock is plentiful at the florists and is inexpensive." Poehlman also marketed a "Hughes Shamrock Box" as "A Bit of Old Ireland." This 5.5" × 3" × 3" gift idea included a scene of Blarney Castle on the cover and was filled with live shamrocks, which sold for $2.40 per dozen or a hundred for $20. Likewise, the floral industry trade journal admired the display of gilded wooden harp stands for small pots of shamrock in the windows of Pennock Bros., the Philadelphia cut-flower giant.[26]

Although a variety of clover could pass for shamrock, authenticity was more problematic when such a ritual object was made in the image and likeness of the real thing.[27] Under the Tariff Acts of 1897 and 1909, imitation shamrocks were considered artificial leaves, subject to a duty of "sixty per cent ad valorem." Several attempts were made in the American courts to classify such shamrocks as toys or silk goods, both taxable at lower rates, 35 and 50 percent respectively. In November 1911, witnesses called on behalf of Tuska, Son & Co.—importers of metal and silk shamrocks from the Far East—testified before the U.S. Court of Customs Appeals that the articles in question were "bought and sold all over the United States as toy shamrocks" and were "pretty generally worn as the emblem of the shamrock by men, women, and children, mainly of Irish parentage, on St. Patrick's Day." Nevertheless, the company also argued that these same articles bore "no resemblance to the natural shamrock and bore no similitude to any natural leaf whatever." After consulting *A Standard Dictionary of the English Language* and "various other lexicographers," the judges upheld the original Tariff Act classification. "We think it is common knowledge that the leaves of the shamrock are of trefoil shape and of green color," they wrote in the decision, thus ". . . it follows that these leaves do simulate and resemble the shamrock leaves and that the importations are artificial shamrocks."[28] Legal arguments like this mattered little in practice when imitations were cheaper than the real plant; in 1916, teachers could purchase silk shamrocks at a dozen for twenty cents from March Brothers of Lebanon, Ohio—sixteen cents less than the live shamrocks sold by Poehlman Bros. and reusable too.[29]

Penny postcards also played a role in raising the profile of St. Patrick's Day for Americans who were not Irish. Between 1898 and the First World War, they were such a popular means of mass communication that six hundred million passed through the U.S. Post Office in 1907 and 1908.[30] A distinct subset of these were holiday greeting cards, and several major companies brought out souvenir lines for St. Patrick's Day, extending the reach of March 17 far beyond the Irish community. The images on such postcards, unlike the commercial market for shamrocks, were unmoored from St. Patrick's Day traditions like parading or religious observance; instead, they were extrapolated from older conceits in Moore's *Irish Melodies* as well as newer ones from Tin Pan Alley songs and sheet music, which were readily mixing in the green space.[31] American and English postcard artists used the color green, clovers, children, and cloying sentiments in designs that were then manufactured in Europe, most often by German lithographers, for firms like the International Art Company and Raphael Tuck & Sons.[32] In a 1910 example, a cartoonish man and woman in outdated attire dance, surrounded by vaguely trefoil shapes, accompanied by a nonsense verse: "A true Irishman can jig a bit And sing 'the wearing of the green' And cheer for Erin's Emerald flag And make love to his sweet colleen."[33] All the word cues—green, shamrocks, jig, Erin, emerald, and colleen—distract from an otherwise unrealistic depiction of the Irish. In this way, postcards became critical ethnic texts for ordinary Americans. The consumers of such cards, Daniel Gifford argues, were largely in rural small towns, but examples survive of urban Irish Americans embracing them too.[34] In 1911, Mamie Madden sent Willie Donovan a note on the back of a whimsical postcard depicting a small boy in stage Irish dress made by the International Art Company: "Top of the morning to ye Willie. St. Patrick told me to send this. Don't forget to kiss the Blarney Stone." The recipient was most likely the four-year-old American-born son of New York Irish immigrants, John and Margaret Donovan, suggesting that exposure to American popular culture's interpretation of the holiday as early as childhood fostered a hybrid understanding of ethnic identity.[35]

Not all postcards were so harmless. Efforts to stop the sale of offensive cards—old vaudeville jokes like "How Bridget served the potatoes undressed," "vulgar caricatures" with "hideous featured monstrosities," stage Irish speech ("Good Luck to Hooroo you're a broth of a Boy; There's no blarney in this now begorra"), or pigs and four-leafed clovers rather than the true three-leafed shamrock—coincided with their emergence.[36] In 1910 and again in 1911, the AOH asked the Post Office to destroy any souvenir postcards "which ridicule the Irish race." P. J. Haltigan, editor of the AOH's national publication, justified the request because "it was against the law to use the mails in defamation of private or public characters."[37] In response, the Hayes Lithographing Co. of Buffalo felt compelled to advertise that its series of twelve postcards were "THE St. Patrick's art subjects, beautiful Irish scenery, shamrocks, harps, flags, etc.," containing "nothing to offend the most sensitive taste."[38] So

Figure 6.1. The enduring romantic influence of Thomas Moore is reflected in this turn-of-the-twentieth-century St. Patrick's Day postcard by Raphael Tuck & Sons, an English firm with offices in London, Berlin, and New York. The stage curtains pulled back to reveal ruins on a moonlit night reference the popular melodramas of Dion Boucicault. Credit: Mick Moloney Irish-American Music and Popular Culture Irish Americana Collection (AIA 031.004), box 52, folder SPD298, Archives of Irish America, Special Collections, Bobst Library, New York University.

too did the Drysdale Company, whose nine St. Patrick's Day cards were said to "meet a long felt want." Its ad read, "Clean, good, wholesome Irish sentiment; appealing to the best class of trade."[39] But the *Novelty News* printed a lengthy chastisement that accused Irish resentment of being "far-fetched" and the AOH as full of "false pride" about "all the cute and good-natured little novelties." It challenged the Irish to embrace "glorious symbols of honest toil" like the "pick, shovel, wheelbarrow and hod" because "these little primitive 'souvenirs' . . . of racial types are surely not things to be hidden away when a great race has formally arrived at the dignity of maturity and power." Protests should hardly be about such "innocent little holiday souvenirs."[40]

To understand this non-Irish writer's point of view as well as the presumed general right to use the emerald sheen for profit, readers of *Novelty News* needed to already be familiar on some level with Irish. As those various and distinct images—historical, cultural, racial—encountered one another in the green space, they were amalgamated or disassembled as needed, enabling astute business interests to invent items for what was then America's only ethnic holiday. The argument that "maturity and power" required the Irish to turn a blind eye to reminders of their working-class roots was disingenuous; it was merely a convenient cover for commodification around St. Patrick's Day.

Postcards were only the cusp when it came to the holiday. Greeting cards, hidden inside envelopes, soon supplanted postcards as both Rustcraft (established in 1906 in Kansas City) and Norcross (founded in New York City in the 1920s) began to market major lines for March 17. Rustcraft encouraged people to "keep friendship green, don't let it dry up," by sending St. Patrick's Day greetings.[41] Predictable as well as new Irish cues were used on these cards too: shamrocks, green, pipes, hats, donkeys, castles, and the words "blarney," "top of the morning," and "begorra." Other cards referenced favorite Tin Pan Alley songs like "Sweet Rosie O'Grady" (1896), "My Wild Irish Rose" (1897), and "When Irish Eyes Are Smiling" (1912), clearly reflecting the alchemy of the green space. One 1928 Norcross card captured the growing popular sentiment that everyone could be Irish on St. Patrick's Day: "English, Dutch, American, It matters not a pin, Any mixture is the best, 'Wid a bit o Irish in.'"[42] During the 1920s and 1930s, the word itself was increasingly used on cards as an adjective rather than a noun, for example, "'Tis the Irish heart that's warm, 'Tis the Irish heart that's sweet, 'Tis the Irish wish I'm sending you, To make this day complete."[43] The extent to which exchanging such greetings was integrated into the celebration of March 17 is reflected in an exercise for ten children published in 1936 that begins, "We're a group of greeting cards Made just for St. Patrick's Day; We make you very, very happy When the postman brings us your way."[44]

In the 1930s, Norcross cards also gave consumers a new American definition for Irish symbols that cleansed them of ethnic meaning. Any real-world association of Ireland with economic distress, civil war, and emigration conveyed in newspaper headlines, as discussed in chapter 2, was a holiday sales disadvantage. Instead, the shamrock stood for "best wishes" as well as "good luck to you"; the horseshoe for "good fortune" or "many happy birthdays"; the pipe for "good cheer"; the harp for "happy hours" or "a song in your heart"; the hat for "good friends" or "high hopes for the future"; and the jaunting cart pulled by a donkey for "sunny days."[45] Jack Santino observes that such interpretations—"the slip between intention and reception"—are only possible when symbols are polysemous and multivocal.[46] When transformed into novelty items, Irish symbols became pervasive. A description of the retail trade along the New York City parade route in 1926 concluded that March 17 was a "prosperous day" for "hundreds of peddlers": "So much so that before the parade was under way everything that bore a superficial resemblance to a shamrock was gone." Even the old legend that St. Patrick banished serpents from Ireland was not immune from being transformed into cash. As the *New York Times* observed, "The laughing peddler who is arrested now and then for scaring nervous women and children with artificial snakes was scaring them yesterday with green snakes."[47]

One of the major distributors of these kinds of holiday items was B. Shackman & Co. in New York City. Its 1932 spring catalog devoted eight full pages to favors and novelties for St. Patrick's Day (up from four pages in 1912), such as two-inch, green silk shamrocks at a bargain $0.80 per gross or two for a penny, an affordable price that enabled street peddlers to mark up and still be able to sell in volume on the seventeenth of March.[48] Irish silk flags, crowd favorites in some form or another on parade sidelines from the 1870s, were available in four sizes, ranging in wholesale price from under a dollar to nearly eight dollars for twelve dozen. These continued to bear the nineteenth-century favorite golden harp on a dark green field, sometimes with shamrocks and "Erin Go Bragh" printed on them, although Shackman did offer a two-inch paper "Irish Republic" flag pin with green, white, and orange stripes as was more politically accurate at the time.[49]

The Shackman line of Irish favors also included white clay pipes; emerald-green cardboard suitcases; wooden jaunting carts with tiny donkeys; frogs made of celluloid, rubber, or wooden beads; pigs made of papier-mâché or china or covered in velvet; snakes formed out of hard cotton, metal wire, or rubber balloons; and papier-mâché potatoes and harps. Which came first, the postcards or such novelties? Clearly, they mutually reinforced each other. Moreover, despite Prohibition's ban on the real export item, the old association of Irish with whiskey emerged from the green space in the form of paper "Blarney Castle

Irish Whiskey" bottles. One hundred and forty-four cost $4.80 (or three cents apiece); "pull cork," the catalog description says, "and Irish flag fan appears."[50]

There were three kinds of "Mother Machree" dolls made of celluloid and china, described as an "old fashioned woman with white hair; has green dress with white collar and green hat."[51] Nearly a dozen kinds of Kewpies—small, fat-cheeked, wide-eyed baby dolls—became Irish men and women when dressed in green hats or skirts.[52] Painted papier-mâché or metal traffic cops, assorted boys and girls, comic figures, and "dudes" and "dandys" were for sale. If you wound up the "Dancing Irishman" and hung it by a string, its feet would tap on a hard surface.[53] These kinds of toys were generic, and it was only the application of the emerald sheen that repurposed them for St. Patrick's Day.

Not everyone was amused. Emmet O'Reilly, president of the Celtic Fellowship, felt St. Patrick's Day was shamelessly debased by such novelties. "The realist may keenly appreciate the economic [value] and sympathize with the human place of the pig, the potato or even the tall green hat, blackthorn, brown jug and swallow-tail coat, in the nation's life," he wrote, "while failing to perceive their value in miniature as tokens of Irish art or fellowship or promise."[54] But it was too late to stop the craze for such items. Aside from being sold by peddlers along parade routes, many of these novelties were also used as props in a genre of one-act plays intended for the classroom or local amateur dramatic productions all across America. The Eldridge Entertainment House of Franklin, Ohio, published *The Saint and the Fairies* by Jean Ross (the Scottish science fiction writer Irene Dale Hewson) as well as Rebecca L. Bloodworth's *Meet Saint Patrick: An Informative Play for St. Patrick's Day* and the *Story of the Life and Work of St. Patrick, Together with a Hymn, a Short Drama, and Other Interesting Material* by Hubert M. Skinner, PhD. The latter was available for fifteen cents through the Eldridge school supplies catalog.[55] Among the selections in *St. Patrick's Day Plays and Pieces*, published by the Willis N. Bugbee Co. of Syracuse, New York, in 1932, was "A St. Patrick's Day Parade" that required children to march around the stage "to a lively Irish tune" with novelties as props. The action that follows includes a dialogue that incorporates several symbols into a master explanation of the holiday illustrating the stunning interplay occurring in the green space:

NELLIE: Who's St. Patrick?
WILLIE: Why, don't you know? He lived almost a million years ago and he killed all the snakes in Ireland.
EDDIE: And he smoked a clay pipe like this. (Puffs)
SAMMY: And planted potatoes—lots and lots of 'em.
MICKIE: And he dug peat with a spade like this.
TOMMY: Pete who?
MICKIE: Pete nobody, you silly. Peat is something they burn like coal.
MINNIE: And I guess he must have raised shamrocks like this, only maybe not so big.
ELSIE: And he kept the pig in the parlor.
TOMMY: Oh gee!
JENNIE: And he wasn't a bit afraid of the Banshees.
NELLIE: What are they?
JENNIE: Something like spooks.
NELLIE: O-o-oh! Spooks and snakes. I wouldn't want to live there.
TOMMY: Say, how'd he kill the snakes?
LOTTIE: With a shelalah [sic]. See—like this. (Holds up club)
TOMMY: Goodness! How'd you find out?
WILLIE: From Mr. and Mrs. Pat O'Shaughnessy. I guess he was some relation to St. Patrick.[56]

Although the historical St. Patrick was an excuse for dramatic license, some basic facts endured as the holiday became integrated into the American calendar season, appearing in collections of books alongside Washington's Birthday, Arbor Day, and April Fool's Day. Mary Curtis's *Why We Celebrate Our Holidays*, published in 1924, begins, "I fancy that all the information a good many of us have about St. Patrick is that he was an Irish saint on whose birthday we like to wear a green ribbon, or necktie, or a bit of Irish shamrock, if we can get it." She then informs her young readers of the three main ideas associated with St. Patrick. First, that he was not born in Ireland but, as a teenager, was sold into slavery there for six years; second, that he later returned as a Christian missionary to Ireland and there used the three-leafed shamrock to symbolically represent the Trinity; and third, that he drove all the snakes "and similar vermin" out of Ireland.[57] The same story of St. Patrick—reinforcing myths over facts—was related in *The Playground* in 1926, in *Good*

Housekeeping in 1930, and in *The American Book of Days* in 1937.[58] In *Special Pageants for Little People*, published in New York in 1929, a child is selected to recite a rhyme about St. Patrick that concludes with "Apostle of the Emerald Isle, We wear the green for you" as boys and girls do a simple march that is part animated greeting card, part novelty showcase. They form arches using green covered pointers with eighteen-inch green streamers and wear white shirts, green ties, and headbands with "a large shamrock leaf of the same shade as the ties."[59]

Music and dance (at a minimum, an Irish jig) were frequently incorporated into suggestions for observing St. Patrick's Day. *St. Patrick's Eve* by Dorothy Reynolds (1931) opens with an old Irish couple (played by children) dozing by the fire. Dream sequences of their childhood, youth, and courtship then follow. The stage directions incorporate five dances, with the movements for each described as well as specific music—namely, popular tunes like "Mother Machree," "The Low-Backed Car," "The Kerry Dances," "The Wearing O' the Green," "The Highland Fling," "Killarney," "Come Back to Erin," and "My Wild Irish Rose." There are roles for fairies, a leprechaun, and a fiddler. Its dialogue is written in an Irish patois familiar from the vaudeville stage: "Oh, indade, what I meant to be sayin' was, those were the grand days, before ye left for America, and afther, when I was joinin' ye there—but, oh, it was a weary long time atween!"[60] Amalgamating such scattered, vaguely familiar references for young people had the effect of inventing holiday traditions that could then be continued into adulthood. As Eric Hobsbawm points out, with such traditions, the "strength of an 'hallucination' . . . is sustained by an economic interest." Falling between Christmas and Easter, holidays whose extensive commercialization was already established and widely accepted, the immigrant traditions of March 17 "now intermingled with commercially constructed and manipulated holiday rituals centered on mass consumption."[61]

During the 1930s, Samuel French, Inc. of 25 West Forty-Fifth Street in New York City licensed performance rights for plays on Irish themes. These were comedy-dramas for grown-ups, such as Edward E. Rose's *Irish Eyes* (1921), *The Blarney Stone* (1923), and *Maytime in Erin* (1933). Amateurs could present these plays for a royalty fee of twenty-five cents per performance. As the synopsis for *The Blarney Stone* reveals, these plays were no less contrived than those written for children: "The spirit of youth pervades the story, yet it has its moments of pathos, its passages of heart-touching eloquence, its dashes of Irish humor, and its splashes of charming folly which render the Irishman at once delightful and incomprehensible. The play is a breath of 'Old Erin' in a modern setting." All the plays included music, and for fifty cents a copy, French also provided clever songs like "Arrah Go On, I'm Gonna Go Back to Oregon," "When the Robert Emmet Comes A-Sailin' Down the Shannon," "When John McCormack Sings a Song," and "I've Been Floating Down the Old Green River."

The depiction of two Irish immigrants in Rose's *Irish Eyes*, which opens in "John Brady's apartment on Riverside Drive, New York City," on St. Patrick's Day, is typically forced. Brady is described as "a large man of fifty-five" with "the indefinable air of a self-made man, one who has worked and fought his way up from the bottom." In the first scene, he implores his seventy-year-old butler, Lanty Lanigan, a native of County Galway, to lose his Irish accent only to hear, "I give it up, Mister Brady! Sure an' I tries to catch the new ways, but the Galway brogue hangs to me tongue like a limpet to a rock." Despite such stereotypical dialogue, the paperback copies of Rose's scripts contain "Publicity Notes" and "Testimonials" from all over the United States and Canada. The Bridgeport (CT) *Evening Star*'s endorsement declared, "The characters in [*The Blarney Stone*] are true to life and many times during the performance it was hard to realize that one was in a theatre watching a play." Catholic parishes and organizations were also earnest in their praise, contributing yet another influence to the green space. For example, the pastor of St. Agatha's in West Philadelphia wrote, "Your play *Irish Eyes* proved one of the most successful entertainments ever given on our parish stage." Rev. M. A. Harris of St. Bernard's in Moncton, New Brunswick, was so pleased with *Irish Eyes* that he wrote to request another Rose play because "I am now preparing for St. Patrick's Day." Likewise, M. J. Mulvihill of the Knights of Columbus Council #235 in Orange, New Jersey, "decided to do *Maytime in Erin* on the 17th of March."[62] Since such Catholic audiences in the 1920s were not homogeneous either in ethnicity or ancestry, impressions about the Irish gleaned from these dramas were only heightened by the imprimatur of the church.

With humor as their mainstay, plays like these encouraged the belief that St. Patrick's Day was about having a good time. "Every year, on March seventeenth, the shamrock, symbol of good luck to Erin's sons and daughters the world over, is worn by Irish men and women wherever they may be," *Parties for Young Americans* instructed. "And so why not give a Shamrock Party, with plenty of games, music, and jolly Irish fun? This is one way in which young Americans may help keep the friendly tradition of Saint Patrick and his day."[63] Likewise, the Fitzgerald Publishing Corporation of New York City (formerly Dick and Fitzgerald) published *Shamrocks for St. Patrick's Day* by Marie Irish, a four-part collection of things to do on March 17. Part 1 contains "readings, recitations, monologues, toasts, and quotations"; part 2, "plays, dialogues, songs, drills, tableaux, pantomimes, and a pageant"; part 3, "parties, decorations, games, and contests"; and part 4, "An Irish Minstrel Show." "Marie Irish," a pseudonym for Evelyn Simons, was the author of no less than 117 holiday-related titles that even extended the emerald sheen into December with *Christmas Eve at Mulligan's* and *Patsy Duggan's Christmas* (both 1922).[64] Her introduction to *Shamrocks for St. Patrick's Day* (1932) is yet another clear example of green space pastiche:

> Everyone knows the grand old Irish songs, and every one [sic] likes the good Irish jokes. Pat and Mike—you remember them? Naturally, for there's something unforgettable about the Emerald Isle and its sons and daughters. So we think that even if you've never seen the "ould sod," even if you don't know all the words to "The Wearin' O' the Green," even if you're not quite sure what a shillalah [sic] is, you'll enjoy this new collection of Irish entertainment. There's a little of everything in it, and a lot of laughter and fun. We don't believe there's any collection quite like it, and we know that as sure as the Shannon flows you'll be after likin' it intirely![65]

As parties and classroom activities on March 17 became more popular among non-Irish Americans, the range of items available for purchase (most of them green) reflected the holiday's extensive exploitation. An early advertisement for the Dennison Manufacturing Company announced that March 17 was the "chance for a new kind of party," the "chance to use new colors, quaint designs, real 'old country' games and stunts," and asked customers to "let us help you plan this 'different' party."[66] *Recreation*, published by the National Recreation Association, suggested sending out invitations using this verse: "The 17th of March in the avenin' / Has been chosen by a few / To have a good old Irish fight / And we're inviting you. / Please come all ready for the fray; / We want you on the scene. / You'll find the place quite aisily; / 'Twill all be trimmed in green."[67] Readers of *Good Housekeeping* were told in 1930, "Ireland is called the Emerald Isle, and green is the color of the shamrocks, so green must be used lavishly in the decorations."[68] For classrooms, teachers could choose stencils to chalk designs on the blackboard, such as "Erin Go Bragh," "Saint Patrick," "Irish Lad and Lassie," and a border of shamrocks and harps. Shackman's sold "Irish High Hats," "St. Patrick Salted Nut Cases" (also available for ice cream), and "St. Patrick Candy Boxes" in several sizes, some decorated with ribbon bows and clay pipes, which could be filled with party confections. Shackman's carried candles, electric light shades, napkins and tablecloths, place or tally cards, invitations, and party hats—all in green—as well as "St. Patrick Noisemakers." These latter were siren horns, whistles, and rattles decorated with "comic" faces.[69] Dressing Irish was also an option. In a throwback to stage Irish depictions, *Good Housekeeping* offered ten-cent instructions for "A Pat and Patsy Party, An Irish Affair," suggesting outfits for the adult St. Patrick's Day host and hostess: "He should wear a bushy fringe of red whiskers and a large green bow tie. The hostess might wear an Irish costume made up of a short, green skirt, white blouse, and a tight green bodice laced together in front."[70] Such a specific woman's Irish costume was directly inspired by images already in circulation for at least twenty years on St. Patrick's Day greeting cards, while the man's costume, an exaggeration of older, offensive vaudeville Irish cues, had been resurrected by *Life* magazine as recently as 1927.[71]

One of the more troublesome associations to adhere to Irish was the pig. *Good Housekeeping* advised readers that "little china pigs with table numbers pasted on their backs make amusing [table] markers" for St. Patrick's Day parties.[72] By 1936, the source of the toy pig supply was Germany, where the pig had long been a symbol of good luck.[73] Shackman's carried pigs made from a variety of materials in its St. Patrick's line of novelties. A "China Pig Family"—including a 2½ inch "Mother Pig" and three 1¼ inch piglets—sold for $1.50 for a dozen sets. A green unbreakable papier-mâché pig, 7½ inches "with shaking wire tail," could be bought wholesale for twenty-five cents.[74] These little pigs proved to be a sore point with Irish immigrants. The United Irish Societies of Brooklyn and Long Island passed a unanimous resolution calling upon German interests to stop their manufacture and sale in the United States. The *New York Times* reported that the resolution was the result of "resentment against toy green pigs as emblematic of St. Patrick's Day and the Irish race." The pigs typically wore top hats and smoked a clay pipe. Facts were useless against such misinformation, as John T. Rogan, president of the AOH of Kings County (Brooklyn), wrote, "When we celebrate St. Patrick's Day we are not glorying the memory of a pigherd. We are extolling the great apostle of our memory and our delegate in heaven."[75]

The porcine problem was not limited to novelty items. By this time, St. Patrick's Day provided a conceit upon which a seemingly endless variety of games were created for both adults and children. Sometimes these were simply adaptations of musical chairs or pin the tail on the donkey with clever new names like "Irish Potato Snatch" or "Pat's Hat" or word games such as rhyming Pat or using clues to guess words that included Pat like *patriotic* or *patent*. *Good Housekeeping* connected a party to the Irish sweepstakes, during which adults would race one another on children's hobby horses.[76] More often though, they were a jaded continuation of the association of Irish with shamrock, green, and pig. In 1933, for example, *Recreation* magazine suggested dividing children into four families named Murphy, Maloney, Mulligan, and McCarthy to play games: "Each group forms one side of a large square. From left to right each family is numbered or given such names as Pat, Mike, Jerry, Kitty, Maggie, Kathleen, etc.," were the directions for "Pig in the Parlor" or "Snatch Paddy's Pig." They continued, "The leader calls out the numbers or names and four players respond, one from each family or group who attempts to get the 'pig' back to his side. Score is kept. One point is scored each time the pig is brought over the line or if one side catches the snatcher."[77]

While the game itself is innocent enough, it packaged St. Patrick's Day in slighting ways that already pervaded party activities. In 1926, *Playground*, the magazine of the Playground Association of America, recommended that girls be given "scissors and a piece of cork out of which they are asked to cut a shamrock, and the men [that is, boys] are given a potato and asked to cut out a pig with their penknives. A prize is given for the best shamrock and the best pig."[78] Marie Irish's *Shamrocks for St. Patrick's Day* gave the following directions for an "artistic stunt": "Cards are passed and each person is given a stick of gum to chew—the chewing to begin at a given time; at a second signal each one uses the gum, drawing it into a thread, to outline a pig on the card."[79] The theme was even carried over into edible suggestions for "Irish club sandwiches . . . consisting of toast, roast pork and lettuce." Indeed, for children's St. Patrick's Day parties, green mints and lollipops could be game prizes and place cards could be made out of gumdrops "with little shamrocks stuck in them." Marie Irish recommended a more savory option: green pepper sandwiches decorated with "pipes" made from cucumber pickles as refreshments. The liberal use of green vegetable coloring magically transformed vanilla ice cream and plain frosted cakes into Irish confections, and trefoil-shaped cake cutters gave new meaning to ordinary sugar cookies and mint gelatin.[80] "It's a poor St. Patrick's Day party without shamrock cookies, I'm thinking," says Mrs. O'Grady in a 1934 one-act play, one of several holiday dramas that reinforced such ideas. "The children will love them," her neighbor replies, "'specially the green frosting."[81]

Recipe suggestions for grown-up lunch and dinner on St. Patrick's Day also appeared in magazines read by middle-class American women. Although *Good Housekeeping*'s "Menu for St. Patrick's Day" in 1915 suggested thin sliced boiled ham, potato salad, oaten bread and butter, whole-wheat pancakes with bottled honey, raisin pudding with hard sauce, cake, Irish Moss (carrageen served with wine and cream), tea, sweetmeats, and apples, by the 1930s holiday menus bore no resemblance to that relatively authentic standard, instead reducing Irish cuisine to the use of green foods such as pistachio ice cream, sweet gherkins, asparagus, string beans, avocados, and pea soup. "Green is the flavor of green vegetables," wrote Phyllis Carr in *Ladies' Home Journal* in March 1934, "and a luncheon in green is just the way to entertain at bridge when March brings around St. Patrick's Day."[82] Newspapers like the *Dallas Morning News* and Memphis's *Commercial Appeal* took their cues from the magazines: "Whether the family tree includes an Irishman or not, do take the opportunity of introducing a few of the gaily colored St. Patrick's Day motifs either by decorations or by colored foods, in the menu this weekend." Culinary creativity was strained in the effort to come up with new recipes such as "Jellied Cabbage Salad," a concoction of chopped celery, shredded cabbage, sliced olives, and almonds in lime-flavored Jell-O, served cut into squares on a bed of lettuce![83]

While *Playground, Recreation, Ladies' Home Journal, Good Housekeeping,* and the *Saturday Evening Post* had a select readership, the viewpoints in these same journals had an exponential influence as purchases from novelty catalogs and the local stationery store transformed the meaning of St. Patrick's Day. Children's impressions of an immigrant people were spoon-fed to them by teachers who brought these games and activities into the classroom, just as mothers brought decorations and recipes into the home. The appropriation and then exploitation of the holiday's symbols for profit remade the character of St. Patrick's Day observations, created connections with products like china pigs that otherwise might not have existed, and thus perpetuated a saccharine and demeaning image of Irish. For children in the heartland, where Irish immigrants were increasingly a rarity, there was no other major ethnic holiday in the American calendar to challenge the faux Irish hegemony of St. Patrick's Day.[84] As it became homogenized at the national level, the holiday even lost religious connotations for Catholics. Only one of the four St. Patrick's Day plays offered by the Catholic Dramatic Guild, founded in 1922 and "devoted to clean, inspirational plays," dealt with the life of the saint; the others—*A Bit O' Blarney, An Irish Memory,* and *Mr. O'Grady's Party*—were predictably formulaic in plot and music.[85]

What the Irish from Ireland thought of this American artifice is revealed by the reaction of Tim Costello to his post–St. Patrick's Day parade clientele in the early 1950s. An immigrant from County Offaly who owned a bar on Third Avenue in New York City and had been in business since 1929, Costello declared "in anguished astonishment, 'This is the end. Will you look?'":

> Mr. [William] Peer turned and saw two men, both covered with literally hundreds of shamrocks, white clay pipes and other tokens of Erin. Both were a little wobbly on their pins as, with arms entwined and misty eyes, they gave a soulful rendition of Mother Machree. One man could have been Irish, but the other was unmistakably Chinese.

According to the *Saturday Evening Post,* "Tim closed the place for the rest of the day—even for the advertising men."[86]

* * *

Figure 6.2. On the cover of this 1909 sheet music edition of "The Wearing of the Green," Ireland meets Irish America on an Irish country lane. The woman wears a traditional shawl, while the man is incongruously attired in clothing familiar from American stage depictions of the Irish. The other Irish cues, of course, are the word *green* and the thatched cottage. T. H. Glenney is not the composer; he is the actor who played Shaun the Post in the original Broadway production of Dion Boucicault's melodrama *Arrah-na-Pogue* (1865) and introduced the song to America. Credit: Mick Moloney Irish-American Music and Popular Culture Irish Americana Collection (AIA.031.004), box 40, folder 7, Archives of Irish America, Special Collections, Bobst Library, New York University.

The chronology of this commercialization is striking. While St. Patrick's Day souvenirs were sold in the nineteenth century, especially in cities with large Irish populations, the pivotal decades for American mass consumption of the holiday came later. Judging by the dates of newspaper stories and magazine advice columns as well as novelty catalogs, the 1920s and 1930s appear to be the critical period. Because this is *after* protests about objectionable postcards in 1911 and *after* the establishment of the Irish Free State in 1921 but *during* the implementation of national origins restrictions, the Depression, and Prohibition—all of which undercut Irish immigration and exports—it raises the question about what else in the green space fueled America's adoption of St. Patrick's Day as the March holiday. The answer is the movies.

As the popularity of vaudeville theater faded, motion pictures became an accepted form of mass entertainment for all ages and sexes, driving demand for content.[87] Simultaneously, advances in technology enabled longer films with more time for narrative action, character development, dialogue, and music. Older Irish stage representations, Robert Snyder observes, gave way to new cinematic ones as Irish American prosperity and concerns about respectability increased.[88] At the turn of the twentieth century, for example, theaters in urban Irish neighborhoods offered films about Ireland or with Irish plots, like *Shamus O'Brien* (1908) and *Robert Emmet* (Thanhouser, 1911), which were adaptations of dramas about patriots.[89] Beyond such specific examples for the ethnic market, film producers scrambled for all kinds of Irish content that had a proven track record. *For the Wearing of the Green* (1911, 1913), *Kathleen Mavourneen* (1906, 1913),[90] *The Banshee* (1913), *A Sprig of Shamrock* (1915), *The Cry of Erin* (1916), *Rosie O'Grady* (1917), *Top O' the Morning* (1922), *Blarney* (1926), and *Mother Machree* (1928) demonstrate how familiar phrases as titles could pique interest and sell tickets. As Gary Rhodes observes, these kinds of films "needed to have mass appeal" in order to recoup production costs. This meant "large audiences, far more than what one particular subgroup of Americans could generally offer."[91]

Filmmakers also relied on the iconography of St. Patrick's Day cards and novelties to broadcast Irish. Before the advent of sound pictures, they were a convenient shorthand to distinguish Irish characters from white Anglo-Saxon Protestant ones. *The Shamrock Handicap* (1926), an early film by director John Ford, used holiday symbols to represent the key players in the film: shamrocks and a harp for the O'Haras, a caubeen (battered old hat) and pipe for the O'Sheas. The film's dialogue titles were garbled English, as in "Please, Your Honor, an' my man Mike has sint the passage money—an' my boy—an' herself—are goin' to Americky"; and recycled associations such as "Well, he sure made me feel at home! It's just like the Old Country—always fightin'," or "It's the Shamrock that brought us everything—luck and faith and hope—and love!"[92] In *Variety*'s review, this approach was so familiar that it was unremarkable: "The scene is Ireland and America. That let the director, John Ford, in in all his glory. He loves anything Irish, and he made the most of the little human-interest touches."[93]

Engaging with audiences extended beyond such content into the promotional aspects of films. New York City retained control of motion picture financing, advertising, and distribution after production shifted in the 1920s from the East Coast to Hollywood.[94] The movies, notes Robert Sklar, forged "many of the techniques of modern publicity and commercial exploitation."[95] One of these, the ballyhoo, became an industry standard for the promotion of motion pictures like Cecil B. DeMille's *The Ten Commandments* (1923).[96] While the *Oxford English Dictionary* defines the noun as "blarney" or "bombastic nonsense," in practice, the ballyhoo was "designed and slated to evoke advance public interest and to pre-sell through channels untapped by" regular publicity.[97] The ballyhoo was a comprehensive campaign for audience attention to "compel them to stop, look, and listen." A producer whose publicity department helped to create ballyhoos told *Outlook* magazine in 1925 that "big picture specials absolutely require this sort of thing today. We cheerfully put a fortune into a picture, and we've had to learn how to wake up the country to the picture, because only in that way could we be sure of getting a fortune out."[98] Films with Irish plots quickly adopted the new techniques. The press book for Paramount's *Irish Luck* (1926) reasoned, "In every community there is a large Irish element. They will flock to it. So will the non-Irish, for there's an appeal about the Emerald Isle that attracts."[99] When Warner Brothers released *Irish Hearts*, starring Mary McAvoy and Jason Robards, in the late spring of 1927, the public relations spin was similar: "You don't need to be Irish to like it. You simply need to be human."[100]

Such promotional campaigns were not without their troubles, as the example of *Irish Hearts* reveals. The studio described the plot as "The other side of New York—not the gay supper clubs and roof gardens, but New York as it is lived by thousands of wage earners. *Irish Hearts* is REAL because it's about the kind of people you see every day."[101] In fact, *Irish Hearts* differed little from the stage depictions protested by the Irish over twenty years earlier, and the *Gaelic American* indignantly declared, "*Irish Hearts* depicts the Irish as a low, ignorant, vulgar, drunken and disorderly race."[102] Within a month of its release, complaints about *Irish Hearts* reached the offices of James Wingate, director of the Motion Picture Division of the New York State Department of Education. He had the film rescreened and on July 1, 1927, wrote to Albert S. Howson, the scenario editor at Warner Brothers, to suggest that changing the title and eliminating some scenes might quiet criticism.[103] Howson replied a few days later, "It would be a Herculean task, if not an impossible one, to recall all the prints and recut them" because the film had been nationally released on May 21: "I therefore, very regretfully, must tell you that *Irish Hearts* will have to run its course as it is."[104] This was not the last word. Wingate asked for a meeting with Howson, and Warner Brothers eventually agreed to make cuts to the dozen prints in New York State theaters.[105] Among the eliminations made were obvious references to the ethnicity of the main characters, including titles like "How 'bout me an' you goin' to the Hibernian dance tonight?" However, Warner Brothers' initial hesitation to make any changes at all was most likely rooted in the extensive ballyhoo it had undertaken—an "exploitation" campaign that directly linked the film with Irish in every conceivable manner.

Even if one never actually saw *Irish Hearts*, it was difficult to avoid it in small cities and towns across America. Warner Brothers' promotional literature suggested that theater owners cooperate with local haberdashers, confectioners, tobacconists, florists, and ten-cent stores to combine their green merchandise with film stills in attractive window displays.[106] Exhibitors were instructed to run a "Big Ad Smash," a four-column illustrated advertisement, with this copy: "For Feelings, Frolicking and Fights! From the bogs of County Cork to the sidewalks of New York, Patsy followed the lad who left her behind him. A playboy he was.—Ah, but Tim! Tim had daring and fun, with two fists to him." The press book listed ballyhoo gimmicks informed by the same merchandise so firmly embedded in St. Patrick's Day consumption:

FOR THE STREETS

1. A whiskery little old Irishman, with a stub clay pipe in full steam, a battered hat and sandwich sign of 'Irish Hearts.'
2. A youth with good voice, dressed as Chauncey Olcott Irishman, green silk trousers, red silk shirt, tall hat, to parade twirling cane and pausing to sing Irish songs, "Mother Machree," etc.
3. Young man and girl, the girl dressed in green. As man plays Irish jig on mouth organ, girl jigs!
4. A balloon man with green and red balloons, stamped 'Irish Hearts,' date of play and place of showing on his coat.

FOR THE LOBBY

Ticket booth draped in green with red hearts. Accordion player doing Irish airs as crowds are passing . . .

COSTUMES FOR USHERS

Dressed as Irish colleens. Short green skirt with white binding. White shirt-waist with full sleeves. Short green laced jacket. Heads bound with green ribbons tied in big butterfly bows in front or on side.

PROLOGUE

Medley of Irish airs. Irish songs by some local person. Irish dances, contestants from the Irish Jig Tournament, mentioned on this page.[107] Old man who plays the fiddle or accordion or mouth organ, or a player of the harp, meet with tremendous applause. Ballyhoo keeps 'em talking about you!

DON'T BE CONTENT!
KEEP YOUR THEATRE ON THE MAP!

Publicity campaigns like this prepared audience expectations. *Variety* reported that Baltimore's fifteen-hundred-seat Metropolitan theater took in six thousand dollars during the first week's run of *Irish Hearts*, although "neither picture nor business anything to brag about."[108] Nevertheless, producers and distributors ran the risk of offending Irish sensibilities as had happened with St. Patrick's Day postcards. That same summer, *The Callahans and the Murphys* was released, a film the *New York Times* characterized as "full of fights and broad slapstick."[109] Coming on the heels of *Irish Hearts*, it appeared to confirm an "outbreak of anti-Irish films." In New York, an American Irish Vigilance Committee, composed of representatives from sixteen Irish and American Irish organizations, pressured theaters to withdraw certain films from exhibition because "every means of convincing the producers that these films are indecent in themselves, and particularly offensive and misrepresentative of the people of Irish ancestry and birth has been exhausted."[110]

When Metro-Goldwyn-Mayer refused to withdraw *The Callahans and the Murphys*, a series of demonstrations ensued that were reminiscent of the 1911 protests against *The Playboy of the Western World*. According to the *New York Times*, at a screening in Yorkville on August 25, "a man near the front rose in his seat and shouted, 'My mother never acted like that.' . . . A number of electric light bulbs were then thrown against the screen and malodorous chemicals were poured on the floor, to the accompaniment of exploding torpedoes."[111] Irish neighborhoods popular with new Irish immigrants—like Harlem and Washington Heights in Manhattan, the Ninth Ward in Brooklyn, the Bronx, and Yonkers—were soon enlisted in the action.[112] The police made arrests and arraigned mostly young men, born in Ireland, who were working at jobs as carpenters, bricklayers' helpers, and laborers.[113] The American Irish Vigilance Committee perceptively accused Loew's Theatres, the chain exhibiting the film in the metropolitan area, of being in league with the police so that the arrests of protesters would generate greater publicity. The *New York Times* ran at least six stories as well as an editorial reminiscent of *Novelty News*'s attitude toward Irish protests against "innocent little holiday souvenirs": "There is so much natural fun in the Irish that it is not surprising to find searchers after comedy using them in plays and movies. But it is a pity that they take their own magnificent humor so solemnly."[114]

The brains behind these ballyhoos—and, of equal importance, studio damage control—were men like Winfield Sheehan. Sheehan worked for Fox Studios, which owned a chain of vaudeville theaters that had been converted "into comfortable movie houses for middle-class audiences."[115] He was vice president, general manager, and production chief from 1916 through 1934, earning $300,000 a year. During this period, Fox released twenty-five Irish feature films.[116] According to one of the industry's early chroniclers, Benjamin Hampton, "Sheehan had acquired an uncanny understanding of the popular mind and a sure hand in devising entertainment that would please it. Fox pictures again leaped into the first rank of popularity, and his profits increased half a million to a million dollars a year."[117] Sheehan's savvy is evident in another Fox film directed by John Ford in 1928. Released within a year of the negative publicity garnered by *Irish Hearts* and *The Callahans and the Murphys*, *Mother Machree* was the antithesis of the Warner Brothers' approach to community relations. *Variety* commented, "It may serve to put up the quietus on the Irish societies which have been up in arms against Hollywood of late.... It's for the mob, and they'll like it.... And not least of *Mother Machree* is the score. The song, of course, is the basis."[118]

In contrast, First National Vitaphone Productions ran into trouble with *Smiling Irish Eyes* in 1929. *Motion Picture News* wondered how such a poor picture ever got released and thought that if its "comedy relief" didn't "bring down the wrath of the Irish societies in America on the heads of everyone connected with the picture then we are very much mistaken."[119] The *Irish World* and various Irish societies duly protested. They were undermined, however, by the International Federation of Catholic Alumni. Calling Irish objections "over-sensitive" and "unjust," this organization of college-educated young women gave its stamp of approval to the Motion Picture Producers and Distributors of America. *Smiling Irish Eyes* was subsequently booked into schools as well as theaters.[120] There are two explanations: first, it starred the popular actress Colleen Moore, the epitome of a model minority since her turn as a young Irish American several years earlier in *Come On Over* (1922); second, *Smiling Irish Eyes* was Vitaphone's first sound picture.[121] Newspaper ads declared "She Sings—She Talks."[122] To promote the film, they made a short trailer that was approved by the New York State censor on July 13, and within two months thirty prints of this trailer were in circulation.[123] It depicted three scenes, including one of Moore's character talking to her pet pig and another of her bidding farewell to her emigrating sweetheart with this sentimental exchange:

KATHLEEN O'CONNOR: But Rory, with all the Queens and fine ladies in America you won't be forgetting to come back, will ye?

RORY O'MORE: The devil a girl from hell to Connaught can keep me from comin' back to Ireland and my Kathleen.[124]

The release of *Smiling Irish Eyes* demonstrates how ballyhoos could draw on the musical silo in the green space. The film had two theme songs, "Smiling Irish Eyes" and "A Wee Bit O' Love," both of which, so theater owners were told, "already have been sung and played into popularity by leading orchestras and radio bands. They are sung and played throughout the picture and will be sung by your customers long after the picture has had its run." Motion picture exhibitors were encouraged to tie in *Smiling Irish Eyes* with local sales of the sheet music (published by M. Witmark) and 78 rpm records (on the Victor label). Suggested "stunts" included using a loudspeaker to play the music over the marquee; hiring girls to dress in costume and wander the streets with a portable victrola; getting phonograph and radio stores to give away Colleen Moore's photograph to the first two hundred persons to buy the theme song on a certain morning; and holding a contest for amateur lyricists for the best second chorus to the theme songs (with *Echoes of Erin*, a book of Irish songs, offered as the prize). Theaters were advised to have the sheet music covers (which were "beautifully laid out with shamrocks") tacked up in their lobby frames, since "theme songs are a tremendous box-office influence these days and it is up to you to make the most of it."[125] Audiences thus engaged with the film on multiple levels that were reminiscent of earlier St. Patrick's Day promotions.

By the 1930s, "if a picture was expensively produced, with handsome sets and costumes, big-name stars and plenty of ballyhoo, it was likely to make out all right even if it was mediocre—and if it was good, it could make a fortune," Robert Sklar concludes.[126] *The Irish in Us* was a Warner Brothers vehicle to showcase the actors Pat O'Brien and James Cagney, who by 1935 had become Hollywood's representative Irishmen. According to the publicity package, it was "the story of a typical New York Irish family, a mother and three sons. The boys are always in a continuous wrangle, but with a deep love for each other underneath. It is filled with riotous comedy, tense drama and pathos, and a most unusual romance."[127] Nevertheless, the exploitation campaign for *The Irish in*

Figure 6.3. This magazine advertisement was part of the ballyhoo for the controversial film *Smiling Irish Eyes* (1929). Credit: author's collection.

Us, a summertime release, pushed the threshold of Irish gimmicks with which to pack the theaters. It capitalized on the film's title with advertising catchlines like "Howling St. Patrick! If it ain't thim two divils Jimmy and Pat again! You can't keep two good Irishmen down . . . for long! And here they are . . . scrapping over a skirt again . . . in Warner Bros.' Hilarious Hibernian hit."[128] A double-page spread in the film's press book provided a menu of twenty-four ideas enclosed in shamrock-shaped balloons, such as these:

> Telling All the Kellys—Let the Irish know you're playing this picture . . . post heavily in Irish neighborhoods, distribute heralds at Irish dances, plant publicity stories and ads in Irish papers and periodicals, window cards in stores owned by Irishmen . . . *oh you know the rest of the angles on this one* . . .
>
> A Posie to Patrons—If you can get a slew of Shamrocks, announce in ads and front displays that you'll hand 'em to first 100 persons to enter theatre on opening night. Few nifty lookin' gals handing out these Irish orchids wouldn't hurt the stunt. *Better make a note to call that florist contact of yours before you forget about the stunt.*
>
> Green in Yer Lobby—*Alright so you've already thought of it* . . . but just in case . . . give your lobby the works on this one with plenty of green paint and lights. It's the color that best fits your displays on this film and besides it looks oh so cool.[129]

In addition, the names of three novelty companies that manufactured banners, heralds, tire covers, bumper stickers, doorknob hangers, and mesh wire shamrocks at $7.50 for a thousand were included in the publicity package. The Economy Novelty Co. on West Thirty-Ninth Street in New York City could even supply throwaways resembling Irish sweepstakes tickets that were printed with the name of the film and the theater where it was playing.[130] *Variety* called the campaign "effective," noting that 150,000 promotional napkins were distributed to the city's drug stores, restaurants, and bars. As a result, the first week's box office take was $32,000, despite stiff competition from Shirley Temple's *Curly Top*, which at $80,000 was the top grosser. *The Irish in Us* cleared $24,000 in Philadelphia, $21,000 in Detroit, $10,000 in Buffalo, and $7,000 apiece in Baltimore and Kansas City during first runs that same week. By early September, it was the top-grossing film at the 3,940-seat Chicago Theatre.[131]

Warner Brothers used similar techniques to promote *Three Cheers for the Irish* (1940), the story of a retired New York Irish cop concerned about his daughter's romance with a young Scottish patrolman.[132] One jaded New Yorker declared, "Is nothing sacred?" when she discovered that a press agent had planted a shamrock in the sidewalk at Broadway and Forty-Eighth Street near the theater playing the film.[133] But it is quite possible that Selma Goldstein's letter to the *New York Times* was also planted as part of the ballyhoo. "The job of the Home Office exploiter in New York is an extremely vital one," the Screen Publicists Guild explained in 1944: "These first engagements are frequently the dress rehearsal for nation-wide exploitation, more often than not the yardstick by which exhibitors measure the value of a picture. The Home Office exploiter either aids in the direction of, or actively participates in, the supervision of the first 150 engagements of a motion picture. In addition he initiates and creates material for the national exploitation of the picture."[134]

Department stores were enlisted to promote the release of *My Wild Irish Rose* in 1947, a biopic about the Irish American actor-songwriter Chauncey Olcott. Akin to the trademark registrations discussed in chapter 5, the film's stars associated Irish with products by endorsing Ronson cigarette lighters, Deltah pearls, Gruen watches, Marxsman pipes, Resistol hats, and Dancing Twins hosiery in window display stills. Such merchandising tie-ins were not new to Hollywood, but the introduction of a "sensational new color," Irish Rose, to Westmore Cosmetics' lipstick line and a negligee ensemble christened "Hushabye, Wee Rose of Killarney" after one of the movie's theme songs were exploitation innovations. The nationally circulated magazines *Life*, *Look*, *Photoplay*, *Modern Screen*, *Mademoiselle*, *Band Leaders*, and *Seventeen* carried advertisements for RCA Victor's *Songs from "My Wild Irish Rose"* album, and every week the network radio program *The RCA Show* gave the film a plug.[135]

Small motion picture companies, and occasionally the major studios, made "B" movies like *Laughing Irish Eyes* (Republic, 1936), *Irish Luck* (Monogram, 1939), and *Leave It to the Irish* (Monogram, 1944) to meet audience demand for double features (two movies for the price of one). Although far less profitable than the big feature films discussed above,

"B" movies were made as cheaply as possible, often in less than a week with minimal sets and screenplays that were plot-driven.[136] There was little economic incentive to develop characterization as producers knew their audiences were "loyal, enthusiastic, and, by and large, undiscriminating."[137] Sales managers like Monogram's Steve Broidy recalled that exploitation and advertising were "very important. You see, most of our material was original material. We'd start with a title, sometimes, and write a story around the title." In these films, cues and comedy were substituted for any accurate depiction of ethnicity, and in some cases, "the little companies [were] shameless."[138]

In neighborhood theaters in some parts of the country, exhibitors played the "B" movie as a single feature on Saturdays, the day many working people had off or came into town, to ensure a maximum gross.[139] Here, too, attracting audiences through the ballyhoo was the key to success. Just like the major studios, Monogram supplied theater owners with pages of instructions for drawing in a crowd. "Give 'em the old Irish 1–2 punch in your exploitation campaign," theaters booking *Leave It to the Irish* were told. A murder-mystery solved by private eye Terry Moran and his girlfriend Nora O'Brien, the daughter of a cop, the characters were only nominally Irish. But the exploitation pulled out all the Irish stops, from newspaper ads in which the title was enclosed in a shamrock to decorating the lobby with St. Patrick's Day accessories from the local greeting card store and "a good sized 'Blarney Stone' . . . made out of scrap sandstone or other kind of rock" from the nearest stone dealer.[140] For 1945's *There Goes Kelly*, another murder-mystery, Monogram suggested trying to find the "largest family of Kellys in your community" as well as staging a "Most Popular Irish Cop" contest—after all, they said, "In almost every city large enough to have a police force there are several Irish cops. . . . And when cops are involved it will be easy to get merchant cooperation."[141] Aiming for a March release date, when St. Patrick's Day was always some kind of newspaper story, was also good for business.

Hollywood honed these exploitation campaigns at precisely the same time that film content was regulated by the Production Code Administration and the threat of boycott from the Legion of Decency, a nationwide Catholic organization established in 1934 and said to be able to influence eleven million at its peak. Every stage of film development, from outline to final cut, was supervised, and a $25,000 fine was levied on any producer who violated the code.[142] But the work of the studio advertising man who drew upon the emerald sheen skirted such policing. *My Wild Irish Rose*—recall that 1947 was within a year of President Truman's March 17 visit to Fifth Avenue—passed the New York State censor (in operation since 1921) and the Production Code Administration as well as the Legion of Decency, yet its ballyhoo used St. Patrick's Day hype such as "Put on Your Kelly Green—Give Your Bowler an Irish Tilt—Don't Forget Your Lucky Shamrock—Because Here Comes Warner Brothers' Big Parade of Color Colleens and Kilarney [*sic*]! Starring Dennis Morgan as Chauncey Olcott, the Rogue with the Brogue."[143]

Even though the Production Code was increasingly sensitive to stereotyping and racial prejudice about African Americans and Jews, by the 1940s the Irish screen image had been normalized through the combined influence of St. Patrick's Day and the Catholic Church.[144] The latter had had a cozy relationship with the Fox Film Corporation since 1926 when the studio produced a ninety-six-minute documentary about the Twenty-Eighth International Eucharistic Congress held in Chicago. The two men who later wielded censorship control over Hollywood, Joseph Breen and Martin J. Quigley, worked with Fox's Winfield Sheehan (all Irish Catholics) on the project.[145] Breen's career with Catholic public relations and Quigley's influential industry journal, the *Motion Picture Herald*, combined to make the Eucharistic Congress film a success for Fox. Thomas Doherty writes, "Breen oversaw the thousands of commercial and logistical details attendant to the Congress, galvanizing the tom-tom network of Catholic newsweeklies from Boston to Los Angeles, planting stories in secular newspapers and magazines, credentialing hordes of international journalists, and certifying truckloads of commemorative buttons, pennants, postcards, picture books, and votive candles." Fox, in turn, donated "exclusive copyright and all profits from the film to the Catholic Church," an arrangement "brokered by" Quigley, and the Catholic clergy made sure seats were filled.[146]

The experience of these same ambitious and powerful men, who subsequently controlled motion picture production during the 1930s and 1940s, helps explain why organized protests against Irish screen images dwindled even as the embrace of a commercialized St. Patrick's Day rose in the United States. Cinema was a better means for Catholicism to influence American popular culture and social mores than an ethnic holiday that was increasingly secular. Gradually, Hollywood equated Irish with an alternative—cool Catholicism, as in *Angels with Dirty Faces* (1938), *Going My Way* (1944), or *The Bells of St. Mary's* (1945)—that was in fact less overtly ethnic or belittling than early films like *Smiling Irish Eyes* and *Irish Hearts*.[147] The promotional campaign for *Going My Way* was also ambiguous, giving theater owners the option to play the Catholic angle up or down: "Local conditions should dictate which of the treatments to use."[148] Irish and Catholic, like "commerce and morality," could be "mutually exclusive" or not.[149] As in the plays the church endorsed for parish holiday productions, Irish could be indulged as long as it was relatively harmless, no matter how detached from the reality of modern Ireland.

* * *

The early inclusion of St. Patrick's Day in the calendar of official American holidays and the development of profit streams built around its celebration sped the adoption of symbols like the shamrock as a visual cue for Irish. Holiday commercialization and, later, motion picture ballyhoos converged with Catholic interests to make the emerald sheen a very powerful force in the United States. It directed non-Irish consumers to a specific, albeit shallow, means of "being and feeling" Irish, even if only on one day a year, and it provided a more tempting mainstream substitute than ethnic organizations or ethnic culture for late-generation Irish Americans, especially when endorsed by the Catholic Church.[150] The template that emerged in the process was central to the ability of a capitalist system to commodify ethnicity. Most non-Irish Americans celebrated St. Patrick's Day lightheartedly and with exuberance because the commercialization of holidays, Jack Santino argues, comes "from the top down and so reinforce[s] the social structure as it exists."[151] The adoption of March 17 was a mercantile opportunity seized in much the same way as when florists promoted Mother's Day as the May holiday after 1908.[152] Consequently, St. Patrick's Day in the United States rose in popularity in direct proportion to its trivialization in movie theaters, schools, and suburban living rooms. This seductive emerald sheen distracted everyone from the fact that a group with foreign ancestry was now upwardly mobile and, in some parts of the country like Worcester, Massachusetts, preferred to express their Catholic faith on Columbus Day rather than their Irish ethnicity on March 17.[153] It also seriously undercut nativist opposition in the 1920s to celebrating a Catholic foreigner, St. Patrick, whom they had deemed unworthy of an annual American holiday.[154] While commercialization generally had little practical effect on Irish American social mobility, the widespread inversion of Irish pride into ethnic exploitation had consequences for Ireland.

The American spin put on St. Patrick's Day was so pervasive that it was widely conflated as genuinely representative of Ireland and the Irish by the middle of the twentieth century. Norcross experimented with realism rather than comedy on some of its greeting cards when it combined a portrait of St. Patrick with a blessing, rosary beads, and a Celtic cross in 1950, the same year that the company produced its first card depicting an Irish landscape.[155] After 1953, Rustcraft artists created sentimentalized illustrations of Irish landmarks such as St. Patrick's Cathedral in Dublin, St. Finbarr's Cathedral in Cork, the Avonmore River in County Wicklow, the Arch of Claddagh, and Galway Bay.[156] Both companies also tried maps of Ireland, the names of Irish counties, Irish coins, and Celtic interlacing.[157] But significantly, this was the same decade that launched a new phase for the Irish image that demonstrates how the green space enabled various elements to interact, eclipsing such attempts at such realism while co-opting others.

Two examples of the latter will suffice. The first time Norcross associated beer with its St. Patrick's Day cards occurred in 1957; leprechauns followed in 1958. It was no coincidence that "Golden Leprechaun Light Beer"—brewed by Carnes of Drogheda, County Louth, and imported by Reiter's Beer Distributors of Brooklyn, New York—was registered as a U.S. trademark in March 1957.[158] Likewise, the reintroduction of Irish whiskey to the postwar American market made possible a 1960 card on which a tipsy cartoon character carried a shillelagh and a bottle of "Olde Millbrush Irish Spirits—100 proof" while declaring: "Me name's not O'Malley but still you can see . . . I've got a wee bit o' the IRISH in me!"[159] The wordplay on a genuine Irish whiskey, "Old Bushmills," was as obvious then as it is now.

In contrast, downplaying merrymaking suited modern Ireland. St. Patrick's Day there was such a nondescript, sober anniversary for most of the twentieth century that holiday kitsch in the United States was rendered irrelevant to Ireland's Catholic nation-building agenda at home or image-making abroad until the 1950s.[160] When the first direct commercial flights between Shannon and New York inaugurated a new era in Ireland's official relationship with the United States in 1952, it had to play by American holiday rules: a hundred thousand fresh shamrocks were delivered just in time for St. Patrick's Day. The following year, President Dwight D. Eisenhower accepted a Waterford Crystal bowl of shamrocks from John J. Hearne, the new Irish ambassador to the United States.[161] The bowl was compliments of the company, a bit of strategic product placement. Eisenhower wrote, "[It] graced my desk all day, and each visitor to my office took away with him a small bit of the emblem of your country."[162] When Ireland's *taoiseach* John A. Costello visited Washington, DC, in 1956, he was feted with a green-drenched luncheon by the American Newspaper Women's Club: "Decorations Chairman Jane Marilley and her committee had outdone themselves with maps of Ireland, leprechauns suspended from the ceiling, a bit of stone said to be part of the Blarney Stone, Gaelic slogans and Irish flags."[163] Then he went to New York City to review the parade, where he was struck by the contrast between St. Patrick's Day in Ireland ("not such a big day") and St. Patrick's Day in America. The *New York Times* estimated Costello witnessed 110,000 marchers "with others who were Irish for the occasion," prompting the exclamation that he "had never seen so many Irish men and women at one time before."[164]

Ireland and its official representatives understood by then that dignified diplomacy and clear-eyed pragmatism rather than protests could harness the green space and its various echo chambers. The development during these same years of an Irish image that could be embraced by tourists is the next chapter in this story.

7

Come Back to Erin

As American popular culture embraced St. Patrick's Day—aided in no small part by holiday accoutrements, songs, and motion pictures—Irish was transformed into something generic and fun. It also meant a witty, genial, and sentimental people who prized old-fashioned virtues like filial affection and innocent romance.[1] Simultaneously—as a result of different but related interactions in the green space—the old image of Ireland as a troubled country of successive famines, political unrest, and endemic emigration was replaced by an idealized pastoral land that rivaled any for breathtaking scenery. This astonishing new profile was an image too irresistible for modern Ireland to ignore, given a transatlantic feedback loop that progressively grew stronger over the course of the twentieth century.

Tourism was a fraught subject for the Irish Free State in general, principally for financial and ideological reasons, and it continued to be so for the Republic of Ireland into the 1950s.[2] Despite official efforts to present an alternative image, like the Tailteann Games in the 1920s and the Eucharistic Congress in 1932, Ireland eventually drew from the green space to make itself a desirable destination for tourists from the United States.[3] It could not compete with 1952's *The Quiet Man*, filmed on location in glorious technicolor. The image Americans expected was cemented by this motion picture, full of a familiar visual and aural vocabulary that needed no explanation given all that preceded it in popular culture. Thereafter, as tourism became a reliable barometer of economic success for Ireland, the question of what was Irish was settled. By 1961, Ireland's aim was "to make sure that the qualities that make the tourist want to come here are those that he finds when he comes."[4]

* * *

The ambitious New York publisher Thomas Kelly had three editions of *Picturesque Ireland*, edited by John Savage, in print by 1885 as well as three editions of Martin Haverty's *The History of Ireland from the Earliest Period to the Present Time*. Savage's book, at seven hundred pages, contained "one thousand engravings and thirty colored maps of the counties"; it was priced "within the means of every intelligent family." The Haverty tome was nearly nine hundred pages before lengthy appendices; it too was "beautifully illustrated with chromolithographs and steel engravings."[5] In the decades to follow, the development of photography and then film also spread knowledge about Irish geography, topography, history, antiquities, and folklore in the United States. But the version of Ireland thus visualized was a highly selective one that created a common frame of reference out of an endless repetition of specific landmarks and themes.

The ability to see this condensed Ireland from the armchair was reinforced by the hibernicon, an Irish version of the moving panorama / variety stage shows that entertained Americans all across the country in the second half of the nineteenth century. The highlight of the hibernicon was a guided tour of Ireland.[6] Audiences virtually traveled to the island by viewing a series of 5′ × 8′ canvas paintings framed by a curtain "with an opening just large enough" for a vantage point. Because the panorama was "attached to two upright spools" that were wound by hand, scenes changed at the pace they were described by a narrator-cum-guide.[7] The most famous, as well as the most widely imitated, was *MacEvoy's Tour through Ireland*, renamed *MacEvoy's Hibernicon* in 1863 and later *Erinopion, or Erin Illustrated* in 1880. Barney, a comic character John MacEvoy introduced, was the jaunting car driver who guided the audience on their excursion.[8] Significantly, MacEvoy also used Thomas Moore's well-known Irish songs to match certain scenes. "Hibernicon companies reinvented and reframed key elements of travel books through their performances," Michelle Granshaw argues, "which allowed for multi-layered readings of the 'real' Ireland and stage Irish convention."[9] Patsy Touhey, who was later castigated by some for his performances at the 1904 World's Fair in St. Louis, began his career as a professional musician with *Harrigan's Double Hibernian Co., Irish and American Tourists* in 1885. This show was advertised using a jaunting car pulled through the streets by ponies, upon which Touhey and another uilleann piper played, a scene also depicted on the cover of *Harrigan's Hibernian Tourist Songster*.[10]

Just as hibernicons nurtured an emotional connection to specific Irish places, so too did inexpensive, decorative Irish color prints produced by Currier and Ives, the most influential of the nineteenth-century American lithographers.[11] Their 1868 "The Meeting of the Waters," just one example, not only referenced Moore's song about the Vale of Avoca in County Wicklow, where three rivers converge that had been popular in America since 1811, but also a scene already featured in *MacEvoy's Hibernicon*.[12] In the same way, audiences who saw Dion Boucicault's *The Colleen Bawn* (1860), a runaway theatrical success that played on a variety of American stages for decades, saw scenes of County Kerry said to have been written around "a specific set of steel engravings of Killarney." These were most likely the sixteen views by Currier and Ives already in circulation because Boucicault commissioned the melodrama's "elaborate scenery" in advance of finishing his script.[13] Many featured natural settings that later appeared with frequency on respectable St. Patrick's Day postcards, then became sites of pilgrimage for tourists visiting the Killarney region: O'Sullivan's Cascade, the Gap of Dunloe, Ross Castle, the Lakes, the Old Weir Bridge. In the green space, the longevity of associating sites like these with Irish in the nineteenth century provided a readymade template for Irish tourist development in the twentieth.

By the time of the World's Fairs described in previous chapters, tangible experiences of Ireland were possible too. In 1893, visitors to Chicago could kiss "a piece of the genuine Blarney Stone from Ireland" that was intentionally built into the reproduction of the castle: "Here the adventurous or the romantically inclined may kiss it and obtain the gift of tongues which belongs to every true Irish man or woman." This was a performative dimension, as was sitting in a replica of the "Wishing Chair" at County Antrim's Giant's Causeway that stood "on real Irish soil." Sod maps of Ireland, with its thirty-two counties clearly demarcated, were popular features of subsequent Irish fairs. A 60' × 90' map "warranted to kill snakes in less time than it takes to kiss the Blarney stone" was built for New York and Chicago in 1897; San Francisco's required fifty tons of imported soil in 1898. For only ten cents, thousands of "delighted" visitors could "walk across Ireland" in miniature.[14]

This was hyperreality, something only aspirational for hibernicons and travel books, like *The Isle of the Shamrock* (1901) and *On an Irish Jaunting-Car through Donegal and Connemara* (1902).[15] It also suggests an appeal to multiple audiences: those seeking novel entertainment or a form of education about an exotic island as well as those for whom seeing home in these ways had to substitute for the Ireland they left behind. For the latter, the landscapes of their childhoods carried deep meaning that was far more than nostalgic.[16] The *Irish World* described how eighty-year-old Kate Murphy kissed soil from County Fermanagh in New York, then knelt to say her prayers "unmindful of the crowd around her."[17] Olfactory memories of the bog and recollections of summer days bringing home the turf that was cut there were also triggered, so much so that pieces of turf were popular souvenirs. When Luna Park opened on New York's summer resort Coney Island in 1903, sods from every Irish county formed its "Little Ireland" attraction.[18] Naturally, "The soil used in the village is imported from Ireland," noted *The World's Fair Bulletin* about St. Louis in 1904: "The ground is even carpeted with Irish sod. . . . The famous rocky road to Dublin gives the visitor the well-known rough ride in a jaunting car." It added that "jaunting cars are provided for a rare drive through the panorama of the Lake Killarney region, and other bits of fine Irish scenery, disclosing historic places celebrated by the Bards of Erin and her later poets."[19]

Killarney and Blarney dominated this discourse. That these place names rhymed was no small factor in easily privileging them over other Irish places, as were a web of additional connections facilitated by the green space. Michael Balfe's *Killarney*, with lyrics by Edmond Falconer, debuted on the London stage in 1861 and was available on sheet music in Michigan within four years. It remained a favorite in the American song repertoire into the twentieth century, recorded in 1897 and hundreds of times thereafter, most famously by the Irish tenor John McCormack in 1910. Its notes and lyrics became a leitmotif on penny postcards for St. Patrick's Day: "By Killarney's lakes and fells, Em'rald isles and winding bays, Mountain paths, and woodland dells, Mem'ry ever fondly strays." Also buttressing popular affinity for "that Eden of the west" was the 1862 opera *The Lily of Killarney*, which was on the American stage by 1867, another import from England based on Boucicault's melodrama *The Colleen Bawn*.[20] Later, the news that the Herberts sold their County Kerry estate, complete with its legendary views of the lakes, inspired headlines as well as a Tin Pan Alley song, *Why Did They Sell Killarney?* (1899).[21]

These examples illustrate how long transatlantic cross-fertilization could linger, ultimately foreshadowing Bing Crosby's 1949 hit *How Can You Buy Killarney?* The last stanza of that song succinctly entwines place and image with commerce: "Nature bestowed all her gifts with a smile / The emerald, the shamrock, and the Blarney / When you can buy all these wonderful things / Then you can buy Killarney."[22]

Likewise, part two of Thomas Edison's film *European Rest Cure* (1904) was little more than a motion picture hibernicon. Following a rough ocean crossing, tourists arrive in Ireland and visit Blarney Castle, where they have a comic encounter with the local guide on its parapet. The film actually reflects the principal tourist route that Americans took after disembarking from their ocean liners in Queenstown, County Cork. That same year, Burton Holmes debuted the first Irish travelogue.[23] The American daughters of ultra-Irish nationalists Jeremiah and Mary Jane O'Donovan-Rossa most likely saw his *Beautiful Ireland* before they sailed because their path was as predictable as their description:

> The one thing we could not fail to do in Ireland was to kiss the Blarney Stone, so one gloriously sunny morning, with an escort of two stalwart young Irishmen, Jane and I set forth for Blarney Castle. . . . Picturesque and alone it stands, looking with time-dimmed eyes on great vistas of lovely wooded country. We climbed the little winding stairs that reached its turret and held our breath in wonder at the beauty of the view, but we held our breath in earnest when we saw the precipitous wall over which we had to hang, heads down, to kiss the Blarney Stone. Mighty thankful were we for the strength of those young men who held our ankles in bars of iron as we hung suspended over that frightening drop. It was in truth with trembling hearts we sought the 'Gift of Blarney.' . . . So to Killarney we went, but to describe its beauty needs far more eloquence than the Blarney Stone imparted. Spellbound we stood, at the foot of old Ross Castle, and feasted our eyes on the gorgeous panorama of shimmering lakes and unbelievably green slopes that lay before us. Never have I seen grass so vitally green as the grass of old Killarney.[24]

Beyond mere cliché, such language is indicative of the extent to which early tourists from the United States were thoroughly indoctrinated with a romantic image of Ireland, as well as with a must-see checklist.

Figure 7.1. The slogan "Kiss Me, I'm Irish" first appeared on buttons worn at the 1963 St. Patrick's Day parade in South Boston. It went mainstream via a 1968 Norcross greeting card that featured the Blarney Stone with "Kiss Me, Baby, I'm Irish!" The genesis for the idea of obtaining blarney by proxy was souvenir postcards for the Irish tourist market. This example combines three images dating from 1909 to 1913 and was created by Fergus O'Connor of Dublin, whose company logo was a harp and shamrock linked by a ribbon declaring "Erin go Brái" (Ireland Forever). It was still in circulation in 1933. Credit: Mick Moloney Irish-American Music and Popular Culture Irish Americana Collection (AIA 031.004), box 53, folder H16, Archives of Irish America, Special Collections, Bobst Library, New York University.

The first American company to film on location abroad was Kalem, and Ireland was its destination for a number of years between 1910 and 1915. In addition to its travelogues *The Irish Honeymoon: A Trip through Ireland* (1911) and *The O'Kalems' Visit to Killarney* (1912), it was its screen adaptation of *The Colleen Bawn* (1911) that helped further promote American tourism to Killarney. Kalem shot many of the sites traditionally associated with the plot, and its United States ballyhoo—although new for the motion picture world—echoed that earlier novelty: genuine Irish soil, in four-foot square trays, with certificates of authenticity from the parish priest at Killarney. Theater owners were advised to use the slogan "Come and Tread on Irish Soil" to "attract every Irish son and daughter to the theatres."[25] Burton Holmes made a second travelogue about Ireland in 1914, this time starting in Ulster before proceeding to the west "to the spots where life is hard among the people and the peat-bogs. . . . Killarney was not overlooked."[26] Irish scenery emerged from the background to become a star central to the entertainment.

Kalem inspired the Film Company of Ireland to also shoot on location for the American market. Its most notable film was *Knocknagow* (1918), adapted from the popular nationalist novel by Charles Kickham. When picked up for distribution by American management during the politically turbulent years of 1920 and 1921, *Knocknagow* was frequently packaged with the two-reel travelogue *Beautiful Ireland* (1918) and marketed using the same sure methods that promoted plays for St. Patrick's Day—that is, through the extensive network of Catholic parishes and schools and the pastors in charge of them.[27] In fact, its immediate predecessor was a late hibernicon of the same name that featured "the Irish Bernhardt" Kathleen Mathew, grandniece of the famous Catholic temperance advocate, Father Theobald Mathew. Her *Beautiful Ireland* (1916) included "picture, wit, humor, and impersonations."[28]

The Film Company of Ireland's *Beautiful Ireland* (sometimes advertised as *Here and There in Ireland*) was therefore and in many ways unsurprising, which was part of its appeal. The first reel featured scenes in County Limerick, especially the Shannon River, as well as "Views of the lower Lakes of Killarney, taken from Muckross House" with notes that indicate these "must be tinted green." Reel two focused on Dublin landmarks like the Botanical Gardens and St. Stephen's Green, the Custom House and the Four Courts, "A Jaunting Car Comedy," Donnybrook,

Glasnevin, and the "Dublin Mountains under snow."²⁹ Screened as *The Emerald Isle* for St. Patrick's Day in Salt Lake City in 1921, the beauty of Killarney and Blarney was endorsed by the General Federation of Women's Clubs.³⁰ That fall, the Irish American actor/singer Emmet Moore leased the rights for three years to promote Film Company of Ireland titles in twenty-two states west of the Mississippi. There, *Beautiful Ireland* was sometimes renamed *Forty-Five Minutes in Ireland* as a prelude to Moore's vocal segment "Merry Ramble 'Round Ireland" and was followed by the main audience draw, a five-reel "highly charged political melodrama" called *Ireland, a Nation* (1914). In general, the inclusion of travelogues in such large entertainment programs—in Moore's case, a three-hour show—was not confined to ethnic audiences; rather, they appealed to the typical moviegoer in this period.³¹

The *Boston Herald* described *Forty-Five Minutes in Ireland* as "a cross section of Irish life today interspersed with a breath of the past, given by the ancient ruined abbeys, the alluring lake scenes, and the desolate quiet of bog and mountain side."³² Obviously, celluloid Ireland was, even then, defined by its landscape and antiquities, scenic and historic assets ripe for exploitation in the right hands. F. W. Crossley, one of the pioneers of the tourism industry in Ireland, included "many well-produced illustrations of Irish scenery" in each issue of the *Irish Tourist*.³³ Accused of suddenly being "tourist mad in Ireland," Crossley replied, "We are not mad, but only just coming to our senses."³⁴ Indeed, his attitude was prescient with regard to American tourists: "They have money, we have not; We *must* get, well, all they've got."³⁵

* * *

In Ireland, progress in tourism development was interrupted by the outbreak of the First World War, then prolonged by the War of Independence and the Civil War. Michael Hayes, speaker of Dáil Éireann, following a tour of the United States in 1925, observed that "generations of hostile propaganda have created a certain impression about Ireland on the minds of Americans who are not of Irish birth or extraction. . . . Ireland is to them the wild country which unfriendly critics have painted it."³⁶ He was pointing to the negative media discussed in chapter 2, not to the power of Irish to engage or entertain tourists. Recognizing the potential of film, the Irish Tourist Association (ITA), a voluntary organization, arranged for the Fox Film Corp. to tour Ireland that same year. *Irish Travel* reported that test screenings in American theaters were enthusiastically received. "The use of the screen to illustrate the attractions of Ireland as a holiday-land is unquestionably a very effective form of publicity," the ITA's magazine wrote, "and there is every reason to hope that the fruits of the film tour . . . will be apparent in the increased volume of tourist traffic to Ireland next and each succeeding summer."[37]

The ITA's efforts were cautiously encouraged by the Irish Free State's new Department of Industry and Commerce. Eric Zuelow sees this as an important milestone: the first time Ireland had "the opportunity to define Irishness for itself."[38] Yet Ireland was simultaneously competing against Hollywood. Dublin's *The Irish Statesman* opined, "It threatens to blow almost everything native out of the soul, and the images of humanity which replace what is native are invented in Los Angeles."[39] *Irish Luck* (1925), a light romantic drama about an Irish American who returns to visit family in Ireland only to find himself impersonating a wealthy titled man, was probably one of the culprits. Despite filming its exteriors on location in Ireland, the prime audience for this Paramount picture was not ethnic. An Alabama newspaper reviewer remarked on the scenes shot in modern Dublin but also in "beautiful Killarney with its lakes, antique castles and picturesque countryside," where most of the action takes place. The lead actor, of course, kisses the Blarney Stone in a close-up shot. Despite the fact that less than a dozen Irish-born people lived in Lauderdale County, Alabama, where the *Florence Times-News* was published, a big audience turnout was anticipated for the 1926 St. Patrick's Day screenings.[40]

In contrast, the ITA was run by a small group of men who were modestly underwritten by a government that was actually ambivalent about tourist development. There were perceptions that tourism was not a modern industry in the way that building Ardnacrusha to harness the Shannon was, and some feared catering to foreign visitors "would have the effect of making the Irish people servile and obsequious" or "destroy timeless ways of life."[41] But businesses with direct commercial interests such as hotels, railways, and shipping companies supported the ITA as it grappled with how "to induce a still larger number of Americans to include Ireland in their travel plans." Among the association's earliest publicity decisions were at least one hundred thousand folder maps of Ireland; brochures on aspects of Irish holidays such as fishing, hunting, health, and scenic and seaside resorts; plus "a Complete Guide to Ireland on 'Baedeker' lines." One thousand new photographs were ordered to illustrate these, and designs were invited for "a series of illustrated posters for display in foreign countries."[42] The *Gaelic American*'s summary of the purpose of these efforts was straight out of the green space: "to popularize Ireland" as "a place where life was easy and pleasant, with a genial people, whose hospitality was seldom met with elsewhere."[43] Indeed, the key to tourism success was juxtaposing Irish with hospitable—a transformation already well underway with St. Patrick's Day in the United States—and the Irish landscape with certain vistas long familiar to Americans. "Erin has scenic beauty, romantic history and legend and always has a thousand welcomes for the stranger," the *New York Times* agreed. "Ireland, always sentimental, would be overjoyed to see a stream of visitors come to her from the shores of America, whither so many of her sons and daughters went during the course of the nineteenth century. Aside from the business aspect of tourists on a holiday, there is a soft spot in Ireland's heart for Americans."[44]

While touring Ireland for the U.S. State Department in 1926, Professor Towne Nylander of the Department of Economics at Princeton University told authorities in Dublin that "there was tremendous sympathy in America towards Ireland. The Americans admired the Irish for their perseverance, good nature, good humour, and independence. . . . There was no reason why Ireland should not have tourists for eight months of the year." In his opinion, Ireland was an attractive tourist destination for three types: "the elderly and more sedate, who would consciously go around to all the buildings and ruins, and make notes of all they saw; the younger group, who would like any amusement there was; and writers, dramatists, and poets, who would come primarily to meet the people, and learn something of their folklore traditions and habits."[45]

To encourage this, the ITA published a guidebook, *Ireland*. The first two pages of the 1929 edition are advertisements for Irish linen and John Jameson whiskey, items a tourist might purchase as souvenirs of their visit. After a brief introduction that addressed climate, scenery, sport, hotels, and railway and motor coach travel, *Ireland* devoted nineteen pages to "Antiquities." It called Killarney "that picture of delight . . . so famous that no detailed description of it is called for." It pointed out the tradition of the Blarney Stone and recommended a visit "even if one does not try to kiss" it.[46] In the descriptions broken down by province, tourists were also encouraged to see the Book of Kells in Dublin's Trinity College, Glendalough in County Wicklow, the Rock of Cashel in County Tipperary, the Aran Islands in County Galway, the Shannon River in County Limerick, and the Giant's Causeway in County Antrim. Nevertheless, Ireland's attempt to educate potential tourists was undercut by the business needs of transatlantic travel. The White Star Line's advertisement on page 120 spoke a language Americans already understood:

> VISIT IRELAND. See for yourself the romantic 'Emerald Isle'—the dear Country of the Shamrock, with its jaunting cars, its castles, relics of bygone ages, its exquisite scenery of mountains and lake—enjoy its charming hospitality. KISS THE BLARNEY STONE!

The ripple effect of such hype was soon apparent.

"All our friends wondered at our going to Ireland," George Davison, an American, recalled in 1930. He tried to describe "Why Ireland?": "A multitude of reasons: but to clarify and put in words how difficult! Like so many Irish things it is more a matter of feeling than logic or thinking; of impression rather than perception." He and his wife prepared for their visit by reading Padraic Colum's *The Road Round Ireland* and *An Irish Rambler* by C. F. Howell "with considerable profit," although he also recommended Stephen Gwynn's *Ireland* as "most sympathetic." "Our greatest help," Davison wrote, "came from a friend who went into a tourist office in New York and collected all the pamphlets they had." His most memorable impression of Ireland was provided by his Killarney jaunting car driver, Dan Hogan, "whose stories regaled every minute of our drive, fact and story in glorious confusion":

> [He] also told us the story of Colleen Bawn and showed us the rock from whence she was drowned. He explained that the exact height of McGillicuddy's Reeks was "3,414 feet, 9¾ inches, and from the top on just the right day you can see the trolleys running around the streets of New York." He added that he had told that once to a lady from New York and the worst of it was she believed him.[47]

As with the hibernicon guides in America, those like Dan Hogan "invariably adopted whatever role was expected of him, so that instead of actually seeing what was, the tourist very often saw something which he himself had created"—obviously culled from the Irish amalgam in the green space.[48]

Alison Barstow Murphy, a fifteen-year-old Girl Scout who published *Every Which Way in Ireland* in 1930, also felt compelled to answer "Why Go to Ireland?" in her first chapter.[49] Like countless visitors before and after her, Murphy proceeded to enumerate Ireland's principal attractions: "Irish hospitality is famous. . . . In ancient monuments, Ireland abounds. . . . Castles fairly popped out of the roadside." As for folklore, she wrote, "Ireland is one of the few places where fairies live today—live, in reality, as well as in imagination. People we met have seen fairies, and their spirit is in every hill and lake, in every bit of colourful landscape. The country makes a fitting setting for the fairy tales and the wonderful ancient mythology."[50] How could she possibly know this? Perhaps her parents—"her father was a naturalist on the staff of the American Museum of Natural History and her mother was a member of the Society of Woman Geographers"—read to her from Jeremiah Curtin's *Tales of the Faeries and the Ghost World, Collected from the Oral Tradition in Southwest Munster*? It had been serialized in *The New York Sun* for its Sunday Edition in 1922 and 1923 when she was seven or eight.[51]

Blarney got yet another high-profile boost in 1930, this time from Johnson Brothers, the British manufacturer of popular tableware. The castle adorned the "all-important dinner plate" and coffeepot on the company's affordable open stock series, *Old Britain Castles*, a strategic decision to enhance its "romantic" appeal to prospective American buyers.[52] The fact that the County Cork landmark was now part of the Irish Free State rather than Great Britain was conveniently sidestepped by using a 1792 engraving. Surprisingly, there seem to have been no Irish or Irish American objections. The Blarney plate sold for forty cents in 1931 just as the ITA opened an office on Fifth Avenue in New York City.[53] To mark the occasion, its executive vice president, John P. O'Brien, presented "an authentic chip off the old block at Blarney Castle"—supposedly one of only two in the United States—to Mayor John P. O'Brien in a City Hall ceremony. This guaranteed news coverage; according to the *New York Times*, "In political circles the news that Mayor O'Brien would go into the Mayoralty campaign with a bit of the real Blarney Stone in his possession spread like wildfire. It was hailed as an omen of success at the polls in November."[54]

It was quite natural, then, for James A. Fitzpatrick's 1932 travel talk *Come Back to Erin*, filmed with ITA cooperation, to open with a jaunting car passing Blarney Castle. Fitzpatrick, a second-generation Irish American, followed this with two more travelogues filmed on location under the auspices of MGM: *Ireland, the Melody Isle*, and *Ireland, the Emerald Isle* (both 1934).[55] Describing the latter, Darragh O'Donoghue concludes, "Images of medieval religious settlements, an impoverished rural district, and a colonial fortress, each found in different parts of the country, are brought together—not to show the variety of Irish life, experience, and history, but to collapse them into a generic travel agent's idea of Ireland." He dismisses Fitzpatrick's narration as romantic "blubber" and the focus on "picturesque poverty" as designed "to appeal to 'Irish exiles.'"[56] But like Burton Holmes before him, Fitzpatrick gave all Americans, regardless of ethnicity, what they expected to see: "How would I have gained admittance to those countries if I had commented on their social problems? . . . I don't recall anyone ever requesting a tour of slums and prisons."[57] Indeed, *Ireland, the Melody Isle* opens with a wide shot of the Lakes of Killarney; then, after a flowery testimonial to the historic connections between Irish landscape and song, the first verse of Balfe's *Killarney* leads off the soundtrack for scenes in Kerry.[58]

Irish travelogues like these primed many non-Irish Americans to receive Robert Flaherty's *Man of Aran*, one of the top foreign films of 1934, as realistic. Here again was a subject matter—"the bleak coast of Ireland"— that Kalem had experimented with back in 1911 with *Among the Irish Fisherfolk* and *The Fishermaid of Ballydavid*, in which the sea is as much the protagonist as the Irish people. According to the ethnographer John Messenger, "Flaherty was so influenced by primitivism and his philosophy of esthetics that he . . . seriously distorted numerous indigenous [customs] in order to make Aran culture fit his preconceptions."[59] These were, of course, built upon the widely read literary work of John Millington Synge and others that had promoted western Ireland as the source of unsullied Irishness for decades. The ITA was actually pleased with the news that Flaherty was filming on Aran.[60] Likewise, the fieldwork conducted in rural County Clare between 1932 and 1934 by the American social anthropologists Conrad Arensberg and Solon Kimball—which was encouraged by Éamon de Valera—reaffirmed an image of Ireland associated with the simplicity of cottage and village life. Because of this, "tourists visiting Aran come armed with" many "misconceptions," Messenger concludes.[61] *Man of Aran* tapped into the growing thirst for leisure tourism much better than, for example, 1935's *The Informer*, winner of four Academy Awards, which was set in Dublin during the War of Independence although filmed in Los Angeles. RKO acknowledged that *The Informer* could just as easily be set "in the collieries of Pennsylvania, in the grim salt mines of Siberia," as in Ireland.[62] Not so *Man of Aran*, which inspired prose for travel writers like Diana Rice: "Ireland's west coast . . . is a good show, especially when storms sweep in from the Atlantic," she wrote in 1938. "Then clouds of spray dash high over jagged cliffs and waters churn in secluded coves."[63]

Ireland's Department of Industry and Commerce boosted the efforts of the private ITA when it created the semi-state Irish Tourist Board (ITB) in 1939.[64] Once again, the need to advertise in America was embraced, and four tons of literature were distributed that year at the World's Fair in New York.[65] Although Seán Lemass, the department's minister, declared that there was more to Ireland than the "overrated Blarney Stone," the ITB announced plans that "spots of great natural beauty, villages retaining primitive customs, and historic castles now difficult to access will be fetched into tour circles."[66] Equally formulaic, the ITA's emphasis on traditions of Irish hospitality and friendliness was continued by the ITB, even as it struggled to upgrade roads and hotel accommodations.[67] The ITB opened a tourist office at 33 East Fiftieth Street in New York in 1947 with a mandate "to sell to the visitor, not merely a beautiful view or a good cuisine, but a favorable impression of the country as a whole." Ten thousand Americans visited Ireland in 1948, the same year President Truman reviewed New York's St. Patrick's Day parade; there were twenty thousand in 1949.[68]

Being in the tourist spotlight was not, however, without its challenges. In December 1949, *Holiday* magazine published a feature story on Ireland by the noted author Frank O'Connor. Not only was *Holiday*'s circulation enormous (425,000 per issue and counting), but its reputation was also growing. "What *Vogue* did for fashion, *Holiday* did for destinations," Michael Callahan concludes. And for O'Connor, it was an opportunity for the substance of his 1947 travel book *Irish Miles* to reach a wider American audience as well as to become part of "the magazine's starry roster" of authors.⁶⁹ Even though Ireland had only recently banned two books by O'Connor—*Midnight Court* (1946) and *The Common Chord* (1947)—the government no doubt expected, not unreasonably, something similar to the May 1940 issue of *National Geographic*, "When Irish Skies Are Smiling."⁷⁰

That feature was by Harrison Howell Walker, a staff writer and photographer whose next assignment was the Amish in Lancaster County, Pennsylvania. He was "enchanted by picturesque rural vistas, by men who farm or fish and by women who spin or bake bread, and always by the language, music and dance of Ireland." Walker emphasized those aspects of Ireland that were unchanged by nearly twenty years of independence, including tourist landmarks like Blarney Castle and the Rock of Cashel. Clearly, Walker had seen an Irish travelogue or two and read Arensberg's *The Irish Countryman* before going on assignment. He took photographs of thatched cottages, donkeys, pigs, turf, children, and shawled women that were intentionally more primitive than modern, as was his text. The writer Peig Sayers, for example, is pictured standing before her delph-laden dresser with the caption "Because there is no electricity on Great Blasket, natives collect as curiosities discarded bulbs that wash ashore." Mrs. Geary, after nine years in Boston, is posed next to her spinning wheel in Connemara, where "now her heart beats warm again as her bare feet tread softly on the cool stone floor."⁷¹

In 1940, the Irish government still had little interest in the potential of American tourists, but by 1949 things were different. Therefore, O'Connor's essay for *Holiday* came as a shock because its rather lighthearted account of the course of Irish history was wrapped in a dark, sardonic portrait of contemporary Irish economic and social problems. "Ireland contains slums you have not seen the like of elsewhere in Europe," O'Connor wrote in his second paragraph, "with sickly-looking children playing barefoot in the streets." He continued,

> As you travel you will see that the towns are thinly spaced, have little industry or none, and no reason for existence except fair or market days when farmers come in with cattle, or with butter and eggs, our main exports; that the villages are mere hamlets and the old parish churches all in ruin. There

will be occasional country houses, but many of these will be gutted, and most of the remainder in various stages of decay. The treeless landscape will be broken up by an extraordinary, and indeed, incomprehensible, network of roads and lanes; and along each of these in a sort of rural ribbon development, a couple of cottages will have sprung up, well apart from their neighbors, without electricity, gas, water, plumbing and probably without a school, church, dance hall or social meeting place within miles of them. In such a landscape public services like transport and telephones will be a nightmare.[72]

This indictment, in the very introduction to the feature, was devastating for the ITB and the legacy of the ITA. It undermined steps even then being taken to develop Shannon Airport in County Clare as the European anchor for air travel, with pressure from the American government to see tourism "in Ireland's national interest, in terms of both improving dollar earnings and ensuring the continued receipt of Marshall Plan aid."[73] The Department of External Affairs, which was just coming around to seeing tourism as "cultural propaganda"—not unlike the cultural currency Irish Americans had wielded as discussed in chapter 3—demanded an explanation from *Holiday*. From Ireland's perspective, readers were deceived and tourists discouraged, given O'Connor's emphasis on Irish poverty and the searing image of "slum children" who lived in a crumbling Dublin tenement.

The magazine explained that it had expressly asked O'Connor to "steer well clear of the sentimental and corny approach."[74] However, O'Connor's text was juxtaposed with color photographs by *Holiday*'s staff photographer, Thomas Hollyman, and his wife, Jean. Many of these delivered what Americans had long been conditioned to expect of Ireland, such as the very first image, in which smoke rises from the chimney of a small, thatched cottage nestled amid hills. In addition to de rigueur castles, round towers, kissing the Blarney Stone (a four-photograph spread), and Killarney's "lakes and fells" (a full page), their editors slipped in some new elements to the tourist lexicon: the imposing Anglo-Irish wealth of Powerscourt in County Wicklow (a four-page spread) and horses and hounds ready for racing or the hunt (a two-page spread) are counterpoints to the subsistence life on the Stack family farm in County Kerry and at the Catholic monastery at Mount

Melleray, County Waterford (both two-page spreads). While *Holiday* thus documented wealth disparity in 1940s Ireland, its photographs of the republic's capital, Dublin, contained familiar echoes from the green space too: de Valera, Seán Ó Faoláin, Padraic Colum, the Abbey Theatre, a jarvey on a jaunting car, and Guinness. The issue's cover, a watercolor by John Cullen Murphy, was nothing less than a tourist postcard: a jaunting car full of happy children moving along a country lane past a thatched cottage and a shawled woman holding a baby, with the top of a Celtic stone cross filling the lower right foreground.

Although the thatched cottage and the jaunting car were old tropes, they were soon raised to iconic levels by John Ford's *The Quiet Man*

Figure 7.2. Irish tourism supported the domestic production of souvenirs like this one made by Arklow Pottery in County Wicklow, 1955, which features a jarvey and his jaunting car carrying tourists at the Lakes of Killarney. The little ceramic pot carried a secondary meaning for its purchaser: it was made to resemble a *scilléad*, the ubiquitous three-legged cast iron skillet that hung over the open fire in every rural cottage into the early twentieth century. Arklow Pottery opened in 1935 and presented a black and gold china coffee set to New York's mayor Robert Wagner in honor of St. Patrick's Day, 1954. Credit: author's collection.

(1952). Pan American World Airways was quick to take advantage, obviously inspired by *Variety*'s first review in May: "Republic has an excellent money picture," the critic wrote. "The lush green scenery, gentle streams, quaint cottages and customs add a travelog [*sic*] interest to the plot. In fact, Ford evidences such a fondness for the picturesque values that he goes overboard on them, stretching the picture out to an unnecessary 129 minutes."[75] With help from Padraic Colum, the travelogue *Wings to Ireland* was completed by June just as Ireland's president attended the first screening of *The Quiet Man* in Dublin (it wouldn't premiere in the United States until late August). The narration of *Wings to Ireland* took the form of a letter describing what an American family encountered as they drove around Ireland. Their first stop was Cong in County Mayo to stay in Ashford Castle—one of the few first-class hotels in the west of Ireland at the time, where members of the *Quiet Man* cast and crew were based during filming—followed by a visit to a "quaint old thatched cottage." They smelled "the incense of Ireland, the sweet smell of burning turf" and "cycled out to an old Franciscan Friary, built in 1474." The voice-over continues, "All Ireland is dotted with such ruins." A striking conclusion was the observation "And the girls! Well, I see why people get sentimental about Ireland."[76] Since Pan American was then one of the few carriers on the New York–Shannon route, a sneak preview like this for American passengers was very good for its summer business.

*   *   *

At its most essential, *The Quiet Man* is the story of an Irish American who comes back to Erin, a theme that runs through all the iterations of travel genres previously discussed. Seán Thornton, the principal character, is a "Returned Yank" who sees Ireland through American eyes—that is, through the lens of the green space. The opening credits of *The Quiet Man* roll over a castle silhouetted by a sunset, immediately triggering Irish associations. Next, the audience is drawn into a one-act play by actors from the Abbey Theatre that begins as Thornton gets off the train and asks for directions to Inisfree (a fictional location that references Innisfree, a lake island in County Sligo immortalized in an 1890 poem by Yeats). They are loquacious locals, full of blarney. Adrian Frazier calls this "a Hollywood cover version of a popular hit," Lady

Gregory's *Spreading the News* (1908).⁷⁷ Thornton's disorientation, and that of the film's viewers, is quickly dispelled as, within minutes, Ford recreates the hibernicon: a jaunting car framed by the window of the station's waiting room. Its driver becomes Thornton's guide then and throughout the rest of the film as he explains Ireland and the Irish to the American.

In the United States, audiences did not require such tutelage because Ford delivers all the necessary Irish cues before any of the central plot unfolds. The setting is obviously rural Ireland, with its greenness heightened by Technicolor. The jaunting car moves through a tourist landscape to its first stop, a stone bridge from which Thornton sees the thatched cottage where he was born and remembers how his mother waxed poetic about her humble home. Next, as it traverses the manicured parkland of Ashford Castle, a Celtic cross leans askew in the foreground. Eamonn Slater identifies this as a folly rather than an actual ruin, one that adds little value to the scene.⁷⁸ However, anyone familiar with *Holiday*'s Irish feature would remember the cottage and stone cross on the cover as well as that they were the very first images on the title page of Frank O'Connor's controversial essay.

Ireland's Department of Industry and Commerce knew that there were millions of Irish Americans it needed to target in any tourist campaign and that nearly 50 percent of all Irish Americans lived in a compact geographical area (New York and six neighboring states) that coincided with the source of most transatlantic traffic.⁷⁹ It made sense to encourage and facilitate the production of *The Quiet Man* because it was "advantageous to the national interest." The Department of External Affairs was warier after its experience with *Holiday*. As Roddy Flynn astutely notes, in the early 1950s Ireland was, "arguably for the first time, pursuing a concerted image control campaign" and *The Quiet Man* "threatened to undermine" Irish efforts to present "alternative perspectives."⁸⁰ It was, after all, a Hollywood film made by an American director with long experience dating back to the silent era. The Irish government worried that there might be backlash because of certain scenes, particularly the long donnybrook that leads to the film's conclusion. "The Irish of another generation—and I well know their attitude—might have looked askance at Ford's somewhat violent depiction of the Emerald Isle's people," Edwin Schallert recalled in the *Los Angeles Times*, a sentiment echoed by the Irish ambassador in Washington, who feared there would be protests as there had been over *The Playboy of the Western World* in 1911 or over *Irish Hearts* in 1926.[81] But there were none because the green space had conditioned an entire generation in how to see Irish. "Everybody, but everybody loves it!" screamed a full-page ad in *Variety* in September 1952.

Although John Ford could boast of his Irish heritage and that filming on location in Ireland had long been an ambition, he knew only too well how to deploy the green space to the advantage of *The Quiet Man*.[82] He sent his writer, Frank Nugent, a copy of Arensberg and Kimball's *Family and Community in Ireland* (1940).[83] He selected "The Isle of Innisfree" (1950) as the main theme song used throughout the film; it had just been recorded for Decca by Bing Crosby in January 1952. He hired the same cinematographer who had won the 1950 Academy Award for his use of Technicolor in a Ford film; Winton Hoch won again for the Ireland depicted in *The Quiet Man* with its redheaded heroine. *Variety* declared that Barry Fitzgerald, an established Abbey actor in Hollywood since 1936, held the film together with the "socko punching of the Irish type with which he has become identified. . . . While his character and those of a number of others might not be realistic Irish, they are along the lines of popular conception and add to the film's enjoyment."[84] Fitzgerald, who plays Seán Thornton's guide, refers to himself twice as "The Shaughraun," an Irish rogue from Dion Boucicault's eponymous comic melodrama that Americans had laughed with for more than eighty years. When Fitzgerald also famously remarks early in the film, "I think I'll go and join me comrades and talk a little treason," he obliquely reminds U.S. audiences of recent newspaper headlines about Ireland. Likewise, Vic Young's score is reminiscent of Victor Herbert's *Irish Rhapsody* (written in 1892, published in 1910, and subsequently "played to death" in the United States).[85] Thornton's love interest, Mary Kate Danaher, declares that she was "no pauper to be going to him in [her] shift," and Thornton himself is revealed to have actually killed a man—both good-natured references to what had once been objectionable in *The Playboy of the Western World*. The couple cycle to a ruined abbey, where they embrace while sheltering from the rain. Boucicault always used ruins, and they were perennial favorites in guidebooks, magazines, and travelogues about Ireland. After their marriage, Seán and Mary Kate move into Thornton's restored thatched cottage with its emerald-green door that "only an American would have thought of," as is remarked in the film.

The green space suffuses *The Quiet Man* like this to such an extent that the *Washington Post* reviewer had to remind readers that the film was not modern Ireland: "The Ireland Mr. Ford is giving us is the Ireland of a joyful mind, an inspired dreamland of timelessness and lavishly green fields, of ivory-skinned women with flaring red hair, of lusty, brawling men, friendly taverns, violent energies and lush plenty," wrote Richard Coe. "This is the Ireland we all want to believe in . . . all this Ireland of the imagination never quite collapses into the cliché class. When it seems on the verge, there's a wonderful line or situation to fly over that chasm."[86] In fact, this is the position the Irish government took too: the film was fantasy, but because Irish scenery looked so good in it, the principal benefit for Ireland would be more tourists. Frank Aitken, the minister for external affairs, called it excellent publicity.[87]

Nevertheless, Ireland continued to worry about its image abroad—sensitive to any suggestions that it was backward rather than progressive—without fully understanding the powerful rip current of the green space.[88] There was a repeat of the *Holiday* fiasco when CBS television aired "Ireland: The Tear and the Smile" in February 1961. The title derived from one of Thomas Moore's melodies, but it also referenced a Somerville and Ross book of Irish sketches published by Houghton Mifflin in 1933. The Irish government was upset to learn that the script was written by Elizabeth Bowen, a novelist "with very distinct cultural and political prejudices" like Frank O'Connor. The reviewer for the *Pittsburgh Post-Gazette*, on the other hand, thought it was a well-done documentary about a "fascinating land." Other publicity focused on its interviews with the actress Siobhan McKenna and the designer Sybil Connolly, as well as that familiar American media spokesman for Ireland, the writer Seán Ó Faoláin. CBS claimed it received mostly letters of praise, including from the AOH and the Knights of Columbus.[89]

By that autumn, in a special tourism issue of *Administration*, T. J. O'Driscoll, director-general of the state-run agency Bord Fáilte (heir to the ITA and ITB), had come around to the 1890s pragmatism of F. W. Crossley: "The hard fact is that it is the tourists' money we are all after, and the more they spend the better we are pleased."[90] The future implications of this attitude were profound. As Linda King notes, Aer Lingus was well ahead of the Irish government when it came to tourism strategies. When the national carrier inaugurated service between New York and Shannon in 1958, its use of "Irish International Airlines" and the shamrock on the tail of its planes was an intentional appeal to the American market, where the word Irish and the trefoil had a very long history. It commissioned a poster inspired by *The Quiet Man*—thatched cottage and jaunting car, of course—and it paid *Holiday* magazine for a full-page ad to promote itself as "the friendly airline" with "gracious Irish colleens" to welcome you aboard.[91] Irish like this not only matched the tourist image; it confirmed that there was still plenty of room in the green space for Ireland if it was willing to play by the rules. Those rules were American.

Conclusion

One night in the spring of 1977, Noel Rice could not hear himself over the din at the Irish Village, a pub on West Diversey Avenue in Chicago. The Concannon Folk Group, visiting musicians from Ireland, were performing "popular Irish rebel songs" and "lively dance music." Rice was there to be interviewed as president of the North Side Comhaltas Ceoltóirí Éireann Branch for the Library of Congress's Chicago Ethnic Arts Project. Its field notes record that the main disruption came from a television producer who "was charging about coercing the audience into states of hysterical appreciation of the entertainment (including standing on tables, wild cavorting, and frenetic hand clapping)." Rice's interviewer, the folklorist Mick Moloney—a native of Ireland only five years in the United States—was clearly annoyed by the American film crew's efforts to create a party-like atmosphere, describing conditions as "atrocious" and the entire scene as "chaos."[1] Moloney was recording Irish for the premiere repository of American history and culture; the crew was recording Irish for an American television broadcast.

The Concannon Folk Group and the Irish Village were cultural derivatives: the former was inspired by the Clancy Brothers and Tommy Makem, Irish musicians who played the American folk circuit before and after skyrocketing to national fame in 1961 on *The Ed Sullivan Show*; the latter was a direct descendant of the Irish Villages that Americans had explored at several World's Fairs since 1893. As such, they tapped into a memory bank more intricate than immediately obvious, even to Moloney. On the other hand, the purpose of the Chicago Ethnic Arts Project was to survey the "status of ethnic art traditions," and Moloney was hired to document Irish for this initiative.[2] The first- and second-generation men and women he interviewed—and others like them in Boston, New York, Philadelphia, Detroit, St. Paul, and San Francisco—were part of a small, networked subculture in an otherwise vast America that understood Irish quite differently. The Concannon

Folk Group was in the Windy City because touring the Irish American diaspora was a good source of income. Patrons of the Irish Village were there because a group from Ireland was entertaining, bringing tradition and the allure of authenticity closer. Noel Rice, a flute player from Geashill, County Offaly, who emigrated to Chicago in the 1950s, abandoned the pub for a diner where he could speak with Mick Moloney about traditional music as serious folk culture rather than popular culture until four in the morning.[3] All of this was irrelevant to the nonethnic audience who would see the performance on television because Americans had already learned exactly what to expect of anything presented to them as Irish.

To make sense of this requires understanding the tangled web of associations, preconceptions, and self- and national identification that are in the green space; the invested parties who first introduced images to it; and the influence of Irish that resulted. Timing is also critical to comprehending what happened. *Moore's Melodies*, Dion Boucicault, and St. Patrick's Day spread with ease throughout the United States, connecting Irish with generally positive codes. Music, melodrama, and the March holiday were counterweights to the far more negative images rife in American media, politics, and society in the nineteenth century. Even corned beef, that iconic dish served up every March 17 all across America, was a useful distraction from the hated association of Irish with pigs. Not only was it from a different animal, but it was a hearty yet inexpensive cut of beef, a favorite of miners, heavyweight boxers, and frugal housewives stretching a dollar—whether they were Irish or not. Although Ireland exported hams and bacon for a quality niche market in the United States, it was corned beef that ultimately prevailed as Irish. Likewise, well-meaning Irish American elites and Anglo-Irish gentry, each with different agendas, added new images to the matrix. The former focused on heroes and respectability to demonstrate Irish contributions to the United States as well as the right of Ireland to political self-determination; the latter emphasized craftwork, brewing, and distilling as the means to raise Ireland's economic profile while simultaneously distinguishing Irish from English. During the decades that straddled the turn of the twentieth century, these efforts succeeded in banishing the most egregious stereotypes from the stage as well as showcasing Irish ability at two World's Fairs in the United States.

CONCLUSION * 213

Thereafter, the range of images expanded so rapidly that it puts a year like 1911 in perspective. Nonethnic consumers heard and saw fresh iterations of Irish through new media, such as Chauncey Olcott's sentimental "Mother Machree"—written, performed, and recorded in the United States—as well as from silent film adaptations of Boucicault, like Kalem's *The Colleen Bawn*, a drama-cum-travelogue shot in Killarney for American cinema screens. They also saw and heard Seumas MacManus on the lecture circuit; his captivating storytelling made him the personification of an Irishman for a new generation of Americans. Irish American efforts to place a statue of Commodore John Barry in Washington, DC, moved forward at the same time that there were objections to demeaning representations on St. Patrick's Day postcards and in the Abbey Theatre's *The Playboy of the Western World*. Meanwhile, a tariff case in the court of customs appeals debated whether the American public recognized imitation trefoils as shamrocks. The true impact of any one of these requires situating all in relation to one another as well as to what came before and what would follow.

The advent of the Irish Free State added another agenda involving image-making to the green space. However, in the 1920s and 1930s, Ireland encountered even more competition because news of its nation-building in Ireland faced entrenched pro-British attitudes among journalists and politicians. Control of Irish in other arenas was harder too. Ireland took on the promotion of legacy products like linen and battled trademark violations, while Irish America fought against immigration restrictions, superficial holiday novelties, and tasteless movies. But anti-Catholic nativism, Prohibition, and the Hollywood ballyhoo overwhelmed or undercut those efforts. Even the United Irish Counties Association Feis and the 1939 World's Fair were no match against rampant commercialization and an American media hungry for English-language content. There were only so many fronts on which contesting what was Irish could be sustained—either by a small nation, its declining immigrant communities in America, or its Americanizing diaspora. As the image increasingly gravitated toward the profitable, the utility and power of the green space fused transatlantic interests. The embrace of *The Quiet Man* in the 1950s and *Riverdance* in the 1990s are good examples of this symbiosis at work.

Much of what is thought of as Irish today is not new. It all has a history that reflects perceptions that have been developing for close to two

Figure C.1. This 1919 promotional brochure promised, "The songs of Ireland, famous for their plaintive sweetness, are presented by *The Colleens* as one of the features of an evening replete with interest and variety. *The Colleens* program opens with a village scene in Ireland, and the four young ladies who comprise the company are appropriately dressed in Irish costumes." Such entertainment foreshadows the twenty-first-century world tours of Celtic Woman. Credit: Redpath Chautauqua Collection, University of Iowa Libraries, Iowa City, Iowa.

centuries. The codes that visibly support consumption and particular genres of popular culture are not confined to them; they can be wielded politically and socially too. The equation of Irish with fun—a direct consequence of St. Patrick's Day—tempted Ireland's Bord Fáilte to tap the green space in 1989. A sophisticated and successful television ad proclaimed Ireland as the "ancient birthplace of good times" by using dreamy Irish scenery, New Age Celtic music, and a young girl with red hair, freckles, and a roguish smile. Ireland paid for and approved the ad, but its conception took place in the New York office of the Hill Holliday agency, and it debuted in the first commercial break during the Super Bowl, the nationally broadcast American football championship.[4] Although critics in Ireland protested its lack of realism, the advertisement won eight coveted industry awards, beating out corporate giants like American Express and American Airlines.[5] One New Yorker's attitude was both jaded and prescient: "Let's bury realism. We live in reality with all its pluses and minuses. Let the Irish tourism campaign have its fling with an appeal to the emotions of those far-flung descendants of Ireland who, while attracted by a campaign of castles and comely maidens, would not be at all disappointed by the reality of the beautiful, vibrant Ireland of the 1990s."[6]

Communicating a particular image like this has more utility for modern Ireland in the twenty-first century than it once had for its American diaspora. The historian Joe Lee sees the late twentieth century as a hinge moment for being Irish: "If identity increasingly depends on imagination rather than inheritance, how inheritance is used is critical to the nature of creativity."[7] This helps explain Killarney Town in Virginia, a simulation of Irish that met expectations just like the good times ad campaign. This modern iteration of the World's Fairs' Irish Villages is in the Europe theme park at Busch Gardens Williamsburg, formerly part of the entertainment division of Anheuser-Busch, brewers of Budweiser beer. During the creative process before opening day in 2001, Busch Gardens had a reciprocal relationship with officials from Killarney in County Kerry and hired Irish university students as summer workers. The result continues to be attractions like Castle O'Sullivan, Emerald Isle Gifts, Grogan's Pub and Grill, and the Abbey Stone Theatre, where the Celtic Fyre stage show features Irish music and step dancing.[8] For decades now, visitor presumptions about Irish have been confirmed by such hyperreality.

Indeed, what people think, or will think, is critical to image-making. Irish as a multidimensional discourse is now so elastic and time-tested that its historical, ethnic, racial, linguistic, religious, and cultural challenges have faded. Ireland, including Northern Ireland since 1998, and the United States also have the advantage of a positive political and economic relationship in recent decades.[9] This enables images made on both sides of the Atlantic to influence how people understand Irish around the world today. The takeaway is mixed: the duty-free store in Shannon Airport sells "Kiss Me, I'm Irish" buttons, "Luck of the Irish" magnets, and "Shamrock Boxer Shorts" next to its premium Irish whiskey display. Dublin's Guinness Storehouse and Titanic Belfast are major tourist attractions. Irish Americans a century ago would have been perplexed, but now they and others embrace these juxtapositions, as do the Irish in Ireland. Therefore, one cannot underestimate the green space; when Americans celebrate Cinco de Mayo or Lunar New Year, its dynamic expands and adapts not unlike how it did with St. Patrick's Day.[10] The green space is a portfolio easily accessed by those who create images, challenge them, remake them, co-opt or subvert them. What else, then, might be possible—and for whom?

ACKNOWLEDGMENTS

Gestation is invaluable to intellect and perseverance in a project such as this one. Family, friends, colleagues, and students have sustained and inspired me for many years. Everyone helped, for which I am most grateful, but I take the liberty of naming a few. My dear friends Linda Dowling Almeida, Miriam Nyhan Grey, and Barbara B. Haws are scholars who have been generous to me in ways too numerous to count. Peter Knapp's interest and help in the home stretch was critical, and his steadfastness in recent times was a godsend. I also thank Francis S. Casey Sr., Sean and Diana Casey, Hasia R. Diner, Maura A. Doherty, Virgina Ferris, Loretta Brennan Glucksman, Mary J. Hickman, John and Eileen Kennedy, Shafeez and Sharda Khan, J. J. Lee, Anjali Mehta, Timothy J. Meagher, Patrick J. Mullins, Cormac Ó Gráda, Cormac K. H. O'Malley, John T. Ridge, James S. Rogers, Robert J. Scally, Kelly Sullivan, Thomas M. Truxes, Sarah Waidler, Walter J. Walsh, Nicholas M. Wolf, and the Advisory Board and staff of Glucksman Ireland House. I could not have begun nor finished this book without you.

David M. Reimers came into my life at a key moment and has been a mentor whom I treasure for his kindness and erudition. His confidence in me was unfaltering. He perceptively read everything through multiple iterations and was patient while waiting to see this bound volume. I hope it makes him smile.

When Kevin Kenny left Boston College and came to New York University, it was a turning point for this book. He encouraged me to keep pen to paper with rallying advice, editorial skill, and warm friendship that will not be forgotten. I am thrilled to be published as part of the Glucksman Irish Diaspora series at New York University Press under the wing of Clara Platter and her team. This book is so much better because of input from two anonymous reviewers. I thank them for their time and insights, and I hope to shake their hands someday. For very skillful copyediting and patience, I am also grateful to Alvaro Estrada and everyone at Scribe Inc. Life interrupted a previous contract I once had with Johns Hopkins University Press, so I sincerely remember, with deep gratitude, Robert J. Brugger.

The work of the New York Irish History Roundtable and the Irish Institute of New York was always inspirational. Grants from the Irish American Cultural Institute, the Cushwa Center for the Study of American Catholicism at Notre Dame, and the Hagley Museum and Library enabled me to travel to visit collections in California, Delaware, and Wisconsin. I acknowledge all the archivists and librarians who have digitized material and made it available online. Research for a book like this was so much easier, especially during the pandemic, as a result of your efforts. For permission to publish images, I thank Lynne Swanson at Michigan State University Museum; Brad Ferrier at the University of Iowa, Special Collections & Archives; and Shannon O'Neill at the Tamiment Library, Special Collections, New York University.

Of course, nothing compares to listening to those who made things happen at the time. I was fortunate to learn so much from Dorothy Hayden Cudahy, Frank Durkan, Rosaleen Cahill Fitzgibbon, Rita McLaughlin Fitzpatrick, John Garvey, Joan Moriarty Gilroy, Mary McTaggart McMullan, Kathleen Mulvey (née Bergin), and Paul O'Dwyer. I would be remiss if I didn't acknowledge the prescient motivation to collect Irish Americana of Mick Moloney as well as the intellectual foresight of David N. Doyle, who originally pointed me in the direction of Irish American Studies. *Ar dheis Dé go raibh a n-anamacha.*

I wrote this book without a sabbatical. That meant the loss of precious family time. I thank them for understanding and always being there for me anyway, especially my beautiful mother and first teacher, Joan Dineen Casey; my first "book," Hannah Dineen Smith, who has lived with my piles of paper, folders, books, and Irish kitsch her entire life; and David Boldt Smith, who won't read this book but suggested a great title that I really couldn't use: *Erin Goes Braless*.

Bay Ridge, Brooklyn, New York, December 2023.

ABBREVIATIONS

- AIA: Archives of Irish America, Special Collections, Bobst Library, New York University
- AIHS: American Irish Historical Society
- AOH: Ancient Order of Hibernians
- BPL: Department of Rare Books and Manuscripts, Boston Public Library, Boston, MA
- DATI: Department of Agricultural and Technical Instruction for Ireland
- DIB: *Dictionary of Irish Biography*
- DORIS: Municipal Archives, Department of Records and Information Services, NY, NY
- FOIF: Friends of Irish Freedom
- GAA: Gaelic Athletic Association
- HAGLEY: Center for the History of Business, Technology, and Society, Hagley Museum & Library, Wilmington, DE
- IIDA: Irish Industrial Development Association
- ITA: Irish Tourist Association
- ITB: Irish Tourist Board
- LC: Library of Congress, Washington, DC
- MIA: *Making the Irish American: History and Heritage of the Irish in the United States*
- MPPDA: Motion Picture Producers and Distributors of America
- NA: National Archives, Washington, DC
- NAI: National Archives of Ireland, Dublin

NMAH: National Museum of American History, Smithsonian Institution, Washington, DC

NYPL: New York Public Library, NY, NY

NYSA, MPD: New York State Archives, Motion Picture Division, Albany, NY

NYU: New York University, NY, NY

TESS: Trademark Electronic Search System, United States Trademark and Patent Office

NOTES

INTRODUCTION

1. Sarah Burns, "Aran Jumper Chosen as World Fashion Icon," *Irish Times*, August 5, 2017, 2; Deirdre McQuillan, "From Mayo to MoMA: Iconic Aran Jumper Heads to New York: The Emblematic Piece of Irish Clothing Gets a Starring Role in a New Exhibition," *Irish Times*, August 22, 2017, 11.
2. "A particular set of cultural and economic pressures has rapidly transnationalized Irishness" and made it "a form of discursive currency" involving a wide "variety of heritage narratives and commercial transactions." Negra, *Irish in Us*, 1. See also Negra, "Consuming Ireland," 76–97.
3. Trade card for Schultz's Irish Soap, circa 1870, Calvert Lithographing Co. (Detroit, MI), in American Broadsides and Ephemera, series 1, no. 29551 (American Antiquarian Society and NewsBank, Inc., 2005). An alternative version (AIA31.004, M20) is in the Mick Moloney Collection of Irish-American Music and Popular Culture, Archives of Irish America, Special Collections, Bobst Library, New York University (hereafter Moloney, AIA). On Irish Spring, see Negra, "Consuming Ireland," 83–88.
4. O'Barr, "Brief History of Advertising," 15.
5. Ruffins, Calafell, O'Barr, Tchen, Ng, and Mak, "Roundtable Issue"; Halter, *Shopping for Identity*; Gambrinus advertisement, *Irish Voice*, March 17, 1998, 85; Casey, "'Best Kept Secret,'" 84–109; Rains, "Celtic Kitsch," 52–57.
6. Maureen O'Hara, box 1, folder 3, Sandra & Gary Baden Collection of Celebrity Endorsements in Advertising (#611), Advertising, Marketing, and Commercial Imagery Collections, NMAH, Smithsonian.
7. Kimball, "Replicating Authenticity."
8. Cronin and O'Connor, *Irish Tourism*; Negra, *Irish in Us*; Rains, *Irish-American*; Clancy, *Brand New Ireland?*; Barton, *Screening Irish-America*; Dowd, *Irish and the Origins*. See also essays by Edward Hagan, Stephanie Rains, and James Rogers in Rogers and O'Brien, *After the Flood*. Important exceptions are Meagher, "Abie's Irish Enemy," 45–60; Kibler, "Paddy, Shylock, and Sambo," 259–80. Compare their approach with that of Lloyd, *Ireland after History*; Negra, "Consuming Ireland"; Rains, "Celtic Kitsch"; Negra, *Off-White Hollywood*, 25–54; and Casey, "Riverdance," 9–25.
9. Most recent scholarship in American studies, performance studies, and cultural studies, by contrast, has tied "Irishness" to self-identification by Irish Americans, using a number of older theoretical frameworks: cultural hegemony, invented traditions, the invention of ethnicity, imagined communities, symbolic ethnicity, ethnic options, and semiotics. Those popular theorists are Gramsci, *Selections from the*

Prison; Hobsbawm and Ranger, *Invention of Tradition*; Sollors, *Invention of Ethnicity*; Anderson, *Imagined Communities*; Gans, "Symbolic Ethnicity," 1–20; Waters, *Ethnic Options*; Barthes, *Semiotic Challenge*; and Baudrillard, *Consumer Society*.

10 Lee and Casey, *Making the Irish American*, 691 (hereafter *MIA*); "Happy St. Patrick's Day," United States Census Bureau, accessed May 28, 2023, www.census.gov.
11 Such leprechaun costumes are sold in Ireland by Carrolls Irish Gifts (www.carrolls irishgifts.com) and in the United States by Oriental Trading (www.orientaltrading .com) among others. Accessed October 15, 2022.
12 Andrew M. Greeley, "The Last of the American Irish Fade Away," *New York Times*, March 14, 1971, SM32.
13 "Pioneering Marketer in US Committed to Irish Roots: Michael J Roarty," *Irish Times*, April 27, 2013, 12; Nigel Brown, "US Brewery Takes over Irish Derby Sponsorship," *Irish Times*, October 5, 1985, 1; "Derby Extends Deal with Dubai Duty Free," *Sport for Business*, January 31, 2018, accessed October 15, 2022, https:// sportforbusiness.com.
14 Oboler, *Ethnic Labels, Latino Lives*, 2.
15 "St. Patrick's Festival, Dublin, Ireland," accessed May 25, 2023, https://stpatricks festival.ie.
16 Miriam Lord, "Natives Join New Irish in Jamboree of Silly Hats," *Irish Times*, March 19, 2007, 7.

1. VESTED INTERESTS

1 Kenny, *American Irish*, 7.
2 Miller et al., *Irish Immigrants*, 268; Truxes, *Defying Empire*; Doyle, "Irish in North America," in *MIA*, 171–83.
3 Carter, "'Wild Irishman,'" 178–89.
4 Casey, "Limits of Equality," 45–49.
5 Miller, "Ulster Presbyterians," in *MIA*, 255–60.
6 Blessing, "Irish in America," table 1, 454.
7 Quoted in Casey, "Limits of Equality," 49.
8 Knobel, *Paddy and the Republic*; Curtis, *Apes and Angels*. Quotes are from Phelim Lynch, editor of the *Irish American*, letters to the *New York Times*, April 28, 1853, 8; August 30, 1854, 2.
9 Williams, *'Twas Only an Irishman's Dream*, 40–42.
10 Blessing, "Irish in America," table 1, 454.
11 Schrier, *Ireland and the American Emigration*, 111. On remittances in general, see Schrier's chapter 6. Also Marion R. Casey, "Friends in Need: Financing Emigration from Ireland—the Irish Emigrant Society and the Emigrant Industrial Savings Bank," *Seaport: New York's History Magazine*, May 1996, 30–33; Ridge, "Irish County Societies," 286–89.
12 "First- and Second-Generation Irish in the United States, by Region and State, According to the Census of 1890," in *MIA*, table 1, 689.
13 Doyle, "Irish as Urban Pioneers," 36–59.

14 Barrett, *Irish Way*; Bayor and Meagher, *New York Irish*; Meagher, *Inventing Irish America*; Meagher, *From Paddy to Studs*; McCaffrey, Skerrett, Funchion, and Fanning, *Irish in Chicago*; Skerrett, *Irish Parish in Chicago*; McMahon, *What Parish Are You?*; O'Connor, *Boston Irish*; Clark, *Irish in Philadelphia*; Thernstrom, *Other Bostonians*; Vinyard, *Irish on the Urban Frontier*; Mitchell, *Paddy Camps*; Byron, *Irish America*; Kelly, *Shamrock and the Lily*.

15 Doyle, "Remaking of Irish America," in *MIA*, 213–52; Greeley, "Success and Assimilation," 229–36.

16 O'Riordan, *Catholicity and Progress*, 292, quoted in Fitzpatrick, "Emigration, 1871–1921," 637.

17 "We Never Looked Back," *Irish Echo*, February 7, 1987, 17.

18 Ó Cadhain, *Road to Brightcity*, 33; Whelan, "'Idea of America,'" 76–81.

19 "Irish-Born for Selected Years in Fifteen Cities of Largest Irish Population in 1890," in Blessing, "Irish in America," table 2, 460.

20 Binder, Reimers, and Snyder, *All the Nations*; Barrett, *Irish Way*; McMahon, *What Parish Are You?*; McGreevy, *Parish Boundaries*.

21 Greeley, *Why Can't They Be?*, 30–31.

22 Golden, preface to Hapgood, *Spirit of the Ghetto*, ix; Barrett and Roediger, "Irish and the 'Americanization,'" 3–33.

23 Doyle, *Irish Americans, Native Rights*, 62; McNickle, "When New York Was Irish," 342.

24 Hayes won the marathon and Sheridan won the discus throw at the 1908 Olympic Games. In his brief athletic career (he died at the age of thirty-seven), Sheridan competed in three Olympics, winning five gold, three silver, and one bronze medals. Roger D. McGrath, "The Irish Olympics: Running Rings 'round the Empire," *Irish America Magazine*, September 1988, 38–42; James S. Mitchel, "The Celt as a Baseball Player," *The Gael*, May 1902, 151–55.

25 "Irish in America for Period Indicated or at the End of Decade Indicated," in Blessing, "Irish in America," table 1, 454; Lee, "Emigration: 1922–1998," 263–66; Lambert, "Irish Women's Emigration," 181–87; Almeida, *Irish Immigrants*, 23, 25.

26 Kennedy, "Irish Free State," 134.

27 *Cork Weekly Examiner* quoted in *Literary Digest*, February 28, 1925, 20; Whelan, "'Idea of America,'" 76–81.

28 Based on a survey of advertisements in the oldest extant copy of the *Irish Echo*, November 30, 1929, AIA.

29 Rates are based on a sample of display ads from the *New York Times* for 1892 and 1911; the *Irish World*, March 13, 1926; and *Old Castle Garden*, March 1931, June 1931, March 1938, and September 1939. Quote from Flood Travel Agency advertisement, *Gaelic American*, June 15, 1929.

30 Quoted in Almeida, *Irish Immigrants*, 26; "Irish Emigration," *Chicago Tribune*, November 5, 1949, 10.

31 Brown, *Ireland*, 184; Whelan, "'Idea of America,'" 80–81; William P. Clancy, "Not 'Going My Way,'" *New York Times*, January 3, 1954, BR26; O'Brien, *Vanishing Irish*; Daly, *Slow Failure*, 179–82.

32 Between 1941 and 1950, 26,967 emigrated from Ireland to the United States, then 57,332 between 1951 and 1960. See Blessing, "The Irish," table 1, 528.
33 "Irish Emigration," *Chicago Tribune*, November 5, 1949, 10.
34 O'Brien, "Wartime Revisions," 95; Herbert L. Matthews, "Population Drop Alarms the Irish," *New York Times*, July 28, 1956, 19.
35 Hamill, "Once We Were Kings," in *MIA*, 528–29.
36 The Anglo-Irish Treaty was signed on December 6, 1921, and ratified January 7, 1922. The British formally recognized the Irish Free State on December 6, 1922.
37 Nash, "'Embodying the Nation,'" 86; Rockett, "Documentaries," 73.
38 Arensberg's work was part of a Harvard anthropological study that was approved by the Irish Free State. "Harvard Anthropological Survey," 482; Arensberg, *Irish Countryman*; Arensberg and Kimball, *Family and Community*; *Man of Aran*, dir. Robert Flaherty (Gaumont-British Picture Corporation, 1934).
39 Miller, "Assimilation and Alienation," 88.
40 Ní Bhroiméil, *Building Irish Identity*; Brown, *Ireland*, 84.
41 Gronow, "Ethnic Recordings," 13.
42 Almeida, "Great Time to Be Irish," 206–20; Nyhan, "Comparing Irish Migrants"; Nyhan, "County Associations," 27–36.
43 Casey, "Keeping the Tradition Alive," 24–30; Miller, "Irish Traditional and Popular," 481–507. Quote is from *From Shore to Shore: Irish Traditional Music in New York City*, dir. Patrick J. Mullins (New York: Cherry Lane Productions, 1993).
44 In the decade from 1930 to 1940, the circulation of these newspapers went from 80,000 to 100,000 for *The Irish World*; 33,000 to 60,000 for *The Gaelic American*; and 29,350 to 43,000 for *The Irish Advocate*. Circulation figures are from Ayer, *American Newspaper Annual and Directory* (1930, 1935, 1940). *The Irish Echo* is not listed in this source.
45 As the population of New York City increased from three to eight million, the number of Irish-born in the city dropped from 275,102 to 114,008. This is consistent with the drop in the number of all foreign-born in the city's population, which decreased from an estimated 37 percent in 1900 to 20 percent in 1960. The percentages are based on 275,102 of 1,615,459 in 1900 and 114,008 of 338,722 in 1960. See tables 2 and 3 in Blessing, "The Irish," 528, 531; and Bayor and Meagher, *New York Irish*, table A.1, 551. The city's population increased from 3,437,202 in 1900 to 7,781,984 in 1960. Salvo and Lobo, "Population," 1019.
46 P. J. Drudy, "Population Change," in Drudy, *Irish in America*, 76; C. Robertson, "Irish Occupations & Professions, including Statistics" (1937), box 3579, folder 5, "Occupations and Locations," 14, in *WPA Historical Records Survey: Federal Writers Project, "Irish in New York,"* Municipal Archives, Department of Records and Information Services, New York City (hereafter DORIS).
47 Shelley, "Twentieth-Century American Catholicism," in *MIA*, 575–90.
48 Doyle, *Irish Americans, Native Rights*, 6–7, 12, 15, 18, 342–45. There were 201 English-language Catholic periodicals published in the United States in 1911. Meehan, "Periodical Literature."

49 The timing of this phenomenon is interesting considering retention theories about ethnic identity and its reduction to symbolism the further one is removed from the immigrant generation. See Alba, *Ethnic Identity*, 76–77; Gans, "Symbolic Ethnicity"; Waters, *Ethnic Options*; Kennedy, "Irish Free State," 132–52.
50 "Poetical Works of Thomas Moore," 135.
51 Cohen, *Making a New Deal*, 100–155.
52 "Race of Hibernian Cooks and Housemaids Will Soon Be Extinct," *New York Daily Tribune*, September 18, 1905, 5.
53 Dell, "Representation of the Immigrant," 115–221.
54 Miller, "Assimilation and Alienation," 89; Doyle, *Irish Americans, Native Rights*, 46.
55 Rowland, "Irish-American Catholics," 3–31; McDannell, "'True Men,'" 19–36.
56 Moynihan, "The Irish," in *MIA*, 493.
57 Drudy, "Irish Population Change," 73.
58 Olcott, Graff, and Ball, *When Irish Eyes*; Weatherly, *Danny Boy*; Young, Olcott, and Ball, *Mother Machree*; Shannon, *Too-Ra-Loo-Ra-Loo-Ral*.
59 "Press: Jiggs and Maggie," *Time*, February 1932, 26.
60 Zim, Lerner, and Rolfes, *World of Tomorrow*; "Ireland Express Pride in Fair Role," *New York Times*, May 14, 1939, 40. "Special Irish Air Liner Leaves New York with Mayor Wagner Aboard," Aerlinte Eireann–Aer Lingus press release, April 24, 1958, part of a press kit for the inaugural flights between Dublin and New York (photocopy in possession of the author, courtesy of the late Liam Dunphy).
61 O'Neill, "Star-Spangled Shamrock," 118–38.
62 John F. Kennedy, "Address before the Irish Parliament," Dublin, Ireland, June 28, 1963, John F. Kennedy Presidential Library and Museum, accessed May 29, 2023, www.jfklibrary.org.
63 "Ireland: New Spirit in the Ould Sod," *Time*, July 12, 1963, 37.

2. MEDIA MATTERS

1 Muriel Sperry, "Try Your Hap against the Irishmen," *Atlantic Monthly*, August 1934, 167–68; Seaburg, "Learned Minister at Harvard," 181–82.
2 Emery and Emery, *Press and America*, 323, 330.
3 Chase, *New York 1932*, 11–12.
4 Emery and Emery, *Press and America*, 320, 377. See U.S. Station Information in Key, *Pierre Key's Radio Annual*, 22, 277–309. A 1938 Gallup poll estimated that 77 percent of American families owned radios. Gallup, *Gallup Poll*, 129.
5 Doorley, *Irish-American Diaspora Nationalism*, 17–20; Brundage, *Irish Nationalists in America*; Carroll, "Collapse of Home Rule," 31–42; Janis, *Greater Ireland*.
6 Roberts *Ireland in America*, 197; Mugridge, *View from Xanadu*, 34–36.
7 Gavan, "Old Fenians," 19–20; Clarke, *My Life and Memories*; Cummins, *My Irish Colleagues*; Blair, "Newsreel Politics," 59–70.
8 Doorley, *Irish-American Diaspora Nationalism*, 30–31.

9. John V. Kelleher, "Ireland . . . and Where Does She Stand?," *Foreign Affairs*, April 1957, 485; Marion R. Casey, "Ireland in Arms and America's Reaction," *Irish Echo*, April 17–23, 1991, 33.
10. Doorley, *Irish-American Diaspora Nationalism*, 83, 93. See also Hannigan, *De Valera in America*.
11. Copies of these radio addresses are in the Nation's Forum Collection at the Library of Congress and can be heard online as part of the American Memory Historical Collection "American Leaders Speak: Recordings from World War I and the 1920 Election, 1918–1920," accessed May 30, 2023, http://memory.loc.gov.
12. Lewis S. Gannett, "The Nation and Ireland," *The Nation*, January 31, 1942, 125.
13. The subject has been covered by Buckley, *New York Irish*; Carroll, *American Opinion*; Ward, *Ireland and Anglo-American*.
14. White and Rouse, "Francis Hackett," in *Dictionary of Irish Biography* (hereafter *DIB*).
15. See dedication to Swopes in Hackett, *Story of the Irish Nation*; for *Washington Post* coverage, see February 5, 9, 12, and 26, 1922.
16. Gaughan, *Memoirs of Senator Joseph*, 233, 239; *The Nation*, March 22, 1922, 343; Gibney, "Occupation of the Irish Consulate," 323–28.
17. *The Irish Press*, founded in Philadelphia by Joseph McGarrity to support the Irish War of Independence, was only published from March 23, 1918, to May 6, 1922.
18. Doorley, *Irish-American Diaspora Nationalism*, 37, 151.
19. Golway, *Irish Rebel*, 298–301.
20. Éamon de Valera to Arthur Griffith, February 17, 1920, quoted in Davis, "Éamon de Valera's Political Education," 75.
21. William T. Cosgrave, "Backbone of the Irish Revolt Broken," *Chicago Tribune*, February 26, 1923, 12.
22. Emery and Emery, *Press and America*, 282.
23. Foreign Office minute, May 25, 1920, cited in Hachey, *Britain and Irish Separatism*, 24.
24. "De Valera Visit Recalls Scoop by Tribune Man," *Chicago Tribune*, March 18, 1948, 12.
25. O'Drisceoil, *Censorship in Ireland*, 204.
26. Ayer, *American Newspaper Annual* (1930). Much of the following discussion of Irish subjects covered by New York City newspapers is based, for convenience's sake, on a survey of the *New York Times Index* for the years 1920 to 1950 and supplemented by ProQuest Historical Newspaper searches. While their editorial positions on Ireland may have been different, it is likely that all the newspapers picked up the same Irish news from the press associations.
27. Conklin, "Chicago Tribune," 94.
28. "Irish Difficulties," *New York Times*, January 31, 1925, 12.
29. "Scores Irish Famine Tales," *New York Times*, February 14, 1925, 5. Also *New York Times*, February 1, 1925, 5; February 18, 1925, 18; March 20, 1925, 21.
30. *Chicago Tribune*, January 31, 1925, 4; and February 2, 1925, 14.
31. Cronin, *McGarrity Papers*, 75. For more details on the Irish Bond Drive, see Carroll, *America and the Making*, 64–81; Carroll, *Money for Ireland*; Macardle, *Irish Republic*, 986–87.

32 For details on de Valera's time in the United States and on his fundraising efforts there, see McCartan, *With De Valera*; Tansill, *America and the Fight*; O'Doherty, *Assignment America*; Hannigan, *De Valera in America*; Sullivan, "Éamon de Valera," 98–115.
33 *New York Times*, February 10, 1929, 1; December 20, 1932, 1; March 28, 1935, 1; *Christian Science Monitor*, May 12, 1927, 4B.
34 "There was a growing impatience with the continuation of fighting in Ireland and Irish-American clamour in the United States. . . . Americans had little interest in the intricacies of Irishmen fighting among themselves." Carroll, *American Opinion*, 189.
35 John J. McCarthy, "The Irish Sweeps," *Harper's*, June 1934, 50, 57. At the time, *Harper's* circulation was approximately 100,000.
36 McCarthy, "Irish Sweeps," 58; "Americans Win Fortunes" and "Irish Hospital Sweepstakes," *Newsweek*, November 4, 1933, 16; and November 10, 1934, 19; "Dublin and Other Lotteries," *Fortnightly Review*, October 1932, 519–22. See also the *New York Times*, 1931, 1934–40, 1949 (2 articles), and 1950 (5 articles). The 1931 draw had a turnover of nearly £3 million, "the biggest lottery in the world." Gray, *Ireland This Century*, 117.
37 *Good Housekeeping*, March 1934, 34; "*Sweepstakes*, Columbia Workshop," CBS (October 31, 1937), and "Town Hall Tonight," NBC Red (March 30, 1938), Fred Allen Papers, MS. 2033, box 72, folder 1, Boston Public Library (hereafter Allen, BPL); also Rockett, *Irish Filmography*, 349; and *Cinema Pressbooks from the Original Studio Collections of United Artists (1919–1949), Warner Brothers (1922–1949), and Monogram Pictures (1937–1946)* (Woodbridge, CT: Research Publications and the Wisconsin Center for Film and Theater Research, 1988) (hereafter *Cinema Pressbooks*), part 1, reel 16, "Sweepstakes Winner."
38 A 1938 Gallup poll found that 51 percent of Americans thought that "government lotteries would produce an unwholesome gambling spirit in this country." Survey #119-A, May 18, 1938. Gallup, *Gallup Poll*, 103.
39 Coleman, "Irish Hospitals Sweepstake," 220–37; Corless, *Greatest Bleeding Hearts Racket*, 62–74.
40 Page 1 stories appeared in the *New York Times* on March 17, 19, 23, 24, 25, 28, 31, and April 1, 12, 13, 17, 18, 25, 28, 29, 30. The feature articles ran in part 5 on April 3 and May 1. There were editorials on February 29 and May 15. The *Chicago Tribune* ran stories on page 1 on March 17, 21, 23, 24, 27; others were progressively deeper inside the paper.
41 NBC radio "broadcast seven consecutive hours of live coverage of the coronation ceremonies of George VI" on May 12, 1937. MacDonald, *Don't Touch That Dial!*, 300. Not surprisingly, 25 percent of Americans named the Windsor marriage as the most interesting event of 1937. Survey #105, December 26, 1937, Gallup, *Gallup Poll*, 80. For the foreign policy aspects of this period, see Whelan, *De Valera and Roosevelt*.
42 Not to be confused with the Christian Front, an American organization, although its purpose was anti-communist too.
43 Cronin, *McGarrity Papers*, 162; *Chicago Tribune*, January 18, 1939, and January 19, 1939.

44 "De Valera was regularly taunted with reneging on his own earlier persona." Lee, *Ireland, 1912–1985*, 223; "De Valera Asks Dictator Power; Fears Uprising," *Chicago Tribune*, January 3, 1940, 6.

45 Andrew Bushe, "Diplomatic Uproar over Insulting NBC Radio Play," *Irish Echo*, January 17, 1996, 7.

46 De Valera's February 1939 announcement that Ireland would try to remain neutral during the European hostilities was on page 6. *New York Times*, February 23, 1939, 12. For comparison, when Ireland recognized Franco's authoritarian government in Spain it was reported on page 3 of the February 13, 1939, edition.

47 Raymond J. Raymond, "The Marshall Plan and Ireland, 1947–1952," in Drudy, *Irish in America*, 297.

48 Hanley, "'No English Enemy,'" 245–64. The subject has been covered by Dwyer, *Irish Neutrality*; Cronin, *Washington's Irish Policy*; Fisk, *In Time of War*; Kennedy, *Ireland and the League*; Raymond, "David Gray," 55–71; Davis, *Dublin's American Policy*; Wills, *That Neutral Island*; O'Halpin, *Spying on Ireland*; Quigley, *U.S. Spy in Ireland*.

49 Raymond, "American Public Opinion," 26.

50 O'Hara and Nicoletti, *'Tis Herself*, 63.

51 Raymond, 28–29, 35. Some smaller magazines were also less circumspect; for example, "Myopia in Éire," *Living Age*, December 1940, 304–5.

52 Dwyer, *Irish Neutrality*, 118–27, 134–37; Dwyer, *Strained Relations*, 190–95; O'Drisceoil, *Censorship in Ireland*, 207; Davis, "'Irish Movement,'" 39–40.

53 For example, the NBC Blue network broadcast a report from Dublin by Dennis Johnson on Ireland's "refusal to fight against the Nazis." July 5, 1940, NBC Radio Collection, Library of Congress (hereafter LC).

54 "Irish Americans Want Éire Ports Open to Britain," *Chicago Tribune*, March 10, 1941, 2; Dwyer, "American Friends of Irish," 36–37.

55 Published on January 13, 1941; February 22, 1942; January 8, 1943; April 5, 1944; and April 22, 1944. Historians have also frequently conflated the vocal Irish American societies with "Irish America" and their passionate Irish nationalism with Irish American identity. The problem is (1) generally an overreliance on the *Gaelic American* and *Irish World* as fully representative source material even though the *Irish Advocate* and *Irish Echo* are also on microfilm and (2) an interpretation of Irish American nationalism that is overly colored by pre-1922 activism. Matthew O'Brien unfairly and simplistically characterizes post-1922 Irish advocates such as Paul O'Dwyer as "fractious and disreputable 'professional Irishmen'" who epitomized "the failure of isolationism and Anglophobia as the basis for Irish ethnicity in the U.S." O'Dwyer represented a generation of immigrants whose ethnic orientation was derived from independent Ireland and who were organized along distinctly different principles than the more Irish American members of the Ancient Order of Hibernians. See O'Brien, "Wartime Revisions," 77; and O'Brien, "'Hibernians on the March,'" 175.

56 "72% of Irish in U.S. Want Bases in Éire," *New York Times*, February 22, 1942, 12.

57 Survey #227-K, January 13, 1941, Gallup, *Gallup Poll*, 260.

58 "Would you like to see Éire let the Allies use war bases along the Irish coast?" Survey #260-K, February 22, 1942, Gallup, *Gallup Poll*, 323.
59 Aiken portrayed "neutrality as the 'crown & symbol' of Ireland's independence" in *American Magazine*, August 1941, cxxxii, cited in Rosenberg, "1941 Mission of Frank," 177. *American Magazine* circulation from Ayer, *American Newspaper Annual* (1940).
60 Dwyer, "American Friends of Irish," 36–37.
61 Cole, *Propaganda*, 66; Rosenberg, "1941 Mission of Frank," 169, 174–75. Thousands turned out for a New York rally to object to Colonel William J. Donovan's position on the use of Irish ports, and there were stories in the *New York Times*, November 24, 1941, 5; and the *Chicago Tribune*, November 24, 1941, 6.
62 Cole, *Propaganda*, 88. Circulation figures are from Ayer, *American Newspaper Annual*.
63 Cole, *Propaganda*, 106.
64 "U.S. Troops Land in a Trouble Spot," *New York Times*, January 27, 1942, 4; the Paramount newsreel is in the collection of the Motion Picture, Sound, and Video Branch, National Archives, Washington, DC (hereafter NA). See also Carroll, "United States Armed Forces," 15–36; Mary Pat Kelly, *Home Away from Home*; "Yanks in Ireland," *National Geographic*, August 1943. In contrast, Matthew O'Brien concluded that the February 1942 Gallup poll clearly indicated "willful blindness" about Irish neutrality among the Irish American community. O'Brien, "Wartime Revisions," 87.
65 On the propagandist wars around Ireland's various name changes in this period, see Daly, "Irish Free State / Éire," 72–90.
66 "Ireland: A New Flag Brings Hope to an Old and Pious Land," *Life*, July 24, 1939, 61.
67 Eithne Golden, "Ireland," *Life*, August 14, 1939, 2; Eithne Golden Saxe, November 2, 2006, Ireland House Oral History Collection (AIA.030), Archives of Irish America, Special Collections, Bobst Library, New York University (hereafter AIA).
68 William Bayles, "Report from Éire," *Reader's Digest*, March 1942, 78.
69 Bayles, "Report from Éire," 78–81.
70 *Reader's Digest* went from a circulation of three million in 1938 to nine million in 1946. Emery and Emery, *Press and America*, 343; Tebbel and Zuckerman, *Magazine in America*, 184–85.
71 Wills, *That Neutral Island*, 187; Ferriter, *Judging Dev*, 308; Gaughan, *Memoirs of Senator Joseph*, 284.
72 "Irish Spies Are Smiling," *Newsweek*, April 3, 1944, 44.
73 "Mr. De Valera's Neutrality," *New York Times*, March 12, 1944, IV, 8. The editorial is unsigned.
74 *New York Times*, March 25, 1934, IV, 3; March 17, 1937, 5; March 17, 1940, 43; March 18, 1946, 1; March 18, 1947, 9.
75 Survey #314-K, April 5, 1944, and #315-K, April 22, 1944, Gallup, *Gallup Poll*, 439, 442.
76 "Majority Favors More American Pressure to Force Éire to Send Away Axis Diplomats," *Washington Post*, April 5, 1944, 9.
77 "Talk of the Town: Neutral News," *New Yorker*, September 2, 1944, 13–14; Hanley, "'No English Enemy,'" 245–64.
78 Thomas Sugrue, "The Newsreels," *Scribner's Magazine*, April 1937, 9, 10, 14, 17.

79 The newsreels cited are all in the collection of the Motion Picture, Sound, and Video Branch, NA.
80 Kennedy, *Dreams and Responsibilities*, 52–53.
81 Ayer, *American Newspaper Annual* (1940); Raymond, "American Public Opinion," 31.
82 Anne O'Hare McCormick, "Abroad: Ireland Not Excited over Its Election," *New York Times*, December 31, 1947, 14. A *New York Times* colleague preferred "confirmed Irish Puritan" for a 1946 book review headline; Richard Watt's review, however, noted that de Valera's "case is almost never presented with sympathy to the outside world." *New York Times*, October 27, 1946, 155.
83 Anne O'Hare McCormick, "Abroad: Éire Assumes a New Status in the World Community," *New York Times*, December 27, 1947, 12. Under the Marshall Plan, Ireland received $150 million.
84 "Irish Medal Goes to Mrs. M'Cormick," *New York Times*, May 8, 1949, 10. For biographical information on McCormick, see *Current Biography Yearbook*, 530–31; and her *New York Times* obituary, May 30, 1954, 1.
85 Raymond, "American League," 46–47; Marion R. Casey, "Irish," in Jackson, *Encyclopedia*, 659. At the time, the Irish government tried to distance itself from the subject of partition so that Marshall Plan funds would not be jeopardized. See Whelan, *Ireland and the Marshall*, 398.
86 "Brooke Opposes U.S. Action," *New York Times*, March 30, 1950, 11. On Brooke's visit as a British experiment to test the depth of Irish American support for partition, see Davis, "'Irish Movement,'" 46.
87 "U.S. House Action Delights Ireland," *New York Times*, March 31, 1950, 18.
88 *New York Times*, March 18, 1950, 30; Sarro, "William O'Dwyer," 30.
89 *New York Times*, March 9, 1948, 1. In an editorial that was atypical for a newspaper in a major Irish American urban center, the *Tribune* called O'Dwyer a "professional Irishman" and suggested that the place for people "wrapped up" in partition was "back in Éire." "A Guest of Chicago," *Chicago Tribune*, May 4, 1950, 20. Davis reports that the British Ambassador to Washington thought this editorial was "remarkable." Davis, "'Irish Movement,'" 49.
90 Marion R. Casey, "American-Irish Men Picket, 1950," AIA, accessed May 31, 2023, https://digitaltamiment.hosting.nyu.edu.
91 "Irish Picket Ulster Premier on His Arrival at Idlewild," *New York Times*, April 7, 1950, 1. Relying solely on the archives of the British Foreign Office, Troy Davis has unconditionally accepted the British interpretation of this protest as "a handful of demonstrators." Davis, "'Irish Movement,'" 48. Davis also underestimates the seriousness and commitment of the participants. See the videotaped recollections of the picket by Kathleen Mulvey and Dorothy Hayden Cudahy in the documentary short *New York Stories* (produced and directed by Marion R. Casey for AIA, 2000), accessed May 31, 2023, https://vimeo.com/269261270.
92 Casey, "American-Irish Men Picket."
93 O'Dwyer, *Counsel for the Defense*, 173. O'Dwyer advised Chicago politicians to make no arrangements to welcome Brooke, since the Illinois State Legislature had

condemned partition in 1949. "Deny Any Plans to Snub North Ireland Leader," *Chicago Tribune*, April 11, 1950, A7.

94   This culminated in the media wars surrounding the representation of the 1981 Hunger Strikes in the United States. See *1981 Hunger Strike: America Reacts* (curated by Marion R. Casey, Meaghan Dwyer, and Katie Senft for AIA, 2001), accessed May 31, 2023, https://gih.hosting.nyu.edu/hungerstrikes.

95   The following discussion of American magazine coverage of Ireland is based on a survey of the *Reader's Guide Retrospective* database (H. W. Wilson Company, 2010). The chronological breakdown of feature articles on Ireland by date range/period is as follows: 1890–1915 Home Rule (1,470); 1916–22 Revolution & War (766); 1923–32 Irish Free State (393); 1932–49 de Valera, WWII, and Republic (537); 1950–63 Post-War and JFK (350). The total for 1890–1963 is 3,516 articles. According to Tebbel and Zuckerman, magazine content for the mass market was primarily information, entertainment, escape, and opinion formation at this time. *Magazine in America*, 190.

96   During the 1930s, *Time* did nine articles on the IRA (mostly on its bombing campaign in England), while *Newsweek* printed six on the same subject. This greatly pleased the Philadelphia-based Clan na Gael leader Joseph McGarrity, who, in 1939, recalled that "the action of the [Irish Republican] Army after all was the newsmaker" and "even *Time*, the weekly magazine, has taken the Army to its bosom as it were." Cronin, *McGarrity Papers*, 169–70. The *Chicago Tribune* published three stories on the detention by U.S. authorities of IRA leader Seán Russell on June 4, 6, and 7, 1939.

97   Herbert L. Matthews, "The Partition of Ireland," *Harper's*, August 1948, 108, 113, 114.

98   Matthews, 109, 111.

99   "'Home Town' Greets de Valera with Parade, City Hall Reception," *New York Times*, March 10, 1948, 1.

100   Survey #446-K, August 14, 1949, Gallup, *Gallup Poll*, 851–52. Fred Allen's show, which from 1942 included the "Allen's Alley" sketch, "attracted a weekly audience of three out of four radio households." Taylor, *Fred Allen*, 16–17. Fred Allen's name at birth was John Florence Sullivan.

101   Morton Downey (1901–85) was a popular singer/actor at the time known as the "Irish Nightingale." Jackson, Markoe, and Markoe, *Scribner Encyclopedia*, s.v. "Morton Downey," 242–43.

102   "Main Street Walk—Ajax Cassidy Stop," Fred Allen Papers, MS.2033, box 75, folder 25 (transcript for April 24, 1949), Allen, BPL. Ajax Cassidy was a regular character, described by Allen's biographer as a "bibulous Irish coot."

103   "Reeks from the Reeks," *Time*, December 28, 1942, 74; and "A Hanging in Belfast," *Time*, September 14, 1942, 30. These examples are characteristic of *Time*'s "brash, idiosyncratic style" and "obvious political biases." Tebbel and Zuckerman, *Magazine in America*, 174.

104   Robert Shaplen, "Letter from Dublin," *New Yorker*, June 14, 1952, 85.

105   George Brett Jr. to Stephen Gwynn, August 29, 1923; and Stephen Gwynn to George Brett Jr., May 13, 1925, box 75, Macmillan Company Records, New York Public Library (hereafter Macmillan, NYPL).

106 Stephen Gwynn to George Brett Jr., October 15, 1923; and George Brett Jr. to Stephen Gwynn, October 31, 1924, box 75, Macmillan, NYPL.
107 Stephen Gwynn to George Brett Jr., October 15, 1923, box 75, Macmillan, NYPL.
108 Stephen Gwynn, "A Decade of Ireland," *Living Age*, May 15, 1926. During the 1930s, Gwynn published five articles on Ireland in the *Fortnightly Review*, plus pieces in *Foreign Affairs*, *Living Age*, and *Current History*. He also wrote for the *New York Times* in 1932, summing up Ireland's first decade as a Free State under President Cosgrave's administration.
109 After *Angela's Ashes* (Frank McCourt, 1996) and *Let the Great World Spin* (Colum McCann, 2009) won the Pulitzer Prize and National Book Award, respectively, both authors stepped into a similar role as the go-to commentator on both Ireland and Irish America. The choice of writers like McCourt and McCann rather than, for example, an historian or sociologist was predetermined by the legacy created between journalism and Irish literary culture at the beginning of the twentieth century.
110 "Heyday of Short Story Writers; Prices Fabulous to Old Timers," *Chicago Tribune*, June 4, 1911, B4; Meehan, "Seumas MacManus," in *DIB*; Cusack, "'Seanachie to the New World,'" 1–26.
111 Promotional brochure, "Sixth American Lecture Tour of Seumas MacManus," *Travelling Culture: Circuit Chautauqua in the Twentieth Century*, Iowa Digital Library, accessed May 31, 2023, http://digital.lib.uiowa.edu/tc/; biographical sketch in Kunitz and Haycraft, *Junior Book of Authors*, 244–45; "Seamus [sic] MacManus Gives Interesting Lecture," *Notre Dame Scholastic* 68, no. 11 (December 7, 1934): 2.
112 "Seumas MacManus Lectures," *Irish American*, March 22, 1913, 4.
113 In November 1912, he presented "Rollicking Ramble in Ireland" [sic] to the National Geographic Society in Washington, DC, where their president was smitten by MacManus's personality, "which breathes the spirit of Ireland itself, with its humor, its naivete and its mysticism." "Sixth American Lecture Tour," *Travelling Culture*. "No Real Promise of Home Rule, Declares Seumas MacManus, Irish Writer," *New York Times*, December 12, 1909, C5; "Seumas MacManus Sees Gain by Dublin Shooting," *Washington Post*, August 3, 1914, 9; "Seumas MacManus Gives Out Statement on Conditions in Ireland," *Chicago Tribune*, July 19, 1915, 3; "New Reign of Terror in Ireland Owing to Drastic Measures Taken, Says Seumas MacManus, Novelist," *Washington Post*, August 15, 1915, R11; "Erin in Uproar against Britain; Seumas MacManus Gives Out Statement on Conditions in Ireland," *Chicago Tribune*, July 19, 1915, 3.
114 Seumas MacManus, "The Birth of Sinn Féin by One Who Was There," *New York Times*, February 2, 1919, 68; Meehan, "Seumas MacManus," in *DIB*.
115 Strand, "W. B. Yeats's American Lecture," Appendix I: Itineraries, 239–49.
116 Charlotte Canning, "What Was Chautauqua?" (December 2000), University of Iowa Libraries Special Collections, accessed May 31, 2022, www.lib.uiowa.edu/sc/tc. Among the other speakers on the circuit who had contemporary Ireland and the Irish in their repertoire were Gertrude M. O'Reilly, Gabriel Reid Maguire, and H. G. Scott.
117 Canning, "What Was Chautauqua?"

118 Strand, "W. B. Yeats's American Lecture," 247.
119 "Death of Padraic Colum at 90," *Irish Times*, January 12, 1972; "Lee Keedick Presents Padraic Colum," *Travelling Culture*, promotional brochure (1924), Iowa Digital Library, accessed May 31, 2023, https://digital.lib.uiowa.edu.
120 Colum, *Life and the Dream*, 238; Padraic Colum, "The Trouble with Ireland," *New Orleans Item*, June 25, 1916, 50; and *Washington Post*, June 22, 1916, 7.
121 Ayer, *American Newspaper Annual*, vol. 2 (1916), 1192, UNT Digital Library, University of North Texas, accessed July 18, 2016, http://digital.library.unt.edu/; *Watertown Daily Times*, September 9, 1916, 6.
122 Murray, "Padraic Colum," 104–23.
123 Padraic Colum to George Brett Jr., April 26, 1933, box 67, Macmillan, NYPL.
124 "Mr. Colum on Mr. [Bennett] Cerf," Letters to the Editor, *Saturday Review of Literature*, January 29, 1944, 13.
125 B. W. Maxwell, April 23, 1953, box 67, Macmillan, NYPL. Ultimately, the manuscript was published in 1959 as *Ourselves Alone! The Story of Arthur Griffith and the Origin of the Irish Free State* in the United States and as *Arthur Griffith* in Ireland.
126 Harmon, "Seán O'Faolain," in *DIB*.
127 Ray C. B. Brown, "Seán Ó Faoláin's Novel Graces the Field," *Washington Post*, January 14, 1934, SM10; John Chamberlain, "Seán Ó Faoláin's Fine Tales of the Irish Rebellion," *New York Times*, March 27, 1932, BR7.
128 "Mr. Yeats at Seventy," *New York Times*, June 30, 1935, E8; "A Dublin Monument in Homage to AE," *New York Times*, October 6, 1935, 88; "St. Patrick's Day: Thoughts about Ireland," *New York Times Magazine*, March 11, 1956, 223–24; "Roger Casement," *American Mercury*, February 1936, 160–67; "How to Acquire a 'Brogue': Seán Ó Faoláin in the Commonweal," *Washington Post*, December 27, 1939, 6.
129 Seán Ó Faoláin, "An Unhappy Report from Ireland by an Irish Novelist," *New York Times*, October 10, 1948, BR3.
130 *Boston Globe*, July 24, 1949, A12; *Christian Science Monitor*, September 29, 1949, 15; Ó Faoláin, "Explanation," *The Irish*, x.
131 Orville Prescott, "Books of the Times," *New York Times*, August 1, 1949, 15.
132 Whelan, "Adopting the 'American Way,'" 30–33; Whelan, "Marshall Plan Publicity," 321–22.
133 R. M. Fox, "Censorship in Ireland," *The Nation*, May 8, 1929, 571.
134 Milton Marmor, "Ireland Stages Vigorous Drive to End Emigration," *Advocate*, March 15, 1954, 5; and *Milwaukee Journal-Sentinel*, March 14, 1954, 59.
135 Seán Ó Faoláin, "Love among the Irish: A Catholic Blames Celibacy and Censorship for Fostering Racial Decay in His Country," *Life*, March 16, 1953, 140–57; Brian Inglis, "The Vanishing Irish," *Spectator*, April 24, 1953, 9.
136 John P. Shanley, "TV: A Little Bit of Ireland," *New York Times*, January 30, 1961, 47; Savage, *Ireland in the New*, 155–62.
137 "Ireland Pushes Bid for Dollars: New Incentives and Larger Free-Trade Zone Offered to U.S. Investors," *New York Times*, March 12, 1958, 43; "Briscoe to Spearhead Irish Drive in U.S.," *Boston Herald*, March 9, 1958, 52; "Investments in Éire Urged,"

San Diego Union, June 8, 1951, 30; "Ireland to Seek American Capital," *Springfield Union*, June 26, 1955, 24.

138 "U.S., Ireland Sign Friendship Treaty," *New York Times*, January 22, 1950; Hugh G. Smith, "Dublin Welcomes Capital from U.S.," *New York Times*, February 7, 1950, 8; *Treaty Series 1950 No. 7 Treaty of Friendship, Commerce and Navigation, with Protocol, between Ireland and the United States of America* (Dublin: Department of Foreign Affairs and Trade, 1950), accessed May 31, 2023, www.dfa.ie.

139 "Ireland Not Stagnant, Poet Colum Reports," *Evening Star*, April 14, 1959, A16.

140 Leo Sullivan, "Such Was Ireland in Her 'Troubles,'" *Washington Post*, June 10, 1959, D7. Emphasis in original.

141 "Terror of Irish Student Unwillingly Drawn into Revolution Is Depicted," *Dallas Morning News*, February 4, 1934, III, 13; "Cagney Film Made in Ireland," *Boston Globe*, July 26, 1959, A5.

142 John Beaufort, "'Shake Hands with the Devil' Arrives on Orpheum Screen," *Christian Science Monitor*, August 5, 1959, 5; Amy Loveman, "The Clearing House," *Saturday Review of Literature*, July 21, 1934, 15; "Cagney Irish Rebel in Film at Delman," *Dallas Morning News*, September 10, 1959, 10; "Irish Film Tells Story of Rebels," *Richmond Times Dispatch*, June 12, 1959, 28; "Movie Pushed by Producers," *Times-Picayune*, May 6, 1959, 24.

143 "Cagney Film Made in Ireland," *Boston Globe*, July 26, 1959, A5; "All-Ireland Picture Producers to Visit," *Dallas Morning News*, April 23, 1959, 26; Rockett, "Irish Cinema," 23.

144 "Big screen success eclipsed the fact that the novel had been banned by the Irish Censor in 1934, a convenient anomaly for the studio's pre-release publicity in 1959." *Trenton Evening Times*, April 10, 1959, 26; "Irish Books Banned under the Censorship of Publications Acts, 1929–67," Hutton, *Oxford History*, 644–49.

3. CULTURAL CURRENCY

1 "Saints' Names for Apes," *Sun and New York Press*, April 12, 1893, 3; "Irish Indignant Because of the Naming of Central Park Zoo Animals," *Cincinnati Post*, April 12, 1893, 3; "How the Central Park Hippopotamus Came to Be Called 'Miss Murphy,'" *Evening Star*, April 14, 1893, 8; "Why All Irish Names? Isn't It Time for Some Variety at the Zoo?," *Irish World*, April 22, 1893, 8; "Irishmen Protest. They Want New Names Given to the Animals in the Menagerie," *New York Herald*, May 1, 1893, 11.

2 Tessier, *Bard of Erin*, 111–12; White, "Thomas Moore," in *DIB*; Sarah McCleave, "The Irish Melodies: Songs That Still Speak," *Thomas Moore in Europe*, accessed August 3, 2020, https://blogs.qub.ac.uk/erin.

3 Quoted in the advertisement for *Moore's Celebrated Irish Melodies* in the *New York Musical Review and Choral Advocate*, February 16, 1854, 62.

4 Williams, *'Twas Only an Irishman's Dream*, 28–29.

5 "Thomas Moore," *Irish American*, December 21, 1850, 1.

6 "Moore's Irish Melodies," *Musical Times and Singing Class Circular*, May 1, 1859, 42.

7 Knobel, "Vocabulary of Ethnic Perception," 45–71.

8 "The Minstrel of Ireland, Honors to the Memory of Moore," *New York Tribune*, May 29, 1879, 5. The Brooklyn statue cost $3,500 in 1879.
9 "Thomas Moore," *Art Inventories Catalog*, Smithsonian American Art Museum, accessed January 31, 2021, https://siris-artinventories.si.edu; Murphy and Mannion, *History of the Society*, 349–50; "The Poet of Ireland. Unveiling the Bust of Moore. Simple Exercises in Central Park," *New York Tribune*, May 29, 1880, 5.
10 Berger, *Ways of Seeing*, 135.
11 Clarke, "Irish Share," 124.
12 Beckert, *Monied Metropolis*, 240, 254.
13 "Crimmins, Mr. John D.," *Social Register, New York, 1911* 25, no. 1 (November 1910), 136; Marion R. Casey, "John D. Crimmins," in Jackson, *Encyclopedia*, 331; "John D. Crimmins, Ward 19, Manhattan, New York County," *1910 U.S. Federal Census*, Ancestry.com; Susan Nova, "Crimmins Estate Boasts Vast Waterfront," *Stamford Advocate*, April 15, 2010, accessed May 19, 2016, http://www.stamfordadvocate.com/.
14 As a boy, Crimmins was regularly taken to visit the graves of the United Irishmen Dr. MacNeven and William Sampson in Astoria. O'Donovan Rossa, *Rossa's Recollections, 1838–1898*, 392, 396–97.
15 Crimmins, *Irish-American Historical Miscellany*, 227; "1911 Dinner Program," *Society of the Friendly Sons of St. Patrick in the City of New York*, accessed January 31, 2021, www.friendlysonsnyc.com; "1919 Dinner Program," *Society of the Friendly Sons of St. Patrick in the City of New York*, NMAH.AC.0398, Smithsonian; O'Shaughnessy, "Rough Rider & Friendly Sons," 3.
16 Sullivan, "Community in Print," 44; Rowland, "Irish-American Catholics," 3–31; McDannell, "'True Men,'" 19–36.
17 Marion R. Casey, "Catholic Club of the City of New York," in Jackson, *Encyclopedia*, 215; Madigan, "Catholic Club of New York," 412–28; "John D. Crimmins, Financier, Dies at 73 of Pneumonia," *New York Tribune*, November 10, 1917, 8.
18 Clarke, "The Hudson-Fulton Celebration," 125, 130; "The Hudson-Fulton Celebration," *Irish American*, September 18, 1909, 4.
19 Clarke, "The Hudson-Fulton Celebration," 130, 137; "The Irish Concert: Appreciative Audience Crowd Carnegie Hall to Listen to Ireland's Songs," *Irish American*, October 2, 1909, 1.
20 McGrath, *John Barry*, xiii–xv, 511–12. Barry is one of four Irish Catholic men who surround Moses in the fountain; the others are Charles Carroll, John Carroll, and Father Theobald Mathew. The sculptor was Herman Kim. "The Centennial Fountain," Catholic Historic Research Center of the Archdiocese of Philadelphia, June 18, 2018, accessed August 18, 2020, https://chrc-phila.org; Gasparini, "Celebration of Moral Force," 3, 12.
21 Murphy and Mannion, *History of the Society*, 402.
22 "St. Patrick's Sons Honor 'Fighting John' Barry by Unveiling Statue in Independence Square," *Philadelphia Inquirer*, March 17, 1907, 1, 8; "Last Chapter in Capt. Barry Controversy," *Washington Herald*, November 24, 1913, 5.

23. "An Urgent Appeal," *John Barry Memorial* (New York: Friendly Sons of St. Patrick, 1906), Joseph McGarrity Books, Joseph McGarrity Collection, Digital Library at Villanova University, accessed May 31, 2023, https://digital.library.villanova.edu (hereafter McGarrity, Villanova); Chester, "Morgan J. O'Brien," 121–26. O'Brien, who earned his law degree from Columbia University, was the son of an Irish immigrant.
24. Murphy and Mannion, *History of the Society*, 402–3; "Commodore John Barry (sculpture)," *Art Inventories Catalog*, Smithsonian.
25. Soderman, *Sculptors O'Connor*, 43.
26. "Don't Like Barry Statue," *Evening Star*, March 7, 1909, 23. The original design for the Centennial Fountain in Philadelphia was more "Irish" too: "the allegorical union of Ireland and America" was to be depicted in "two figures, representing Erin and the Goddess of Liberty," but in the end, Moses striking the rock to bring forth water became the centerpiece of the monument to temperance. Gasparini, "Celebration of Moral Force," 7.
27. "O'Connor Explains Design," *Evening Star*, March 26, 1909, 19; "Rejected Statue for France," *Evening Star*, June 4, 1909, 12; "Barry Statue Passes National Commission. J. J. Boyle's Model Found to Be Acceptable," *Irish American*, October 11, 1913, 1; Neil Flanagan, "How Politics Sank a Radical Monument 105 Years Ago," *Greater Greater Washington*, April 16, 2014, accessed August 7, 2020, https://ggwash.org.
28. "Statues in Capital, 29 Erected, 1 Building, 7 Authorized," *Evening Star*, December 5, 1909, 11.
29. "Commodore John Barry (sculpture)," *Art Inventories Catalog*, Smithsonian; "Barry Statue Passes National Commission. J. J. Boyle's Model Found to Be Acceptable," *Irish American*, October 11, 1913, 1.
30. Murphy and Mannion, *History of the Society*, 426; "'Father of U.S. Navy' Honored," *Arkansas Gazette*, May 17, 1914, 10.
31. For biographical information on Dowling, see Murphy and Mannion, *History of the Society*, 435.
32. Fanning, "Robert Emmet," 53.
33. Ó Murchú, *Jerome Connor*, 36–37, 75. For the story of how Robert Emmet's death mask came to New York and into the possession of the Emmet family (now in the collection of the American Irish Historical Society, New York City), see Emmet, *Incidents of My Life*, 269.
34. "Robert Emmet," *Internet Broadway Database*, accessed August 9, 2020, www.ibdb.com; Ó Murchú, *Jerome Connor*, 40. "Robert Emmet," *Art Inventories Catalog*, Smithsonian. The quote is excerpted from Emmet's famous "speech from the dock" (September 19, 1803) prior to his execution. Connor's statue was later replaced by an elephant and put into storage until 1966 when, to mark the fiftieth anniversary of the Easter Rising, it was relocated to Massachusetts Avenue and Twenty-Fourth Street NW in Washington, DC.
35. "Irish Hero's Statue Unveiled at Museum," *Evening Star*, June 29, 1917, 3; "Wilson Will Pay Honor to Emmet," *Washington Post*, June 27, 1917, 7.
36. "Robert Emmet," *Art Inventories Catalog*, Smithsonian; Ó Murchú, *Jerome Connor*, 75.
37. Szpila, "Lest We Forget," 30–40.

38 "Monument to 'Nun of the Battlefield' Is Planned for Arlington National Cemetery by Roman Catholic Women of Country," *Evening Star*, August 19, 1916, 16.
39 Ó Murchú, *Jerome Connor*, 40; "Nuns of the Battlefield," *Art Inventories Catalog*, Smithsonian.
40 Ó Murchú, *Jerome Connor*, 40, 75; "Prince of Church Dedicates Token," *Evening Star*, September 20, 1924, 5; "Nuns of the Battlefield," *Art Inventories Catalog*, Smithsonian.
41 For biographical details on these men, see Casey, "John D. Crimmins"; Rouse, "William Bourke Cockran," in *DIB*; White, "John Quinn," in *DIB*; Reid, *Man from New York*; American-Irish Historical Society, "Memorial of Thomas Hamilton Murray," 80–87; "Thomas H. Murray Dead," *Pawtucket Times* (Rhode Island), June 6, 1908, 8.
42 The best discussion of second-generation Irish Americans at the turn of the twentieth century is Timothy J. Meagher, *Inventing Irish America*.
43 Captain John O'Connell, President, Irish Brigade Association to Thomas Hamilton Murray, June 7, 1904, quoted in DATI, *Handbook and Catalogue*, part 3, p. 79.
44 "Irish Village's Rare Treasures," *St. Louis Republic*, September 24, 1904, 7; Potterton, "Letters from St. Louis," 249.
45 Ní Bhroiméil, "Creation of an Irish Culture," 87–88; Wolf, "Irish-Language Community," 239–40.
46 The concession for the Irish Village was obtained by Thomas F. Hanley, a wealthy Irish entrepreneur and master plumber in St. Louis. It was intended to showcase the products of the Irish industrial revival; this is discussed further in chapter 5. Potterton, "Letters from St. Louis," 245; "National Association of Master Plumbers," *Engineering Review* 11 (September 1904): 2.
47 "Pikers Planning a Great Parade," *St. Louis Republic*, April 21, 1904, 5; "Stalwart Men and Pretty Girls Represent Ireland at the Fair," *St. Louis Republic*, April 28, 1904, 2; "Irish Village Interests Visitors to the Exposition," *St. Louis Republic*, May 29, 1904, 17.
48 Walsh, "Narelle, Marie (Molly)." Ireland also sent "The Young Kellys," a dancing troupe, and the "Workmen's Club Band," a group of forty musicians who performed as the "Dublin Band" in St. Louis. "Famous Irish Dancers Sent to the St. Louis Fair," *Duluth News-Tribune*, May 22, 1904, 9.
49 Nick Whitmer, "Patrick (Patsy) Touhey" and "Charles Mack," *Lives of the Pipers*, accessed August 16, 2020, http://livesofthepipers.com; Dowling, *Traditional Music*, 136–37; O'Neill, *Irish Minstrels and Musicians*, 344. The County Kerry piper Daniel O'Keefe was also hired "to play on the porch of the McKinley cottage in the Irish Village." O'Neill, *Irish Minstrels and Musicians*, 349.
50 "Delightful, Impression Made on a Louisville Visitor to the St. Louis Exposition," *Kentucky Irish American*, July 16, 1904, 2.
51 T. W. Rolleston to John Quinn, May 14, 1904, quoted in O'Connor, *Art, Ireland*, 56.
52 "Does Not Caricature Irish," *St. Louis Republic*, June 18, 1904, 9.
53 Myles J. Murphy, "Ireland at the Fair," *The Gael*, April 1904, 141. The other announced Irish dramas were "Robert Emmet," by Henry Mangan, and "An Posadh"

(The Marriage); see "Famous Irish Dancers Sent to the St. Louis Fair," *Duluth News-Tribune*, May 22, 1904, 9.
54. "Trouble in Irish Village," *Boston Journal*, June 21, 1904, 12; "Apology Is Price for Return to Erin," *St. Louis Post Dispatch*, June 17, 1904, quoted in White, "Blarney in St. Louie," 54.
55. "Stay Away from the Show," *Gaelic American*, June 11, 1904, 5; "The 'Pike' Is Attraction at St. Louis," *Fairmont West Virginian*, June 4, 1904, 8; Whitmer, "Trouble in the Irish Village," 26–28. "It Takes the Irish to Beat the Dutch" might have played well in St. Louis, given that the fair took place in a section of the country where German Americans outnumbered Irish Americans.
56. T. W. Rolleston to John Quinn, May 14, 1904, quoted in O'Connor, *Art, Ireland*, 55.
57. T. W. Rolleston to John Quinn, June 3, 1904, quoted in O'Connor, *Art, Ireland*, 56; "Stay Away from the Show," *Gaelic American*, June 11, 1904, 5; "The 'Stage Irishman,'" *Irish World*, June 25, 1904, 8; White, "Blarney in St. Louie," 54–60. Among the three actors was Dudley Digges (1879–1947), who went on to a career on Broadway and in Hollywood. Doyle, "(John) Dudley Digges," in *DIB*. The Irish Exhibit Company paid the salaries and transportation costs for those who wanted to go back to Ireland. O'Leary, "St. Patrick Meets St. Louis," 168.
58. Seumas MacManus, "All Ireland Goes on Pilgrimage to Shrine," *Saint Paul Globe*, July 31, 1904, 28. The *Gaelic American* supported the actions of the Irish players; see O'Leary, "St. Patrick Meets St. Louis," 142, 167–69.
59. "Gaelic Notes," *Irish World*, June 25, 1904, 8; White, "Blarney in St. Louie," 58; Doyle, "Mary Digges (née Quinn)," in *DIB*; Doyle, "(John) Dudley Digges," in *DIB*; O'Connor, *Art, Ireland*, 54–57.
60. Kibler, "Pigs, Green Whiskers," 490–91.
61. O'Dea, *History of the Ancient*, 1286, 1470–71; McCarthy, *Respectability and Reform*, 114–17; Meagher, *Inventing Irish America*, 249–50.
62. "The Stage Irishman," in *The Clansman: Souvenir of Celtic and Emmet Clubs, Clan na Gael Irish Picnic and Games, Celtic Park, Long Island City, New York, June 17, 1905*, McGarrity, Villanova, 43–44; *Gaelic American*, March 16, 1907, quoted in Golway, *Irish Rebel*, 184.
63. "Crusade against 'The Stage Irishman.'" *The Gael*, May 1903, 145; Harrington, *Irish Play*, 61; "Caricature Was an Insult," *Cleveland Leader*, April 18, 1904, 2.
64. "Hibernians in Session," *Plain Dealer*, July 21, 1904, 7; "Order of Hibernians, 900 Delegates Assemble in St. Louis Today," *Evening News*, July 19, 1904, 1.
65. O'Neill, "Patrick J. Touhey," in *Irish Minstrels and Musicians*, 313, 315.
66. "Stay Away from the Show," *Gaelic American*, June 11, 1904, 5.
67. "Stage Irishman Goes," *Milwaukee Journal*, August 13, 1904, 3.
68. "Irish Village Entertainers," *St. Louis Republic*, August 20, 1904, 17; "The Irish Theater at Ireland on the Pike," advertisement, *St. Louis Republic*, August 14, 1904, 32; "Oriental Scenes on the Pike," *Rochester Democrat and Chronicle*, June 12, 1904, 3; Murphy, "Ireland at the Fair," 141.

69 According to T. W. Rolleston, "an average Pike audience" was a "miscellaneous crowd of Sioux, cowboys, demi-mondaines, and pleasure-seekers of all kinds." T. W. Rolleston to John Quinn, May 14, 1904, quoted in O'Connor, *Art, Ireland*, 55. "Patsy Touhey, Irish-American Piper on Cylinder, 1900s," *Irish Traditional Music Archive*, accessed January 19, 2021, www.itma.ie.
70 Tomás Mac Anna, "How the Abbey Theatre Really Began," *Irish Times*, April 1, 2002, accessed August 21, 2020, www.irishtimes.com.
71 McDiarmid, "Abbey and the Theatrics," 57–71; Kane, "'Staging a Lie,'" 111–45; Harrington, *Irish Play*, 55–74.
72 McDiarmid, "Abbey and the Theatrics," 60.
73 Kibler, "Stage Irishwoman," 5–30.
74 Moynihan, "The Irish," in Glazer and Moynihan, *Beyond the Melting Pot*, 247–48.
75 Quote is from a *New York Evening Post* review (February 25, 1908) of Lady Gregory's *The Rising of the Moon*, reproduced in Kenneth Cox Lyman, "Critical Reaction," 105–6.
76 Harrington, *Irish Play*, 65.
77 "Riot in Theatre over an Irish Play," *New York Times*, November 28, 1911, 3.
78 Kane, "'Staging a Lie,'" 120.
79 Golway, *Irish Rebel*, 186.
80 Gregory, *Our Irish Theatre*, 204.
81 "A Stormy Page of Dramatic History: When *The Playboy* Caused Terrible Riots," original source and date unknown, clipping in *Playboy of the Western World* file, Theatre Collection, Museum of the City of New York; "Riot in Theatre over an Irish Play," *New York Times*, November 28, 1911, 1.
82 John Devoy to Daniel F. Cohalan, November 29, 1911, quoted in Tansill, *America and the Fight*, 123–24; McDiarmid, "Abbey and the Theatrics," 65.
83 "Irish Players Act 'Playboy' in Riot," *New York Tribune*, November 28, 1911, 1.
84 McDiarmid, "Abbey and the Theatrics," 62, 64–66; Gregory, *Our Irish Theatre*, 180, 221–22.
85 Ridge, "Irish County Societies," 288–89.
86 Mayo Men's Patriotic and Benevolent Association, "History of the Mayo Men's," 16–18, 28. To add insult to injury, in Synge's *Playboy*, Christy Mahon's "prowess at local sports confirms him in the role of hero." Welch, *Oxford Companion*, 474.
87 Harrington, *Irish Play*, 65. George Russell (Æ) actually "reasoned that the *Playboy* itself would have been found quite acceptable if the actors had played it more for poetry and fantasy, less for realism." Reid, *Man from New York*, 68.
88 McElroy, *Red Bricks*, 45.
89 Ridge, *St. Patrick's Day Parade*, 97.
90 Lyman, "Critical Reaction," 54.
91 "The Comic Irishman," *The Gael*, April 1902, 140.
92 John Redmond's support of the Parliament Act of 1911 had only just extracted a promise from the British government of a third Home Rule Bill for Ireland. Also, Harrington (*Irish Play*, 68) notes that, unlike in Dublin, the New York protests came

early in the play and, significantly, after dialogue that implies a blind subservience to "the Holy Father and the Cardinals of Rome." Harrington calls this "an especially cruel libel on the Irish [in New York] when played before a mixed rather mandarin audience in one of the Shubert houses on Broadway."

93 "Poet Yeats Defends the Irish Players," *New York Times*, October 12, 1911, 9.
94 "Gaelic League Condemn the Abbey Theatre Plays," *Irish American*, October 14, 1911, 1; Letter to the Editor, "In Hibernia," *Irish American*, October 21, 1911, 5.
95 "The 'Playboy' Row," *New York Times*, November 29, 1911, 10. The second editorial called the Irish protests an "absurd resentment of a play that doesn't minister to their racial illusions and conceits." It chastised, "It isn't true? What isn't true? That there are not in Ireland, as in every other country on earth, fool women who have a morbid admiration for criminals, or fool men who drink too much whisky? Who is to say what vices, weaknesses, and imbecilities are not to be found in or around a miserable, low-down drinking-place, even in Ireland? And if genius discovers and reveals poetry and humor even there, is it his fitting reward to be lynched as a traitor and liar?" "Falsity Not the Grievance," *New York Times*, November 30, 1911, 12.
96 Cronin, *McGarrity Papers*, 36.
97 Kibler, *Censoring Racial Ridicule*, 109
98 Maura Anand, Andrew S. Hicks, and R. Bryan Willits, "The Man in Philadelphia: Joseph McGarrity and 1914," in Nyhan Grey, *Ireland's Allies*, 109–23.
99 Cronin, *McGarrity Papers*, 35; Reid, *Man from New York*, 117; McDiarmid, "Abbey and the Theatrics," 66–69; Kibler, *Censoring Racial Ridicule*, 102–10. Lady Gregory had advance knowledge of the possibility of arrests in Philadelphia, and her reaction speaks volumes: "I should like to avoid arrest, because of the publicity; one would feel like a suffragette." Gregory, *Our Irish Theatre*, 224.
100 "The 'Playboy,'" *Irish American*, April 20, 1912, 4.
101 "Judge Dismisses Suit on 'Playboy,'" *Philadelphia Inquirer*, January 24, 1912, 11.
102 "Oriental Scenes on the Pike," *Rochester Democrat and Chronicle*, June 12, 1904, 3; Dean, *All Dressed Up*, 33–34, 48, 73, 83; Ryan, "Performing Irish-American Heritage," 105–20; "The Significance of the Gaelic Art Revival," *Current Opinion*, June 1913, 492. The Chicago Irish held a modest pageant, *The Feis of King Guaire*, in 1910. "Will Revive Old Irish Dances," *Chicago Daily News*, May 28, 1910, 15. For more on this unique form of public history, see Glassberg, *American Historical Pageantry*.
103 "Grand Historical Pageant," *Irish American*, March 22, 1913, 5. Dr. Kelly was born in Ireland, and Dr. McGuinness was the daughter of Irish immigrants. "Madge McGuinness," 1920 U.S. Federal Census, New York County, Assembly District 9, Ancestry.com; "Dr. McGuinness, 75, A Physician Here," *New York Times*, December 11, 1959, 34; Nyhan Grey, "Dr. Gertrude B. Kelly," 75–89.
104 "500 in Pageant of Irish History," *New York Times*, May 8, 1913, 11.
105 The Spectator column, *Outlook*, May 31, 1913, 258–59.
106 For other media coverage of the pageant, see *New York Times*, March 23, 1913, III, 11; and April 2, 1913, 20; *New York Tribune*, May 8, 1913, 7; "Erin of Old in Pageant

Scenes: Opens in Blaze of Glory at Sixty-Ninth's Armory," *Sun and New York Press*, May 8, 1913, 7. The pageant was reportedly to move to Boston in November, where Mayor John F. Fitzgerald was selected as chairman of the supervising committee. "Pageant of Ireland: Beautiful Spectacle to Be Seen in Boston," *Boston Globe*, September 11, 1913, 3.

107 "500 in Pageant of Irish History," 11. The Irish Historic Pageant realized $20,000 for the benefit of the Gaelic League in Ireland. The money was for the Irish Research and Language Work Fund. The pageant was produced by W. F. Hamilton, John J. Coleman was the stage director, and costume design was by John Campbell. "Grand Historical Pageant," *Irish American*, March 22, 1913, 5; "500 in Pageant of Irish History," 11.

108 Saunders and Kelly, *Joseph Campbell*, 100–101; Harrington, "Joseph Campbell, Exile," 42–43.

109 Harrington, *Irish Play*, 73. It is also doubly ironic that the legal defender of the Abbey players in 1911, the art patron / lawyer John Quinn, was unable in 1921 to persuade the courts that chapters from James Joyce's *Ulysses* were "art" akin to cubism and not a portrait of real Irish men and women. For an analysis of legal objections to *Ulysses*, see Gillers, "Tendency to Deprave," 259–64.

110 There were group exhibitions of Irish art each year from 1929 to 1934 that garnered a modest degree of press coverage and attention from art critics. O'Connor, *Art, Ireland*, 179–92; O'Connor, "America Called," 16, 20–21, 30; "Irish Exhibition Hits Modernism," *Charleston News and Courier*, May 5, 1929, 31.

111 "The Opening of the Exhibition of Contemporary Irish Art," *New York Times*, April 7, 1929, 32; O'Connor, *Art, Ireland*, 241–43.

112 "Exhibition of Contemporary Irish Art," *Boston Herald*, Rotogravure Section, May 5, 1929, 89; "Irish Exhibition Hits Modernism," *Charleston News and Courier*, May 5, 1929, 31.

113 McCarthy, "Irish Americans in Sports," in *MIA*, 457–71.

114 "Tipperary Terrors Score 44 to 17 Victory over S.F. All-Star Hurlers," *San Francisco Chronicle Sporting Green*, June 14, 1926, 1.

115 Éimear O'Connor, "The Tipperary Hurler," Hugh Lane Gallery, accessed October 24, 2022, https://hughlane.emuseum.com.

116 Comerford, "History of the United," 20; McElroy, *Red Bricks*, 85.

117 Comerford, "History of the United," 13–20.

118 "Concerning the Feis," *Irish World*, May 16, 1942. Clipping in Rita McLoughlin Fitzpatrick's scrapbook, United Irish Counties Association Collection (AIA.056), box 3, folder 17–19, AIA, hereafter Fitzpatrick scrapbook (AIA.056), AIA.

119 "Concerning the Feis," Statistics are as reported in the *New York Journal American*, June 13, 1942; the *Bronx Sentinel*, June 12, 1942; and the *New York Sun*, June 15, 1942, Fitzpatrick scrapbook (AIA.056), AIA.

120 Rosa Pringle, "Irish Societies," 1939, box 3579, folder 13 "Organizations," 18, in *WPA Historical Records Survey: Federal Writers Project, "Irish in New York,"* DORIS.

121 *Irish Echo*, May 30, 1942, Fitzpatrick scrapbook (AIA.056), AIA.

122 Comerford, "History of the United," 36.
123 Flanagan, "'Dance and Song,'" 23; "A Brief History of the National Folk Festival," *National Folk Festival* (U.S.), accessed January 19, 2021, https://nationalfolkfestival.com.
124 Éamonn Ó Gallchobhair, quoted in Kennedy, *Dreams and Responsibilities*, 74.
125 Miller, "Irish Traditional Music," in *MIA*, 504.
126 Souvenir Program, UICA Feis, 1940; and Syllabus, UICA Feis, 1945 (photocopies in possession of the author). The Central Council of Irish Clubs began an annual feis in Boston in 1950. See advertisement in the program for the UICA Feis, 1952. The UICA Feis records are preserved in the UICA Collection (AIA.056), box 2, folders 14–17; and box 3, folders 1–5, AIA.
127 Fanning, "Hidden Flowering," 44.
128 "Tune in on This," *Irish World*, June 16, 1928; "Will Tint Ether," *Kentucky Post*, March 10, 1929, 6.
129 Moloney, "Irish Ethnic Recordings," 85–86.
130 Declan McCormack, "Saving Mayo's Lost Tenor from Obscurity," *Irish Independent*, September 28, 2003; *Scribner Encyclopedia*, s.v. "Morton Downey," 242–43.
131 "A Bing Crosby Discography," *International Club Crosby*, accessed October 18, 2022, http://www.bingmagazine.co.uk/; Fanning, "Hidden Flowering," 18.
132 Murphy and Mannion, *History of the Society*, 442–516.
133 O'Leary, "Manufacturing Reality," 268, 270. An embarrassing 1915 attempt to recreate Ireland is discussed in Elizabeth Creely, "Shamrock Isle at the Panama Pacific International Exposition and the end of the Irish Village," *FoundSF: The San Francisco Digital Archive*, accessed June 4, 2023, www.foundsf.org.
134 O'Leary, "Manufacturing Reality," 272, 275–76, 277n72.
135 Fanning, "Dueling Cultures," 100.
136 Fanning, "Hidden Flowering," 43–44; Fanning, "Dueling Cultures," 105.
137 "Irish Army Team Excels at Chicago," *New York Times*, October 24, 1933, 29; "Irish Champions Invade Chicago," *Chicago Tribune*, July 20, 1933, 19.
138 Program, "Irish Day at a Century of Progress, August 15, 1934," Hagley Museum and Library (hereafter HAGLEY); Charles Bradley and Edward Paulson, *There's Only One Ireland* (New York: Leo Feist, 1912), *Irish Sheet Music Archives*, accessed October 30, 2022, https://irishsheetmusicarchives.com.
139 "Irish Day Speech," A Century of Progress Publicity Division press release, Chicago, August 15, 1934, HAGLEY; "Irish Celebrate in Rain at Fair," *Chicago Tribune*, August 16, 1934, 5; Fanning, "Dueling Cultures," 105–6. A new feature for Irish Day in 1934 was the selection of "Miss Shamrock I," nineteen-year-old Margaret McCormick. "Beauty Winner," *Chicago Tribune*, August 15, 1934, 8.
140 Program, *The Pageant of the Celt* (1934), HAGLEY, 40; Fanning, "Dueling Cultures," 101; William Shortall, "The Pageant of the Celt," *RBSC at ND*, University of Notre Dame, accessed October 30, 2022, https://sites.nd.edu/rbsc.
141 White, "Michael Scott," in *DIB*; Sheaff, "Shamrock Building," 27.
142 Malloy, "Exhibiting Ireland," 262–64.

143 O'Connor, *Art, Ireland*, 313.
144 "Double Irish Show Turns Clock Back," *New York Times*, May 14, 1939, 40.
145 "Colorful Ceremonies Mark Opening of Irish Pavilions at the Fair," *Gaelic American*, May 20, 1939. Sheaff ("Shamrock Building," 28) incorrectly associates MacGonigal's mural with the Shamrock Building.
146 "Double Irish Show Turns Clock Back," *New York Times*, May 14, 1939, 40; O'Connor, *Art, Ireland*, 318.
147 Unsourced newspaper clipping, 1939, headlined "Columbia College Irish Day at the World's Fair," Fitzpatrick scrapbook (AIA.056), AIA.
148 "Record Crowd Attend Ireland's Celebration Day Ceremonies at the World's Fair Sunday Last," *Irish Advocate*, June 22, 1940. That summer, the Irish tenor Jack Feeney broadcast an "Irish Review" live over the radio station WINS from the Gas Building at the World's Fair. "Jack Feeney's Broadcast at the World's Fair," *Irish Advocate*, August 24, 1940.
149 Malloy, "Exhibiting Ireland," 268–72.
150 "Irish Singers to Appear Here," *Detroit Tribune*, January 22, 1955, 4.
151 "Irish Festival Singers to Present Favorite Songs," *Marietta Journal*, March 14, 1956, 2; "Disc Shops Break Out of the Green with Gala Parade of Irish Airs," *Advocate*, March 17, 1957, 46.
152 "Irish Singers in City on 23rd," *Springfield Union*, January 5, 1955, 20; "DeVally Shares Honor as Tenor," *Springfield Union*, January 14, 1955, 26; "Irish Festival Singers Distill Emerald Isle Enchantment," *Plain Dealer*, February 11, 1955, 11. "The Foggy Dew" was written by Fr. Charles O'Neill in approximately 1918, while "The West's Awake" was composed by Thomas Davis in the early nineteenth century; both are considered Irish nationalist songs.
153 "Good Irish Songs Badly Arranged," *San Francisco Chronicle*, February 27, 1956, 6.
154 "The Ed Sullivan Show," *Detroit Times*, March 11, 1956, 19; O'Donovan, *Dreamers of Dreams*, 57–59. See also Dorothy Hayden Cudahy, interview by Rebecca S. Miller, March 4, 1992 (transcript in possession of the author). In the 1950s, the Smith Family, five Irish step dancers, regularly had thirteen-week contracts to perform on the RKO and Loew's theater circuits. Cullinane, *Aspects of the History*, 54.
155 Miller, "Irish Traditional and Popular," 492.
156 "Edward Sullivan, E.D. 0171, Port Chester, Westchester County, New York," 1920 U.S. Federal Census, Ancestry.com.
157 "Charm of the Irish," *New York Times*, March 16, 1959, 55; "March 15, 1959: St. Patrick's Day Show, CBS, Episode Details and Credits," *Metacritic*, accessed January 26, 2021, www.metacritic.com/tv; "Irish Dancing Teacher 1964," *RTE Archives*, accessed January 26, 2021, www.rte.ie.
158 Miller, "Irish Traditional Music," in *MIA*, 412–13, 497–98; Moloney, "Irish-American Popular Music" and "Irish-American Festivals," in *MIA*, 399–403, 429–30; Tom Deignan, "The History of the Clancy Brothers," *Irish America Magazine*, April/May 2009, accessed January 2021, https://irishamerica.com.
159 Clancy, *Mountain of the Women*, 279–80; Carden, "Cable Crossings," 260–75.

4. RACIAL RECKONING

1. Cuddy, "'Are the Bolsheviks?,'" 23.
2. Zimmerman, "'Each "Race" Could Have,'" 92–100.
3. Quoted in Cuddy, "'Are the Bolsheviks?,'" 17.
4. Cuddy, 29.
5. Jacobson, *Whiteness of a Different*, 7–8.
6. 873,662 between 1891 and 1920 according to Blessing, "Irish," 528. See also West and Roland, *If They Don't Want*.
7. After 1917, every immigrant over the age of sixteen was required to read a thirty-to-forty-word passage in the language of their choice. Hutchinson, *Legislative History*, 433, 589; Commons, *Races and Immigrants*, 234; Blessing, "Irish," 529.
8. "Immigrants who wish to avoid Ellis Island should travel cabin. They would thus have better food and a more comfortable berth on the voyage, an earlier examination on arrival, and less delay in meeting relatives or proceeding to their destination." This advice was offered by the Mission of Our Lady of the Rosary for the Protection of Irish Immigrant Girls in New York City. See *Irish Advocate*, October 11, 1924; and Murphy, "Mission of Our Lady," 228. Also Chermayeff, Wasserman, and Shapiro, *Ellis Island*, 110. "Frank claimed me at the dock (U.S. immigration requirements had been completed in Ireland)." O'Dwyer, *Counsel for the Defense*, 57.
9. Malcolm, "Tuberculosis," 583; Hutchinson, *Legislative History*, 138. For a detailed history see Jones, *"Captain of All These."*
10. Bennett, *American Immigration Policies*, 18, 25, 28. A one-way fare from Ireland to New York was about $85 in the 1920s.
11. U.S. Department of State, *Immigration Work*, 2; Hutchinson, *Legislative History*, 586–87; O'Grady, "Irish Free State Passport," 396–405.
12. O'Dwyer, *Counsel for the Defense*, 50.
13. These figures do not include income from Belfast. Whelan, *United States Foreign Policy*, 500.
14. Foster, "'No "Wild Geese"?,'" 120–21; Whelan, *United States Foreign Policy*, table 12.2, 491.
15. Delaney, "Diaspora," 496.
16. Whelan, *United States Foreign Policy*, 461, 502.
17. "Irish Emigrants Will Be Examined at Home by U.S. Officials," *Gaelic American*, June 6, 1925, 8; "New American Regulations for Irish Immigrants; Medical Examinations Abroad," *Irish Advocate*, August 8, 1925; O'Brien, "Transatlantic Connections," 41.
18. "Irish Immigrants Landed at Cunard Company's Pier," *Gaelic American*, August 22, 1925, 2; "Praise Immigrants Here from Ireland: Inspectors Say That 65, Examined Abroad, Are as Fine a Type as Ever Came Over," *New York Times*, August 17, 1925, 15.
19. Anderson, *American Census*, 133–35.
20. "Immigration from Ireland," *Irish Trade Journal* 2, no. 4 (January 1927): 56; Whelan, *United States Foreign Policy*, table 12.2, 491.
21. Leak and Priday, "Migration," 195.
22. Leak and Priday, 196–97.

23 Bernard, "Immigration," 492.
24 The Emergency Quota Act was effective May 19, 1921, yet it was not among the top stories in the May 21, 1921, edition of the *Irish Advocate* or the *Gaelic American*.
25 In 1924, for example, only 12,016 left Ireland for the United States. "Migration to and from Saorstát Éireann," *Irish Trade Journal* 1, no. 1 (October 1925): 19; Leak and Priday, "Migration," 196.
26 The Johnson-Reed Act was effective May 26, 1924. Again, the *Irish Advocate* headlines for its May 31 edition do not address the restrictions; "Immigration Law in America: Mother and Child Deported Refused to Remain at Ellis Island," *Irish Times*, June 16, 1924, 5.
27 Hutchinson, *Legislative History*, 483–84.
28 Ngai, "Architecture of Race," 69–72.
29 "England Will Get Bulk of Immigration Quota under the New Rules," *Gaelic American*, May 15, 1926, 1.
30 Department of Commerce, *Statistical Abstract*, tables 28, 31, pp. 31, 33.
31 Anderson, *American Census*, 144–45; Ngai, "Architecture of Race," 78–80.
32 Leak and Priday, "Migration," 196; United States Congressional Serial Set, Volume 8227, John B. Trevor, "A Preliminary Study of Population," Appendix A of House Reports 68th Congress, 1st Session (December 3, 1923, to June 7, 1924), Vol. 2 (Washington, DC: U.S. Government Printing Office, 1924), 26–31; Congress, House, Committee on Immigration and Naturalization, *National Origins Provision Immigration Act of 1924*, 69th Cong., 2d sess., 1927. CIS No. H455-7 (published hearing), 26; John S. Murphy to the Congress of the United States, March 12, 1928, reproduced in *Repeal of the 'National Origins' Clauses of the Immigration Act of 1924*, pamphlet, Maloney Collection, Manuscript and Archives Division, Center for the Humanities, New York Public Library (hereafter cited as *Repeal* pamphlet–NYPL), 2.
33 John Bond Trevor Papers, Bentley Historical Library, University of Michigan, accessed July 16, 2021, https://quod.lib.umich.edu.
34 "Free State Emigrants," *Irish Times*, December 15, 1924, 6.
35 Bennett, *American Immigration Policies*, 35.
36 Anderson, "Census, Political Power," 93; see also note 4 in Ngai, "Architecture of Race," 68.
37 *New York Times*, March 1, 1924, quoted in Bennett, *American Immigration Policies*, 53.
38 American Irish Historical Society, "Immigration Law," 9.
39 "Free State Friends Oppose New Quotas," *New York Times*, June 6, 1926, 26.
40 "Friends of Irish Freedom Make Protest against Discriminatory Features of the 1924 Immigration Act," *Gaelic American*, June 19, 1926, 2.
41 "Hibernians Protest: Juggling of Emigration Quotas," *Irish Advocate*, July 17, 1926; "Michael Donohoe Assails Trevor's Immigration Quota," *Gaelic American*, June 19, 1926.
42 Edward F. McSweeney to Daniel F. Cohalan, December 5, 1926, Daniel F. Cohalan Papers, American Irish Historical Society (hereafter AIHS), quoted in Doorley, "Friends of Irish Freedom," 257. See also McSweeney, *Racial Contribution*.

43 Doorley, *Justice Daniel Cohalan*, 189.
44 Perlmann, *America Classifies the Immigrants*, 30; Meagher, *Columbia Guide*, 227.
45 Jacobson, *Whiteness of a Different*, 9–11.
46 Testimony of Joseph Carey, January 26, 1927. Congress, House, Committee on Immigration and Naturalization, *National Origins Provision Immigration Act of 1924*, 69th Cong., 2d sess., 1927. CIS No. H455-7 (published hearing), 65.
47 "New Immigration Quota for the Irish Free State; If New Law Report Is Accepted by Congress," *Irish Advocate*, September 24, 1926.
48 "New Quota Is an Affront to the Irish Race in America," *Gaelic American*, May 22, 1926, 2. This article was reprinted from the *Boston Pilot* of May 11, 1926. "National Origin Quota Is Based on Fraud, Jugglery, Prejudice and Imagination," *Gaelic American*, May 22, 1926, 2.
49 Murphy to Congress, March 12, 1928, *Repeal* pamphlet–NYPL, 2.
50 On the extent of the inaccuracies, see Donald H. Akenson, "Why the Accepted Estimates of Ethnicity of the American People, 1790, Are Unacceptable," *William and Mary Quarterly* 41, no. 1 (January 1984): 102–19.
51 "New Quota Is an Affront," 1.
52 "Assuming that an honorable past would convey respectability, [the Irish] made it their mission to document their honorable past, usually employing American middle-class standards of respectability." Moynihan, "History as a Weapon," 34.
53 Jacobson, *Whiteness of a Different*, 8.
54 See U.S. Bureau of the Census, *Century of Population Growth*, table 48, 121. Also Bennett, *American Immigration Policies*, 298. Census schedules for six states were missing, so these figures included estimates to compensate for the gap. The actual number for the surviving records of seven states was 44,273 Irish, comprising 1.6 percent of the white population, compared with 6.7 percent Scotch and 83.5 percent English. See tables 45–46 in *Century of Population Growth*.
55 Joseph I. C. Clarke, introduction to O'Brien, *Hidden Phase*, xiii. Clarke was a veteran journalist, public relations chief for Standard Oil, and president of the Friendly Sons of St. Patrick and of the AIHS. Murphy and Mannion, *History of the Society*, 411.
56 "Irish Societies Oppose National Origins Clause of Immigration Act," *Gaelic American*, January 15, 1927, 1.
57 O'Brien, *Hidden Phase*, 375.
58 O'Brien, 379–80.
59 Clarke in O'Brien, *Hidden Phase*, xi.
60 In addition to Lodge, L. Perry Curtis Jr. lists John Fiske, John W. Burgess, Albert B. Hart, Andrew D. White, Moses C. Tyler, and Francis Walker; see Curtis, *Anglo-Saxons and Celts*, 94. Also Edward F. McSweeney, "The 'National Origins' Myth," in *Repeal* pamphlet–NYPL, 26–27.
61 Freeman had lectured in Boston and privately expressed a desire "to eliminate from the English-speaking world all the Irish along with the still worse Negroes and Jews." Solomon, *Ancestors and Immigrants*, 65.
62 Altschul, *American Revolution*, x.

63 Kauffman, "Edward McSweeney," 55.
64 Curtis, *Anglo-Saxons and Celts*, 94; Higham, *Strangers in the Land*, 323. Lodge chaired the Senate Immigration Committee for a time and pushed for restrictive legislation. Edward F. McSweeney later charged, in an address delivered to the AIHS in 1927, that "in 1906 under the leadership of Senator Lodge, then the dominant factor in Immigration matters in Congress, a law was passed authorizing the director of the Census to analyze and make a report on the first census taken by the U.S. in 1790. . . . The report of Director North in 1909 was a voluminous one. North followed almost identically Lodge's 'Distribution of Ability' theory and presumed to demonstrate that approximately 90% of the American people in 1790 were of British origin." McSweeney, "'National Origins' Myth," 27–28. "Director North" was the statistician Simon Newton Dexter Norton, who became census director in 1903. Anderson, *American Census*, 113.
65 McSweeney, "'National Origins' Myth," 27; and Commons, *Races and Immigrants*, 22–23. In 2002, David N. Doyle determined that 2.4 percent of the entries in the *Dictionary of American Biography*, planned in the 1920s, were for the Irish-born and that that percentage was "fairly proportionate" to the total Irish-born population in the United States between 1800 and 1920; see Doyle, "Irish Elites," 35.
66 Maginniss, *Irish Contribution*, 3; Haltigan, *Irish in the American*. The Irish were correct in their assessment that the Irish stock population of the United States in 1790 had been undercounted, probably for political reasons. In the 1980s, after a thorough and impartial reexamination of the figures and all contributing factors, David Doyle found that the real number was around 447,000 but concluded that "historians such as Michael O'Brien [had] so strained the evidence to prove that there were [significant numbers of Irish Catholics], that they lost the case with the body of dispassionate observers." Doyle, *Ireland, Irishmen and Revolutionary*, 60, 73.
67 Zimmerman, "'Each "Race" Could Have,'" 101.
68 Kauffman, "Edward McSweeney," 58–59.
69 The exceptions were three books on African Americans, Jews, and Germans produced for the Knights of Columbus's Racial Contribution Series in 1924. Kauffman, "Edward McSweeney," 60–61. By 1920, Woodrow Wilson and Warren G. Harding both possessed copies of *A Hidden Phase of American History*. Dunkak, "Papers of an Unheralded," 121.
70 James McGurrin to Edward F. McSweeney, January 10, 1927, box 6, Joint Committee on the Immigration Act of 1924, Correspondence; and "Addressing, Mailing and Distributing Company," January 5, 1927, Maloney Collection, NYPL; "Irish Societies Oppose National Origins Clause of Immigration Act," *Gaelic American*, January 15, 1927, 1.
71 Murphy to Congress, March 12, 1928, *Repeal* pamphlet–NYPL, 1. President Coolidge also received letters from Irish organizations urging him to oppose the national origins system. See Divine, *American Immigration Policy*, 31–32.
72 Emphasis in original. McGurrin to McSweeney, January 10, 1927. The *Gaelic American* circulation figure is for 1930 from Ayer, *American Newspaper Annual* (1930).

73 Testimony of Joseph A. Hill, January 18, 1927. Congress, House, Committee on Immigration and Naturalization, *National Origins Provision Immigration Act of 1924*, 69th Cong., 2d sess., 1927. CIS No. H455-7 (published hearing), 22–24.
74 Johnson was an "unusually energetic and vehement nativist." Higham, *Strangers in the Land*, 307.
75 Testimony of John B. Trevor, January 19, 1927. Congress, House, Committee on Immigration and Naturalization, *National Origins Provision Immigration Act of 1924*, 69th Cong., 2d sess., 1927. CIS No. H455-7 (published hearing), 48–49.
76 "John Trevor Dies; Urged Alien Law," *New York Times*, February 21, 1926, 33; Willits, "Stereopticon," 185–99.
77 John P. Buckley, "The New York Irish: Their View of American Foreign Policy, 1914–1921" (PhD diss., New York University, 1974), 179, 181; Mick Mulcrone, "The Treasonous Irish: Vigilantes, Conspiracies and the Mainstream Press, 1917–1918," 19th Annual Ernie O'Malley Lecture, Glucksman Ireland House, NYU, accessed July 26, 2021, www.youtube.com.
78 Testimony of Joseph Carey, January 26, 1927. Congress, House, Committee on Immigration and Naturalization, *National Origins Provision Immigration Act of 1924*, 69th Cong., 2d sess., 1927. CIS No. H455-7 (published hearing), 67–68.
79 Delaney, "Diaspora," 495.
80 Akenson, "Why the Accepted Estimates," 113.
81 Ford, *Scotch-Irish in America*, 520; Delaney, "Diaspora," 495.
82 Bryson, "Scotch-Irish People," 102; Bolton, *Scotch Irish Pioneers*, iii; and Ford, introduction to *Scotch-Irish in America*.
83 Dunkak, "Papers of an Unheralded," 119–20.
84 O'Brien, *Hidden Phase*, 289–90. This was a particularly galling insult, since, as discussed in chapter 3, the Irish had had the privilege of the *Clermont* float at the 1909 Hudson-Fulton celebration in New York City.
85 Abramovitch, "America's Making Exposition," 139; James T. Fulton, "The Genealogy of the Scots-Irish Fultons of North America Derived from the Fultons of Lisburn & Beith," *Fultons of North America*, accessed August 26, 2021, https://neuronresearch.net/genealogy.
86 Testimony of John B. Trevor, January 19, 1927. Congress, House, Committee on Immigration and Naturalization, *National Origins Provision Immigration Act of 1924*, 69th Cong., 2d sess., 1927. CIS No. H455-7 (published hearing), 36, 41, 42. The phrase "filiopietist acrimony" is David Doyle's; see Doyle, *Ireland, Irishmen and Revolutionary*, 57.
87 *Repeal* pamphlet–NYPL, 20.
88 "The Immigration Law," *New York Times*, January 19, 1927, 22; "Benedict Fitzpatrick Dies at 83," *New York Times*, February 6, 1964, 29.
89 O'Connor, *Art, Ireland*, 326–27; "Prizes Awarded in IBM Shows at the Fairs," *Dallas Morning News*, October 4, 1939, 8.
90 Murray and Lawler, "American-Irish Historical Society," 1.
91 Moseley, "Letter from Edward A. Moseley, the Retiring President-General, to the AIHS," 54.

92 For a contemporaneous and critical assessment of the theories of Ripley, Grant, and Burgess, see Hankins, *Racial Basis of Civilization*, 176.
93 Knobel, *Paddy and the Republic*, 125; Jacobson, *Whiteness of a Different*, 48–49.
94 Winter, *Notes on Criminal Anthropology*.
95 "Blames Stew and Buttermilk for Irish Fighting Nature," *New York Times*, March 2, 1922, 1; and "More Than Diet Is Involved," *New York Times*, March 3, 1922, 12. Edwards was a Boston physician and an advocate for preventative medicine.
96 "Irish Came from Eskimos, German Professor Suggests," *New York Times*, October 28, 1925, 1; Julius Pokorny's name (1887–1970) was misspelled "Porkory" in this article. Also Ó Dochartaigh, *Julius Pokorny*, 66–68; "Eskimo Ancestry of Irish Traced by German Professor," *Boston Globe*, November 22, 1925, B3.
97 Jacobson, *Whiteness of a Different*, 87.
98 "Topics of the Times: He'll Soon Hear from Dublin," *New York Times*, October 29, 1925, 24.
99 Douglas, "Anglo-Saxons and Attacotti," 44.
100 Douglas, 46.
101 Douglas, 41.
102 *Repeal* pamphlet–NYPL, 21; *New York Times*, June 6, 1926, 26; Testimony of John B. Trevor, January 19, 1927. Congress, House, Committee on Immigration and Naturalization, *National Origins Provision Immigration Act of 1924*, 69th Cong., 2d sess., 1927. CIS No. H455-7 (published hearing), 48. According to John Higham (*Strangers in the Land*, 314), in 1921 Trevor, a "member of New York's nativist elite," had voluntarily testified before Congress "about the overwhelmingly foreign character of New York radicals . . . Before long Trevor was drawn into intimate association with the [House] committee [on Immigration]. He sat in on informal meetings of the restrictionist majority, fed ideas to it, and contributed to the drafting of reports, all on a voluntary, unpaid basis."
103 Testimony of Francis H. Kinnicutt, February 13, 1929. Congress, Senate, Committee on Immigration, *National Origins Provision of Immigration Law*, 70th Cong., 2d sess., 1929. CIS No. S318-6 (published hearing), 155.
104 Quote from Condon, *Irish Race in America*, 12. All the broadsides were published by the FOIF in 1920.
105 Bernard, "Immigration," 493.
106 "Will Anglomaniacs Control Bi-Centennial of George Washington?," *Gaelic American*, January 22, 1927, 4.
107 "Where Are the Anglo-Saxons?," *Gaelic American*, February 12, 1927, 4. On the wide influence of Carnegie money in higher education, see Berman, "View from the Top," 455–63, especially note 5.
108 "American Bloc Is Needed to Oppose Alien Propaganda Says Congressman," *Illinois Fiery Cross*, March 7, 1924, 1; "Protest New Limit for Alien Quotas," *New York Times*, May 11, 1926, 19; and "Irish Object to Insult to Race under Quota Law," *Irish World*, May 29, 1926, 11.
109 Higham, *Strangers in the Land*, 290–91.

110 "Irish-Catholic Claim to Valor in Revolutionary War Is Refuted by Figures of U.S. Census Bureau," *Illinois Fiery Cross*, February 29, 1924, 1.
111 "Wisconsin Klan in Drive against National Anthem," *Badger American*, March 1, 1924, 2.
112 "Key and the Irish," *American Standard*, May 1, 1924, 8.
113 This is reproduced in Appel and Appel, *Pat-Riots to Patriots*, 22.
114 Frank de Sales Casey, "The Dare-Devil," *Life*, March 12, 1925, MSU Museum Cultural Collections, Object ID 7572.784, Michigan State University.
115 Frank de Sales Casey, "It Seems There Were Two Irishmen—," *Life*, March 11, 1926, MSU Museum Cultural Collections, Object ID 7572.782, Michigan State University.
116 A play on the well-known Irish nationalist song "The Wearing of the Green." Cover by Frank de Sales Casey, "The Wearing of the Grin," *Life*, March 17, 1927, MSU Museum Cultural Collections, Object ID 7572.1095, Michigan State University.
117 Brooks E. Hefner and Edward Timke, "Circulating American Magazines Dataset from the Audit Bureau of Circulations Publisher's Reports," Center for Open Science, accessed July 26, 2021. https://doi.org/10.17605/OSF.IO/533CK.
118 Curtis, *Anglo-Saxons and Celts*, 109, 112. See especially chapter 7, "Anglo-Saxonism in America," and chapter 9, "Celticism: The Irish Response." C. J. Herlihy published *The Celt above the Saxon* in Boston in 1890.
119 Doorley, *Justice Daniel Cohalan*, 171–72.
120 Jacobson, *Whiteness of a Different*, 87.
121 Observations of Secretary on H.R. 6540 (later H.R. 7990), Charles Evans Hughes to Albert Johnson, February 2, 1924, in Hughes, *Correspondence with Executive Departments*, 1204.
122 Whelan, *United States Foreign Policy*, 447–54, 460. Smiddy's credentials would not formally be presented to President Coolidge until October 1924.
123 Doorley, *Justice Daniel Cohalan*, 171–72; Whelan, *United States Foreign Policy*, 462–63.
124 Akenson, "Why the Accepted Estimates," 108.
125 Murphy to Congress, March 12, 1928, *Repeal* pamphlet–NYPL, 2; Divine, *American Immigration Policy*, 32.
126 American Council of Learned Societies, "Report of Committee," 124. Donald Akenson later concluded that the ACLU surname analysis was nothing but "a fool's errand" that "[in] dealing with the Irish . . . did almost nothing right." Akenson, "Why the Accepted Estimates," 106, 115, 188. The 1940 U.S. Census was the first to recognize the partition of Ireland under "Place of Birth."
127 Murphy to Congress, March 12, 1928, *Repeal* pamphlet–NYPL, 2.
128 "Ireland and America," *Old Castle Garden*, December 1938, 93.
129 Almeida, *Irish Immigrants*, 28.
130 O'Brien, "Transatlantic Connections," 41–42.
131 Ninety-one of those 338 were preference visas.
132 Almeida, *Irish Immigrants*, 23–26. The number leaving Ireland for Great Britain was much higher during the same period: 463,104.
133 Almeida, 27–28.

134 Delaney, "Diaspora," 496.
135 Daly, "Nationalism, Sentiment, and Economics," 264; O'Hanlon, *Unintended Consequences*, 20.
136 Loftus, "Politics of Cordiality," 143; O'Hanlon, *Unintended Consequences*, 122.
137 O'Hanlon, *Unintended Consequences*, 20–21, 118–20; "U.S. May Cut Irish Immigrant Quota: Kennedy Proposes New Laws," *Irish Times*, July 24, 1963, 1; Hennessy, "American Irish Immigration Committee," 44.
138 Almeida, *Irish Immigrants*, 48–54; Casey, "Twentieth Century Irish Immigration," 28.
139 Loftus, "Politics of Cordiality," 147.
140 Loftus, 149–50.
141 O'Hanlon, *Unintended Consequences*, 21–22.
142 Testimony of James B. Carey, *Hearings before the Subcommittee on Immigration and Naturalization of the Committee on Judiciary, United States Senate, 89th Congress, 1st Session on S. 500 "to Amend the Immigration and Nationality Act, and for Other Purposes, Part 1"* (Washington, DC: U.S. Government Printing Office, 1965) (hereafter *S. 500 Hearings 1965*), March 15, 1965, 477.
143 O'Hanlon, *Unintended Consequences*, 110. Carey was born in 1912, and at the time of this hearing he was the president of the International Union of Electrical, Radio & Machine Workers of America (IUE), and secretary-treasurer of the Industrial Union Department, American Federation of Labor and Congress of Industrial Organizations. *S. 500 Hearings 1965*, March 15, 1965, 467. For Ireland as the birthplace of Carey's grandparents, see "James B. Carey," Bainbridge Street, District 0973, Philadelphia Ward 30, Philadelphia, Pennsylvania, U.S. Federal Census 1920, Ancestry.com.
144 Testimony of Dr. James H. Sheldon, *Hearings before the Subcommittee No. 1 of the Committee on the Judiciary, House of Representatives, Eighty-Ninth Congress, 1st Sess., on H.R. 2580 to Amend the Immigration and Nationality Act, and for Other Purposes* (Washington, DC: U.S. Government Printing Office, 1965) (hereafter *H.R. 2580 Hearings 1965*), May 27, 1965, 366, 367.
145 *S. 500 Hearings 1965*, March 15, 1965, 480, 482, 483.
146 *S. 500 Hearings 1965*, 67, 276, 512.
147 Senate Vote #232 in 1965 (89th Congress), *To Pass H.R. 2580, Immigration and Nationality Act Amendments. Sep 22, 1965*, accessed August 15, 2021, www.govtrack.us/congress/votes.
148 O'Hanlon, *Unintended Consequences*, 12.
149 Casey, "Twentieth Century Irish Immigration," 28.
150 Almeida, *Irish Immigrants*, 54.
151 O'Hanlon, *Unintended Consequences*, 21–22.
152 Adrian Flannelly, quoted in O'Hanlon, *Unintended Consequences*, 122.
153 Cathy Hayes, "Trying to Help the Undocumented Irish in an Earlier Generation," *Irish Central*, July 1, 2012, accessed August 13, 2021, www.irishcentral.com.
154 Moynihan, "The Irish," in *MIA*, 509.
155 Hayes, "Trying to Help"; Almeida, *Irish Immigrants*, 56.
156 Moynihan, "The Irish," in *MIA*, 497.

157 John Collins, "Seeking Help from Senator Robert Kennedy on Changing 1965 Immigration Act," *Irish Central*, July 4, 2012, accessed August 13, 2021, www.irishcentral.com; Hennessy, "American Irish Immigration Committee," 43–46; Hayes, "Trying to Help."
158 Moynihan, "The Irish," in *MIA*, 511; Meagher, *Columbia Guide*, 150, 157.
159 "Open U.S. Immigration to Irish," flyer, American Irish National Immigration Committee, 1969, Irish America Vertical Files (AIA.013), AIA; *Congressional Record*, January 3, 1969, 58, accessed August 19, 2021, www.govinfo.gov; *Amendments to the Immigration Laws (1965): Hearings, Ninety-First Congress . . . by United States. Congress. House. Committee on the Judiciary. Subcommittee No. 1* (Washington, DC: U.S. Government Printing Office, 1970), 3, hereafter *Amendments to the Immigration Laws (1965)*.
160 *Amendments to the Immigration Laws (1965)*, 10.
161 *Amendments to the Immigration Laws (1965)*, 14.
162 Wu, *Color of Success*, 3; Hsu, *Good Immigrants*.
163 *Amendments to the Immigration Laws (1965)*, 3.
164 Griffin, "American Irish Historical Society," 42; Rodechko, "Michael J. O'Brien," 190–92.
165 Lee, "Introduction: Interpreting Irish America," in *MIA*, 7–9.
166 David Dempsey, "Their Story Has Become a Living Legend: *The American Irish*. By William V. Shannon," *New York Times*, January 12, 1964, BR12.
167 Lee, "Introduction: Interpreting Irish America," in *MIA*, 10.
168 Hamill, "Once We Were Kings," in *MIA*, 528; Meagher, *Columbia Guide*, 159.
169 O'Brien, "Irish America, Race," 88, 91; Matthews, *Bobby Kennedy*, 286–87.
170 O'Brien, "Devlin's 1969 American Tour," 94.
171 Holland, *American Connection*, 27–28; Meagher, *Columbia Guide*, 226.
172 Promsias Mac Aonghusa, "The Split among Irish-Americans," *Irish Times*, December 9, 1969, 10. See also "National Association for Irish Justice," *Irish Left Archive*, accessed August 20, 2021, www.leftarchive.ie; Seán Prendiville Papers (AIA.005), AIA.
173 Jerry Carroll, "No-Nonsense Visit: Bernadette's S.F. Mission," *San Francisco Chronicle*, August 29, 1969, 11.
174 Meagher, *Columbia Guide*, 161.
175 Henry Raymont, "Ulster 'Truth Squad' Pursues Miss Devlin to U.S.," *New York Times*, August 30, 1969, 8.
176 Mac Aonghusa, "Split among Irish-Americans"; O'Brien, "Irish America, Race," 100.
177 Seán Maxwell, "Forever Green," *Irish Echo*, January 3, 1970, 10.
178 O'Brien, "Irish America, Race," 94.
179 Raymont, "Ulster 'Truth Squad' Pursues"; Carroll, "No-Nonsense Visit"; "Is She Joan of Arc or Joan of Moscow?," *Omaha World-Herald*, September 7, 1969, 37; Richard J. H. Johnston, "O'Dwyer Debates Unionists," *New York Times*, September 6, 1969, 12.
180 Judy Barden, "Home-Front Critics: Everyone Isn't Wild about Bernadette," *Chicago Daily News*, August 23, 1969, 16.

181 O'Brien, "Irish America, Race," 98.
182 John Chamberlain, "Keys to Destruction," *Augusta Chronicle*, March 14, 1970, 4.
183 "Campaign in U.S., Bernadette's Plea for Ulster," *San Francisco Chronicle*, August 22, 1969, 13.

5. SELLING VALUE

1 Black, "Branding Trust," xiii.
2 DATI, *Report on the Trade* (1912), 126.
3 *The Gael*, July 1902, 239; DATI, *Report on the Trade* (1914), 102.
4 Gribbon, "Economic and Social History," 298.
5 DATI, *Report on the Trade* (1914), 101; Gribbon, "Economic and Social History," 300; Cullen, *Economic History of Ireland*, 159; Truxes, *Irish-American Trade*, 186.
6 O'Connor, *Art, Ireland*, 4–20.
7 "From Bleak Donegal: Fascination of Mrs. Hart's Irish Village for Visitors," *Daily Inter Ocean*, August 16, 1893, 6; "Ireland at Chicago: A Picturesque Scene from Erin's Green Isle," *Idaho Falls Times*, August 3, 1893, 3; Kate Field, "An Irish Village: One of the Most Striking Exhibits at the Fair," *Plain Dealer*, August 13, 1893, 13.
8 Teresa Dean, "White City Chips, Ireland as Represented at the Donegal Irish Village," *Daily Inter Ocean*, August 18, 1893, 7.
9 Map in *A Week at the Fair* (Rand, McNally & Co., 1893), accessed October 10, 2021, https://commons.wikimedia.org.
10 "The Irish Village," *Irish World*, May 20, 1893, 1; "Ireland at Chicago," *Irish American*, May 6, 1893, 1.
11 "The Exhibit of the Irish Industries Association," in *Guide to the Irish Industrial Village and Blarney Castle: The Exhibit of the Irish Industries Association at the World's Columbian Exposition, Chicago* (Chicago: Irish Village Book Store, 1893), 12, accessed September 26, 2021, http://livinghistoryofillinois.com/.
12 *Guide to the Irish Industrial Village and Blarney Castle*, 2, 11–15; Sheehy, *Rediscovery of Ireland's Past*, 85–89; Akhtar, "Cultural History of Irish."
13 "The Irish Village," *Irish World*, May 20, 1893, 1.
14 Ishbel Aberdeen, "Ireland at the World's Fair," *North American Review*, July 1893, 22–23.
15 Advertisement for A. Shuman & Company, *Boston Herald*, April 30, 1893, 27.
16 *The Gael*, December 1899, 269; and February 1900, 42.
17 *The Gael*, April 1902, 143; August–September 1900, 225. See also advertisement for the Irish Poplin Scarf House, Dublin, in the July 1902 issue.
18 *The Gael*, September 1902, 273.
19 Gribbon, "Economic and Social History," 302; Cullen, *Economic History of Ireland*, 163.
20 *The Gael*, June 1903, 198, mistakenly calls this the "Irish Agricultural League of America." It is the same organization described in *The Gael*, April 1904, 149; October 1903, 331; July 1901, 201–5.
21 DATI, *Handbook and Catalogue*, part 3, 10.

22 "Pike Leader a Native of St. Louis," *St. Louis Republic*, September 11, 1904, 27.
23 *The Gael*, June 1903, 198: "The Irish Department of Agriculture has decided to organize a special exhibit of Irish industries for the St. Louis Exposition. The Secretary for Ireland, Mr. [George] Wyndham, in making this announcement in the House of Commons, said that the Department had been informed that if it undertook the organization of an Irish exhibit a special pavilion would be provided from American sources."
24 "Ireland at the Fair," *Dallas Morning News*, September 18, 1904, 24; M. J. Murphy, "Ireland at the Fair," *The Gael*, April 1904, 141.
25 O'Connor, *Art, Ireland*, 51; "Ireland as It Is," *The Gael*, February 1904, 75; DATI, *Handbook and Catalogue*, part 2, 37; "The Irish Village at Madison Square Garden," *The Gael*, November 1904, 376; "Irish Arts and Crafts," *New York Times*, October 7, 1905, 7; Potterton, "Letters from St. Louis," 249.
26 T. W. Rolleston, "Progress in Ireland as Shown at the Fair," *Harper's Weekly*, November 5, 1904, 1707.
27 "Dun Emer Art Industry," *The Gael*, February 1904, 74.
28 DATI, *Handbook and Catalogue*, part 2, 6.
29 "Ireland at the Fair," *Dallas Morning News*, September 18, 1904, 24.
30 "Irish Exposition Opened," *Irish World*, September 30, 1905, 4.
31 "The Irish Village at Madison Square Garden," *The Gael*, November 1904, 376.
32 "The Irish Exposition," *Irish World*, September 16, 1905, 2; "The A.O.H. Irish Exposition," *Irish World*, September 30, 1905, 4; Reid, *Man from New York*, 39. Dun Emer was run by the sisters of William Butler Yeats. "Dun Emer Art Industry," *The Gael*, February 1904, 74.
33 "Irish Arts and Crafts," *New York Times*, October 7, 1905, 7.
34 "Irish Trade with the United States. Unfair Competition. Reputation of Irish Goods. Methods of Marketing," *Irish Trade Journal* 1, no. 1 (October 1925): 13; "Trade with the United States," *Irish Trade Journal* 2, no. 3 (May 1928): 93.
35 "Irish Homespuns," *New York Times*, March 18, 1927, 5.
36 Daly, *Industrial Development*, 11.
37 See Blessing, "Irish," table 2, 528.
38 John T. Ridge, "Irish Shop Around," 38–40; "Hibernians Want Wine and Beer Back: Convention Also Urges the Buying Here of Irish-Made Goods," *New York Times*, July 24, 1925, 3. In the 1950s, there was another "Buy Irish" promotion; see "Buy Irish: An Idea Taking Hold in America," *Irish Illustrated* 1, no. 6 (January 1957): 8–10.
39 Eileen Phillips, "Copy of a Talk on Belleek China, Belfast, June 1931," pamphlet in Ms. 1091/5/20, National Archives of Ireland (hereafter NAI).
40 "Irishwomen's Co-operative League of America," *Irish World*, February 25, 1922, 10; "Contribute to Irish Independence," advertisement, *Irish World*, March 18, 1922, 2. This organization, founded in December 1920, was also known as the Irish Women's Purchasing League.
41 "Lindsay Crawford Is Very Hopeful for Future of Ireland," *Gaelic American*, June 19, 1926, 3. Crawford served as the Irish Free State trade representative from

December 1922 until October 1929. Dempsey and Boylan, "(Robert) Lindsay Crawford," in *DIB*.

42 This committee eventually became Córas Tráchtála (the Irish Exports Board) in 1959. The Irish Free State also opened a trade bureau in Montreal in 1926. "Ireland to Foster Trade with Canada," *New York Times*, May 11, 1926, 41; Craig, "Córas Tráchtála." For an economic history of Ireland after independence, see Ó Gráda, *Rocky Road*.

43 "Staged Irish Exhibition," *Irish World*, March 20, 1929; "People of Varied Nationalities Mingle in International Village," *Christian Science Monitor*, March 29, 1929, 5; "Ireland Express Pride in Fair Role as Twin Exhibits Are Dedicated in Rain," *New York Times*, May 14, 1939, 40; "Irish Exhibit Spins Romance of Linen," *New York Times*, May 17, 1939, 21; "Wares of Ireland to Be Put on View," *New York Times*, October 13, 1949, 31; Annette Sara Cunningham, "Córas Tráchtála / The Irish Export Board in North America 1978–1987: The Branding of Ireland," unpublished essay, copy in possession of the author.

44 "Chicago Exhibition, 1933: Report on Saorstát Exhibit," *Irish Trade Journal* 9, no. 1 (March 1934): 10. On the potential of linen, Rosalind Abercorn, the wife of the governor of Northern Ireland, declared, "Curtains, furniture coverings and bedspreads can all be now had and the artistic effects arrived at are quite lovely." Rosalind Abercorn, *Irish Linen, New York World's Fair, 1940*, pamphlet (Belfast, Ireland: Irish Linen Guild, 1939), 12, author's collection.

45 Black, "Branding Trust," 8–9.

46 DATI, *Handbook and Catalogue*, part 2, 37; O'Connor, Art, Ireland, 52.

47 Mary Gorges, "Industries of Ireland: Belleek Pottery," *The Gael*, October 1900, 285–88.

48 Sheehy, *Rediscovery of Ireland's Past*, 76.

49 Eileen Buckley, "An Appreciation of Belleek," *Antiques*, October 1922, 165–66.

50 Cunningham, *Story of Belleek*, 58, quoting Barber, *Pottery and Porcelain*, 216. In contrast, see Buckley, "Appreciation of Belleek": "Within recent years a porcelain of somewhat similar pattern and glaze has been manufactured in New Jersey. It is, however, a far coarser product than the Irish original, which latter is further distinguished by its mark."

51 "John J. Gavigan, Potter, Is Dead Well Known in Trade throughout Country—Highly Regarded in City," *Trenton Evening Times*, January 10, 1911, 2; "Many Regrets for Late John J. Gavigan," *Trenton Evening Times*, January 15, 1911, 32.

52 Harriet E. Brewer, "American Belleek," *New Jersey Historical Society Proceedings* 52, no. 2 (April 1934): 108.

53 "Brief for Final Hearing on Behalf of the IIDA," U.S. Patent Office, Opposition No. 949, Irish Industrial Development Authority (hereafter IIDA) vs. Dennis D. Barrett, March 19, 1912, 4, 14, 19, Ms. 1091/5 (legal correspondence), NAI.

54 Phillips, "Copy of a Talk on Belleek China, Belfast, June 1931," NAI. Eugene Sheerin, a Belleek Pottery artist, wrote a poem in 1885 called "Trademark on Belleek China Ware" from which the following lines are appropriate to quote here:

"A trademark may appear a prosy thing, But such is not this one of which I sing; For if your cup in beauty be unique, Twill bear the well-known stamp of famed Belleek. . . . With emblems dear to Irish patriot's heart, And meet to signalize our Celtic Art. . . . Fair-famed Belleek, long may thy products be Unrivalled here, and far beyond the sea! For to the world they silently convey What Celtic brain and hand can do to-day!" Quoted in Cunningham, *Story of Belleek*, 59.

55 IIDA, *Fifth Annual Report* (1911), 9; Riordan, *Modern Irish Trade*, 277; *Irish Trade Journal* 1, no. 2 (November 1925): 31; McMahon, *Grand Opportunity*, 148–49. The Irish trademark remained in use until 1967.

56 N.F., Inspector, IIDA to Messrs. Belleek Pottery, Ltd., September 21, 1925, Ms. 1091/5/20, NAI; IIDA, *Sixth Annual Report* (1912), 15; IIDA, *Fifth Annual Report* (1911), 7; Riordan, *Modern Irish Trade*, 275–76. In 1918, France adopted "Unis France" as its national trademark, and over eight hundred manufacturers registered their products with this trademark during its first year; see IIDA, *Twelfth Annual Report* (1918), 7.

57 Francis J. Dolan, Belleek Pottery, Ltd. to E. Towers, Secretary, IIDA, September 22, 1925, Ms. 1091/5/20, NAI.

58 See advertisements in the *Boston Herald*, November 26, 1923, 4; *Dallas Morning News*, November 16, 1923, 8; *Times-Picayune*, June 17, 1925, 17; *Plain Dealer*, March 13, 1924, 4; *Omaha World-Herald*, May 20, 1923, 4.

59 IIDA to Belleek Pottery, 21 September 1925, Ms. 1091/5/20, NAI.

60 E. Riordan, Department of Industry and Commerce (Commerce and Technical Branch) to the secretary of the IIDA, September 30, 1926, Ms. 1091/5/20, NAI.

61 Cunningham, *Story of Belleek*, 58; Scandinavia Belting Co. v. Asbestos and Rubber Works, 2 Circ., 257 F. 937 (March 3, 1919) 950 established that it was objectionable to use a geographical name if it did not reflect a product's origin, manufacture or ownership.

62 "Maddock One of Trenton's Pottery Pioneers; City Leads U.S. in Ware," *Trenton Evening Times*, October 27, 1929, 92.

63 D. D. Barrett to W. J. Branagan, secretary, Dublin Industrial Development Association, received December 26, 1909, Ms. 1091/5 (correspondence), NAI.

64 Barrett to Brannigan [sic], December 26, 1909, Ms. 1091/5 (correspondence), NAI, and D. D. Barrett to W. J. Branagan, secretary, Dublin Industrial Development Association, March 11, 1910, Ms. 1091/5 (correspondence), NAI.

65 D. D. Barrett to Kevin J. Kenny, editor, *Contract Gazette*, September 12, 1909, Ms. 1091/5 (correspondence), NAI. Barrett had a sixth-grade education according to the 1940 U.S. Federal Census, E.D. 84-45, Terre Haute, Vigo, Indiana, Ancestry.com.

66 Deposition of Michael Fahey, July 24, 1911, 2–3, included with "Brief for Final Hearing on Behalf of the IIDA" (1912), NAI. "The Irish Trade Mark, Efforts to Register It in America," *Irish American*, August 17, 1912, 1.

67 IIDA, *Fifth Annual Report* (1911), 7; "Trade Mark Bill Urged," *New York Times*, October 26, 1912, 4.

68 Riordan, *Modern Irish Trade*, 313–14. The IIDA was also able to prevent an Ohio firm from registering "Irish Washing Soda" on a non-Irish product. "The Irish Trade Mark Protected in U.S.," *Irish American*, September 7, 1912, 1.
69 "Successful Action in the U.S.A.," [1912], 4, Ms. 1091/5 (Legal Papers), NAI.
70 IIDA, *Eleventh Annual Report* (1917), 8.
71 Because the IIDA pre-dated the Irish Free State by nearly twenty years, the Irish Trade Mark was applied to manufactures produced on the island, regardless of the border. "Marking of Irish Goods. American Customs Requirements," *Irish Trade Journal* 1, no. 1 (October 1925): 14.
72 Rev. S. E. Nicholson, Society of Friends, April 15, 1914, 5, *Amendment to the Trademark Laws, Hearing before the Committee on Patents, House of Representatives, 63rd Congress, 2nd Session on H.R. 15403, a Bill Reviewing and Amending the Statutes Relative to Trademarks* (Washington, DC: U.S. Government Printing Office, 1914), 5.
73 "Irish Trade with the United States. Unfair Competition. Reputation of Irish Goods. Methods of Marketing," *Irish Trade Journal*, 1, no. 1 (October 1925): 13.
74 Paynter, *Psychological Study of Trade-Mark*, 5, 39.
75 See advertisements in *Modern Stationer and Bookseller* 2, no. 1 (September 25, 1920): 47; 2, no. 3 (October 25, 1920): 37; 3, no. 3 (April 25, 1921): 37; *Irish Tourist* 2, no. 6 (1895): 18; and McBrinn, "Marcus Ward," in *DIB*.
76 *Modern Stationer and Bookseller* 6, no. 2 (October 10, 1922): 3; Black, "Branding Trust," 8–16. The H. H. Tammen Company of Denver listed "Irish Linen Old Style Finish" writing paper in its school supplies catalog as late as 1941. H. H. Tammen Company, *1941 School Supplies Catalog*, 3, Colorado Historical Society, Denver.
77 IIDA, *Eleventh Annual Report* (1917), 5.
78 IIDA, *Tenth Annual Report* (1916), 6–7.
79 "Two Sue on Trade-Marks," *New York Times*, March 10, 1927, 33; "Files Dry Goods Libel Suit," *New York Times*, April 13, 1927, 27. The case was most likely settled out of court because neither company appears in the Lexis-Nexis online database.
80 Black, "Branding Trust," 16.
81 "The Irish Trade Mark," *Irish American*, August 30, 1913, 6.
82 "Irish Lace and Crochet Industry," *Irish American*, December 20, 1913, 1.
83 Advertisement for Simpson, Crawford & Simpson, "Real Irish Laces," *Irish World*, October 5, 1901, 2.
84 IIDA, *Sixth Annual Report* (1912), 11; *Seventh Annual Report* (1913), 7; *Ninth Annual Report* (1915), 7; also, letter from John Byrne on "Foreign 'Irish' Manufacturers," *Irish World*, September 9, 1905, 4.
85 "Irish Trade with the United States," *Irish Trade Journal* 1, no. 1 (October 1925): 13.
86 "Trade Name 'Irish' in United States. Judicial Decision Establishing Exclusive Right," *Irish Trade Journal* 1, no. 9 (June 1926): 175; Grant, *International Directory of Company Histories*, s.v. "Bardwil Linens," 15–16.
87 "Irish Lace Wins the Fight before Federal Trade Commission," *Gaelic American*, May 8, 1926, 1, 5.
88 "Trade Name 'Irish' in United States," *Irish Trade Journal* 1, no. 9 (June 1926): 175.

89 "Irish Lace. Important Judicial Decision in United States," *Irish Trade Journal* 4, no. 2 (February 1929): 56.
90 "Indirect Exports to the United States," *Irish Trade Journal* 1, no. 4 (January 1926): 77.
91 "Irish Trade with the United States," *Irish Trade Journal* 1, no. 1 (October 1925): 13.
92 "Irish Trade with the United States," 13; the portion of the quote after the ellipsis is from "American Embroidery Trade," *Irish Trade Journal*, 1, no. 4 (January 1926): 77–78.
93 "Patric [*sic*] M. Sweeney," 1910 U.S. Federal Census, Brooklyn Ward 22, Kings County, New York and "James Johnson Sweeney," U.S. Passport Application #178366, May 25, 1922, Ancestry.com. Patrick's son, James (1900–1986), became the second director of the Guggenheim Museum in New York City. "James Johnson Sweeney Dies; Art Critic And Museum Head," *New York Times*, April 15, 1986, B8.
94 Correspondence with Manufacturers, folder 9; "*You* want the highest quality," folder 19; and "The Old Standby—Medallion Levers Laces," folder 20, Promotional Materials, Sweeney and Johnson Company Records #5345, Southern Historical Collection, The Wilson Library, University of North Carolina at Chapel Hill [hereafter Sweeney Johnson UNC–Chapel Hill].
95 Sweeney and Johnson to Office of Price Stabilization, Export-Import Branch, Washington, DC, January 30, 1952, Sweeney Johnson UNC–Chapel Hill.
96 "Prices and Description—Chinese Hand-Embroidered," folder 20, Promotional Materials, Sweeney Johnson UNC–Chapel Hill.
97 Paynter, *Psychological Study of Trade-Mark*, 5.
98 Trademark Electronic Search System, United States Trademark and Patent Office (hereafter TESS), accessed January 15, 2022, www.uspto.gov/trademarks.
99 Advertisement, "Chesterfield Cigarettes," *Liberty Magazine*, August 8, 1936, Picture ID 1191726019, Gallery of Graphic Design, accessed February 14, 2022, http://gogd.tjs-labs.com.
100 The cases are Smiling Irishman, Inc., et al. v. Juliano et al., 45 NYS 2d 361 (December 8, 1943), 361–70; and Smiling Irishman, Inc., et al. v. McDonald, 52 NYS 2d 211 (December 18, 1944), 211–14.
101 Smiling Irishman, Inc., et al. v. Juliano et al., 366.
102 Advertisement, "The Smiling Irishman, Automobile Dealer, 921 South Hoover Street, Los Angeles, California," *Manzanar Free Press*, April 14, 1943, 5; "An Unsmiling Irishman: N.Y. Supreme Court Bans Use of Trademark by Used Car Dealer Holzer," *Automotive News*, July 2, 1945, 13.
103 "Squabbling 'Irishmen' Evidently Talk with Accents Old Erin Never Heard," *Beaumont Journal*, September 28, 1943, 2.
104 "Smiling Irishman's Grin Gone in Gaelic Lawsuit," *Plain Dealer*, March 11, 1948, 1, 4.
105 Brendan O'Shaughnessy, "What's in a Name: How Notre Dame Became the Fighting Irish," University of Notre Dame Office of Public Affairs and Communications, August 2018, accessed January 22, 2022, www.nd.edu/stories.
106 Brendan O'Shaughnessy, "A Clash over Catholicism," University of Notre Dame Office of Public Affairs and Communications, August 2018, accessed January 22, 2022, www.nd.edu/stories; Tucker, *Notre Dame vs. the Klan*, 211.

107 Registration Number 1264894, TESS, accessed January 22, 2022, www.uspto.gov/.
108 Registration Number 1229591, TESS, accessed January 23, 2022, www.uspto.gov/.
109 Mark J. Mitchell IV, "Over the Hill," *Notre Dame Scholastic*, February 16, 1995, 10–11; Chris Bowman, "Irish Items Worth a Million," *South Bend Tribune*, September 4, 1993, A1.
110 J. Christopher Murphy, "ND's Spirit All in the Leprechaun," *Observer*, March 14, 1986, 2; Mary Goddard, "'Tis True—He's No Irishman," USVA: VP Student Affairs, "Cheerleaders and Prep Rallies, 1966–67," PNDP 3020-L-2 "Fighting Irish Leprechaun Symbol," Archives of the University of Notre Dame.
111 "Buy Irish Goods to Help Employment in Ireland," *Irish Advocate*, June 13, 1964, 9.
112 Rev. Edward A. Malloy, "In Brief," *President's Newsletter* 40, no. 9 (Summer 1997); "Fighting Irish Leprechaun Symbol," Archives of the University of Notre Dame.
113 Arthur Donn Piatt, "American Trade with Ireland," in United States Department of Commerce and Labor, *Monthly Consular and Trade Reports*, 291 (December 1904): 92–93, 4681 H.doc.788 (58-2).
114 DATI, *Handbook and Catalogue*, part 2, 23–24; "Ireland Rules the Garden," *New York Daily Tribune*, September 19, 1905, 14.
115 Advertisement, *Irish American*, February 8, 1851. Also, advertisements, *Richmond Whig*, February 17, 1860; *Daily Advocate*, March 27, 1861; *Irish American*, November 25, 1871.
116 Grant, *International Directory*, vol. 96, s.v. "Irish Distillers," 204; Registered Trademark No. UK0000004474B, April 1, 1876, Intellectual Property Office (hereafter IPO), accessed February 7, 2022, https://trademarks.ipo.gov.uk; Dennison and MacDonagh, *Guinness 1886–1939*, 9; Registered Trademark No. UK00000025819, March 5, 1881, IPO, accessed February 7, 2022, https://trademarks.ipo.gov.uk; Registered Trademark No. UK00000029942, 8 December 1882, IPO, accessed 7 February 2022, https://trademarks.ipo.gov.uk.
117 Dennison and MacDonagh, *Guinness 1886–1939*, 62–72; advertisement, *Irish American*, October 18, 1879. Even Burke's eventually succumbed to piracy; in 1903, it took out a warning notice to advise the public that its bottles were being illegally refilled. Advertisement, *Sun and New York Press*, May 1, 1903, 5.
118 Dennison and MacDonagh, *Guinness 1886–1939*, 67–72.
119 Registration Numbers 0063040 and 0321014, TESS, accessed January 23, 2022, www.uspto.gov.
120 Registration Number 0544232, TESS, accessed January 23, 2022, www.uspto.gov.
121 Registration Numbers 0517883, 0521209, and 0899349, TESS, accessed January 23, 2022, www.uspto.gov.
122 Registration Number 0030705, TESS, accessed January 23, 2022, www.uspto.gov.
123 Riordan, *Modern Irish Trade*, 163; "Irish Distillers," *International Directory of Company Histories*, 205–6; Humphreys, "Issue of Confidence," 96–97.
124 "Irish Distillers," *International Directory of Company Histories*, 206; Humphreys, "Issue of Confidence," 106.
125 "Old Dublin Whiskey" (1934) and "Irish American Whiskey" (1938), advertisements, William Jameson & Son, Seagram Museum Collection, box 112, HAGLEY.

126 Humphreys, "Issue of Confidence," 107–10; Evans, "'Pint of Plain,'" 36–38.
127 Dennison and MacDonagh, *Guinness 1886–1939*, 198.
128 Callanan, *Ireland's Shannon Story*, 44–46; O'Connell with O'Carroll, *Brendan O'Regan*, 71, 77, 125; Fiona Redden, "The Irish 'Father of Duty Free' and Saviour of Shannon," *Irish Times*, October 4, 2018, accessed February 12, 2022, www.irishtimes.com.
129 Ward Morehouse, "Broadway after Dark," *Staten Island Advance*, May 9, 1958, 16; "James J. Downey, 65, Restaurateur, Dies," *New York Times*, June 1, 1972, 46; Earl Wilson, "How to Patch Up Frankie-Desi Feud," *New Orleans States-Item*, April 13, 1961, 23; Kelly, "Nationalism by Design," 125–28.
130 *Beverage Retailer Weekly*, May 8, 1961, 1, Jim Downey's Steakhouse: Clippings, box 1, folder 26, Rosaleen Cahill Fitzgibbon Papers (AIA.007), AIA; John Jameson, advertisement, *New Yorker*, December 2, 1961, 116.
131 Quote reproduced in Kelly, "Nationalism by Design," 137.
132 "New Irish Stylist Is Noted," *New York Times*, August 4, 1959, 18; Caroline Mitchell, "The Evelyn Gaughan Collection," *Irish Times*, July 25, 1962, 4; Irish Pavilion: Uniform Sketches and Notes, box 1, folder 25, Fitzgibbon Papers, AIA.
133 Irish Pavilion: Coffee Bar Menu, box 1, folder 18, Fitzgibbon Papers, AIA.
134 Havel, *Maestro of Crystal*, 236–40. Waterford Crystal, established in 1783, was not produced after the middle of the nineteenth century as a consequence of the Act of Union. *Waterford Crystal* (promotional book, no author, Dublin: Brown and Nolan, n.d.); also, Ida Grehan, *The Collector's Guide: Waterford, an Irish Art* (Huntington, NY: Robert Campbell / Portfolio Press, 1981), 25, 39; "Try One of the World's Truly Great Ones," advertisement no. 7908, Tearsheets and Proofs, Old Bushmills, Seagram Museum Collection, box 112, HAGLEY.
135 Richard J. H. Johnston, "Myths from Past Beset Ireland's Future at Fair," *New York Times*, September 22, 1964, 18; "Irish Whisky [sic]," export label, 1967, B. Standen Scrapbooks, vol. 232, Seagram Museum Collection, HAGLEY.
136 "The Company Image of United Distillers of Ireland: A Qualitative Enquiry" prepared for United Distillers of Ireland Ltd. by I.C.R. Ltd., 24 Ely Place, Dublin 2 (April 1969), 16, 46, Ernest Dichter Papers, series I, accession 2407, box 183, HAGLEY. United Distillers (later Irish Distillers) included John Jameson, John Power, Paddy (Cork Distilleries), and in 1972, Old Bushmills. "Irish Distillers," *International Directory of Company Histories*, 206.
137 "Proposal for a Motivational Research Study on Increasing Sales of Irish Whiskey in the USA" submitted to United Distillers of Ireland by the Ernest Dichter International Institute for Motivation Research, November 1969, Ernest Dichter Papers, series I, accession 2293A, box 101, HAGLEY.
138 *A Motivational Research Study on Increasing Sales of Irish Whiskey in the United States* (Institute for Motivational Research, Inc., Croton-on-Hudson, New York, 1970), 2–7, HAGLEY.
139 *Motivational Research Study*, 122, 130, 131, HAGLEY.

140 "Hospitality and Recipe Guides—Irish Whiskey, Jameson," 1975, Seagram Museum Collection, box 199, HAGLEY.
141 Eden, *Touchdown Jesus*, 180.

6. EMERALD SHEEN

1 "1,500,000 Cheer Colorful N.Y. St. Patrick's Day Parade," *Bridgeport Telegram*, March 18, 1948, 1. On earlier observances of the holiday in the United States, see Crimmins, *St. Patrick's Day*; Ridge, *St. Patrick's Day Parade*; Fitzgerald, "St. Patrick's Day Parade"; Cronin and Adair, *Wearing of the Green*; Moss, "St. Patrick's Day Celebrations," 125–48; Meagher, "'Why Should We Care?,'" 255–69; Marston, "Public Rituals and Community," 255–69; Ryan, "American Parade," 131–53.
2 "Allen's Alley," Fred Allen Papers, MS.2033, box 67, folder 12 (transcript for March 21, 1943), Allen, BPL; Ramsburg, *Network Radio Ratings*, 112, 119, 229.
3 "The Shamrock," *The Gael*, March 1900, 94. "Saint Patrick's Day was not made a national holiday [in Ireland] until 1903 when a bill introduced by the Earl of Dunraven in the House of Lords was passed by the Westminster parliament." Hopkin, *Living Legend*, 120.
4 "A St. Patrick's Day Party and a History of St. Patrick" by "Elaine," *Good Housekeeping*, March 1930, 104.
5 "Truman Arrives in Serious Mood, but Crowd's Good Humor Dispels It," *New York Times*, March 18, 1948, 32; "Truman and Dewey Watch St. Patrick's Day Parade in N.Y.," *Chicago Tribune*, March 18, 1948, 2; "Truman Stands beside Dewey at Irish Parade," *Los Angeles Times*, March 18, 1948, 1.
6 Nelson, *Shamrock*, 113, 134; Hopkin, *Living Legend*, 109.
7 Schmidt, *Consumer Rites*, 18–37.
8 De Breffny, *In the Steps*, 151.
9 De Breffny, *In the Steps*, 148.
10 Hopkin, *Living Legend*, 118–21, 132; Hill, "National Festivals," 30–51.
11 Bankhurst, "Early Irish America," 17–38. On symbols of a negative Irish stereotype circulating in Britain—including St. Patrick, Paddy, brogue, and shillelagh—that were inverted by Irish nationalists, see Higgins, "Paddies Evermore," 61–86.
12 O'Connor, "*Shamrock* of New York," 4–5.
13 Crimmins, *St. Patrick's Day*, 174–89; Quinn, "Toasting King William," 27–51.
14 Williams, *'Twas Only an Irishman's Dream*, 19, 27–29.
15 "Mr. Bernard's Advertisement," *Salem Observer*, November 20, 1852, 2; Nelson, *Shamrock*, 67–68.
16 Nelson, *Shamrock*, 61. "The Wearing of the Green" was originally popularized by Irish nationalists in the late eighteenth century.
17 "Green on Every Side," *New York Times*, March 18, 1886, 3.
18 Crimmins, *Irish-American Historical Miscellany*, 348.
19 "St. Patrick's Day," *New-York Tribune*, March 18, 1869, 5; "St. Patrick's Day," *New York Times*, March 18, 1869, 8; "St. Patrick's Anniversary," *New York Times*, March 18,

1879, 5; "St. Patrick's Day," *Chicago Tribune*, March 18, 1877, 2. Note that this is a phenomenon distinct from the vogue for shamrock decorations in late-nineteenth-century Ireland; see Nelson, *Shamrock*, 90–114.
20 John Reid, *St. Patrick's Day in America*, lithograph (Philadelphia: Duval & Hunter, 1872), accessed June 2, 2023, www.loc.gov/item/2015647829.
21 Marriott, *Nearly 300 Ways*, 198.
22 "Gay Irish Airs Stir 5th Avenue Throng," *New York Times*, March 18, 1927, 3.
23 "Gov. Smith Wears Green from Neck to Ankles," *New York Times*, March 18, 1927, 1.
24 *Irish World*, March 26, 1898, quoted in Ridge, *St. Patrick's Day Parade*, 81. The nurseryman William Baylor Hartland of County Cork supplied "one thousand pots of shamrock for the Irish village" at the Chicago World's Fair in 1893. In 1899, he advertised packets of three thousand shamrock seeds as "A St. Patrick's Day Present for the Irish Abroad" but "the [export] market was never lucrative because it was too seasonal and could easily be over-supplied." Nelson, *Shamrock*, 124–25.
25 "Shamrocks," *New Yorker*, March 12, 1932, 12–13; "Staten Island," *American Florist*, 50 (June 8, 1918): 1034.
26 *American Florist* 44 (January 23, March 6, and March 13, 1915): 13, 330, 374; "A Menu for St. Patrick's Day," *Good Housekeeping*, March 1915, 337.
27 Nelson, *Shamrock*, 6–7, 85–89; Santino, *New Old-Fashioned Ways*, 155.
28 Tuska, Son & Co. v. United States, 2 U.S. Cust. App. 325, 21 Treas. Dec. 615 (1911), 326. An earlier case was United States v. Cattus, 167 Fed. Rep. 532 (2d Cir. 1909), 532. On Japan as one of Tuska's foreign sources, see *The Pottery, Glass and Brass Salesman*, 7 (February 6, 1913), 32.
29 *The Teachers Year Book* (Lebanon, OH: March Brothers, 1916), 70 and *The Teachers Year Book* (Lebanon, OH: March Brothers, 1925), 73, both in the Romaine Trade Catalog Collection, Mss 107, Special Research Collections, Davidson Library, University of California at Santa Barbara (hereafter Romaine, UC Santa Barbara). See the series "Trade Catalogs of School and School Supplies, 1874–1930."
30 Ames, review of *American Holiday Postcards*, 286.
31 Moloney, "Irish-American Popular Music," in *MIA*, 393–98.
32 "The History of Greeting Cards from John Calcott Horsley to Hallmark," Postcard and Greeting Card Museum, accessed August 30, 2022, http://www.emotionscards.com; Roy Nuhn, "Celebrating America's Irish-American Past: Postcards Recall St. Patrick's Days of Yesteryear," *MidAtlantic Antiques*, March 1994, C2.
33 Collection of the author.
34 Ames, review of *American Holiday Postcards*, 287.
35 "St. Patrick's Day in the Morning," New York Public Library Digital Collections, accessed August 13, 2022, https://digitalcollections.nypl.org; William Donovan, East 94th Street, Manhattan Ward 12, ED 0361, New York County, 1910 U.S. Census, Ancestry.com. Myles J. Murphy, a veteran of the St. Louis Irish Village, sold more realistic postcards at his Irish Store on West Twenty-Third Street. "Irish Industries," *Irish American*, February 3, 1906, 5.

36 Descriptions are based on series 5 of the Mick Moloney Irish-American Music and Popular Culture Irish Americana Collection (AIA.031.004), Moloney, AIA; "The Anti-Irish Campaign. Artless, Witless Atrocities Sent Round by the Rotograph Company," *Gaelic American*, February 9, 1907, 1; McElroy, *Red Bricks*, 46.
37 "Killing the Caricatures," *Irish American*, March 14, 1908, 4; "Irish War on Post Cards," *New York Times*, March 1, 1910, 3.
38 Advertisement, *The Novelty News* 12, no. 1 (January 1911): 90.
39 Advertisement, *The Novelty News* 12, no. 2 (February 1911): 106.
40 "A.O.H. Bans Comic Irish Novelties and Post Cards," *Novelty News* 12, no. 3 (March 1911): 96, 98.
41 Advertisement for Rust Craft's St. Patrick's Day Cards in Karl Bros.' pamphlet, "What's New: St. Patrick's Day Number," n.d., box 14, folder 8, Warshaw Collection of Business Americana, NMAH.AC.0060, Archives Center, National Museum of American History [hereafter cited as Warshaw/NMAH]; Earl Ruiter, "The Norcross Greeting Card Company," Postcard and Greeting Card Museum, accessed August 30, 2022, http://www.emotionscards.com.
42 Card 3V4 (1928), series 5 (Permanent Files), subseries 21 (St. Patrick's Day), box 1435, Norcross Greeting Card Collection, NMAH (hereafter cited as Norcross/NMAH).
43 Card 3SP14 (1930), box 1435, Norcross/NMAH. On Manhattan's Upper West Side, the largely Irish American parishioners of Holy Trinity R. C. Church picketed the St. Patrick's Day greeting card display in the windows of the new Woolworth's at Seventy-Ninth Street and Broadway in the early 1930s. Author interview with Dorothy Hayden Cudahy, December 16, 1997. Mrs. Cudahy recalled being one of many children who participated in the Woolworth's picket.
44 Docter, *Celebrating St. Patrick's Day*, 23.
45 Card 15SP5 (1931), box 1435; card 15SP7 (1936), box 1436; card 10SP14 (1933) Norcross/NMAH. For perspective, in 1802, the three leaves of the shamrock stood for Faith, Hope, and Charity. Hopkin, *Living Legend*, 138.
46 Santino, *New Old-Fashioned Ways*, 154.
47 "Great Throng Views St. Patrick's Parade," *New York Times*, March 18, 1926, 25.
48 *A Catalog of Shackman's Favors for All Occasions* (New York: B. Shackman & Co., 1912), Internet Archive, accessed June 2, 2023, https://archive.org/details/catalogofshackma00bsha. There were as many as one thousand unlicensed peddlers distributing such notions in New York City in 1941. See "The Roving Street Peddler," *City Affairs Committee Bulletin* (April 1941), 8, in "New York City Pushcarts, Peddlers" (vertical file), New York City Municipal Reference Library.
49 "St. Patrick's Day: The Celebration Yesterday," *New-York Tribune*, March 18, 1871, 5; "St. Patrick's Day," *Philadelphia Inquirer*, March 18, 1874, 2. The green flag with the golden harp endured in miniature even through contentious debates over flying full-size ones in New York City between the 1880s and 1890s. Fitzgerald, "St. Patrick's Day Parade," 150–201; *Shackman's Wholesale Catalog No. 69* (New York: B. Shackman & Co., 1932), 19, 20, Romaine, UC Santa Barbara; see the series "Trade Catalogs of

Celebration Paraphernalia, 1879–1950." Also, Francis Joseph Biggar, "The Arms and Flags of Ireland," *Irish American*, June 14, 1913, 4.
50 *Shackman's Wholesale Catalog No. 69*, 16–23, Romaine, UC Santa Barbara.
51 At least seven years earlier, the Irish Art Co. of 112 East Forty-First Street in New York had marketed a "Mother Machree" statuette. This was an old woman seated in a rocking chair akin to "Whistler's Mother," complete with "cap, 'Galway Shawl,' Tara Brooch, [and] Rosary Beads." Advertisement, *Irish World*, circa 1925 (courtesy of John T. Ridge).
52 The Kewpies were conceived in 1905 by avant-garde artist Rose O'Neill, and their adventures were syndicated as a comic strip beginning in 1917. See Callahan, *Big Book of American*, 115, 129.
53 *Shackman's Wholesale Catalog No. 69*, 16–23, Romaine, UC Santa Barbara.
54 Emmet O'Reilly, "Irish Ideals and Culture; Objection Is Raised to Features of the Celebrations of St. Patrick's Day," *New York Times*, March 15, 1925, II, 6.
55 Ross, *Saint and the Fairies*; Bloodworth, *Meet Saint Patrick*; *Descriptive Catalog from the House That Helps; The Best Entertainments, Drills and Novelties for the Use of Schools, Churches, Clubs, etc.* (Franklin, OH: Eldridge Entertainment House, [circa 1920s]), 43, Romaine, UC Santa Barbara; see box 5, "Trade Catalogs of School and School Supplies, [1849?]—1938." "Ross, Jean," *SFE: The Encyclopedia of Science Fiction*, 4th ed., accessed August 6, 2022, https://sf-encyclopedia.com.
56 Irish and Bugbee, *St. Patrick's Day Plays*, 11.
57 Curtis, *Why We Celebrate*, 31–35. Second and third editions were published in 1939 and 1950, respectively.
58 "Suggestions for a St. Patrick's Day Program," *Playground* (magazine of the Playground and Recreation Association of America), February 1926, 628; "A St. Patrick's Day Party and a History of St. Patrick" by "Elaine," *Good Housekeeping*, March 1930, 104; Douglas, *American Book of Days*, 162–63.
59 Kennedy and Bemis, *Special Day Pageants*, 14.
60 Hazeltine, *Anniversaries and Holidays*, 43; Reynolds, *St. Patrick's Eve*.
61 Hobsbawm and Ranger, *Invention of Tradition*, 31; Schmidt, "Commercialization of the Calendar," 888.
62 Endorsements are from the scripts for Rose, *Irish Eyes*; and Rose, *Blarney Stone*, copies of which are in the New York Public Library. Samuel French had satellite offices in Los Angeles and London. Even when a contemporary Irish dramatist is rarely offered as a program suggestion, it is invariably a comedy like Lennox Robinson's *The White-Headed Boy* or J. M. Synge's *Tinker's Wedding*.
63 Spicer, *Parties for Young Americans*, 19.
64 Marie Irish's identity was found by accident. See reference in *International Index to Periodicals, Vol. 4 (1924–1927)* (New York: H. W. Wilson Company, 1929), 1276 of part 1. For a list of her books, see the Library of Congress catalog. For the connection to Dick and Fitzgerald, see Fitzgerald Publishing Corporation, *Fitzgerald Publishing Corporation's Descriptive Catalogue of Plays, Entertainments and Books* (New York: Fitzgerald Publishing Corporation, 191[?]). Lawrence R. Fitzgerald (1826–81) was a native of Philadelphia.

65 Irish, introduction to *Shamrocks*. March Brothers Publishing of Lebanon, Ohio, issued a similar guide in 1936, Kathryn Docter's *Celebrating St. Patrick's Day: A Real Irish Collection*.
66 Advertisement (probably circa World War I) for Dennison's St. Patrick's Day Goods in Karl Bros.' pamphlet, "What's New: St. Patrick's Day Number," n.d., box 14, folder 8, Warshaw/NMAH.
67 "On St. Patrick's Day," *Recreation* (magazine of the National Recreation Association), March 1933, 581.
68 "A St. Patrick's Day Party and a History of St. Patrick," *Good Housekeeping*, March 1930, 104.
69 *Shackman's Wholesale Catalog No. 69*, 16–23, Romaine, UC Santa Barbara.
70 "St. Patrick's Day Mystery Party" by "Elaine," *Good Housekeeping*, March 1932, 94.
71 See, for example, cards 5SP5 and 15SP6, box 1436, Norcross/NMAH. This faux look was adapted for the big screen when Scarlett O'Hara sartorially embodied Irish for the barbecue scene of the 1939 film *Gone with the Wind*.
72 "A St. Patrick's Day Party and a History of St. Patrick," *Good Housekeeping*, March 1930, 104.
73 Thijs Porck, "Lucky Pigs and Protective Boars: The Medieval Origins of the Glücksschwein," *Leiden Medievalists Blog, 2017*, accessed September 11, 2022, www.leidenmedievalistsblog.nl.
74 *Shackman's Wholesale Catalog No. 69*, 16, 17, Romaine, UC Santa Barbara.
75 *March of Time*, radio scripts, March 16, 1936, Time Inc. Annex Files, N-YHS Digital Collections, accessed December 19, 2023, https://digitalcollections.nyhistory.org/; "Irish Here Protest on Toy Green Pigs," *New York Times*, April 8, 1936, 2.
76 "Irish Sweepstakes Party" by "Elaine," *Good Housekeeping*, March 1934, 94.
77 "On St. Patrick's Day," *Recreation*, March 1933, 581–82, 593.
78 "Suggestions for a St. Patrick's Day Program," *Playground*, February 1926, 628–30.
79 Irish, *Shamrocks*, 157.
80 "On St. Patrick's Day," *Recreation*, March 1933, 593; see also Spicer, *Parties for Young Americans*, 23; Irish, *Shamrocks*, 141–42; *Playground*, February 1926, 630; *Recreation*, March 1933, 593; Docter, *Celebrating St. Patrick's Day*, 109.
81 Heisenfelt, *Mr. O'Grady's Party*, 1.
82 "A Menu for St. Patrick's Day," *Good Housekeeping*, March 1915, 337; "Green Is the Flavor of Green Vegetables," *Ladies' Home Journal*, March 1934, 34. In Ireland, it was "traditional to kill a pig" on a feast day like March 17, and "pork, ham and bacon" were "the most traditional of all Irish foods, featuring in the diet since prehistoric times." Mac Con Iomaire, "Pig in Irish Cuisine," 210, 214.
83 "St. Patrick's Day in the Morning," *Good Housekeeping*, March 1931, 89; and "St. Patrick's Day in the Morning," *Good Housekeeping*, March 1935, 104. "Today's Menu and Recipes," *Dallas Morning News*, February 26, 1933, 7; "St. Patrick's Day Calls for Green Luncheon Motif," *Dallas Morning News*, March 2, 1934, 9; "Gaily Colored St. Patrick's Day Menu Suggestions Given," *Dallas Morning News*, March 15, 1940, 6; "Everyone Is an Irishman on St. Patrick's Day," *Commercial Appeal*, February 23,

1930, 17. See also "Simple Guest Luncheon for St. Patrick's Day," *Delineator*, March 1909, 442–43; "Emerald Dinner," *Delineator*, March 1912, 252; "Some St. Patrick's Day Luncheons," *Woman's Home Companion*, March 1925, 68–69.

84 A "Mexican Fiesta" was suggested for a novel Father's Day celebration in 1940. "Mexican" was conveyed through sombreros, cacti, pineapples, donkeys, piñata, striped blankets, and pottery bowls. See Spicer, *Parties for Young Americans*, 43–48. This book was copyrighted by the National Board of the Young Women's Christian Associations of the U.S.A.

85 Helfen, *Catholic Theatre Year Book*, 41, Father Alfred Boeddeker Collection, accessed September 1, 2022, https://ecommons.udayton.edu/ml_boeddeker/10; "Catholic Dramatic Movement Expands," *Catholic Transcript*, September 8, 1932, 2. For comparison, see Heinze, *Adapting to Abundance*, 68–85; Zerubavel, "Easter and Passover," 284–89.

86 "Irish Take Over New York; St. Patrick's Day Parade," *Saturday Evening Post*, March 14, 1953, 85; "Old Haunt of Literati, Costello's, Is Closing," *New York Times*, October 3, 1973, 49; "Tim Costello, Saloon Keeper, Pal of 'Name' Writers, Dies," *Connecticut Post*, November 9, 1962, 6.

87 Izod, *Hollywood*, 7–15, 33.

88 Robert W. Snyder, "The Irish and Vaudville," in *MIA*, 408.

89 Rockett (*Irish Filmography*, 244, 252) attributes *Shamus O'Brien* to the poem by Joseph Sheridan LeFanu that was popularized in the United States by Samuel Lover and *Robert Emmet* to an 1884 play by Dion Boucicault. However, much closer in time to the film versions were popular plays called *Shamus O'Brien*, by *Century Magazine* contributor George Jessup, and *Robert Emmet: The Days of 1803*, by Brandon Tynan, which were produced in New York in, respectively, 1898 and 1902. See Fanning, *Irish Voice in America*, 368n36; and "Robert Emmet. Brandon Tynan's Historical Play Achieves Notable Success," *The Gael*, October 1902, 326.

90 Based on the play *Kathleen Mavourneen, or Saint Patrick's Eve* by William Travers, produced in New York City in 1863. Rockett, *Irish Filmography*, 241, 263.

91 Rhodes, "Irish-American Film Audiences," 70–96, 113.

92 *The Shamrock Handicap*, dir. John Ford (Fox Film Corp., 1926). A copy of this film is in the collection of the Museum of Modern Art, New York City, as is *Come On Over*, dir. Alfred E. Green (Goldwyn Pictures, 1922), which used similar techniques four years earlier.

93 "The Shamrock Handicap," *Variety*, July 7, 1926, 17.

94 The subject has been covered by Hampton, *History of the Movies*; Izod, *Hollywood*; Sklar, *Movie-Made America*; and Seldes, *Movies Come from America*, 89–108. See also Screen Publicists Guild, *Role of the Publicity*, 2. A copy of this is in the Tamiment / Robert F. Wagner Labor Archives, Bobst Library, NYU.

95 Sklar, *Movie-Made America*, 233.

96 The word *ballyhoo* used as a verb means to "cajole by extravagant advertisement or praise." As a noun, an early usage dates from 1914 criminal slang for "a free entertainment used for a decoy to attract customers." Ballyhoo is said to be of unknown

origin or derived from Ballyhooly, a village in north County Cork, but it is close in pronunciation and concept to the Irish verb *baileabhair* (pronounced bal´ aur´), meaning to make a fool of a person, which was anglicized as *ballyour*, meaning to shout loudly. I am grateful to the late Barra Ó Donnabháin for etymological materials that helped to substantiate my intuition.

97 Screen Publicists Guild, *Role of the Publicity*, 15.
98 Rufus Steele, "Exploiters Magnificent: The Film Field Has Developed a Propaganda That Takes Its Toll in Millions," *Outlook*, July 15, 1925, 395–96.
99 Dooley, "Irish on the Screen," 214.
100 "Stage and Screen," *State Times Advocate*, August 18, 1927, 19.
101 *Cinema Pressbooks from the Original Studio Collections of United Artists (1919–1949), Warner Brothers (1922–1949), and Monogram Pictures (1937–1946)* (Woodbridge, CT: Research Publications, 1988), part 2, reel 21 (*Irish Hearts*) (hereafter cited as *Cinema Pressbooks*).
102 "'*Irish Hearts*' Vulgar Play, Should Not Be Patronized," [*Gaelic American*?], June 4, 1927. The clipping is in file #2944—box #2614 (*Irish Hearts*), Department of Education Motion Picture Division Film Scripts, NYSA (hereafter cited as NYSA, MPD-FS).
103 James Wingate to Albert S. Howson, July 1, 1927, file #2944—box #2614 (*Irish Hearts*), NYSA, MPD-FS.
104 Howson to Wingate, July 5, 1927, NYSA, MPD-FS.
105 Wingate to Howson, July 8, 1927, NYSA, MPD-FS. Howson to Wingate, July 30, 1927, NYSA, MPD-FS.
106 Examples are from *Cinema Pressbooks*, part 2, reel 21 (*Irish Hearts*).
107 This was an amateur night stunt that "will be much more exciting if some of the old folks can be gotten to take part. Prizes offered for the three best jiggers are given by you on the last night. Suggestions are horseshoe gold pins or enamel shamrocks." *Cinema Pressbooks*, part 2, reel 21 (*Irish Hearts*).
108 "'Irish Hearts'-Vita Fell Down in Balto," *Variety*, June 22, 1927, 7.
109 "A Roughhouse Comedy," *New York Times*, July 12, 1927, 29.
110 "Lay Plans to Fight 'Anti-Irish' Films," *New York Times*, August 18, 1927, 25.
111 "Denies Irish Protest on Movie Was Met," *New York Times*, August 20, 1927, 3; "Irish Film Causes Another Disturbance," *New York Times*, August 26, 1927, 5.
112 "Arrest Four Women in Row over Irish Film," *New York Times*, August 27, 1927, 30; "Shower of Missiles Greets 'Irish Hearts,'" *New York Times*, September 1, 1927, 6; "Assails Film in Theatre," *New York Times*, September 4, 1927, 17; "Seven Held in Yonkers for Irish Film Attack," *New York Times*, September 6, 1927, 18.
113 "Rumpus in Court over Irish Picture," *New York Times*, September 7, 1927, 22.
114 "Now It Is 'the Movie Irishman,'" *New York Times*, July 30, 1927, 14; "Four Women Fined for Film Protest," *New York Times*, August 28, 1927, 23. By October 1927 the New York Irish had lobbied the Board of Aldermen into proposing a new law that could revoke licenses if theaters screened films that disparaged "any race, creed, or nationality." "M'Kee Wants City to Censor Movies," *New York Times*, October 12,

1927, 1. See also Kibler, *Censoring Racial Ridicule*, 204–6; Rhodes, "Irish-American Film Audiences," 70–96, 113.
115 Izod, *Hollywood*, 24.
116 Curran, *Hibernian Green*, 24. Hampton (*History of the Movies*, 335) describes Sheehan as William Fox's "right-hand man and general factotum." For a list of Fox titles, see Rockett, *Irish Filmography*, 699. "Winfield Sheehan, Film Producer, 61," *New York Times*, July 26, 1945, 19.
117 Hampton, *History of the Movies*, 337, 80.
118 "Mother Machree," *Variety*, March 7, 1928, 23. "Mother Machree" was composed in 1910 by Ernest Ball and Chauncey Olcott with lyrics by Rida Johnson Young. Long before Young's "The Story of Mother Machree" (*Munsey's Magazine*, February 1924, 1–32) inspired John Ford's film, the song had become indelibly associated with the tenor John McCormack.
119 *Motion Picture News*, July 27, 1929, 375, quoted in Rockett, *Irish Filmography*, 332.
120 Carl E. Milliken to Ned E. Depinet, August 23, 1929, Motion Picture Producers and Distributors of America (hereafter MPPDA) Record #608, Letters 7-0348 and 7-0349; Rita C. McGoldrick to Carl E. Milliken, November 9, 1929, MPPDA Record #606, Letter 7-0346, MPPDA Digital Archive, Flinders University Library Special Collections, accessed August 11, 2022, https://mppda.flinders.edu.au.
121 Negra, *Off-White Hollywood*, 26, 40–42. Moore endorsed a line of women's beauty products for the Owl Drug Company, including lip stick, face powder and perfumes, that were decorated with green and shamrocks. "A Silent Star's Makeup: Colleen Moore Face Powder (1928–1929)," *Click Americana Vintage & Retro Memories*, accessed August 16, 2022, https://clickamericana.com.
122 See, for example, the *New York Post*, July 27, 1929, III, 5.
123 One original and thirty duplicate seals were issued during this period. NYSA, MPD-FS, file #16249—box #2825 (*Smiling Irish Eyes—Trailer*).
124 Dialogue submitted for *Smiling Irish Eyes—Trailer*, NYSA, MPD-FS, file #16249—box #2825. The film's writer, Thomas J. Geraghty, formerly a New York newspaper reporter, obviously had heard the Irish expression "To hell or to Connaught" that encapsulates the turmoil in Ireland under Oliver Cromwell.
125 *Cinema Pressbooks*, part 2, reel 23 (*Smiling Irish Eyes*).
126 Sklar, *Movie-Made America*, 191.
127 *Cinema Pressbooks*, part 1, reel 9 (*The Irish in Us*).
128 *Cinema Pressbooks*, part 1, reel 9 (*The Irish in Us*).
129 Emphasis added. *Cinema Pressbooks*, part 1, reel 9 (*The Irish in Us*).
130 *Cinema Pressbooks*, part 1, reel 9 (*The Irish in Us*).
131 "Picture Grosses," *Variety*, August 7, 1935, 8–10, 37. That same year, *Variety* reported on the exploitation for a Paramount feature, *Shanghai*, which was implemented by the Fifth Avenue Theatre in Seattle. There, a "Chinese ricksha" was "pulled about downtown streets opening days by a Chinese, with usherette in appropriate garb, getting the ride. Attracted plenty of attention. Also got model of junk that gov. of China had given to president

of American Mail line, and displayed this in foyer. The Fifth Ave. is Chinese motif in architecture and so lends itself well to exploiting this type pix in the house, with the usherettes in Chinese costumes and the doormen as coolies." *Variety*, July 24, 1935, 27.
132 *Cinema Pressbooks*, part 1, reel 17 (*Three Cheers for the Irish*).
133 "Letters to the Times," *New York Times*, March 13, 1940, 22.
134 Screen Publicists Guild, *Role of the Publicity*, 15.
135 *Cinema Pressbooks*, part 1, reel 12 (*My Wild Irish Rose*). Izod, *Hollywood*, 101–3, discusses Hollywood and consumerism. Within the industry, the tie-in was seen as good business for everyone. See also Screen Publicists Guild, *Role of the Publicity*; and Bergman, *We're in the Money*.
136 Flynn and McCarthy, "Economic Imperative," 15, 16.
137 Flynn and McCarthy, "Economic Imperative," 42; and interview with Phil Karlson reproduced in McCarthy and Flynn, *Kings of the Bs*, 344–45. See also Izod, *Hollywood*, 98–101. This assessment applied to some A's as well; *Variety's* review of *The Irish in Us* (August 7, 1935, 21) observed, "A hokum holiday with everything thrown in. Built strictly for laughs, it's in no danger of being included in the Academy awards but it's in for good returns, especially in the nabes [neighborhoods] and those downtown spots whose audiences go for a robust laugh and are not too particular about literary or production values."
138 Interview with Steve Broidy of Monogram, reproduced in McCarthy and Flynn, *Kings of the Bs*, 274; McGee, *Beyond Ballyhoo*, 160.
139 McCarthy and Flynn, *Kings of the Bs*, 270–71; and Izod, *Hollywood*, 100.
140 *Cinema Pressbooks*, part 2, reel 24 (*Leave It to the Irish*).
141 *Cinema Pressbooks*, part 2, reel 24 (*There Goes Kelly*).
142 For background on the production code and the Legion of Decency, see Curran, *Hibernian Green*, 48–52; Sklar, *Movie-Made America*, 173–74; and Izod, *Hollywood*, 105–8. Also Walsh, *Sin and Censorship*; Black, *Hollywood Censored*; Skinner, *Cross and the Cinema*; and Facey, *Legion of Decency*.
143 Trailer copy for *My Wild Irish Rose*. See *Cinema Pressbooks*, part 1, reel 12.
144 Doherty, *Hollywood's Censor*, 213, 233–36.
145 Sheehan's father was from Ireland, and his mother was from Germany. He was buried from Blessed Sacrament Roman Catholic Church in Hollywood in 1945. Winfield R. Sheehan, Buffalo Ward 22, District 0188, 1900 U.S. Federal Census, Ancestry.com; "Service for W. R. Sheehan," *New York Times*, July 30, 1945, 19.
146 Doherty, *Hollywood's Censor*, 23–25, 29.
147 McGregor, *Catholic Church and Hollywood*, 1–43; Smith, *Look of Catholics*, 73.
148 Smith, *Look of Catholics*, 70.
149 Doherty, *Hollywood's Censor*, 25.
150 Gans, "Symbolic Ethnicity," 212.
151 Santino, *New Old-Fashioned Ways*, 152.
152 Schmidt, "Commercialization of the Calendar," 887–916.
153 Meagher, *Inventing Irish America*, 358.

154 "Is St. Patrick's Day a Legal Holiday?," *Illinois Fiery Cross*, April 4, 1924, 6; T. C. Marshall, "The Religion of St. Patrick," *American Standard*, March 8, 1924, 3.
155 See cards 25SP43 (1950) and 15SP16 (1950), box 1438, Norcross/NMAH.
156 See examples in box 2882, series 6 (Permanent Files), subseries IIB (Vollard, St. Patrick's Day), Rustcraft Greeting Card Collection / NMAH. Rustcraft acquired these cards through its merger with the Vollard company.
157 See cards 15SP151 (1952) and 5SP6 (1953), box 1439, and card 15SP42 (1955), box 1440, Norcross/NMAH; also cards 25SP72 (1957) and 10SP49 (1958), box 2882, Rustcraft/NMAH.
158 Golden Leprechaun Beer Bottle, 1950, AG.65.2151, NMAH, accessed August 11, 2022, https://americanhistory.si.edu.
159 Card 25SP35 (1960), box 1442, Norcross/NMAH.
160 Cronin and Adair, *Wearing of the Green*, 114–16; Walker, "St. Patrick's Day," 248–51.
161 Ridge, *St. Patrick's Day Parade*, 144; "Irish Present Shamrocks to Eisenhower," *Chicago Tribune*, March 18, 1953, 6; "Freedoms Guaranteed by State," *Irish Times*, March 18, 1953, 7.
162 Dwight D. Eisenhower to Seán T. O'Kelly, March 17, 1953, and Thomas J. Horan to Maurice Moynihan, May 1, 1953, TAOIS/s/15291, NAI.
163 "Though He Wasn't 'Wearin' of the Green,'" *Washington Post*, March 16, 1956, 69.
164 "110,000 Irish March Here as Chilled 750,000 Watch," *New York Times*, March 18, 1956, 1, 60.

7. COME BACK TO ERIN

1 Fielder, "Chauncey Olcott," 4–26; Williams, *'Twas Only an Irishman's Dream*.
2 Zuelow, *Making Ireland Irish*, 34–71; Furlong, *Irish Tourism*, 37–86, 159–82.
3 Advertisement, *Old Castle Garden*, June 1931, 46; O'Dwyer, "On Show to the World," 42–47; Cronin, "Projecting the Nation," 395–411.
4 O'Driscoll, Introduction to *Administration*, 153.
5 "Books You Want," *The Gael*, November 1899, 240; also, advertisement in Haverty, *History of Ireland*. For the Irish American market for Catholic publishers, also see Sullivan, "Community in Print," 41–76.
6 Granshaw, *Irish on the Move*, 117.
7 "Things We'd Like—," *Plattsburgh Daily Press*, April 15, 1939, 4.
8 Granshaw, *Irish on the Move*, 116–17; advertisement, "Prof. John MacEvoy's Erinopion, or Erin Illustrated," *Gloucester County Democrat*, October 14, 1880, 3.
9 Granshaw, "Hibernicon and Visions," 4, 26, 35–36, 143.
10 Nick Whitmer, "Pat Touhey's Earliest Known Tour," *Touhey Archive*, accessed March 19, 2023, https://www.whitmerpipes.com.
11 O'Rourke, *Currier and Ives*, 11.
12 Granshaw, "Hibernicon and Visions," 29.
13 Film review, *Moving Picture World*, September 30, 1911, 954; Rockett, Gibbons, and Hill, *Cinema and Ireland*, 213; O'Rourke, *Currier and Ives*, 125. See the *New York*

Daily Tribune, March 30, 1860, for opening night review and specific comments on Killarney sets.

14 "Midway Plaisance," in White and Igleheart, *World's Columbian Exposition*, 569, 595; O'Malley, *Beat Cop*, 177, 185; "Chicago's Irish Fair: Map of the Emerald Isle Covered with Virgin Sod," *Evening Star*, December 11, 1897; "Irish Sod: Soil from the Old Country Received Here for Exhibition Purposes," *Plain Dealer*, July 4, 1898, 3; "The Irish Fair Plans Being Made to Make It a Great Success," *Philadelphia Inquirer*, November 20, 1898, 27.

15 "When reproductions of things seem more real, authentic, and powerful to us than the thing being reproduced, then we are in the realm of hyperrealism." Childers and Hentzi, *Columbia Dictionary*, 142; Eco, *Travels in Hyperreality*; Johnson, *Isle of the Shamrock*; Bayne, *On an Irish Jaunting-Car*.

16 Casey, "Cornerstone of Memory," 10–56.

17 Ridge, "Irish County Societies," 285; White and Igleheart, *World's Columbian Exposition*, 595.

18 "Coney's New Resort," *Irish American*, May 9, 1903, 1; "The 'Ould Sod,'" *The Gael*, June 1903, 200.

19 Thomas R. MacMechen, "The True and Complete Story of the Pike and Its Attractions, World's Fair, St. Louis, U.S.A.," *World's Fair Bulletin*, April 1904, 4, HAGLEY; "Dun Emer Art Industry," *The Gael*, February 1904, 74.

20 Bruce Stewart, "Michael Balfe," *Ricorso: A Knowledge of Irish Literature*, accessed March 9, 2023, http://www.ricorso.net; "Balfe, Michael William," *Discography of American Historical Recordings*, accessed March 9, 2023, https://adp.library.ucsb.edu/names/102997; advertisement for Whittemore's Select Catalogue, *Huron County News*, November 9, 1865, 2; Nigel Burton, "The Lily of Killarney," *Grove Music Online*, accessed March 9, 2023, https://www.oxfordmusiconline.com.

21 Horgan, *Echo after Echo*, 76, 78; "Lakes of Killarney for Sale," *The Gael*, June 1899, 67–68; "Sale of Lakes of Killarney," *New York Times*, November 28, 1899, 7.

22 Hamilton Kennedy, Freddie Grundland, Gerald Morrison, and Ted Steels, *How Can You Buy Killarney?* (London: Peter Maurice Music Corp. Ltd, 1948).

23 *Burton Holmes, Extraordinary Traveler* (Hidden Knowledge E-books, 2016), accessed March 8, 2023, www.burtonholmes.org.

24 O'Donovan-Rossa, *My Father and Mother*, 149–50. See also "Kissing the Blarney Stone," *The Gael*, September 1904, 310; and Kathleen Carmody's Travel Diary, 1903, Kathleen Hill Family Collection (AIA.064), AIA.

25 "The Irish Honeymoon," advertisement, *The Film Index*, February 2, 1911; advertisement for *The O'Kalems' Visit to Killarney* at the Odeon Theatre in Canton, Ohio, *Canton Daily News*, March 24, 1912, 18; "The O'Kalems' Visit to Killarney," *Moving Picture World*, January 20, 1912, 202; advertisement, *Moving Picture World*, March 7, 1914; Harner, "Kalem Company, Travel," 191; Slide, "O'Kalems," 15–26, 113.

26 "Holmes in Ireland: Travelogue Interested Large Audience at Academy of Music," *Philadelphia Inquirer*, December 5, 1914, 5.

27 Felter and Schultz, "Selling Memories, Strengthening Nationalism," 10–20; Felter and Schultz, "James Mark Sullivan," 24–40.
28 "Amusements," *Springfield Daily News*, July 5, 1916, 10.
29 "Beautiful Ireland," folder 1–32, Wharton Releasing Corporation Records, #3924, Division of Rare and Manuscript Collections, Cornell University Library (hereafter Wharton, Cornell).
30 "St. Patrick's Day Program," *Salt Lake Telegram*, March 17, 1921, 11.
31 "Agreement between Arthur Feary and Emmet Moore," folder 5, Wharton, Cornell; Rhodes, introduction to *Post Script*, 3–14; Casella, "Ireland a Nation," 27–43; "'Ireland, a Nation' Is Given at Victory," *Evening News*, November 25, 1920, 2.
32 "Arlington Theatre Erin's Isle," *Boston Herald*, January 28, 1929, 13.
33 "Irish Books and Authors," *The Gael*, December 1901, 392.
34 "Hints and Jottings," *Irish Tourist* 2, no. 6 (1895): 17.
35 "Ah!!!," *Irish Tourist* 1, no. 3 (August 1894): 65.
36 "Let America Know," *Irish Travel* 1, no. 3 (November 1925): 53–54.
37 "A Film Tour of Ireland," *Irish Travel* 1, no. 3 (November 1925): 70.
38 "Advertising Ireland as a Tourist Resort in US and Europe," *Gaelic American*, August 29, 1925, 3; Zuelow, *Making Ireland Irish*, xvii.
39 "The Los Angelesation of Ireland," *Catholic World*, August 1927, 686–87.
40 "Irish Luck," *Florence Times-News*, March 14, 1926, 12; U.S. Census Bureau, *Population Density*, 1920, prepared by Social Explorer, accessed March 11, 2023.
41 Kelleher, "Irish Are Coming Home," 244; "British Tourists Flock to Ireland," *New York Times*, October 5, 1934, 11; Furlong, *Irish Tourism*, 42–43; Zuelow, "Tourism Nexus," 24; Zuelow, "National Identity and Tourism," 145–46.
42 "Activities of the ITA: Publicity," *Irish Travel* 1, no. 2 (October 1925): 33.
43 "Ireland Expects Big Influx of Tourists during Next Summer," *Gaelic American*, April 17, 1926, 1.
44 "Ireland Prepares to Receive American Tourists This Year," *New York Times*, March 27, 1927, VII, 22.
45 "American Professor Give His Views on Irish Tourist Industry," *Gaelic American*, March 20, 1926, 1.
46 Irish Tourist Association (hereafter ITA), *Ireland*, 51, 56.
47 Davison, *Our Fortnight in Ireland*, 3, 22.
48 Horgan, *Echo after Echo*, 76, 92.
49 Murphy, *Every Which Way*, 3; catalog description for MS 21,849, letter from Pat Mullen, Kilronan, Aran Islands to Alison Murphy, April 29, 1930, National Library of Ireland, accessed March 11, 2023, https://catalogue.nli.ie/Record/vtls000836394.
50 Murphy, *Every Which Way*, 4. "Though her journal inevitably borrows a little from the guide-books, it is a fresh and charming account of a happy pilgrimage." *Times Literary Supplement* (London) quoted in *Book Review Digest* (New York: H. W. Wilson, 1930), 756.
51 Curtin, "Jeremiah Curtin," 67.
52 Zarucchi, *Material Culture of Tableware*, 43–46.

53 Marshall Field & Company advertisement, *Chicago Tribune*, July 15, 1931, 15. By 1933, the Association had also opened temporary offices in Chicago and San Francisco, but only the New York office survived the effects of the Depression. "Free State Gaining Tourists," *New York Times*, April 29, 1934, IV, 2.
54 Some wits speculated whether La Guardia might have the other piece. *New York Times*, August 16, 1933, 19.
55 Educational Screen and Greene, *1000 and One*, 39–40; "British Tourists Flock to Ireland," *New York Times*, October 5, 1934, 11; "As America Sees Us! Have They Kissed It?," *Irish Travel* 7, no. 3 (November 1931): 56; "Film Publicity for Ireland," *Irish Travel* 9, no. 9 (July 1934): 171.
56 Darragh O'Donoghue, review of *Fitzpatrick Travel Talks Vol. 1 (1934–1946)*, *Cineaste* 41, no. 4 (2016), accessed March 10, 2023, www.cineaste.com; O'Toole, *Black Hole, Green Card*, 40.
57 Fitzpatrick quoted in Wilkman, *Screening Reality*, 120.
58 In quick succession, *Dublin of the Welcomes* (1934), *Top of the Morning* (1936), *In Ireland's Garden* (1937), *Wings over Ireland* (1939), *Ireland's Real Gold* (1940), and *Irish Cavalcade* (1941), all filmed on location by a new iteration of the Film Company of Ireland, appeared on American cinema screens. The Film Company of Ireland has no known relation to the company of the same name that made films in Ireland during the 1910s. Information on its travelogues was compiled from the Manufacturer and Exchange (Distributor) Indices, NYSA, MPD.
59 Messenger, "Literary vs. Scientific Interpretations," 47; *How the Myth Was Made: A Study of Robert Flaherty's Man of Aran*, dir. George Stoney (New York: Films, Inc., 1979).
60 Furlong, *Irish Tourism*, 52.
61 Maume, "Conrad Maynadier Arensberg," in *DIB*; Messenger, "Literary vs. Scientific Interpretations," 52; Byrne, Edmondson, and Varley, "Arensberg and Kimball," 4, 21, 34, 48–53, 58. The influence of *Man of Aran*, *The Irish Countryman* (1937), and *Family and Community in Ireland* (1940) on academic perceptions cast an enduring long shadow in the green space. The work of Arensberg and Kimball was part of the Harvard Irish Study (1932–36), which also included gathering "anthropometric data" for a "racial survey" especially in rural locations. "Some 12,000 individuals acquiesced to being measured by the physical anthropologists." The timing is interesting, given that it closely follows the fraught racial debates over American national origins legislation discussed in chapter 4. See also O'Neill, "Harvard Scientist."
62 Significantly, although its ballyhoo was not shamrock-soaked, some reviewers drew from the green space when pointing to the main character's penchant for sentimentality, drinking, and fighting. *New York Sun*, May 10, 1935; Rockett, "Documentaries," 72. Fred Allen spoofed it in a radio sketch called "The Squealer." Allen, BPL, MS. 2033, box 54, folder 16.
63 Diana Rice, "Random Notes for Travelers," *New York Times*, November 6, 1938, X, 5.
64 "Ireland Will Seek Big Tourist Trade," *New York Times*, October 26, 1938, 19. In 1952, the operation was divided into *An Bord Fáilte* (which developed tourist facilities) and

Fogra Fáilte (which handled publicity, publications and information). These names indicate the resurfacing of the "genial" and "hospitable" image; *An Bord Fáilte* and *Fogra Fáilte* mean "Welcome Board" and "Welcome Advertising," respectively.

65 "A special despatch [*sic*] of four tons of Irish Tourist Literature outside the ITA Offices, Dublin, prior to its conveyance per *S.S. Roosevelt*, which left Cobh for New York and the World's Fair on 16th April," photo caption, *Irish Travel* 14, no. 8 (May 1939): 182.
66 Rice, "Random Notes for Travelers," 5.
67 Zuelow, *Making Ireland Irish*, 114.
68 Furlong, *Irish Tourism*, 161, 164; "Campaign to Attract U.S. Visitors," *Irish Times*, October 24, 1947, 3; Jack Deedy, "Ireland's Tourist Trade Booming," *Boston Globe*, July 15, 1949, 12.
69 Fiori, *Holiday*, 21; Sherry, "Frank O'Connor," in *DIB*; Eric Forbes-Boyd, "On an Irish Holiday: The Bookshelf," *Christian Science Monitor*, July 9, 1947, 18; "History," *Holiday Magazine*, accessed March 21, 2023, www.holiday-magazine.com; Michael Callahan, "A *Holiday* for the Jet Set," *Vanity Fair*, April 11, 2013, accessed March 24, 2023, www.vanityfair.com.
70 Donal Ó Drisceoil, "Frank O'Connor: Gamekeeper Turned Poacher," *Irish Examiner*, September 17, 2014, accessed March 25, 2023, www.irishexaminer.com.
71 Harrison Howell Walker, "Old Ireland, Mother of New Éire: By Whatever Name, 'Tis the Same Fair Land with the Grass Growing Green on the Hills of Her and the Peat Smoke Hanging Low," *National Geographic Magazine*, May 1940, 655, 658, 687; Weaver-Zercher, *Amish in the American*, 75.
72 Frank O'Connor, "Ireland: A Haunting Sense of the Past Keeps It Proud, Poetic—and Poor," *Holiday*, December 1949, 35.
73 Furlong, *Irish Tourism*, 105–7; Zuelow, *Making Ireland Irish*, 55–56; O'Connell with O'Carroll, *Brendan O'Regan*, 102–5.
74 Zuelow, *Making Ireland Irish*, xxvi–xxix, 57–58; Furlong, "Through a Mirror, Darkly," 56–58.
75 "The Quiet Man," *Variety*, May 14, 1952, 6.
76 *Wings to Ireland (Ireland, Mother Ireland)*, a Hartley Production for Pan American World Airways, Script #57591, box #1686, NYSA, MPD.
77 Adrian Frazier, "Echoes of *The Playboy*: *The Quiet Man* and the Abbey," in Crosson and Stoneman, *Quiet Man*, 59–60.
78 Eamonn Slater, "The Hidden Landscape Aesthetic of *The Quiet Man*," in Crosson and Stoneman, *Quiet Man*, 144.
79 Department of Industry and Commerce, *Synthesis of Reports*, 28.
80 Roddy Flynn, "Talking a Little Treason: The Irish State and *The Quiet Man*," in Crosson and Stoneman, *Quiet Man*, 174.
81 Edwin Schallert, "Ford's 'Quiet Man' Unique in Interest," *Los Angeles Times*, October 3, 1952, B9; Roddy Flynn, "Projecting or Protecting Ireland? The Department of External Affairs and Hollywood, 1946–1960," in Barton, *Screening Irish-America*, 223.

82 Des McHale, "*The Quiet Man* as Cult Movie," in Crosson and Stoneman, *Quiet Man*, 243.
83 Gibbons, *Quiet Man*, 85.
84 "The Quiet Man," *Variety*, May 14, 1952, 6.
85 Marion R. Casey, "Victor Herbert, Nationalism, and Musical Expression," in Nyhan Grey, *Ireland's Allies*, 167, 407n17.
86 "'The Quiet Man' Is the Year's Most Outstanding Picture," *Variety*, September 17, 1952, 24; Richard L. Coe, "Now Irish Eyes Are Smiling Again," *Washington Post*, October 3, 1952, 30.
87 Flynn, "Talking a Little Treason," 171–72. Equally significant is that many Irish Americans, especially those who emigrated in the 1920s and in the aftermath of World War II, would have recognized the traditional, conservative, religious, and rules-bound post-Famine farming world that lies behind what the *New Yorker* reviewer called the film's "treacle." Philip Hamburger, "The Current Cinema," *New Yorker*, August 23, 1952, 56–57; John Hill, "The Quiet Man: Ford, Mythology and Ireland," in in Crosson and Stoneman, *Quiet Man*, 183–95.
88 Flynn, "Projecting or Protecting Ireland?," 226.
89 Win Fanning, "Television and Radio News," *Pittsburgh Post-Gazette*, February 28, 1961, 29; Savage, *Ireland in the New*, 155, 159, 162. The cover of the March 1961 issue of *National Geographic* channeled a shawled Mary Kate Danaher-type to entice readers to peruse "The Magic Road round Ireland," a title that essentially recycled Padraic Colum's 1926 travel book.
90 O'Driscoll, introduction to *Administration*, 151.
91 King, "Saints, Shamrocks, and Signifying," 139, 141, 143.

CONCLUSION

1 Mick Moloney, field notes: May 4, 1977, 4–5; and Sound Recordings, Logs: Tape 13, Side A, Chicago Ethnic Arts Project Collection (AFC 1981/004), American Folklife Center, LC.
2 Chicago Ethnic Arts Project Collection, LC, accessed October 15, 2022, www.loc.gov/collections.
3 Moloney, field notes, 4–5.
4 "The Power of Sibéal," *Irish Times*, February 23, 1989, 13. One of the founding partners of Hill Holliday was John Connors, a Boston Irish Catholic who broke into the advertising business through BBDO in New York; "The Irish Tourist Board: Invaders" (*The One Show*, 1989), the Paley Center for Media, Catalog ID: AT 21946.001; Stuart Elliott, "Irish Tourist Board Is Back with Hal Riney," New York Times, November 14, 1991, D10; David McPherson to Marion R. Casey, October 10, 2020, in David McPherson, "Irish Tourist Board 'Ancient Birthplace of Good Times,'" Vimeo, April 5, 2019, https://vimeo.com/328712175.
5 "Tiny Budget, Big Win," *Irish Times*, July 19, 1989, 17.
6 "Burying Realism," *Irish Times*, November 6, 1995, 13.
7 Joe Lee, quoted in Logue, *Being Irish*, 123.

8 Kimball, "Replicating Authenticity," 33–60; Theme Park Archive, accessed May 25, 2023, www.themeparkarchive.com.
9 *Brown Is the New Green: George Lopez and the American Dream*, dir. Phillip Rodriguez (213 Projects, Independent Television Service for PBS, 2007). The literature on ethnic imagery in communications and commerce tends to concentrate on racial minorities and is oblivious to the precedents set by the Irish. Dávila, *Latinos, Inc.*; Bondanella, *Hollywood Italians*; Davé, Nishime, and Oren, *East Main Street*; Dávila, *Latino Spin*; Dávila and Rivero, *Contemporary Latina/o Media*; Tharp, *Marketing and Consumer Identity*, especially 294–95. An exception is Halter, *Shopping for Identity*.
10 Marion R. Casey, "Ireland and America: A Special Affinity," *Georgetown Journal of International Affairs* (Walsh School of Foreign Service, Georgetown University), February 2, 2021, accessed July 18, 2023, gjia.georgetown.edu.

BIBLIOGRAPHY

MANUSCRIPT COLLECTIONS
Australia
Motion Picture Producers and Distributors of America Digital Archives, Flinders University Library, Bedford Park, South Australia

California
Romaine Trade Catalog Collection, Davidson Library, University of California, Santa Barbara
UCLA Film and Television Archive, University of California, Los Angeles

Delaware
Center for the History of Business, Technology, and Society, Hagley Museum and Library, Wilmington

Indiana
University of Notre Dame Archives, South Bend

Iowa
Travelling Culture: Circuit Chautauqua in the Twentieth Century, University of Iowa

Ireland
Department of Foreign Affairs and Trade, www.dfa.ie
Irish Industrial Development Authority Papers, National Archives, Dublin
National Library, Dublin
RTE Archives, www.rte.ie

Massachusetts
Fred Allen Papers, Archives and Special Collections, Boston Public Library

Michigan
John Bond Trevor Papers, Bentley Historical Library, University of Michigan, Ann Arbor
MSU Museum Cultural Collection, Michigan State University

New York

Archives of Irish America, Special Collections, Bobst Library, New York University. Department of Education Motion Picture Division Film Scripts, New York State Archives
Division of Rare and Manuscript Collections, Cornell University Library
Manuscripts and Archives Division, New York Public Library
Municipal Archives, New York City Department of Records and Information Services
Paley Center for Media
Tamiment/Robert F. Wagner Labor Archives, Special Collections, Bobst Library, New York University
Theater Collection, Museum of the City of New York
Theater Collection, New York Public Library for the Performing Arts

North Carolina

Southern Historical Collection, University of North Carolina, Chapel Hill

Ohio

Father Alfred Boeddeker Collection, University of Dayton

Washington, DC

American Folklife Center, Library of Congress
Art Inventories Catalog, Smithsonian Art Museum
Motion Picture, Sound, and Video Branch, National Archives
National Museum of American History, Smithsonian
NBC Radio Collection, Library of Congress

Wisconsin

Irish Sheet Music Archives, Milwaukee Irish Fest, Milwaukee
Wisconsin Center for Film and Theatre Research, University of Wisconsin-Madison

NEWSPAPERS

Advocate (Baton Rouge, LA)
Arkansas Gazette (Little Rock, AR)
Augusta Chronicle (Augusta, GA)
Automotive News (Detroit, MI)
Badger American (Milwaukee, WI)
Beaumont Journal (Beaumont, TX)
Boston Globe (Boston, MA)
Boston Herald (Boston, MA)
Boston Journal (Boston, MA)
Boston Pilot (Boston, MA)
Bridgeport Telegram (Bridgeport, CT)
Bronx Sentinel (Bronx, NY)
Catholic Transcript (Hartford, CT)

Charleston News and Courier (Charleston, SC)
Chicago Tribune (Chicago, IL)
Christian Science Monitor (Boston, MA)
Cincinnati Post (Cincinnati, OH)
Cleveland Leader (Cleveland, OH)
Commercial Appeal (Memphis, TN)
Connecticut Post (Bridgeport, CT)
Cork Weekly Examiner (Cork, Ireland)
Daily Advocate (Baton Rouge, LA)
Daily Inter Ocean (Chicago, IL)
Dallas Morning News (Dallas, TX)
Detroit Times (Detroit, MI)
Detroit Tribune (Detroit, MI)
Duluth News-Tribune (Duluth, MN)
Evening News (San Jose, CA)
Evening Star (Washington, DC)
Fairmont West Virginian (Fairmont, WV)
Florence Times-News (Florence, AL)
Gaelic American (New York, NY)
Gloucester County Democrat (Woodbury, NJ)
Huron County News (Port Austin, MI)
Idaho Falls Times (Idaho Falls, ID)
Illinois Fiery Cross (Chicago, IL)
Irish Advocate (New York, NY)
Irish American Weekly (New York, NY)
Irish Echo (New York, NY)
Irish Examiner (Dublin, Ireland)
Irish Independent (Dublin, Ireland)
Irish Press (Philadelphia, PA)
Irish Times (Dublin, Ireland)
Irish World (New York, NY)
Kentucky Irish American (Louisville, KY)
Kentucky Post (Covington, KY)
Los Angeles Times (Los Angeles, CA)
Mail and Empire (Toronto, Canada)
Manzanar Free Press (Manzanar, CA)
Marietta Journal (Marietta, GA)
Milwaukee Journal (Milwaukee, WI)
Milwaukee Journal-Sentinel (Milwaukee, WI)
New Orleans Item (New Orleans, LA)
New World (Chicago, IL)
New York Evening Post (New York, NY)
New York Herald (New York, NY)

New York Journal American (New York, NY)
New York Post (New York, NY)
New York Sun (New York, NY)
New York Times (New York, NY)
New-York Tribune (New York, NY)
Observer (South Bend, IN)
Omaha World-Herald (Omaha, NE)
Pawtucket Times (Pawtucket, RI)
Philadelphia Inquirer (Philadelphia, PA)
Pittsburgh Post-Gazette (Pittsburgh, PA)
Plain Dealer (Cleveland, OH)
Plattsburgh Daily Press (Plattsburgh, NY)
Repository (Canton, OH)
Richmond Times Dispatch (Richmond, VA)
Richmond Whig (Richmond, VA)
Rochester Democrat and Chronicle (Rochester, NY)
Saint Paul Globe (Saint Paul, MN)
Salem Observer (Salem, MA)
Salt Lake Telegram (Salt Lake City, UT)
San Diego Union (San Diego, CA)
San Francisco Chronicle (San Francisco, CA)
San Francisco Chronicle Sporting Green (San Francisco, CA)
Seattle Daily Times (Seattle, WA)
South Bend Tribune (South Bend, IN)
Springfield Daily News (Springfield, MA)
Springfield Union (Springfield, MA)
Stamford Advocate (Stamford, CT)
Staten Island Advance (Staten Island, NY)
St. Louis Post Dispatch (St. Louis, MO)
St. Louis Republic (St. Louis, MO)
Sun and New York Press (New York, NY)
Times-Picayune (New Orleans, LA)
Toronto Evening Telegram (Toronto, Canada)
Trenton Evening Times (Trenton, NJ)
Washington Post (Washington, DC)
Watertown Daily Times (Watertown, NY)

MAGAZINES

Administration (Dublin, Ireland)
Albion
American Florist
American Magazine
American Mercury

American Standard
Antiques
Atlantic Monthly
Beverage Retailer Weekly
Book Review Digest
Catholic World
Current Biography
Current History
Current Opinion
Delineator
Engineering Review
Foreign Affairs
Fortnightly Review
Good Housekeeping
Harper's
Holiday
Irish Illustrated (Dublin, Ireland)
Irish America
Irish Tourist (Dublin, Ireland)
Irish Trade Journal (Dublin, Ireland)
Irish Travel (Dublin, Ireland)
Ladies' Home Journal
Liberty
Life
Literary Digest
Living Age
MidAtlantic Antiques
Modern Stationer and Bookseller
Motion Picture News
Motion Picture World
Munsey's Magazine
National Geographic
New York Magazine
New York Musical Review and Choral Advocate
New York Times Magazine
Newsweek
Novelty News
Old Castle Garden
Outlook
Playground
Pottery, Glass and Brass Salesman
Reader's Digest
Recreation

Saturday Evening Post
Saturday Review of Literature
Scribner's Magazine
Seaport: New York's History Magazine
The Capuchin Annual (Dublin, Ireland)
The Delineator
The Film Index
The Gael
The Musical Times and Singing Class Circular
The Nation
The New Yorker
The North American Review
The Notre Dame Scholastic
The Outlook
The Playground
The Spectator
Time
Vanity Fair
Variety
Woman's Home Companion

GOVERNMENT DOCUMENTS

Amendments to the Immigration Laws (1965): Hearings, Ninety-First Congress . . . by United States. Congress. House. Committee on the Judiciary. Subcommittee No. 1. Washington, DC: U.S. Government Printing Office, 1970.

Amendment to the Trademark Laws, Hearing before the Committee on Patents, House of Representatives, 63rd Congress, 2nd Session on H.R. 15403, a Bill Reviewing and Amending the Statutes Relative to Trademarks. Washington, DC: U.S. Government Printing Office, 1914.

Congress, House, Committee on Immigration and Naturalization. *National Origins Provision Immigration Act of 1924*, 69th Cong., 2d sess., 1927. CIS No. H455-7.

Congress, Senate, Committee on Immigration, *National Origins Provision of Immigration Law*, 70th Cong., 2d sess., 1929. CIS No. S318-6.

Congressional Record, January 3, 1969, 58, www.govinfo.gov.

Department of Agriculture and Technical Instruction for Ireland (DATI). *Handbook and Catalogue of Exhibits, Irish Industrial Exhibition, World's Fair, St. Louis, 1904.* Dublin: Department of Agriculture and Technical Instruction, 1904.

———. *Report on the Trade in Imports and Exports at Irish Ports.* Dublin: H. M. Stationery Office, 1912.

———. *Report on the Trade in Imports and Exports at Irish Ports.* Dublin: H. M. Stationery Office, 1914.

Department of Commerce. *Statistical Abstract of the United States: 1924 (Forty-Seventh Number).* Washington, DC: U.S. Government Printing Office, 1925.

Department of Industry and Commerce. *Synthesis of Reports on Tourism, 1950–1951.* Publication no. 586. Dublin: Stationery Office, 1951.
Hearings before the Subcommittee No. 1 of the Committee on the Judiciary, House of Representatives, Eighty-Ninth Congress, 1st Sess., on H.R. 2580 to Amend the Immigration and Nationality Act, and for Other Purposes. Washington, DC: U.S. Government Printing Office, 1965.
Hearings before the Subcommittee on Immigration and Naturalization of the Committee on Judiciary, United States Senate, 89th Congress, 1st Session on S. 500 "to Amend the Immigration and Nationality Act, and for Other Purposes, Part 1." Washington, DC: U.S. Government Printing Office, 1965.
Senate Vote #232 in 1965 (89th Congress). *To Pass H.R. 2580, Immigration and Nationality Act Amendments. Sep 22, 1965.* www.govtrack.us/congress/votes.
United States Bureau of the Census. *A Century of Population Growth.* Washington, DC: U.S. Government Printing Office, 1909.
United States Congressional Serial Set, Volume 8227, John B. Trevor, "A Preliminary Study of Population," Appendix A of House Reports 68th Congress, 1st Session (December 3, 1923, to June 7, 1924), Vol. 2. Washington, DC: U.S. Government Printing Office, 1924.
United States Department of Commerce and Labor. *Monthly Consular and Trade Reports*, 291 (December 1904): 4681 H.doc.788 (58-2).
United States Department of State. *The Immigration Work of the Department of State and Its Consular Officers.* Washington, DC: U.S. Government Printing Office, 1935.

SECONDARY SOURCES

Abramovitch, Ilana. "America's Making Exposition and Festival (New York, 1921)." PhD diss., New York University, 1996.
Akenson, Donald H. "Why the Accepted Estimates of Ethnicity of the American People, 1790, Are Unacceptable." *William and Mary Quarterly* 41, no. 1 (January 1984): 102–19.
Akhtar, Shahmima. "A Cultural History of Irish Identity on Display." *Historical Transactions* (blog). Royal Historical Society (London), July 31, 2019. https://blog.royalhistsoc.org.
Alba, Richard D. *Ethnic Identity: The Transformation of White America.* New Haven, CT: Yale University Press, 1990.
Almeida, Linda Dowling. "A Great Time to Be Irish in America: The Irish in Post-Second World War New York City." In Keogh and Quinlan, *Ireland in the 1950s*, 206–20.
———. *Irish Immigrants in New York City, 1945–1995.* Bloomington: Indiana University Press, 2001.
Altschul, Charles. *The American Revolution in Our School Text-Books; an Attempt to Trace the Influence of Early School Education on the Feeling towards England in the United States.* New York: George H. Doran, 1917.
American Council of Learned Societies. "Report of Committee on Linguistic and National Stocks in the Population of the United States." In *American Historical Association, Annual Report for the Year 1931.* Vol. 1. Washington, DC: American Council of Learned Societies, 1932.

American Folklife Center. *Ethnic Recordings in America: A Neglected Heritage.* Washington, DC: Library of Congress, 1982.
American Irish Historical Society, "Immigration Law, Resolution Adopted at the Quarterly Meeting of the American Irish Historical Society, Held on May 12th, 1926." *Journal of the American Irish Historical Society* 3, no. 6 (September 1926): 9.
———. "Memorial of Thomas Hamilton Murray." *Journal of the American Irish Historical Society* 8 (1909): 80–87.
Ames, Kenneth L. Review of *American Holiday Postcards, 1905–1915: Imagery and Context* by Daniel Gifford. *West 86th: A Journal of Decorative Arts, Design History, and Material Culture* 21, no. 2 (Fall–Winter 2014): 286–90.
Anderson, Benedict. *Imagined Communities: Reflections on the Origin and Spread of Nationalism.* London: Verso, 1983.
Anderson, Margo J. *The American Census: A Social History.* New Haven, CT: Yale University Press, 1990.
———[Conk]. "The Census, Political Power, and Social Change: The Significance of Population Growth in American History." *Social Science History* 8, no. 1 (Winter 1984): 81–106.
Appel, John, and Selma Appel. *Pat-Riots to Patriots: American Irish in Caricature and Comic Art.* East Lansing: Michigan State University Museum, 1990.
Arensberg, Conrad. *The Irish Countryman: An Anthropological Study.* New York: Macmillan, 1937.
Arensberg, Conrad, and Solon Kimball. *Family and Community in Ireland.* Cambridge, MA: Harvard University Press, 1940.
Ayer, N. W., & Son. *N. W. Ayer & Son's American Newspaper Annual and Directory.* Fort Washington, PA: IMS Press, 1930.
———. *N. W. Ayer & Son's American Newspaper Annual and Directory.* Fort Washington, PA: IMS Press, 1935.
———. *N. W. Ayer & Son's American Newspaper Annual and Directory.* Fort Washington, PA: IMS Press, 1940.
Bankhurst, Ben. "Early Irish America and Its Enemies: Ethnic Identity Formation in the Era of the Revolution, 1760–1820." *Journal of Irish and Scottish Studies* 5, no. 2 (2012): 17–38.
Barber, Edwin. *The Pottery and Porcelain of the United States.* New York: G. P. Putnam's Sons, 1893.
Barrett, James R. *The Irish Way: Becoming American in the Multiethnic City.* New York: Penguin, 2012.
Barrett, James R., and David R. Roediger. "The Irish and the 'Americanization' of the 'New Immigrants' in the Streets and in the Churches of the Urban United States, 1900–1930." *Journal of American Ethnic History* 24, no. 4 (Summer 2005): 3–33.
Barthes, Roland. *The Semiotic Challenge.* New York: Hill and Wang, 1988.
Barton, Ruth, ed. *Screening Irish-America.* Dublin: Irish Academic Press, 2009.
Baudrillard, Jean. *The Consumer Society: Myths and Structures.* London: Sage, 1998.
Bayne, Samuel G. *On an Irish Jaunting-Car through Donegal and Connemara.* New York: Harper & Brothers, 1902.

Bayor, Ronald H., ed. *Race and Ethnicity in America: A Concise History*. New York: Columbia University Press, 2003.

Bayor, Ronald H., and Timothy J. Meagher, eds. *The New York Irish*. Baltimore, MD: Johns Hopkins University Press, 1996.

Beckert, Sven. *The Monied Metropolis: New York City and the Consolidation of the American Bourgeoisie, 1850–1896*. Cambridge: Cambridge University Press, 2001.

Bennett, Marion T. *American Immigration Policies: A History*. Washington, DC: Public Affairs Press, 1963.

Berger, John. *Ways of Seeing*. London: BBC and Penguin, 1972.

Bergman, Andrew. *We're in the Money: Depression America and Its Films*. New York: New York University Press, 1971.

Berman, Edward H. "The View from the Top." *History of Education Quarterly* 24, no. 3 (Autumn 1984): 455–63.

Bernard, William S. "Immigration: History of U.S. Policy." In Thernstrom, *Harvard Encyclopedia*, 486–95.

Binder, Frederick M., David M. Reimers, and Robert W. Snyder. *All the Nations under Heaven: Immigrants, Migrants, and the Making of New York*. New York: Columbia University Press, 2019.

Black, Gregory. *Hollywood Censored: Morality Codes, Catholics, and the Movies*. Cambridge: Cambridge University Press, 1994.

Black, Jennifer M. "Branding Trust: Advertising, Trademarks, and the Problem of Legitimacy in the United States, 1876–1920." PhD diss., University of Southern California, 2013.

Blair, Paula. "Newsreel Politics: Early American Non-fiction and the Irish Question." *Post Script* 32, no. 3 (Summer 2013): 59–70.

Blessing, Patrick. "Irish in America." In *The Encyclopedia of the Irish in America*, edited by Michael Glazier, 453–70. Notre Dame, IN: University of Notre Dame Press, 1999.

———. "The Irish." In *The Harvard Encyclopedia of American Ethnic Groups*, edited by Stephan Thernstrom, 453–70. Cambridge, MA: Harvard University Press, 1980.

Bloodworth, Rebecca L. *Meet Saint Patrick: An Informative Play for St. Patrick's Day*. Franklin, OH: Eldridge Entertainment House, 1932.

Bolton, Charles Knowles. *Scotch Irish Pioneers in Ulster and America*. 1910; repr. Baltimore, MD: Genealogical Publishing Company, 1967.

Bondanella, Peter. *Hollywood Italians: Dagos, Palookas, Romeos, Wise Guys, and Sopranos*. New York: Continuum, 2004.

Bourke, Richard, and Ian McBride. *The Princeton History of Modern Ireland*. Princeton, NJ: Princeton University Press, 2016.

Brewer, Harriet E. "American Belleek." *New Jersey Historical Society Proceedings* 52, no. 2 (April 1934): 96–108.

Brown, Terence. *Ireland: A Social and Cultural History, 1922–1985*. London: Fontana, 1981.

Brundage, David. *Irish Nationalists in America: The Politics of Exile, 1798–1998*. Oxford: Oxford University Press, 2016.

Bryson, J. H. "The Scotch-Irish People: Their Influence in the Formation of the Government of the United States." In *The Scotch-Irish in America: Proceedings and Addresses of the Third Congress of the Scotch-Irish Society of America*, edited by the Scotch-Irish Society of America, 99–122. Nashville, TN: Publishing House of the Methodist Episcopal Church, South, 1891.

Buckley, John P. "The New York Irish: Their View of American Foreign Policy, 1914–1921." PhD diss., New York University, 1974.

———. *The New York Irish: Their View of American Foreign Policy, 1914–1921*. New York: Arno, 1976.

Byrne, Anne, Ricca Edmondson, and Tony Varley. "Arensberg and Kimball and Anthropological Research in Ireland: Introduction to the Third Edition." *Irish Journal of Sociology* 23, no. 1 (May 2015): 22–61.

Byron, Reginald. *Irish America*. Oxford: Oxford University Press, 1999.

Callahan, Bob, ed. *The Big Book of American Irish Culture*. New York: Viking Penguin, 1987.

Callanan, Brian. *Ireland's Shannon Story: A Case Study in Local and Regional Development*. Dublin: Irish Academic Press, 2000.

Carden, Siún. "Cable Crossings: The Aran Jumper as Myth and Merchandise." *Costume* 48, no. 2 (2014): 260–75.

Carroll, Francis M. *America and the Making of an Independent Ireland: A History*. New York: New York University Press, 2021.

———. *American Opinion and the Irish Question, 1920–1923: A Study of Opinion and Policy*. Dublin: Gill & Macmillan, 1978.

———. "The Collapse of Home Rule and the United Irish League of America, 1910–1918." In Nyhan Grey, *Ireland's Allies*, 31–42.

———. *Money for Ireland: Finance, Diplomacy, Politics, and the First Dáil Éireann Loans, 1919–1936*. Westport, CT: Praeger, 2002.

———. "United States Armed Forces in Northern Ireland during World War II." *New Hibernia Review* 12, no. 2 (Summer 2008): 15–36.

Carter, Edward C., II. "A 'Wild Irishman' under Every Federalist's Bed: Naturalization in Philadelphia, 1789–1806." *Proceedings of the American Philosophical Society* 133, no. 2 (June 1989): 178–89.

Casella, Donna R. "Ireland a Nation: A Celebration of All Things Irish-American." *Post Script* 32, no. 3 (Summer 2013): 27–43.

Casey, Marion R. "Cornerstone of Memory: John Hughes & St. Patrick's Cathedral." *American Journal of Irish Studies* 12 (2015): 10–56.

———. "Irish." In *The Encyclopedia of New York City*, 2nd ed., edited by Kenneth T. Jackson, 656–59. New Haven, CT: Yale University Press, 2010.

———. "Keeping the Tradition Alive: A History of Irish Music and Dance in New York City." *New York Irish History* 6 (1991–92): 24–30.

———. "The Limits of Equality, 1789–1836." In Bayor, *Race and Ethnicity*, 41–62.

———. "Twentieth Century Irish Immigration to New York City: The Historical Perspective." *New York Irish History* 3 (1988): 25–29.

———. "Victor Herbert, Nationalism, and Musical Expression." In Nyhan Grey, *Ireland's Allies*, 165–82.
Casey, Natasha. "'The Best Kept Secret in Retail': Selling Irishness in Contemporary America." In Negra, *Irish in Us*, 84–109.
———. "Riverdance: The Importance of Being Irish American." *New Hibernia Review* 6, no. 4 (2002): 9–25.
Chase, W. Parker. *New York 1932: The Wonder City*. New York: Wonder City, 1932.
Chermayeff, Ivan, Fred Wasserman, and Mary J. Shapiro. *Ellis Island: An Illustrated History of the Immigrant Experience*. New York: Macmillan, 1991.
Chester, Alden. "Morgan J. O'Brien." In *Courts and Lawyers of New York: A History, 1609–1925*. Vol. 4, 121–26. New York: American Historical Society, 1925.
Childers, Joseph, and Gary Hentzi, eds. *The Columbia Dictionary of Modern Literary and Cultural Criticism*. New York: Columbia University Press, 1995.
Clancy, Liam. *The Mountain of the Women: Memoirs of an Irish Troubadour*. New York: Doubleday, 2002.
Clancy, Michael. *Brand New Ireland? Tourism, Development and National Identity in the Irish Republic*. Farnham, UK: Ashgate, 2009.
Clark, Dennis. *The Irish in Philadelphia: Ten Generations of Urban Experience*. Philadelphia, PA: Temple University Press, 1973.
Clarke, Joseph I. C. "The Irish Share in the Hudson-Fulton Celebration." *Journal of the American Irish Historical Society* 9 (1910): 113–52.
———. *My Life and Memories*. New York: Dodd, Mead and Company, 1925.
Cohen, Lizabeth. *Making a New Deal: Industrial Workers in Chicago, 1919–1939*. Cambridge: Cambridge University Press, 1990.
Cole, Robert. *Propaganda, Censorship and Irish Neutrality in the Second World War*. Edinburgh: Edinburgh University Press, 2006.
Coleman, Marie. "The Irish Hospitals Sweepstake in the United States of America, 1930–39." *Irish Historical Studies* 35, no. 138 (November 2006): 220–37.
Colum, Mary. *Life and the Dream*. New York: Doubleday, 1947.
Comerford, James J. "History of the United Irish Counties Association of New York, Inc." In *UICA Diamond Jubilee Banquet Program, October 12, 1979*. New York: United Irish Counties Association, 1979. United Irish Counties Association Collection (AIA.056), Archives of Irish America, Special Collections, Bobst Library, New York University.
Commons, John R. *Races and Immigrants in America*. New York: Chautauqua Press, 1907.
Condon, Edward O'Meagher. *The Irish Race in America*. 1887; repr. New York: Ogham House, 1976.
Conklin, Mike. "Chicago Tribune." In *Encyclopedia of American Journalism*, edited by Stephen L. Vaughn, 93–95. New York: Routledge, 2008.
Corless, Damian. *The Greatest Bleeding Hearts Racket in the World: Irish Hospitals Sweepstakes*. Dublin: Gill & Macmillan, 2010.
Craig, Rose Mary. "Córas Tráchtála." In *Encyclopedia of Ireland*, edited by Brian Lalor, 236. New Haven, CT: Yale University Press, 2003.

Crimmins, John D. *Irish-American Historical Miscellany*. New York: printed by the author, 1905.

———. *St. Patrick's Day: Its Celebration in New York and Other American Places, 1737–1845: How the Anniversary Was Observed by Representative Irish Organizations, and the Toasts Proposed*. New York: printed by the author, 1902.

Cronin, Michael. "Projecting the Nation through Sport and Culture: Ireland, *Aonach Tailteann* and the Irish Free State, 1924–1932." *Journal of Contemporary History* 38, no. 3 (July 2003): 395–411.

Cronin, Michael, and Daryl Adair. *The Wearing of the Green: A History of St. Patrick's Day*. London: Routledge, 2002.

Cronin, Michael, and Barbara O'Connor. *Irish Tourism: Image, Culture, and Identity*. Clevedon: Channel View Publications, 2003.

Cronin, Seán. *The McGarrity Papers*, 2nd ed. New York: Clan na Gael, 1992.

———. *Washington's Irish Policy, 1916–1986*. Dublin: Anvil, 1986.

Crosson, Seán, and Rod Stoneman, eds. *The Quiet Man . . . and Beyond*. Dublin: Liffey, 2009.

Cuddy, Edward. "'Are the Bolsheviks Any Worse Than the Irish?': Ethno-Religious Conflict in America during the 1920s." *Éire-Ireland* 11, no. 3 (Autumn 1976): 13–32.

Cullen, L. M. *An Economic History of Ireland since 1660*. London: B. T. Batsford, 1972.

Cullinane, John. *Aspects of the History of Irish Dancing in North America*. Cork: printed by the author, 1997.

Cummins, Thomas J. *My Irish Colleagues of New York: Reminiscences and Experiences of a Journalist, 1861–1901*. New York: printed by the author, 1901.

Cunningham, John B. *The Story of Belleek*. Belleek, Northern Ireland: St. Davog's Press, 1992.

Curran, Joseph. *Hibernian Green on the Silver Screen: The Irish and American Movies*. Westport, CT: Greenwood, 1989.

Curtin, Charles A. "Jeremiah Curtin." *Journal of the American Irish Historical Society* 31 (1937): 55–70.

Curtis, L. Perry, Jr. *Anglo-Saxons and Celts: A Study of Anti-Irish Prejudice in Victorian England*. Bridgeport, CT: Conference on British Studies at the University of Bridgeport, 1968.

———. *Apes and Angels: The Irishman in Victorian Caricature*. Washington, DC: Smithsonian Institution Press, 1997.

Curtis, Mary I. *Why We Celebrate Our Holidays*. Chicago: Lyons & Carnahan, 1924.

Cusack, Christopher. "'Seanachie to the New World': Seumas MacManus and the Transatlantic Appeal of Irish Local Color." *Open Library of Humanities* 8, no. 2 (2022): 1–26.

Daly, Mary E. *Industrial Development and Irish National Identity, 1922–1939*. Syracuse: Syracuse University Press, 1992.

———. "The Irish Free State / Éire / Republic of Ireland / Ireland: 'A Country by Any Other Name'?" *Journal of British Studies* 46, no. 1 (January 2007): 72–90.

———. "Nationalism, Sentiment, and Economics: Relations between Ireland and Irish-America in the Post-war Years." In Kenny, *New Directions*, 263–79.

———. *Slow Failure: Population Decline and Independent Ireland, 1922–1973*. Madison: University of Wisconsin Press, 2006.
Davé, Shilpa, LeiLani Nishime, and Tasha G. Oren, eds. *East Main Street: Asian American Popular Culture*. New York: New York University Press, 2005.
Dávila, Arlene M. *Latinos, Inc.: The Marketing and Making of a People*. Berkeley: University of California Press, 2001.
———. *Latino Spin: Public Image and the Whitewashing of Race*. New York: New York University Press, 2008.
Dávila, Arlene, and Yeidy M. Rivero, eds. *Contemporary Latina/o Media: Production, Circulation, Politics*. New York: New York University Press, 2014.
Davis, Troy D. *Dublin's American Policy: Irish-American Diplomatic Relations, 1945–1952*. Washington, DC: Catholic University of America Press, 1998.
———. "Éamon de Valera's Political Education: The American Tour, 1919–1920." *New Hibernia Review* 10, no. 1 (Spring 2006): 65–78.
———. "'The Irish Movement in This Country Is Now Moribund': The Anti-Partition Campaign of 1948–51 in the United States." In Rogers and O'Brien, *After the Flood: Irish America, 1945–1960*, 38–54.
Davison, George W. *Our Fortnight in Ireland*. New York: privately printed, 1930.
Dean, Joan Fitzpatrick. *All Dressed Up: Modern Irish Historical Pageantry*. Syracuse: Syracuse University Press, 2014.
De Breffny, Brian. *In the Steps of St. Patrick*. New York: Thames and Hudson, 1982.
Delaney, Enda. "Diaspora." In Bourke and McBride, *Princeton History*, 496.
Dell, Robert M. "The Representation of the Immigrant on the New York Stage, 1881 to 1910." PhD diss., New York University, 1960.
Dempsey, Pauric J., and Shaun Boylan. "(Robert) Lindsay Crawford." In Royal Irish Academy, *Dictionary of Irish Biography*. Accessed October 30, 2023. https://doi.org/10.3318/dib.002163.v1.
Dennison, S. R., and Oliver MacDonagh. *Guinness 1886–1939: From Incorporation to the Second World War*. Cork: Cork University Press, 1998.
Divine, Robert A. *American Immigration Policy, 1924–1952*. New Haven, CT: Yale University Press, 1957.
Docter, Kathryn. *Celebrating St. Patrick's Day: A Real Irish Collection*. Lebanon, OH: March Brothers, 1936.
Doherty, Thomas. *Hollywood's Censor: Joseph I. Breen and the Production Code Administration*. New York: Columbia University Press, 2009.
Dooley, Roger B. "The Irish on the Screen (Part I): They Have Been Romanticized More Than Any Other Ethnic Group." *Films in Review* 8, no. 5 (1957): 211–70.
Doorley, Michael. "The Friends of Irish Freedom: A Study of an Irish-American Diaspora Nationalism." PhD diss., University of Chicago, 1995.
———. *Irish-American Diaspora Nationalism: The Friends of Irish Freedom, 1916–1935*. Dublin: Four Courts, 2005.
———. *Justice Daniel Cohalan, 1865–1946: American Patriot and Irish-American Nationalist*. Cork: Cork University Press, 2019.

Douglas, George William. *The American Book of Days*. New York: H. W. Wilson, 1937.
Douglas, R. M. "Anglo-Saxons and Attacotti: The Racialization of Irishness in Britain between the World Wars." *Ethnic and Racial Studies* 25, no. 1 (January 2002): 40–63.
Dowd, Christopher. *The Irish and the Origins of American Popular Culture*. New York: Routledge, 2018.
Dowling, Martin. *Traditional Music and Irish Society: Historical Perspectives*. Farnham, UK: Ashgate, 2014.
Doyle, Carmel. "(John) Dudley Digges." In Royal Irish Academy, *Dictionary of Irish Biography*. Accessed October 30, 2023. https://doi.org/10.3318/dib.002580.v2.
———. "Mary Digges (née Quinn)." In Royal Irish Academy, *Dictionary of Irish Biography*. Accessed October 30, 2023. https://doi.org/10.3318/dib.002582.v2.
Doyle, David N. *Ireland, Irishmen and Revolutionary America, 1760–1820*. Dublin: Mercier, 1981.
———. *Irish Americans, Native Rights and National Empires: The Structure, Divisions, and Attitudes of the Catholic Minority in the Decade of Expansion, 1890–1901*. New York: Arno, 1976.
———. "Irish Elites in North America and Liberal Democracy, 1820–1920." *Radharc* 3 (2002): 29–53.
———. "The Irish in North America, 1776–1845." In Lee and Casey, *Making the Irish American*, 171–83.
———. "The Irish as Urban Pioneers in the United States, 1850–1870." *Journal of American Ethnic History* 10, nos. 1–2 (Fall 1990–Winter 1991): 36–59.
———. "The Remaking of Irish America, 1845–1880." In Lee and Casey, *Making the Irish American*, 213–52.
Drudy, P. J., ed. *The Irish in America: Emigration, Assimilation, and Impact*. Cambridge: Cambridge University Press, 1985.
Dunkak, Harry M. "The Papers of an Unheralded Irish American Historian." *Éire-Ireland* 22, no. 2 (Summer 1987): 115–31.
Dwyer, T. Ryle. "American Friends of Irish Neutrality." In Funchion, *Irish American Voluntary Organizations*, 34–38.
———. *Irish Neutrality and the USA, 1939–1947*. Dublin: Gill & Macmillan, 1977.
———. *Strained Relations: Ireland at Peace and the USA at War, 1941–45*. Dublin: Gill & Macmillan, 1988.
Eco, Umberto. *Travels in Hyperreality*. San Diego: Harcourt Brace Jovanovich, 1986.
Eden, Scott. *Touchdown Jesus: Faith and Fandom at Notre Dame*. New York: Simon and Schuster, 2005.
Educational Screen, and Nelson Lewis Greene. *1000 and One: The Blue Book of Nontheatrical Films*. Chicago: Educational Screen, 1935.
Emery, Michael, and Edwin Emery. *The Press and America: An Interpretive History of the Mass Media*, 6th ed. Englewood Cliffs, NJ: Prentice Hall, 1988.
Emmet, Thomas Addis. *Incidents of My Life: Professional, Literary, Social with Services in the Cause of Ireland*. New York: G. P. Putnam's Sons, 1911.

Evans, Bryce. "'A Pint of Plain Is Your Only Man': How Guinness Saved Ireland during the Emergency." *History Ireland* 22, no. 5 (September/October 2014): 36–38.

Facey, Paul W. *The Legion of Decency: A Sociological Analysis of the Emergence and Development of a Social Pressure Group*. New York: Arno, 1974.

Fanning, Charles. "Dueling Cultures: Ireland and Irish America at the Chicago World's Fairs of 1933 and 1934." *New Hibernia Review* 15, no. 3 (Autumn 2011): 94–110.

———. "A Hidden Flowering: Irish-American Culture in the Depression Era." *American Journal of Irish Studies* 9 (2012): 11–52.

———. *The Irish Voice in America: Irish-American Fiction from the 1760s to the 1980s*. Lexington: University Press of Kentucky, 1990.

———. "Robert Emmet and Nineteenth-Century Irish America." *New Hibernia Review* 8, no. 4 (2004): 53–83.

Felter, Maryanne, and Daniel Schultz. "James Mark Sullivan and the Film Company of Ireland." *New Hibernia Review* 8, no. 2 (2004): 24–40.

———. "Selling Memories, Strengthening Nationalism: The Marketing of Film Company of Ireland's Silent Films in America." *Canadian Journal of Irish Studies* 32, no. 2 (Fall 2006): 10–20.

Ferriter, Diarmuid. *Judging Dev: A Reassessment of the Life and Legacy of Éamon de Valera*. Dublin: Royal Irish Academy, 2007.

Fielder, Mari Kathleen. "Chauncey Olcott: Irish-American Mother-Love, Romance, and Nationalism." *Éire-Ireland* 22, no. 2 (Summer 1987): 4–26.

Fiori, Pamela. *Holiday: The Best Travel Magazine That Ever Was*. New York: Rizzoli, 2019.

Fisk, Robert. *In Time of War: Ireland, Ulster, and the Price of Neutrality, 1939–1945*. Philadelphia: University of Pennsylvania Press, 1983.

Fitzgerald, Marie. "The St. Patrick's Day Parade: The Conflict of Irish-American Identity in New York City, 1840–1900." PhD diss., State University of New York at Stony Brook, 1993.

Fitzpatrick, David. "Emigration, 1871–1921." In Vaughan, *New History of Ireland*, 606–52.

Flanagan, Kathleen M. "'Dance and Song of the Gael': Pat Roche and Irish Dance in Chicago, 1933–1953." *New Hibernia Review* 4, no. 4 (Winter 2000): 9–28.

Flynn, Charles, and Todd McCarthy. "The Economic Imperative: Why Was the B Movie Necessary?" In McCarthy and Flynn, *Kings of the Bs*, 13–43.

Ford, Henry Jones. *The Scotch-Irish in America*. Princeton: Princeton University Press, 1915.

Foster, Gavin. "'No "Wild Geese" This Time?' IRA Emigration after the Irish Civil War." *Éire-Ireland* 47, nos. 1–2 (Spring/Summer 2012): 94–122.

Funchion, Michael F., ed. *Irish American Voluntary Organizations*. Westport, CT: Greenwood, 1983.

Furlong, Irene. *Irish Tourism, 1880–1980*. Dublin: Irish Academic Press, 2009.

———. "Through a Mirror, Darkly—Irish Tourism and the Construction of National Identity, 1922–1960." *International Journal of Regional and Local Studies* 5, no. 2 (2009): 48–67.

Gallup, George H. *The Gallup Poll: Public Opinion, 1935–1971*. New York: Random House, 1972.

Gannon, Darragh, and Fearghal McGarry. *Ireland 1922: Independence, Partition, Civil War*. Dublin: Royal Irish Academy, 2022.

Gans, Herbert J., ed. *On the Making of Americans: Essays in Honor of David Riesman*. Philadelphia: University of Pennsylvania Press, 1979.

———. "Symbolic Ethnicity: The Future of Ethnic Groups and Cultures in America." *Ethnic and Racial Studies* 2, no. 1 (1979): 1–20.

Gasparini, Daria A. "A Celebration of Moral Force: The Catholic Total Abstinence Union of America Centennial Fountain." Master's thesis, University of Pennsylvania, 2002.

Gaughan, J. Anthony, ed. *Memoirs of Senator Joseph Connolly (1885–1961): A Founder of Modern Ireland*. Dublin: Irish Academic Press, 1996.

Gavan, Joseph W. "Old Fenians in New York." *New York Irish History* 7 (1992–93): 19–20.

Gibbons, Luke. *The Quiet Man*. Cork: Cork University Press, 2002.

Gibney, John. "The Occupation of the Irish Consulate, New York: Revolutionary Diplomacy." In Gannon and McGarry, *Ireland 1922*, 323–28.

Gillers, Stephen. "A Tendency to Deprave and Corrupt: The Transformation of American Obscenity Law from Hicklin to Ulysses II." *Washington University Law Review* 85, no. 2 (2007): 215–96.

Gillespie, Raymond, and Brian P. Kennedy, eds. *Ireland: Art into History*. Dublin: Town House, 1994.

Glassberg, David. *American Historical Pageantry: The Uses of Tradition in the Early Twentieth Century*. Chapel Hill: University of North Carolina Press, 1990.

Glazer, Nathan, and Daniel Patrick Moynihan, eds. *Beyond the Melting Pot: The Negroes, Puerto Ricans, Jews, Italians, and Irish of New York City*, 2nd ed. Cambridge, MA: MIT Press, 1970.

Glazier, Michael, ed. *The Encyclopedia of the Irish in America*. Notre Dame, IN: University of Notre Dame Press, 1999.

Gleeson, David T., ed. *The Irish in the Atlantic World*. Columbia: University of South Carolina Press, 2010.

Golden, Harry. Preface to *The Spirit of the Ghetto: Studies of the Jewish Quarter of New York*, by Hutchins Hapgood, i–xiv. New York: Schocken, 1966.

Golway, Terry. *Irish Rebel: John Devoy and America's Fight for Ireland's Freedom*. New York: St. Martin's, 1998.

Gramsci, Antonio. *Selections from the Prison Notebooks of Antonio Gramsci*. Edited by Quintin Hoare and Geoffrey Nowell-Smith. New York: International Publishers, 1971.

Granshaw, Michelle. "The Hibernicon and Visions of Returning Home: Popular Entertainment in Irish America from the Civil War to World War I." PhD diss., University of Washington, 2012.

———. *Irish on the Move: Performing Mobility in American Variety Theatre*. Iowa City: University of Iowa Press, 2019.

Grant, Tina, ed. *International Directory of Company Histories*. Detroit, MI: St. James, 2009.

Gray, Tony. *Ireland This Century*. London: Little, Brown, 1994.

Greeley, Andrew. "The Success and Assimilation of Irish Protestants and Catholics in the United States." *Sociology and Social Research* 72, no. 4 (1988): 229–36.

———. *Why Can't They Be like Us? America's White Ethnic Groups*. New York: E. P. Dutton, 1971.
Gregory, Lady Augusta. *Our Irish Theatre: A Chapter in an Autobiography*. New York: G. P. Putnam's Sons, 1914.
Gribbon, H. D. "Economic and Social History, 1850–1921." In Vaughan, *New History of Ireland*, 260–356.
Griffin, William D. "American Irish Historical Society." In Funchion, *Irish American Voluntary Organizations*, 40–43.
Gronow, Pekka. "Ethnic Recordings: An Introduction." In American Folklife Center, *Ethnic Recordings in America*, 1–50.
Guide to the Irish Industrial Village and Blarney Castle: The Exhibit of the Irish Industries Association at the World's Columbian Exposition, Chicago. Chicago, IL: Irish Village Book Store, 1893.
Hachey, Thomas E. *Britain and Irish Separatism: From the Fenians to the Free State, 1867–1922*. Chicago, IL: Rand McNally College Publishing, 1977.
Hackett, Francis. *The Story of the Irish Nation*. New York: Century, 1922.
Halter, Marilyn. *Shopping for Identity: The Marketing of Ethnicity*. New York: Schocken Books, 2000.
Haltigan, James. *The Irish in the American Revolution and Their Early Influence in the Colonies*. Washington, DC: Patrick J. Haltigan, 1908.
Hamill, Pete. "Once We Were Kings." In Lee and Casey, *Making the Irish American*, 526–34.
Hampton, Benjamin B. *A History of the Movies*. New York: Covici, Friede, 1931.
Hankins, Frank H. *The Racial Basis of Civilization*. New York: Alfred A. Knopf, 1926.
Hanley, Brian. "'No English Enemy . . . Ever Stooped So Low': Mike Quill, de Valera's Visit to the German Legation, and Irish-American Attitudes during World War II." *Radharc* 5–7 (2004–6): 245–64.
Hannigan, Dave. *De Valera in America: The Rebel President and the Making of Irish Independence*. New York: Palgrave Macmillan, 2010.
Harmon, Maurice. "Seán O'Faolain." In Royal Irish Academy, *Dictionary of Irish Biography*. Accessed October 30, 2023. https://doi.org/10.3318/dib.006736.v1.
Harner, Gary W. "The Kalem Company, Travel and On-Location Filming: The Forging of an Identity." *Film History* 10, no. 2 (1998): 188–207.
Harrington, John P. *The Irish Play on the New York Stage, 1874–1966*. Lexington: University Press of Kentucky, 1997.
———. "Joseph Campbell, Exile, American Autobiographies, and Irish Studies." *American Journal of Irish Studies* 14 (2017): 31–49.
"The Harvard Anthropological Survey of the Irish Free State." *Science* 76, no. 1978 (November 25, 1932): 482–83.
Havel, Brian F. *Maestro of Crystal: The Story of Miroslav Havel*. Dublin: Currach, 2005.
Haverty, Martin. *The History of Ireland from the Earliest Period to the Present Time*. New York: Thomas Kelly, 1885.
Hayes, Alan, and Diane Urquhart, ed. *The Irish Women's History Reader*. London: Routledge, 2001.

Hazeltine, Mary Emogene. *Anniversaries and Holidays: A Calendar of Days and How to Observe Them*. Chicago, IL: American Library Association, 1944.

Heinze, Andrew R. *Adapting to Abundance: Jewish Immigrants, Mass Consumption, and the Search for American Identity*. New York: Columbia University Press, 1990.

Heisenfelt, Kathryn. *Mr. O'Grady's Party: A St. Patrick's Day Play in One Act*. Milwaukee, WI: Catholic Dramatic Movement, 1934.

Helfen, Mathias. *The Catholic Theatre Year Book*. Milwaukee, WI: Catholic Dramatic Movement, 1954.

Hennessy, Patrick. "American Irish Immigration Committee." In Funchion, *Irish American Voluntary Organizations*, 43–46.

Higgins, Padhraig. "Paddies Evermore: Stereotypes and Irish National Identity in the Late Eighteenth Century." *Eighteenth-Century Ireland* 33 (2018): 61–86.

Higham, John. *Strangers in the Land: Patterns of American Nativism, 1860–1925*. New York: Atheneum, 1988.

Hill, Jacqueline R. "National Festivals, the State and 'Protestant Ascendancy' in Ireland, 1790–1829." *Irish Historical Studies* 24, no. 93 (1984): 30–51.

Hill, Jacqueline, and Mary Ann Lyons, eds. *Representing Irish Religious Histories: Historiography, Ideology and Practice*. Cham, Switzerland: Springer International AG, 2017.

Hobsbawm, Eric, and Terence Ranger, eds. *The Invention of Tradition*. New York: Cambridge University Press, 1983.

Holland, Jack. *The American Connection: U.S. Guns, Money, and Influence in Northern Ireland*. Boulder, CO: Roberts Rinehart, 1999.

Hopkin, Alannah. *The Living Legend of St. Patrick*. New York: St. Martin's, 1989.

Horgan, Donal. *Echo after Echo: Killarney and Its History*. Cork: Blackface, 1988.

Hsu, Madeline Yuan-yin. *The Good Immigrants: How the Yellow Peril Became the Model Minority*. Princeton: Princeton University Press, 2015.

Hughes, Charles Evans. *Correspondence with Executive Departments, Hearing before the Committee on Immigration and Naturalization, House of Representatives, Sixty-Eighth Congress, First Session on the Immigration Act of 1924 (H.R. 7995), April 17, 1924, Serial 4-A*. Washington, DC: U.S. Government Printing Office, 1924.

Humphreys, Madeleine. "An Issue of Confidence: The Decline of the Irish Whiskey Industry in Independent Ireland, 1922–1952." *Journal of European Economic History* 23, no. 1 (Spring 1994): 93–114.

Hutchinson, Edward P. *Legislative History of American Immigration Policy, 1798–1965*. Philadelphia: University of Pennsylvania Press, 1981.

Hutton, Clare. *The Oxford History of the Irish Book*. Vol. 5, *The Irish Book in English, 1891–2000*. Oxford: Oxford University Press, 2011.

H. W. Wilson Company. *Current Biography Yearbook*. New York: H. W. Wilson, 1940.

Irish, Marie. *Shamrocks for St. Patrick's Day*. New York: Fitzgerald, 1932.

Irish, Marie, and Willis N. Bugbee. *St. Patrick's Day Plays and Pieces*. Syracuse, NY: Willis N. Bugbee, 1932.

Irish Tourist Association. *Ireland*. Dublin: Irish Tourist Association, 1929.

Izod, John. *Hollywood and the Box Office, 1895–1986*. New York: Columbia University Press, 1988.
Jackson, Kenneth T., ed. *The Encyclopedia of New York City*, 2nd ed. New Haven, CT: Yale University Press, 2010.
Jackson, Kenneth T., Karen Markoe, and Arnie Marko, eds. *The Scribner Encyclopedia of American Lives*. Vol. 1, *1981–1985*. New York: Charles Scribner's Sons, 1998.
Jacobson, Matthew Frye. *Whiteness of a Different Color: European Immigrants and the Alchemy of Race*. Cambridge, MA: Harvard University Press, 1998.
Janis, Ely M. *A Greater Ireland: The Land League and Transatlantic Nationalism in Gilded Age America*. Madison: University of Wisconsin Press, 2015.
Johnson, Clifton. *The Isle of the Shamrock*. New York: Macmillan, 1901.
Jones, Greta. *"Captain of All These Men of Death": The History of Tuberculosis in Nineteenth and Twentieth Century Ireland*, 2nd ed. Leiden: Brill, 2016.
Kunitz, Stanley, and Howard Haycraft, eds. *Junior Book of Authors*. New York: H. W. Wilson, 1935.
Kane, Paula M. "'Staging a Lie': Boston Catholics and the New Irish Drama." In O'Sullivan, *Religion and Identity*, 111–45.
Kauffman, Christopher J. "Edward McSweeney, the Knights of Columbus, and the Irish-American Response to Anglo-Saxonism, 1900–1925." *American Catholic Studies* 114, no. 4 (Winter 2003): 51–65.
Kelleher, D. L. "The Irish Are Coming Home." *The Capuchin Annual* (1931): 242–44.
Kelly, Mary C. *The Shamrock and the Lily: The New York Irish and the Creation of a Transatlantic Identity, 1845–1921*. New York: Peter Lang, 2005.
Kelly, Mary Pat. *Home Away from Home: The Yanks in Ireland*. Belfast, Ireland: Appletree, 1994.
Kelly, Neeve. "Nationalism by Design: Reimagining Irish Identity in the American Marketplace." PhD diss., College of William and Mary, 2019.
Kennedy, Brian P. *Dreams and Responsibilities: The State and the Arts in Independent Ireland*. Dublin: Arts Council, 1990.
———. "The Irish Free State 1922–1949: A Visual Perspective." In Gillespie and Kennedy, *Ireland*, 132–52.
Kennedy, Marion, and Katharine Isabel Bemis. *Special Day Pageants for Little People*. New York: A. S. Barnes, 1929.
Kennedy, Michael. *Ireland and the League of Nations, 1919–1946: International Relations, Diplomacy, and Politics*. Dublin: Irish Academic Press, 1996.
Kenny, Kevin. *The American Irish: A History*. New York: Pearson Education, 2000.
———, ed. *New Directions in Irish-American History*. Madison: University of Wisconsin Press, 2003.
Keogh, D., and C. Quinlan, eds. *Ireland in the 1950s: The Lost Decade*. Dublin: Mercier, 2003.
Key, Pierre. *Pierre Key's Radio Annual: A Survey of the Year in Radio*. New York: Pierre Key, 1933.

Kibler, M. Alison. *Censoring Racial Ridicule: Irish, Jewish, and African American Struggles over Race and Representation, 1890–1930.* Chapel Hill: University of North Carolina Press, 2015.

———. "Paddy, Shylock, and Sambo: Irish, Jewish, and African American Efforts to Ban Racial Ridicule on Stage and Screen." In Ross, *Culture and Belonging,* 259–80.

———. "Pigs, Green Whiskers, and Drunken Widows: Irish Nationalists and the 'Practical Censorship' of 'McFadden's Row of Flats' in 1902 and 1903." *Journal of American Studies* 42, no. 3 (December 2008): 489–514.

———. "The Stage Irishwoman." *Journal of American Ethnic History* 24, no. 3 (Spring 2005): 5–30.

Kimball, Sarah. "Replicating Authenticity: The Commercialization of Irish Spaces in the Contemporary United States." Master's thesis, New York University, 2019.

King, Linda. "Saints, Shamrocks, and Signifying Practices: Aer Lingus and the Materialization of Irish Identity." *Éire-Ireland* 46, nos. 1–2 (Spring/Summer 2011): 128–51.

Knobel, Dale T. *Paddy and the Republic: Ethnicity and Nationality in Antebellum America.* Middletown, CT: Wesleyan University Press, 1986.

———. "A Vocabulary of Ethnic Perception: Content Analysis of the American Stage Irishman, 1820–1860." *Journal of American Studies* 15, no. 1 (April 1981): 45–71.

Lambert, Sharon. "Irish Women's Emigration to England 1922–1960: The Lengthening of Family Ties." In Hayes and Urquhart, *Irish Women's History Reader,* 181–87.

Leak, H., and T. Priday. "Migration from and to the United Kingdom." *Journal of the Royal Statistical Society* 96, no. 2 (1933): 195.

Lee, J. J. "Emigration: 1922–1998." In Glazier, *Encyclopedia of the Irish,* 263–66.

———. "Introduction: Interpreting Irish America." In Lee and Casey, *Making the Irish American,* 1–60.

———. *Ireland, 1912–1985: Politics and Society.* Cambridge: Cambridge University Press, 1989.

Lee, J. J., and Marion R. Casey, eds. *Making the Irish American: History and Heritage of the Irish in the United States.* New York: New York University Press, 2006.

Lloyd, David. *Ireland after History.* South Bend, IN: University of Notre Dame Press in association with Field Day, 1999.

Loftus, Paul. "The Politics of Cordiality: Continuity and Change in Irish-American Diplomacy during the Johnson Presidency, 1963–1969." *Irish Studies in International Affairs* 20 (2009): 143–66.

Logue, Paddy, ed. *Being Irish: Personal Reflections on Being Irish Today.* Dublin: Oak Tree, 2000.

Lyman, Kenneth Cox. "Critical Reaction to Irish Drama on the New York Stage, 1900–1958." PhD diss., University of Wisconsin, 1960.

Macardle, Dorothy. *The Irish Republic,* 1st American ed. New York: Farrar, Straus, Giroux, 1965.

Mac Con Iomaire, Mairtin. "The Pig in Irish Cuisine Past and Present." In *The Fat of the Land: Proceedings of the Oxford Symposium on Food and Cookery,* edited by Harlan Walker, 207–15. Bristol, UK: Footwork, 2002.

MacDonald, J. Fred. *Don't Touch That Dial! Radio Programming in American Life, 1920–1960.* Chicago: Nelson-Hall, 1979.

Madigan, Michael J. "The Catholic Club of New York." In *Catholic Builders of the Nation: A Symposium on the Catholic Contribution to the Civilization of the United States*, edited by C. E. McGuire, 412–28. Boston, MA: Continental Press, 1923.

Maginniss, Thomas Hobbs, Jr. *The Irish Contribution to America's Independence.* Philadelphia: Doire, 1913.

Malcolm, Elizabeth. "Tuberculosis." In *The Oxford Companion to Irish History*, edited by S. J. Connolly, 583. Oxford: Oxford University Press, 2002.

Malloy, Caroline R. "Exhibiting Ireland: Irish Villages, Pavilions, Cottages, and Castles at International Exhibitions, 1853–1939." PhD diss., University of Wisconsin–Madison, 2013.

Marriott, J. H. Wilson. *Nearly 300 Ways to Dress Show Windows.* Baltimore: Show Window Publishing, 1889.

Marston, Sallie A. "Public Rituals and Community Power: St. Patrick's Day Parades in Lowell, MA, 1841–1874." *Political Geography Quarterly* 8, no. 3 (July 1989): 255–69.

Matthews, Chris. *Bobby Kennedy: A Raging Spirit.* New York: Simon and Schuster, 2017.

Maume, Patrick. "Conrad Maynadier Arensberg." In Royal Irish Academy, *Dictionary of Irish Biography*. Accessed March 10, 2023. https://doi.org/10.3318/dib.000209.v1.

Mayo Men's Patriotic and Benevolent Association of the City of New York. "The History of the Mayo Men's Association." In *Diamond Jubilee Souvenir Yearbook 1879–1954*. New York: Mayo Men's Patriotic and Benevolent Association of the City of New York, 1954. John and Ann Garvey Papers (AIA.088), Archives of Irish America, Special Collections, Bobst Library, New York University.

McBride, Ian, ed. *History and Memory in Modern Ireland.* New York: Cambridge University Press, 2001.

McBrinn, Joseph. "Marcus Ward." In Royal Irish Academy, *Dictionary of Irish Biography*. Accessed October 30, 2023. https://doi.org/10.3318/dib.008920.v1.

McCaffrey, Lawrence J., Ellen Skerrett, Michael Funchion, and Charles Fanning. *The Irish in Chicago.* Chicago: University of Illinois Press, 1987.

McCartan, Patrick. *With De Valera in America.* New York: Brentano, 1932.

McCarthy, Larry. "Irish Americans in Sports: The Twentieth Century." In Lee and Casey, *Making the Irish American*, 457–71.

McCarthy, Mark, ed. *Ireland's Heritages: Critical Perspectives on Memory and Identity.* Abingdon, UK: Routledge, 2017.

McCarthy, Tara M. *Respectability and Reform: Irish American Women's Activism, 1880–1920.* Syracuse, NY: Syracuse University Press, 2018.

McCarthy, Todd, and Charles Flynn, eds. *Kings of the Bs: Working within the Hollywood System.* New York: E. P. Dutton, 1975.

McDannell, Colleen. "'True Men as We Need Them': Catholicism and the Irish-American Male." *American Studies* 27, no. 2 (1986): 19–36.

McDiarmid, Lucy. "The Abbey and the Theatrics of Controversy, 1909–1915." In Watt, Morgan, and Mustafa, *A Century of Irish Drama*, 57–71.

McElroy, James. *Red Bricks and Green Bushes: The Story of the County Tyrone Society*. New York: County Tyrone Society of New York, 1955.

McGee, Mark. *Beyond Ballyhoo: Motion Picture Promotion and Gimmicks*. Jefferson, NC: McFarland, 1989.

McGrath, Tim. *John Barry: An American Hero in the Age of Sail*. Yardley, PA: Westholme, 2010.

McGreevy, John T. *Parish Boundaries: The Catholic Encounter with Race in the Twentieth Century Urban North*. Chicago, IL: University of Chicago Press, 1996.

McGregor, Alexander. *The Catholic Church and Hollywood Censorship and Morality in 1930s Cinema*. London: I. B. Tauris, 2013.

McMahon, Eileen M. *What Parish Are You From? A Chicago Irish Community and Race Relations*. Lexington: University Press of Kentucky, 1995.

McMahon, Timothy G. *Grand Opportunity: The Gaelic Revival and Irish Society, 1893–1910*. Syracuse, NY: Syracuse University Press, 2008.

McNickle, Chris. "When New York Was Irish, and After." In Bayor and Meagher, *New York Irish*, 337–56.

McSweeney, Edward F. *The Racial Contribution to the United States*. New Haven, CT: Knights of Columbus Historical Commission, 1924.

Meagher, Timothy J. "Abie's Irish Enemy: Irish and Jews, Social and Political Realities and Media Representations." In Barton, *Screening Irish-America*, 45–60.

———. *The Columbia Guide to Irish American History*. New York: Columbia University Press, 2005.

———, ed. *From Paddy to Studs: Irish-American Communities in the Turn of the Century Era, 1880 to 1920*. Westport, CT: Greenwood Press, 1986.

———. *Inventing Irish America: Generation, Class, and Ethnic Identity in a New England City, 1880–1928*. Notre Dame, IN: University of Notre Dame Press, 2001.

———. "'Why Should We Care for a Little Trouble or a Walk through the Mud': St. Patrick's and Columbus Day Parades in Worcester, Massachusetts, 1845–1915." *The New England Quarterly* 58, no. 1 (March 1985): 255–69.

Meehan, Helen. "Seumas MacManus." In Royal Irish Academy, *Dictionary of Irish Biography*. Accessed October 30, 2023. https://doi.org/10.3318/dib.005736.v2.

Meehan, Thomas. "Periodical Literature (the United States)." In *The Catholic Encyclopedia*. New York: Robert Appleton Company, 1911. http://www.newadvent.org.

Messenger, John. "Literary vs. Scientific Interpretations of Cultural Reality in the Aran Islands of Éire." *Ethnohistory* 11, no. 1 (Winter 1964): 41–55.

Miller, Kerby A. "Assimilation and Alienation: Irish Emigrants' Responses to Industrial America, 1871–1921." In Drudy, *Irish in America*, 87–112.

———. "Ulster Presbyterians and the 'Two Traditions' in Ireland and America." In Lee and Casey, *Making the Irish American*, 255–60.

Miller, Kerby A., Arnold Schrier, Bruce D. Boling, and David N. Doyle. *Irish Immigrants in the Land of Canaan: Letters and Memoirs from Colonial and Revolutionary America, 1675–1815*. New York: Oxford University Press, 2004.

Miller, Rebecca S. "Irish Traditional Music in the United States." In Lee and Casey, *Making the Irish American*, 504.
———. "Irish Traditional and Popular Music in New York City: Identity and Social Change, 1930–1975." In Bayor and Meagher, *New York Irish*, 481–507.
Mitchell, Brian. *The Paddy Camps: The Irish of Lowell, 1821–1861*. Urbana: University of Illinois Press, 2006.
Moloney, Mick. "Irish-American Festivals." In Lee and Casey, *Making the Irish American*, 426–42.
———. "Irish-American Popular Music." In Lee and Casey, *Making the Irish American*, 381–405.
———. "Irish Ethnic Recordings and the Irish-American Imagination." In American Folklife Center, *Ethnic Recordings in America*, 85–101.
Moseley, Edward A. "Letter from Edward A. Moseley, the Retiring President-General, to the AIHS, January 17, 1899." *Journal of the American Irish Historical Society* 2 (1899): 53–55.
Moss, Kenneth. "St. Patrick's Day Celebrations and the Formation of Irish-American Identity, 1845–1875." *Journal of Social History* 29, no. 1 (Autumn 1995): 125–48.
Moynihan, Daniel Patrick. "The Irish." In Lee and Casey, *Making the Irish American*, 475–525.
Moynihan, Kenneth D. "History as a Weapon for Social Advancement: Group History as Told by the American Irish Historical Society." *New York Irish History* 8 (1993–94): 34–40.
Mugridge, Ian. *The View from Xanadu: William Randolph Hearst and United States Foreign Policy*. Montreal: McGill-Queen's University Press, 1995.
Murphy, Alison Barstow. *Every Which Way in Ireland*. New York: G. P. Putnam's Sons, 1930.
Murphy, Maureen. "Mission of Our Lady of the Rosary for the Protection of Irish Immigrant Girls in New York City." In Funchion, *Irish American Voluntary Organizations*, 227–28.
Murphy, Richard, and Lawrence Mannion. *History of the Society of the Friendly Sons of St. Patrick in the City of New York*. New York: Society of the Friendly Sons of St. Patrick, 1962.
Murray, Damien. "Padraic Colum: Patriot Propagandist for the Poets' Revolution." *Éire-Ireland* 51, nos. 3–4 (Fall/Winter 2016): 104–23.
Murray, Thomas Hamilton, and Thomas Bonaventure Lawler, eds. "American-Irish Historical Society." *Journal of the American Irish Historical Society* 1 (1898): 1.
Nash, Catherine. "'Embodying the Nation': The West of Ireland Landscape and Irish Identity." In O'Connor and Cronin, *Tourism in Ireland*, 29–43.
Negra, Diane. "Consuming Ireland: Lucky Charms Cereal, Irish Spring Soap and 1-800 Shamrock." *Cultural Studies* 15, no. 1 (2001): 76–97.
———, ed. *The Irish in Us: Irishness, Performativity, and Popular Culture*. Durham: Duke University Press, 2006.

———. *Off-White Hollywood: American Culture and Ethnic Female Stardom.* London: Routledge, 2001.

Nelson, Charles. *Shamrock: Botany and History of an Irish Myth.* Aberystwyth, UK: Boethius Press, 1991.

Ngai, Mae M. "The Architecture of Race in American Immigration Law: A Reexamination of the Immigration Act of 1924." *Journal of American History* 86, no. 1 (June 1999): 67–92.

Ní Bhroiméil, Úna. *Building Irish Identity in America, 1870–1915: The Gaelic Revival.* Dublin: Four Courts Press, 2002.

———. "The Creation of an Irish Culture in the United States: The Gaelic Movement, 1870–1915." *New Hibernia Review* 5, no. 3 (2001): 87–100.

Nyhan [Grey], Miriam A. "Comparing Irish Migrants and County Associations in New York and London: A Cross-Cultural Analysis of Migrant Experiences and Associational Behaviour, Circa 1946–1961." PhD diss., European University Institute, 2008.

———. "County Associations in Irish New York, 1945–1965." *New York Irish History* 22 (2008): 27–36.

Nyhan Grey, Miriam. "Dr. Gertrude B. Kelly and the Founding of New York's Cumann na mBan." In Nyhan Grey, *Ireland's Allies,* 75–89.

———, ed. *Ireland's Allies: America and the 1916 Easter Rising.* Dublin: University College Dublin Press, 2016.

O'Barr, William M. "A Brief History of Advertising in America." *Advertising & Society Review* 6, no. 3 (2005). https://doi.org/10.1353/asr.2006.0006.

Oboler, Suzanne. *Ethnic Labels, Latino Lives: Identity and the Politics of (Re)Presentation in the United States.* Minneapolis: University of Minnesota Press, 1995.

O'Brien, John A., ed. *The Vanishing Irish: The Enigma of the Modern World.* New York: McGraw Hill, 1953.

O'Brien, Matthew J. "'Hibernians on the March': Irish American and Ethnic Patriotism in the Mid-Twentieth Century." *Éire-Ireland* 40, nos. 1–2 (Spring/Summer 2005): 170–82.

———. "Irish America, Race, and Bernadette Devlin's 1969 American Tour." *New Hibernia Review* 14, no. 2 (Summer 2010): 84–101.

———. "Transatlantic Connections and the Sharp Edge of the Great Depression." *Éire-Ireland* 37, nos. 1–2 (Spring/Summer 2002): 38–57.

———. "Wartime Revisions of Irish American Catholicism: Stars, Stripes, and Shamrocks." *U.S. Catholic Historian* 22, no. 3 (Summer 2004): 75–96.

O'Brien, Michael J. *A Hidden Phase of American History: Ireland's Part in America's Struggle for Liberty.* New York: Dodd, Mead and Company, 1920.

Ó Cadhain, Mairtin. *The Road to Brightcity.* Dublin: Poolbeg, 1981.

O'Connell, Brian, with Cian O'Carroll. *Brendan O'Regan: Irish Innovator, Visionary & Peacemaker.* Dublin: Irish Academic Press, 2018.

O'Connor, Barbara, and Michael Cronin, eds. *Tourism in Ireland: A Critical Analysis.* Cork: Cork University Press, 1993.

O'Connor, Éimear. "America Called: The Helen Hackett Gallery and the Irish Art Rooms, 1924–1934." *New Hibernia Review* 15, no. 4 (Winter 2011): 16–33.

———. *Art, Ireland, and the Irish Diaspora: Chicago, Dublin, New York 1893–1939, Culture, Connections, and Controversies*. Dublin: Irish Academic Press, 2020.

O'Connor, John P. "*The Shamrock* of New York, the First Irish-American Newspaper." *New York Irish History* 4 (1989): 4–5.

O'Connor, Thomas H. *The Boston Irish: A Political History*. Boston, MA: Northeastern University Press, 1995.

O'Dea, John. *History of the Ancient Order of Hibernians and Ladies' Auxiliary*. Vol. 3. Philadelphia, PA: Ancient Order of Hibernians, 1923.

Ó Dochartaigh, Pól. *Julius Pokorny, 1887–1970: Germans, Celts and Nationalism*. Dublin: Four Courts Press, 2004.

O'Doherty, Katherine. *Assignment America: De Valera's Mission to the United States*. New York: De Tanko, 1957.

O'Donovan, Donal. *Dreamers of Dreams: Portraits of the Irish in America*. Bray, Ireland: Kilbride, 1984.

O'Donovan Rossa, Jeremiah. *Rossa's Recollections, 1838–1898*. Mariner's Harbor, New York: Jeremiah O'Donovan Rossa, 1898.

O'Donovan-Rossa, Margaret. *My Father and Mother Were Irish*. New York: Devin-Adair, 1939.

O'Drisceoil, Donal. *Censorship in Ireland, 1939–1945: Neutrality, Politics, and Society*. Cork: Cork University Press, 1996.

O'Driscoll, T. J. Introduction to *Administration* (Dublin) 9, no. 3 (Autumn 1961): 153.

O'Dwyer, Paul. *Counsel for the Defense: The Autobiography of Paul O'Dwyer*. New York: Simon and Schuster, 1979.

O'Dwyer, Rory. "On Show to the World: The Eucharistic Congress, 1932." *History Ireland* 15, no. 6 (November–December 2007): 42–47.

Ó Faoláin, Seán. *The Irish: A Character Study*. New York: Devin-Adair, 1956.

Ó Gráda, Cormac. *A Rocky Road: The Irish Economy since the 1920s*. Manchester, UK: Manchester University Press, 1997.

O'Grady, Joseph P. "The Irish Free State Passport and the Question of Citizenship, 1921–24." *Irish Historical Studies* 26, no. 104 (November 1989): 396–405.

O'Halpin, Eunan. *Spying on Ireland: British Intelligence and Irish Neutrality during the Second World War*. Oxford: Oxford University Press, 2008.

O'Hanlon, Ray. *Unintended Consequences: The Story of Irish Immigration to the U.S. and How America's Door Was Closed to the Irish*. Newbridge, Ireland: Merrion, 2020.

O'Hara, Maureen, and John Nicoletti. *'Tis Herself: An Autobiography*. New York: Simon & Schuster, 2004.

Olcott, Chauncey, George Graff Jr., and Ernest R. Ball. *When Irish Eyes Are Smiling*. New York: M. Witmark, 1912.

O'Leary, Jeffrey M. "Manufacturing Reality: The Display of the Irish at World's Fairs and Exhibitions, 1893 to 1965." PhD diss., Kent State University, 2015.

———. "St. Patrick Meets St. Louis: The Display of the Irish at the 1904 St. Louis World's Fair." *Éire-Ireland* 54, nos. 3–4 (Fall/Winter 2019): 142–71.
O'Malley, Michael. *The Beat Cop: Chicago's Chief O'Neill and the Creation of Irish Music*. Chicago, IL: University of Chicago Press, 2022.
Ó Murchú, Giollamuire. *Jerome Connor, Irish-American Sculptor 1874–1943*. Dublin: National Gallery of Ireland, 1993.
O'Neill, Ciaran. "'Harvard Scientist Seeks Typical Irishman': Measuring the Irish Race, 1888–1936," *Radical History Review* 143 (May 2022): 89–108.
O'Neill, Francis. *Irish Minstrels and Musicians*. Chicago, IL: Regan Printing House, 1913.
O'Neill, Kevin. "The Star-Spangled Shamrock: Meaning and Memory in Irish America." In McBride, *History and Memory*, 118–38.
O'Riordan, Michael. *Catholicity and Progress in Ireland*. London: K. Paul, Trench, Trübner, 1906.
O'Rourke, Kevin. *Currier and Ives: The Irish and America*. New York: Harry N. Abrams, 1995.
O'Shaughnessy, Ed. "Rough Rider & Friendly Sons: Theodore Roosevelt Attends the 121st Anniversary Dinner of the Friendly Sons of St. Patrick." *New York Irish History* 33 (2019): 3.
O'Sullivan, Patrick, ed. *Religion and Identity: The Irish World Wide 5*. Leicester, UK: Leicester University Press, 1996.
O'Toole, Fintan. *Black Hole, Green Card: The Disappearance of Ireland*. Dublin: New Island, 1994.
Paynter, Richard H., Jr. *A Psychological Study of Trade-Mark Infringement*. New York: Science Press, 1920.
Perlmann, Joel. *America Classifies the Immigrants: From Ellis Island to the 2020 Census*. Cambridge, MA: Harvard University Press, 2018.
"Poetical Works of Thomas Moore." *Albion: A Journal of News, Politics and Literature* 3, no. 16 (April 17, 1841): 135.
Potterton, Homan. "Letters from St. Louis." *Irish Arts Review Yearbook* 10 (1994): 245–51.
Quigley, Martin S. *A U.S. Spy in Ireland: The Truth behind Irish 'Neutrality' during World War II*. Lanham, MD: Roberts Rinehart, 1999.
Quinn, E. Moore. "Toasting King William and 'Cushla-ma-cree': Irish Verbal Art in America before the Great Famine." In *Consuming St. Patrick's Day*, edited by Jonathan Skinner and Dominic Bryan, 27–51. Newcastle upon Tyne, UK: Cambridge Scholars, 2015.
Rains, Stephanie. "Celtic Kitsch: Irish-America and Irish Material Culture." *Circa* 107 (Spring 2004): 52–57.
———. *The Irish-American in Popular Culture, 1945–2000*. Dublin: Irish Academic Press, 2007.
Ramsburg, Jim. *Network Radio Ratings, 1932–1953: A History of Prime Time Programs through the Ratings of Nielsen, Crossley and Hooper*. Jefferson, NC: McFarland, 2012.
Raymond, Raymond J. "American League for an Undivided Ireland." In Funchion, *Irish American Voluntary Organizations*, 46–49.
———. "American Public Opinion and Irish Neutrality, 1939–1945." *Éire-Ireland* 18, no. 1 (Spring 1983): 20–45.

———. "David Gray, the Aiken Mission, and Irish Neutrality, 1940–41." *Diplomatic History* 9, no. 1 (Winter 1985): 55–71.
Reid, B. L. *The Man from New York: John Quinn and His Friends*. New York: Oxford University Press, 1968.
Reynolds, Dorothy. *St. Patrick's Eve*. Lebanon, OH: March Brothers 1931.
Rhodes, Gary D. "Introduction." *Post Script* 32, no. 3 (Summer 2013): 3–14.
———. "Irish-American Film Audiences, 1915–1930." *Post Script* 32, no. 3 (Summer 2013): 70–96.
Ridge, John T. "Irish County Societies in New York, 1880–1914." In Bayor and Meagher, *New York Irish*, 286–89.
———. "The Irish Shop around the Corner: Manhattan's Irish Import Stores." *New York Irish History* 22 (2008): 37–42.
———. *The St. Patrick's Day Parade in New York*. New York: St. Patrick's Day Parade Committee, 1988.
Riordan, E. J. *Modern Irish Trade and Industry*. London: Methuen, 1920.
Roberts, Edward F. *Ireland in America*. New York: G. P. Putnam's Sons, 1931.
Rockett, Kevin. "Documentaries: Ethnicity and Landscape." In Rockett, Gibbons, and Hill, *Cinema and Ireland*, 71–73.
———. "Irish Cinema: The National in the International." *Cineaste* 24, nos. 2–3 (1999): 23–25.
———, ed. *The Irish Filmography, Fiction Films 1896–1996*. Dublin: Red Mountain Media, 1996.
Rockett, Kevin, Luke Gibbons, and John Hill, eds. *Cinema and Ireland*. Syracuse: Syracuse University Press, 1988.
Rodechko, James P. "Michael J. O'Brien, Irish-American Historian." *New-York Historical Society Quarterly* 54, no. 2 (1970): 173–92.
Rogers, James S., and Matthew J. O'Brien, eds. *After the Flood: Irish America, 1945–1960*. Dublin: Irish Academic Press, 2009.
Rose, Edward E. *The Blarney Stone: A Comedy-Drama in Four Acts*. 1923; repr. New York: Samuel French, 1933.
———. *Irish Eyes: A Comedy-Drama in Three Acts*. 1921; repr. New York: Samuel French, 1933.
Rosenberg, Joseph L. "The 1941 Mission of Frank Aiken to the United States: An American Perspective." *Irish Historical Studies* 22, no. 86 (September 1980): 162–77.
Ross, Jean. *The Saint and the Fairies*. Franklin, OH: Eldridge Entertainment House, 1924.
Ross, Marc Howard, ed. *Culture and Belonging in Divided Societies: Contestation and Symbolic Landscapes*. Philadelphia: University of Pennsylvania Press, 2009.
Rouse, Paul. "William Bourke Cockran." In Royal Irish Academy, *Dictionary of Irish Biography*. Accessed October 30, 2023. https://doi.org/10.3318/dib.001785.v1.
Rowland, Thomas J. "Irish-American Catholics and the Quest for Respectability in the Coming of the Great War, 1900–1917." *Journal of American Ethnic History* 15, no. 2 (Winter 1996): 3–31.

Royal Irish Academy, ed. *Dictionary of Irish Biography*. New York: Cambridge University Press 2009. https://dib.cambridge.org/.

Ruffins, Faith Davis, Bernadette Marie Calafell, William M. O'Barr, Jack Tchen, Zan Ng, and Jennifer Mak. "Roundtable Issue: Conversations about Race and Ethnicity in Advertising." *Advertising & Society Review* 6, no. 2 (2005). https://doi.org/10.1353/asr.2005.0002.

Ryan, Deborah Sugg. "Performing Irish-American Heritage: The Irish Historic Pageant, New York, 1913." In McCarthy, *Ireland's Heritages*, 105–20.

Ryan, Mary. "The American Parade: Representations of the Nineteenth-Century Social Order." In *The New Cultural History*, edited by Lynn Hunt, 131–53. Berkeley: University of California Press, 1989.

Salvo, Joseph J., and Arun Peter Lobo. "Population." In Jackson, *Encyclopedia of New York*, 1018–20.

Santino, Jack. *New Old-Fashioned Ways: Holidays and Popular Culture*. Knoxville: University of Tennessee Press, 1996.

Sarro, Marie. "William O'Dwyer: An Irish Mayor for All New Yorkers." *New York Irish History* 16 (2002): 27–40.

Saunders, Norah, and A. A. Kelly. *Joseph Campbell: Poet and Nationalist, 1879–1944*. Dublin: Wolfhound, 1988.

Savage, Robert J., Jr. *Ireland in the New Century: Politics, Culture and Identity*. Dublin: Four Courts Press, 2003.

Schmidt, Leigh Eric. "The Commercialization of the Calendar: American Holidays and the Culture of Consumption, 1870–1930." *Journal of American History* 78, no. 3 (December 1991): 887–916.

———. *Consumer Rites: The Buying & Selling of American Holidays*. Princeton, NJ: Princeton University Press, 1995.

Schrier, Arnold. *Ireland and the American Emigration, 1850–1900*. Minneapolis: University of Minnesota Press, 1958.

Screen Publicists Guild. *The Role of the Publicity Department in the Industry: The Functions of the Crafts within the Publicity Department*. New York: Screen Publicists Guild, Local #114, United Office and Professional Workers of America, CIO, 1944.

Seaburg, Alan. "A Learned Minister at Harvard: Willard Learoyd Sperry." *Harvard Theological Review* 80, no. 2 (April 1987): 179–92.

Seldes, Gilbert. *The Movies Come from America*. New York: Charles Scribner's Sons, 1937.

Shannon, J. R. *Too-Ra-Loo-Ra-Loo-Ral*. New York: M. Witmark, 1913.

Sheaff, Nicholas. "The Shamrock Building." *Irish Arts Review* 1, no. 1 (Spring 1984): 26–29.

Sheehy, Jeanne. *The Rediscovery of Ireland's Past: The Celtic Revival, 1830–1930*. London: Thames and Hudson, 1980.

Shelley, Thomas J. "Twentieth-Century American Catholicism and Irish Americans." In Lee and Casey, *Making the Irish American*, 575–90.

Sherry, Ruth. "Frank O'Connor." In Royal Irish Academy, *Dictionary of Irish Biography*. Accessed October 30, 2023. https://doi.org/10.3318/dib.006631.v1.

Skerrett, Ellen. *The Irish Parish in Chicago, 1880–1930*. Notre Dame, IN: University of Notre Dame Press, 1981.

Skinner, James M. *The Cross and the Cinema: The Legion of Decency and the National Catholic Office for Motion Pictures, 1933–1970*. Westport, CT: Praeger, 1993.

Sklar, Robert. *Movie-Made America: A Social History of American Movies*. New York: Random House, 1975.

Slide, Anthony. "The O'Kalems." *Post Script* 32, no. 3 (Summer 2013): 15–26.

Smith, Anthony Burke. *The Look of Catholics: Portrayals in Popular Culture from the Great Depression to the Cold War*. Lawrence: University Press of Kansas, 2010.

Soderman, Doris Flodin. *The Sculptors O'Connor*. Worcester, MA: Gundi, 1995.

Sollors, Werner. *The Invention of Ethnicity*. New York: Oxford University Press, 1989.

Spicer, Dorothy Gladys. *Parties for Young Americans*. New York: Woman's Press, 1940.

Strand, Karin. "W. B. Yeats's American Lecture Tours." PhD diss., Northwestern University, 1978.

Solomon, Barbara Miller. *Ancestors and Immigrants: A Changing New England Tradition*. Boston, MA: Northeastern University Press, 1956.

Sullivan, Dennis M. "Éamon de Valera and the Forces of Opposition in America, 1919–1920." *Éire-Ireland* 19, no. 2 (Summer 1984): 98–115.

Sullivan, Eileen. "Community in Print: Irish-American Publishers and Readers." *American Journal of Irish Studies* 8 (2011): 41–76.

Szpila, Kathleen. "Lest We Forget: Ellen Ryan Jolly and the Nuns of the Battlefield Monument." *American Catholic Studies* 123, no. 4 (January 2012): 23–43.

Tansill, Charles Callan. *America and the Fight for Irish Freedom, 1866–1922*. New York: Devin-Adair, 1957.

Taylor, Robert. *Fred Allen: His Life and Wit*. Boston: Little, Brown, 1989.

Tebbel, John, and Mary Ellen Zuckerman. *The Magazine in America, 1741–1990*. New York: Oxford University Press, 1991.

Tessier, Thérèse. *The Bard of Erin: A Study of Thomas Moore's Irish Melodies (1808–1834)*. Salzburg, Austria: Institut für Anglistik und Amerikanistik, Universität Salzburg, 1981.

Tharp, Marye C. *Marketing and Consumer Identity in Multicultural America*. Thousand Oaks, CA: Sage, 2001.

Thernstrom, Stephan, ed. *The Harvard Encyclopedia of American Ethnic Groups*. Cambridge, MA: Harvard University Press, 1980.

———. *The Other Bostonians: 1880 Mobility Study*. Ann Arbor, MI: Inter-university Consortium for Political and Social Research, 1978.

Truxes, Thomas M. *Defying Empire: Trading with the Enemy in Colonial New York*. New Haven, CT: Yale University Press, 2008.

———. *Irish-American Trade, 1660–1783*. Cambridge: Cambridge University Press, 1988.

Tucker, Todd. *Notre Dame vs. the Klan: How the Fighting Irish Defeated the Ku Klux Klan*. Chicago, IL: Loyola Press, 2004.

Vaughan, W. E., ed. *A New History of Ireland*. Vol. 6, *Ireland under the Union, 1870–1921*. Oxford: Clarendon Press, 1996.

Vinyard, Jo Ellen. *The Irish on the Urban Frontier: Nineteenth Century Detroit, 1850–1880*. New York: Arno, 1976.
Walker, Brian. "St. Patrick's Day: Commemoration, Conflict, and Conciliation, 1903–2013." In Hill and Lyons, *Representing Irish Religious Histories*, 248–51.
Walsh, Frank. *Sin and Censorship: The Catholic Church and the Motion Picture Industry*. New Haven, CT: Yale University Press, 1996.
Walsh, G. P. "Narelle, Marie (Molly) (1870–1941)." In *Australian Dictionary of Biography*. Canberra: National Centre of Biography, Australian National University, 2005. http://adb.anu.edu.au/.
Ward, Alan J. *Ireland and Anglo-American Relations, 1899–1921*. Toronto: University of Toronto Press, 1969.
Waters, Mary C. *Ethnic Options: Choosing Identities in America*. Berkeley: University of California Press, 1990.
Watt, Stephen, Eileen Morgan, and Shakir Mustafa, eds. *A Century of Irish Drama: Widening the Stage*. Bloomington: Indiana University Press, 2001.
Weatherly, Fred E. *Danny Boy*. New York: Boosey, Hawks, 1913.
Weaver-Zercher, David. *The Amish in the American Imagination*. Baltimore, MD: Johns Hopkins University Press, 2001.
Welch, Robert, ed. *The Oxford Companion to Irish Literature*. New York: Clarendon, 1996.
West, Eugene, and Clyde Roland. *If They Don't Want the Irish in Ireland, Let's Bring Them over Here*. New York: Shapiro, Bernstein & Co., 1920.
Whelan, Bernadette. "Adopting the 'American Way': Ireland and the Marshall Plan, 1947–1957." *History Ireland* 16, no. 3 (May–June 2008): 30–33.
———. *De Valera and Roosevelt: Irish and American Diplomacy in Times of Crisis, 1932–1939*. Cambridge: Cambridge University Press, 2020.
———. *Ireland and the Marshall Plan, 1947–57*. Dublin: Four Courts Press, 2000.
———. "Marshall Plan Publicity and Propaganda in Italy and Ireland, 1947–1951." *Historical Journal of Film, Radio and Television* 23, no. 4 (2003): 311–328.
———. *United States Foreign Policy and Ireland: From Empire to Independence, 1913–1929*. Dublin: Four Courts Press, 2006.
Whelan, Irene. "The 'Idea of America' in the New Irish State, 1922–1960." In Gleeson, *Irish in the Atlantic World*, 76–81.
White, Cassandra L. "Blarney in St. Louie: Performing Irishness at the Louisiana Purchase Exposition, 1904." Master's thesis, Central Washington University, 2015.
White, Harry. "Thomas Moore." In Royal Irish Academy, *Dictionary of Irish Biography*. Accessed October 30, 2023. https://doi.org/10.3318/dib.005948.v1.
White, Lawrence William. "John Quinn." In Royal Irish Academy, *Dictionary of Irish Biography*. Accessed October 30, 2023. https://doi.org/10.3318/dib.007561.v1.
———. "Michael Scott." In Royal Irish Academy, *Dictionary of Irish Biography*. Accessed October 30, 2023. https://doi.org/10.3318/dib.007950.v2.
White, Lawrence William, and Paul Rouse. "Francis Hackett." In Royal Irish Academy, *Dictionary of Irish Biography*. Accessed October 30, 2023. https://doi.org/10.3318/dib.003698.v1.

White, Trumbull, and William Igleheart. *The World's Columbian Exposition, Chicago, 1893*. St. Louis, MO: P. W. Ziegler, 1893.

Whitmer, Nick. "Trouble in the Irish Village." *An Piobaire* 11, no. 3 (July 2015): 26–28.

Wilkman, Jon. *Screening Reality: How Documentary Filmmakers Reimagined America*. London: Bloomsbury, 2020.

Williams, W. H. A. *'Twas Only an Irishman's Dream: The Image of Ireland and the Irish in American Popular Song Lyrics, 1800–1920*. Urbana: University of Illinois Press, 1996.

Willits, R. Bryan. "The Stereopticon: German and Irish Propaganda of Deed and Word and the 1916 Easter Rising." In Nyhan Grey, *Ireland's Allies*, 185–99.

Wills, Clair. *That Neutral Island: A Cultural History of Ireland during the Second World War*. Cambridge, MA: Belknap Press of Harvard University Press, 2007.

Winter, Henry Lyle. *Notes on Criminal Anthropology and Bio-sociology: Being a Study of Seventy-Three Irish and Irish-American Criminals at the Kings Co. Penitentiary, Brooklyn, NY*. Utica, NY: State Hospitals Press, 1897.

Wolf, Nicholas M. "The Irish-Language Community in New York on the Eve of the Easter Rising." In Nyhan Grey, *Ireland's Allies*, 239–55.

Wu, Ellen. *The Color of Success: Asian Americans and the Origins of the Model Minority*. Princeton: Princeton University Press, 2014.

Young, J. R., Chauncey Olcott, and Ernest R. Ball. *Mother Machree*. New York: Witmark, 1910.

Young, Mitchell, Eric Zuelow, and Andreas Sturm, eds. *Nationalism in a Global Era: The Persistence of Nations*. Hoboken, NJ: Taylor & Francis, 2007.

Zarucchi, Jeanne Morgan. *The Material Culture of Tableware: Staffordshire Pottery and American Values*. London: Bloomsbury, 2018.

Zerubavel, Eviatur. "Easter and Passover: On Calendars and Group Identity." *American Sociological Review* 47, no. 2 (1982): 284–89.

Zim, Larry, Mel Lerner, Herbert Rolfes. *The World of Tomorrow: The 1939 New York World's Fair*. New York: Harper & Row, 1988.

Zimmerman, Jonathan. "'Each "Race" Could Have Its Heroes Sung': Ethnicity and the History Wars in the 1920s." *Journal of American History* 87, no. 1 (June 2000): 92–111.

Zuelow, Eric G. E. *Making Ireland Irish: Tourism and National Identity since the Irish Civil War*. Syracuse, NY: Syracuse University Press, 2009.

———. "National Identity and Tourism in Twentieth Century Ireland: The Role of Collective Re-imagining." In Young, Zuelow, and Sturm, *Nationalism*, 141–57.

———. "The Tourism Nexus: Tourism and National Identity since the Irish Civil War." PhD diss., University of Wisconsin-Madison, 2004.

INDEX

Page numbers in italics refer to figures.

AARIR. *See* American Association for the Recognition of the Irish Republic
Abbey Theatre (Dublin), 51, 65, 69–75, 205, 206, 208, 213, 238nn57–58, 241n109. See also *Playboy of the Western World, The*
Abercorn, Rosalind, 255n44
Aberdeen, Lady (Ishbel), 124–26, 128, 130, 150
Aberdeen, Lord (John Hamilton-Gordon), 126
Aer Lingus, 18, 210, 225n60
AFIN. *See* American Friends of Irish Neutrality
AIHS. *See* American Irish Historical Society
Aiken, Frank, 32–33, 209, 229n59
Allen, Fred, 28, 42–43, 153, 231n100, 231n102
All-Ireland Hurling Champions (1926, Tipperary), 76
All Nations Exposition (Cleveland, 1929), 130
American Association for the Recognition of the Irish Republic (AARIR), 27, 30–32
American Commission on Conditions in Ireland, 22
American Committee for Relief in Ireland, 22
American Council of Learned Societies, 111
American Friends of Irish Neutrality (AFIN), 31–33, 39

American Irish Historical Society (AIHS), 39, 56–58, 62, 63, 81, 87, 96, 104, 118, 246n55, 247n64; U.S. immigration restriction and, 94–95, 99, 103, 110
American Irish Immigration Committee, 116, 117
American Irish Minute Men, 39–41
American-Irish Republican League, 95, 100
American League for an Undivided Ireland, 39, 120
American Legion, 107
Ancient Order of Hibernians (AOH), 59–61, 68, 87, 116, 158, 170, 209, 228n55; Irish product promotion and, 129–30, 134; Ladies' Auxiliary, 61, 67; protests by, 67–68, 72–73, 160–61; U.S. colonial history, 96–97; U.S. immigration restriction and, 94, 103, 116–17. *See also* monuments
An Dhord Fhiann (Craig), 74–75, 83. See also *Fenian Rallying Cry, The*
Anglo-Saxon: bias, 5, *93*; as geographic term, 114; as origin of American identity, 87; as propaganda, 88, *93*, 106–9, 122; Protestants, 108; as race, 96, 98, 104–5, 114, 119; superiority of, 97–98, 113; theorists, 96; U.S. colonial history and, 96, 98, 104, 107–8; U.S. immigration restriction and, 5, *93*, 99, 106–7, 110
Anheuser-Busch, Budweiser, 4; Busch Gardens Williamsburg, 215; Guinness, 4; Irish Derby, 4

309

AOH. *See* Ancient Order of Hibernians
Aran, islands, 199, 201–2; sweater, 1, 86. See also *Man of Aran*
Ardmore Studios (Ireland), 51
Arensberg, Conrad, 201–2, 208, 224n38, 273n61; *The Irish Countryman*, 12, 203
Arklow Pottery, *205*
Arrah-na-Pogue (Boucicault), 156–57, *173*

Balfe, Michael, 55, 192, 201
ballyhoo (advertising technique), 154, 175–86, *181*, 195, 213, 266n96, 267n107, 268n131, 273n62
Bantry, John, 95
Barrett, Dennis D., 134–35, 256n65
Barry, John, 7, 63, 77, 83–84; statues of, 58–60, 62, 71, 78, 213, 235n20, 236n26
Bayles, William, 35
Beautiful Ireland (Film Company of Ireland), 195–96
Beautiful Ireland (Holmes), 193
Beautiful Ireland (Mathew), 195
Belfast. *See* Northern Ireland
Belleek (porcelain), 131–36, *133*, 148, 255n54; imitations, 132–34, 255n50; Irish Trade Mark and, 132; nostalgia and, 130; potters and, 132; potter's mark, 132, 256n61; pottery and, 134, 146
Belleek (village), Ireland, 131
Blarney (village), Ireland, 192, 196, 200
Blarney Castle, 86, 158, 163–64, 193, 200–201, 203
Blarney Stone, 42, 84, 86, 128, 160, 188, 191, 193, *194*, 197–202, 204; imitations, 184, 188, 191
Blarney Stone, The (Rose), 166–67, 264n62
"B" movies, 183–84
Boucicault, Dion, 16–18, *161*, 208, 212–13, 266n89; *Arrah-na-Pogue*, 156–57, *173*; *The Colleen Bawn*, 191–92, 195, 199, 213; *The Shaughraun*, 208
Bowen, Elizabeth, 49, 209; "Ireland: The Tear and the Smile," 49

Boyle, John J., 60
Breen, Joseph, 185
Bringing Up Father (McManus), 18
Bromley, William, 132
Brooke, Basil, 40–41, 47, 230n93
Bryan, William Jennings, 46
B. Shackman & Co., 163–64
Busch Gardens Williamsburg, 215
Bushmills (whiskey), 146–47, 150, 187

Cagney, James, 51, 180
Cahill, Rosaleen, 148–50, *149*, 218
Cahill, William T., 117
Callahans and the Murphys, The (Hill), 178–79
Carey, James B., 113–15, 251n143
Carey, Joseph, 95, 100–101
Catholic Church, United States, 72; Archdiocese of New York, 57; colleges, 15; film promotion, 185–86, 195; Irish Americans, 15; journalism, 15; maturity of, 57; prejudice against, 15, 17, 213; social mobility, 57; St. Patrick's Day, 167; U.S. colonial history and, 103
Catholic Club (New York), 57–58
Catholic Dramatic Guild, 172
Catholic Total Abstinence Union Centennial Fountain, 58
CBS radio, 21–22, 28, 32–33
CBS television, 49–50, 209; "Ireland: The Tear and the Smile" (Bowen), 49
Celt(ic): antiquities, 126, 205, 207; as Irish race, 64, 83, 88, 92, 96, 98, 105, 114, 119, 122; music, 215; symbols, 2, 132, 134, 187
Celtic Fellowship, 164
Celtic Fyre (entertainment), 215
Celtic revival, 126, 132. *See also* Gaelic Revival
Celtic Woman (entertainers), *214*
Central Council of Irish County Associations (Boston), 70
Century of Population Growth, A (U.S. Bureau of the Census), 92, 96–97, 246n54

Century of Progress Exposition, 81–83, 242n139. *See also* World's Fair (Chicago, 1933–34)
Chicago Ethnic Arts Project, 211
Churchill, Winston, 31–33
Cinco de Mayo, 216. *See also* "Mexican Fiesta"
Clancy, Liam, 86
Clancy Brothers and Tommy Makem, 86, 88, 211
Clan na Gael, 21–22, 67, 71, 73, 100, 103, 110, 231n96
Clarke, Joseph, I. C., 96–97, 246n55
Coca-Cola, 37
Cockran, William Bourke, 63
Cohalan, Daniel F., 24, 94, 110
Cohan, George M., 10
Cohen, Myron, 86
Colleen Bawn, The (Boucicault), 191, 192, 195, 199, 213
Colleens, The (entertainers), 214
Collins, John P., 116–18
Colum, Padraic, 44, 46–47, 50, 199, 205, 206, 275n89
Comerford, James J., 78
Comerford, Lily, 85
Comhaltas Ceoltóirí Éireann (Chicago), 211
Comp, Sol ("Smiling Irishman"), 144
Concannon Folk Group, 211–12
Conner, Rearden, 50
Connolly, Charles (*Irish Echo*), 13
Connolly, Joseph, 23–24
Connolly, Sybil, 209
Connor, Jerome, 61–62; "The Nuns of the Battlefield," 62; "Robert Emmet," 61
Coolidge, Calvin, 247n71, 250n122
Córas Tráchtála (Irish Exports Board), 130, 255n42
corned beef, 212
Cosgrave, William T., 24, 26, 232n108
Costello, John A., 188
County Tyrone Society (New York), 72
Craig, Anna Throop, 74

Crawford, Lindsay, 130, 137, 254n41
Crimmins, John D., 10, 56–59, 63, 127
Cronin, Timmy, 85
Crosby, Bing, 17, 81, 85–86, 193, 208
Crossley, F. W., 196, 209–10
Curley, James Michael, 60
Currier and Ives, 191

"Danny Boy" (Weatherly), 85–86
DATI. *See* Department of Agricultural and Technical Instruction for Ireland
Deirdre (Russell), 65, 69
Dempsey, Jack, 10
Department of Agricultural and Technical Instruction for Ireland (DATI), 64–65, 127–28
de Valera, Éamon, 22, 23–24, 26–27, 34–35, 83, 86, 112, 202, 205, 230n82; American tours, 22, 26, 36, 41, 42, 61; bond certificate drive, 26–27; death of Hitler and, 31; Fianna Fáil and, 28–29; Fred Allen sketch (1949), 42–43; Irish Republican Army and, 30; *The Nation*, 22; newsreel featuring, 39; radio broadcasts, 22, 35–36, 38, 42; speech to U.S. Congress (1964), 113; as subversive, 29–30, 41; as *taoiseach*, 28–29; television interview (1959), 86; World War II and Irish neutrality, 32, 36, 228n46
DeVally, Liam (Irish Festival Singers), 84–85
Devane, Andrew, 150
Devlin, Bernadette, 120–22; Black Panthers and, 122
Devoy, John, 13, 24, 70–71, 100; de Valera and, 24
Dichter, Ernest, 151–52
Digges, Dudley, 238n57. *See also* Irish Village (St. Louis, 1904)
Dongan, Thomas, 58, 63
Donohue, Michael, 94
Douglas, John J., 99
Dowling, Victor J., 60–61, 74, 129

Downey, Jim, 148–49
Downey, Morton, 81
Draddy, John G., 55
Dublin (Ireland), 3, 6, 14, 31, 35, 42, 51, 69, 71, 84, 89, 187; exports from, 146–47; souvenirs from, 126; tourism and, 192, 195–96, 197, 198, 199, 204–5
Dunne, Veronica (Irish Festival Singers), 84–85

Edison, Thomas, 193
Ed Sullivan Show, The, 85–86, 211
Edwards, Martin, 105
Éire, 12, 39–40, 83; neutrality of, 31, 33–36. *See also Ireland, specific topics*
Eisenhower, Dwight D., 188
Emerald Isle, 3, 35, 166, 168, 169, 175, 196, 199, 201, 207, 215. *See also Ireland, specific topics*
Emergency Quota Act, 87, 90, 245n24. *See also* national origins quotas
Emmet, Robert: film *Robert Emmet* (Thanhouser), 174; as hero, 60–61, 76–77; play *Robert Emmet* (Boucicault), 266n89; play *Robert Emmet: A History Play in Three Acts* (Mangan), 237n53; play *Robert Emmet: The Days of 1803* (Tynan), 69, 266n89; statue of, 60–62, 78, 236nn33–34
Emmet, Rosina, 71
Emmet, Thomas A. (doctor), 61
Emmet Statue Committee, 60–61, 74
England, 11, 25, 126, 136, 138, 192; Irish nationalism and, 12, 22–23, 30, 35, 45, 46, 70; racial composition, 105, 106; U.S. colonial history and, 98, 107, 108; U.S. immigration restriction and, 95. *See also* Anglo-Saxon; Great Britain; United Kingdom
Erlichman, Martin (Marty), 86
Ervin, Samuel J. (Sam), 113–15

Family and Community in Ireland (Arensberg and Kimball), 208, 273n61

Farley, John M., 57–58
Feeney, John, 81
Feighan, Michael, 118
Feis, United Irish Counties Association, 77–79, 80; syllabus, 78–79
Fenian Rallying Cry, The (Craig), 74–75. *See also An Dhord Fhiann*
Film Company of Ireland, 195–96, 273n58
Fitzpatrick, Benedict, 103
Fitzpatrick, James A., 201
Flaherty, Robert, *Man of Aran*, 12, 201–2
Flannelly, Adrian, 112
Fleming, Frank, *93*
FOIF. *See* Friends of Irish Freedom
Ford, John, 17, 175; *The Informer*, 202; *Mother Machree*, 179; *The Quiet Man*, 189, 205–10, 213; *The Shamrock Handicap*, 174–75
Ford, Patrick (*Irish World*), 13
Fox Film Corporation, 178–79, 185, 196–97
Freeman, Edward, 97, 246n61
Friendly Sons of St. Patrick (New York), 55, 81, 86–87, 246n55; Glee Club of, 86
Friendly Sons of St. Patrick (Philadelphia), 59
Friends of Irish Freedom (FOIF), 22, 27, 30; U.S. colonial history and, 98; U.S. immigration restriction and, 94, 103, 107, 249n104
Fulton, Robert, 57, 72, 103

GAA. *See* Gaelic Athletic Association
Gaelic, culture, 4, 53, 58; folklore, 145, 152, 190, 198, 200; folk music, 79, 152; language, 78, 85, 129. *See also* Ireland, cultural nationalism
Gaelic Athletic Association (GAA), 116
Gaelic League, in Ireland, 35, 64, 71, 77, 241n107; in United States, 67, 72, 74, 75, 130
Gaelic Revival, 12, 64–65, 69, 76
Gaelic Society of New York, 64, 84
Gaffney, Austin (Irish Festival Singers), 84

Gallup, on Irish neutrality, 32–33, 38, 229n64; polls, 225n4, 227n38
Gannett, Lewis (*The Nation*), 23
Garland, Judy, 85
Gaughan, Evelyn, 149
Gavigan, John, 132
Giant's Causeway, 84, 191, 199
Gibbons, James, 62
Gilmore, Patrick Sarsfield, 55
Golden (Sax), Eithne, 34–35
Golden, Peter, 34
Gordon, Ishbel Hamilton. *See* Aberdeen, Lady
Gray, David, 31
Great Britain, 25, 27, 200; *Immigration into the United States* (1909), 92; Ireland and, 5, 21, 29, 61; Irish emigration to, 11–12, 111–12, 250n132; Ulster, 23, 41–42; U.S. and, 87, 89, 107, 115; U.S. quota for, 90, 94–96, 106, 110; World War II and, 31. *See also* England; United Kingdom
Greeley, Andrew, 2–3
green space (matrix), 1–6, 212–13, 215, 216, 273n61; and cultural currency, 53, 69, 75, 81, 83, 85, 86; and emerald sheen, 154, 160, 162–64, 167, 168, 174, 180, 187, 188; and media matters, 43, 51–52; and racial reckoning, 88, 96, 104, 108, 122; and selling value, 123, 145, 150–52; and tourism, 189, 191, 192, 198, 200, 205, 206, 208–10, 273n62; and vested interests, 16, 19
Gregory, Lady (Augusta), 70–71, 73–74, 206–7, 240n99
Griffin, Ambrose M., 82
Guinness (stout), 145–46, 148, 205, 216; Budweiser and, 4; imitations of, 146, 259n117
Gwynn, Stephen, *Ireland*, 44, 199; *The Student's History of Ireland*, 44

Hackett, Francis, *The Story of the Irish Nation*, 23

Hall, A. Oakey, 157
Hanley, Thomas F., 127–28, 237n46
Harp and Shamrock Orchestra, 82
Harrigan's Double Hibernian Co., Irish and American Tourists, 190
Harrigan's Hibernian Tourist Songster, 190
Hart, Alice Rowland, 124–25
Harvard Irish Study, 12, 201–2, 224n38, 273n61
Hayden, Dorothy, 85, 218
Hayes, John J., 10, 223n24
Hayes, Michael, 196
Hearne, John J., 188
Hearst, William Randoph, 21
Helen Hackett Gallery (New York), 76, 241n110
Herbert, Victor, 58, 81, 208
hibernicon (entertainment), 190–93, 195, 200, 207. *See also* Ireland, tourism; *MacEvoy's Hibernicon*
Hidden Phase of American History, A (O'Brien, M. J.), 96–97, 99, 102–3, 107, 247n69
Hill Holliday, 215, 275n4
History of Ireland from the Earliest Period to the Present Time, The (Haverty), 190
Hitler, Adolph, 31
Holaday, William Perry, 95
Holiday (magazine), 202–5, 207, 209–10
Hollyman, Jean, 204
Hollyman, Thomas, 204
Holmes, Burton, 195, 201; *Beautiful Ireland*, 193
Holzer, Leland ("Smiling Irishman"), 139–44
Howson, Albert S., 176
Hudson, Henry, 57
Hudson-Fulton Celebration, 57–58, 72, 103
Hughes, Charles Evans, 58, 110

"If They Don't Want the Irish in Ireland, Let's Bring Them over Here" (Roland and West), 88

IIDA. *See* Irish Industrial Development Association
Immigration Restriction League and Allied Patriotic Society of New York, 106
Informer, The (Ford), 202, 273n62
International Association of Chiefs of Police, 68
IRA. *See* Irish Republican Army
Ireland (Gwynn), 44
Ireland, a Nation (MacNamara), 196
Ireland, Blueshirts, 30; bog(s), 75, 126, 176, 192, 195, 196; censorship, 25; communism and, 29, 31, 48, 121–22; constitution (1922), 29; constitution (1937), 29, 47; Dáil Éireann, 22–23, 26, 196; Department of External Affairs, 204, 207; Department of Industry and Commerce, 131, 134, 197, 202, 207; economy, 12, 50, 112, 115, 123; Éire, 12, 33–36, 39–40, 83; Eucharistic Congress (1932), 189; Famine, Great, 8, 60, 111; famine in (1925), 26, 47; Fianna Fáil, 28; government, 49–50, 83–84, 112–13, 230n85; Irish Christian Front, 30, 227n42; Irish Free State, 12, 23, 29, 30, 87, 88, 224n36; news reporting on, 4, 20, 21, 25, 39, 48–50, 196, 203–4, 213, 231n95; population decline, 10–11, 89, 111; Republic of, 6, 12, 115, 189; tuberculosis, 89. *See also* media; Northern Ireland; *and Ireland, specific topics*
Ireland, cultural nationalism, 53; art as, 76–77; folk (traditional) music, 13, 31, 79, *80*, 152, 212; Gaelic Revival, 12, 64, 65, 69, 76; Golden Age, 53, 74–75, 127; at 1939–40 World's Fair (New York), 83; shamrocks as, 188; sport as, 76–77, 189; step dancing, 85, 243n154. *See also* Gaelic, culture
Ireland, emigration from, 7–8, 9, 10–11, 13, 16, 25, 88, 89, 111–12, 224n32, 244n10, 245n25; U.S. immigration restriction and, 90–92, 250n131

Ireland, exports, 5, 12, 123–29, 130–31, 212, 254n41, 255n42; "Buy Irish," 130–31, 145. *See also* Belleek (porcelain); Guinness; linen, Irish; whiskey, Irish
Ireland, independence, 5, 20, 23, 212; Anglo-Irish Treaty, 12, 23, 26–27; Anglo-Irish War (Irish War of Independence), 23, 25, 47, 51, 90, 92, 104, 202; Easter Rising (1916), 12, 22, 46, 61, 236n34
Ireland, John, 59
Ireland, neutrality, 31, 37, 47, 79; editorial hostility and, 31, 36; espionage and, 31, 36; Irish American support for, 33; propaganda and, 31–33
Ireland, Northern. *See* Northern Ireland
Ireland, partition of, 39–40, 41–42, 88, 120–21. *See also* Northern Ireland
Ireland, political nationalism, 13, 21–22; Civil War, 12, 24, 26, 27, 30, 47, 90, 196; Clan na Gael, 21, 22; Easter Rising (1916) and, 12, 22, 44, 46, 61, 236n34; Fenians, 21; Home Rule, 21, 26, 44, 61, 64, 75, 239n92; Irish Parliamentary Party, 75; Land League, 21, 64; opposition to Act of Union, 155; Sinn Féin, 22; United Irishmen, 54, 56
Ireland, tourism, 5, 21, 37, 189, 198, 204; antiquities, 190, 198, 206, 208; Bord Fáilte, 209, 215; publicity, 197–98, 215; scenery, 190, 195–99, 209; sights, 191, 193, 195–96; souvenirs, 192, *194*, 198, *205*; travelogues, 193, 195–97, 201, 203, 206, 208, 213, 273n58; virtual, 84, 125, 190–92, 195, 215. *See also* Blarney (village), Ireland; Dublin; ITA; ITB; Killarney (town), Ireland
"Ireland: The Tear and the Smile" (CBS), 49, 50, 209
Irish, as a brand, 1, 2, 18–19, 123, 136, 138–44, *140*; counterfeits, 131, 137–39, 147; registered word marks, 136, 141–42, 257n68. *See also* Irish Trade Mark

Irish, as code, 1, 18, 86, 273n62; alcohol, 4, 43, 187; Aran sweater, 1, 86; blarney (speech), 162, 193, *194*, 206; Bridget, 16; Catholic, 8, 9, 15; Celt(ic), 64, 83, 88, 92, 96, 98, 105, 114, 119, 122; Celtic cross, 187, 205, 207; characters, 16, 160; clay pipe(s), 72, 162; corned beef, 212; costumes, *3*, 153, 157, 169, 222n11, 265n71; cottage (thatched), 20, *133*, 202–7, 208, 210; dance, 13, 166; Erin (personification of Ireland), 54; fairies, 34, 35, 164, 166, 200; false red beards, 3; fighting (donnybrook), 43, 105–6, 144–45, 150, 207; genial (fun), 168, 176, 178, 189, 198, 215, 274n64; green (color), 16, 117, 153, 157, *173*; green (flag), 163, 263n49; harp, 12, 15, 54, 108, 146, 162–63, *194*; hat(s), 3, 72, 163; hospitable (friendly), 5, 143, 168, 198, 202, 209, 210, 274n64; jaunting car(t), 163, 190, 192, 195, 205, *205*, 207, 210; leprechaun(s), 6, 123, 145, 152, 166, 187, 188; luck, *140*, 160, 162, 168, 175, 183, 185, 197, 216; music, 13, 166; peasant, 4, 78, 86; pig(s), 160, 163–64, 169–71, 203, 212, 265n82; potato(es), 48, 151, 160, 163–64, 165, 170–71; romantic, 18, 150, 156, *161*, 189, 193, 198, 199, 200, 201; sentiment(al), 54, 189, 198, 206; shamrock(s), 4, 15, 18, 54, 83, 154–56, 162, 169, 182, 210, 213; shillelagh, 72, 187; snakes, 163, 165, 191; speech (brogue), 16, 48, 50, 75, 79, 119, 160, 166, 167, 185, 261n11; St. Patrick, 84; St. Patrick's Day, 16, 189; sweepstakes, 4, 27–28; turf (peat), 130, 165, 192, 195, 203, 206; wit (humor), 18, 45, 68, 167, 178, 189, 195, 198, 232n113, 240n95. *See also* green space; Guinness; race, European hierarchy of

Irish, Marie (Evelyn Simons), 168, 170–71, 264n64

Irish Agricultural Organisations Society, 124, 127

Irish America, 7, 12, 13, 31, 36; anti-Communist, 116, 121; Catholic, 15, 57, 72, 87, 103; census returns on ancestry, 2, 8, 12; chain migration, 8, 11, 88; consumption and, 158; contributions to U.S., 59–61, 116, 212; cultural nationalism, 31, 53, 63–64; cultural tensions, 53, 65–69; disloyalty, 101; filiopietism, 103, 118–19, 248n86; generation gap, 32; heroes, 7, 10, 53, 212; hybrid image, 18; immigration, 7, 8, 10–11, 89–90, 116; leadership, 62, 94; literacy, 10; loyalty, 72, 101; maturation, 4, 9, 30, 53; military service, 30; nationalists, 39, 40, 92; nativism, 7–8, 17, 30, 87, 92, 94–95, 103; networks, 9, 11, 13; opposition to national origins quotas, *93*, 94–96, 101; patriotism, 53, 60, 62, 88, 118, 121, 127; Presbyterians, 7, 102; Protestants, 8, 9, 55, 102, 114; respectability, 17, 72, 78, 86, 88, 127, 212; second-generation, 10, 14, 15, 30, 32, 38, 53, 63, 77, 79, 85, 130, 201, 211; settlement patterns, 8–11; social mobility, 9–11, 55–56, 63; subculture, 10, 13, 38, 211; treasonous, 100; U.S. colonial history and, 96–99, 107–8, 110, 117; World War II and Irish neutrality, 32–34, 38. *See also* race, European hierarchy of

Irish America, population, 14, 96–99, 110–11, 115, 197, 207, 247nn65–66; in Boston, 10, 13, 15, 18, 70, 71, *194*, 211, 242n126; in Chicago, 10, 13, 15, 18, 82, 211–12; in Detroit, 211; in New York, 9–10, 13–15, *14*, 18, 57–58, 70, 71, 74, 116, 211, 263n43; in Philadelphia, 10, 13, 15, 18, 71, 73, 211; in San Francisco, 211; in St. Louis, 65; in St. Paul, 211

Irish American Athletic Club, 75

Irish American Historic Loan Collection, 63

Irish Art Rooms (Museum of Irish Art, New York), 76

Irish coffee, 2, 148–49, *149*
Irish Countryman, The (Arensberg and Kimball), 12, 203
Irish Cream (liqueur), 2
Irish Export Board (Córas Tráchtála), 86, 130, 255n42
Irish Festival Singers, 84–86. *See also individual artists' names*
Irish Free State v. Guaranty Safe Deposit Company, 26
Irish Hearts (Haskin), 175–78, 208
Irish Historic Loan Collection, 127
Irish Historic Pageant, 74. See also *An Dhord Fhiann*
Irish Hospitals Sweepstakes, 27–28
Irish Industrial Development Association (IIDA), 132–37, 144, 257n71
Irish Industrial Exposition and Amusement Company, 129
Irish Industrial League of America, 127
Irish in Us, The (Bacon), 180, 182–83
"Irish Ireland," 12–13, *14*
Irish Melodies (Moore, *Moore's Melodies*), 16–17, 54–55, 57, 61, 75, 79, 156, 159–60, 212; "The Harp That Once through Tara's Halls," 17; "The Minstrel Boy," 17. *See also* Moore, Thomas
Irish Memories Stage Revue (entertainers), 85
Irish Players, The, 72. *See also* Abbey Theatre
Irish Republican Army (IRA), 29–30, 39, 43, 231n96
Irish Sweepstakes. *See* Irish Hospitals Sweepstakes
Irish Tourist Association (ITA), 196–98, 201–2, 273n53
Irish Tourist Board (ITB), 202, 204, 209, 273n64
Irish Trade Mark, 132, 134–37, 257n71
Irish Village (Chicago, 1893): Lady Aberdeen's, 125–26; Mrs. Hart's, 124–25
Irish Village (Chicago, 1933–34), 81–83; cultural tensions, 82; Irish Day, 82; Irish Village Corporation, 82
Irish Village (Chicago, 1977), pub, 211–12
Irish Village (New York, 1939–40), 84
Irish Village (St. Louis, 1904), 64–69, 79, 237n46, 237n48, 237n53; advertisement for, *66*; cultural tensions, 65–69; Irish Day, 68; McKinley cottage at, 62, 237n49. *See also* Touhey, Patrick J.; World's Fair (St. Louis, 1904)
Irish Women's Co-operative League of America, 130
ITA. *See* Irish Tourist Association
ITB. *See* Irish Tourist Board
"It Takes the Irish to Beat the Dutch" (Madden and Morse), 65, 238n55

Jameson, John J. (whiskey), 146–48, 152, 198
Jaunting car(t). *See* Ireland, tourism; Irish, as code
Johnson, Albert, 99–102, 248n74
Johnson, Hiram, 110
Johnson Brothers, 200
Jolly, Ellen Ryan, 61–62

Kalem (film company), 195, 201, 213
"Kathleen Mavourneen" (song, Crouch), 8
Kathleen Mavourneen: film (Brenon), 174; film (Porter), 174; play (Travers), 266n90
Keating, Seán, 76–77, 83, 103–4; *Night's Candles Are Burnt Out*, 83; *Race of the Gael*, 104; *The Tipperary Hurler*, 76–77, 83
Kelly, Gertrude B., 74, 240n103
Kelly, John T., 68
Kennedy, Edward M., 113
Kennedy, John F., 12, 112–13, 119; U.S. immigration restriction and, 116; visit to Ireland (1963), 19
Kennedy, John J. ("Smiling Irishman"), 144
Kennedy, Robert, 120
Kerrymen's Association of New York, 26
Kiernan, Thomas J., 113

Killarney (Balfe), 192, 201
Killarney (town), Ireland, 17, 136; tourism and, 191–95, 197–201, 204, 213, 215
Killarney Town, Busch Gardens Williamsburg, 215
Kimball, Solon, 201–2, 208, 273n61; *The Irish Countryman*, 12, 203
Kinnicutt, Francis H., 106–7
"Kiss Me, I'm Irish," 3, *194*, 216
Knights of Columbus, 15, 45, 98–99, 167, 209, 247n69
Knights of St. Gregory, 57
Knocknagow (O'Donovan), 195
Ku Klux Klan, 107–8, 144

lace, Irish, 123, 124, 125–29, 137–39, 157; imitation, 137–39
Lange, Dorothea, 49
Lemass, Seán, 202
Lennon, Julia (singer), 84
Life (magazine), 34–35, 49, 108, *109*, 169, 183
Lily of Killarney, The (Benedict), 192
linen, Irish, 123–24, 128–29, 157, 198, 213, 255n44; imitations and, 35–36. *See also* Ireland, exports
Lloyd George, David, 25
Lodge, Henry Cabot, 97–98, 101–2, 247n64
Low, Seth, 58
Lunar New Year, 216

Macaulay, William (Bill), 81
mac Cumhaill, Fionn, 74, 84
MacEvoy, John, 190–91
MacEvoy's Hibernicon, 190–91
MacGonigal, Maurice, 83
Mackey, Clarence, 10
MacManus, Seumas, 44–47, 67, 232n113; *Ireland's Case*, 45; Redpath Chautauqua and, 45, 213; *The Story of the Irish Race*, 45–46
Macmillan & Company (publisher), 20, 44, 47
Maginniss, Thomas Hobbs, Jr., 98

Makem, Tommy, 86, 211
Man of Aran (Flaherty), 12, 201–2
Marshall Plan, 48, 204; partition of Ireland and, 39–40, 230n85. *See also* United States, European Recovery Program
Mathew, Kathleen, 195
Mayo Men's Patriotic and Benevolent Association (New York), 71
McCann, Colum, 232n109
McCarthy, Joseph, 116
McCauley, Leo, 84
McCormack, John, 17, 61, 64, 79–81, 192, 268n118
McCormick, Anne O'Hare, 39
McCourt, Frank, 232n109
McDonald, John J. ("Happy Irishman"), 143
McFadden's Row of Flats (play, Townsend), 67, 73
McGarrity, Joseph, 73, 226n17, 231n96
McGrath, Dan, 82–83
McGrath, Matthew, 75
McGraw, John, 10
McGuinness, Madge C. L., 74, 240n103
McGurrin, James, 99
McKenna, Siobhan, 209
McKinley, William, 62
McLoughlin, Rita (singer), 84, 218
McManus, George, 18
McNally, Joseph (Irish Festival Singers), 84
McNurney, Charles (Mack), 64
McSweeney, Edward F., 94–95, 98–99, 247n64
media, 18; books, 18, 20; CBS radio, 21–22, 28, 32–33; CBS television, 49–50, 209; greeting cards, 18; internet, 1; magazines, 18, 20, 31, 34–35, 46, 52; movies, 1, 17, *181*, 183–84; music, 79, *80*; NBC, 21, 28, 30, 227n41, 228n53; newspapers, 18, 21, 31, 226n26; newsreels, 18, 20–21, 34, 38–39, 41; novelties, 18; periodicals, 20, 41; postcards, 159–63, *161*, *194*, 213, 262n35; press associations, 24–25;

media (*continued*)
   radio, 17, 18, 20, 21, 31, 35, 42–43, 52, 79, 225n4; records, 18, 69, 79, 82, 85; sheet music, 18, *173*, 180; television, 1, 18, 85–86, 211, 212, 215. *See also specific titles*
melodramas, 51, 69, 156–57, 196; Boucicault and, 16–18, *161*, *173*, 191–92, 208, 212–13, 266n89
Metro-Goldwyn-Mayer, 178, 201
"Mexican Fiesta," 266n84
MGM. *See* Metro-Goldwyn-Mayer
Miller, Glen, 85
Miller, John, 150
Mission of Our Lady of the Rosary for the Protection of Irish Immigrant Girls, 111, 244n8
Moloney, Michael (Mick), 211–12, 218; Moloney Collection AIA, *37*, *161*, *173*, *194*
Montgomery, Richard, 7
monuments, 63; AOH and, 59–61; Barry and, 58–60, 62, 71, 78, 213, 235n20, 236n26; of Catholic nuns, 62; of Emmet, 60–62, 78, 236nn33–34; T. Moore and, 55, 58, *80*
Moore, Colleen, 179–80, *181*, 268n212
Moore, Emmet, 196
Moore, Thomas, 58, *80*, *161*, 190–91, 196, 209; "Believe Me If All Those Endearing Young Charms," 79; centennial of birth, 55; "Erin! The Tear and the Smile in Thine Eyes," 50, 209; "The Harp That Once through Tara's Halls," 17, 75, 79; *Irish Melodies*, 16–17, 156, 159–60; "The Last Rose of Summer," 79, 84; "Let Erin Remember the Days of Old," 57, 84; "The Meeting of the Waters," 191; "The Minstrel Boy," 17, 57, 79; *Moore's Melodies*, 54–55, 57, 79, 212; "Oh, Breathe Not His Name," 61; "Oh, the Shamrock," 156; "Rich and Rare Were the Gems She Wore," 78; "She Is Far from the Land," 61. *See also* monuments

Moseley, Edward A., 104
Mother Machree (Ford), 17, 174, 179
Mother Machree (novelty item), 164, 264n51
"Mother Machree" (song, Young, Olcott, Ball), 17, 69, 166, 172, 177, 179, 213, 268n118
movies, 174–86, 213; Irish promotions for, 176–84; Irish protests against, 176, 178, 267n114; Legion of Decency, 184–85; Production Code Administration, 184–85; Screen Publicists Guild, 183. *See also* ballyhoo; *and specific titles*
Muldoon, Michael, 64–65
Murphy, Alison Barstow, 200
Murphy, John ("Laughing Irishman"), 143
Murphy, John Cullen, 205
Murphy, John J., 74, 99
Murphy, John S., 95
Murphy, Joseph (Joe), 68
Murphy, Myles J., 65, 128, 262n35
Murray, Don, 51
Murray, Samuel, 59
Murray, Thomas M., 63
Museum of Irish Art (Irish Art Rooms, New York), 76

Narelle, Marie, 64, *66*
Nast, Thomas, 49
National Association for Irish Justice, 120
National Association for the Advancement of Colored People (NAACP), 120
National Commodore John Barry Statue Association, 59–60
National Council for the Traditional Arts (United States), 78
National Geographic (magazine), 41, 203, 275n89
national origins quotas, 91, 115. *See also* United States, immigration restriction
NBC radio, 21, 28, 30, 227n41, 228n53
newsreels, 18, 20–21, 33–34, 38–39, 41
"No Irish Need Apply," 3, 54

Norcross (greeting cards), 162, 187, *194*, 263n43
Northern Ireland, 33, 40, 42, 88, 95, 112, 121–22, 216, 255n44; Belfast, 14, 43, 64, 121, 135–36, 138, 216, 244n13; civil rights in, 120–21; Ireland Act (1921), 39–40; U.S. immigration quotas and, 91, 103, 105, 111; World War II and, 31, 33–34, *37*. See also Ireland, partition of
Northern Ireland Civil Rights Association, 120
Notre Dame, University of, 144, 150, 152; "Fighting Irish," 142, 144–45
Nugent, Frank, 208
Nylander, Towne, 198

O'Brien, John P. (ITA executive), 200–201
O'Brien, John P. (New York City mayor), 200–201
O'Brien, Michael J., 81, 102, 118–19, 247n66; *A Hidden Phase of American History*, 96–97, 99, 102–3, 107, 247n69
O'Brien, Morgan J., 59, 127, 235n23
O'Brien, Pat, 180
O'Brien, Quin, 83
O'Brien, Sylvia (Irish Festival Singers), 84–85
Ó Cadhain, Martin, 9
O'Callaghan, Donald, 116–17
O'Casey, Seán, 19
O'Connell, William, 62
O'Connor, Andrew, Jr., 59–60, 62
O'Connor, Fergus, *194*
O'Connor, Frank, 202–4, 207, 209
O'Connor, John (*Irish Advocate*), 13
O'Connor, Terry (Irish Festival Singers), 84–85
O'Donovan-Rossa, Margaret, 193
O'Driscoll, T. J., 209
O'Dwyer, Paul, 32, 40–41, 77, 89, 120, 218, 228n55, 230n89, 230n93
O'Dwyer, William (Bill), 10; Basil Brooke and, 40

Ó Faoláin, Seán, 11, 44, 47–49, 205, 209; *The Irish: A Character Study*, 48; "Love among the Irish," 49; *The Promise of Barty O'Brien*, 48–49
O'Hara, Maureen, 31
O'Higgins, Kevin, 25
Olcott, Chauncey, 68, 177, 183, 185; *Barry of Ballymore*, 69; "Mother Machree," 213, 264n51
O'Leary, Jeremiah, 100
O'Regan, Brendan, 148
O'Reilly, Emmet, 164
O'Reilly, Leonora, 130
O'Riordan, Conal, "The Piper," 30
Orr, John Herbert, *140*

Pageant of the Celt, The, 83
Pan American World Airways, 206
Phelan, James D., 61
Picturesque Ireland (Savage), 189–90
"Piper, The" (O'Riordan), 30
Playboy of the Western World, The (Synge), 69–74, 208, 213, 239nn86–87, 239n92, 240n95
Plunkett, Horace, 124
Pokorny, Julius, 105, 249n96
Price, Norman, *37*
Promise of Barty O'Brien, The (Ó Faoláin), 48–49

Quiet Man, The (Ford), 189, 205–9, 210, 213, 275n87
Quigley, Martin J., 185
Quill, Michael J. (Mike), 10
Quinn, John, 63, 65, 127, 129, 241n109
Quinn, Mary T., 65–67

race, European hierarchy of, 91–92, 94–95, 104–5, 112, 118; contributions to U.S. and, 98–100, 247n69; Harvard Irish Study and, 224n38, 273n61; Irish as inferior, 95, 103, 105–6; Irish as superior, 112, 114, 116, 118, 161; Irish lampooned as, 108, *109*;

race (*continued*)
  model minority and, 118; politics and, 122; propaganda and, 110; pseudo-science and, 104–6; Scotch Irish as, 102; surnames and, 92, 97, 103, 111, 250n126; white (Caucasian), 115, 119, 122. *See also* Anglo-Saxon; Celt(ic)
radio, 17, 18, 20, 21, 31, 35, 42–43, 52, 79, 225n4; CBS, 21–22, 28, 32–33; film and, 183, 269n135; Irish music and, 79, *80*; NBC, 21, 28, 30, 227n41, 228n53; nostalgia and, 17
Rambles in Erin (radio show), 80
Redmond, John, 22, 239n92
Redpath Chautauqua, 45–46, *214*, 232n116
Reed, David, 92
Republic of Ireland, 6, 12, 40, 115, 145, 150, 189. *See also* Ireland, specific topics
Rice, Noel, 211–12
Ridder, Herman, 57–58
Riverdance, 213
Roarty, Michael, 4
Robyn, Alfred, 75
Roche, James Jeffrey, 98
Roche, Pat, 82
Rodino, Peter, 117, 118
Rolleston, Thomas William (T. W.), 65, 128, 239n69
Rooney, Pat, 86
Roosevelt, Franklin Delano, 31, 38
Roosevelt, Theodore, 57
Rose, Edward E., 166–67, 264n62
Rusk, Dean, 115
Russell, George (Æ), 239n87; *Deirdre*, 65, 69
Russell Brothers (John and James), 69
Rustcraft (greeting cards), 162, 187

Sabath, Adolph, 99, 101
Sayers, Peig, 203
Scanlon, William J. (W. J.), 68
Schlei, Nobert, 115
Scotch (whiskey), 147–48, 152
Scotch Irish (Ulster Scots), 5, 8, 95; as a race, 102–4, 248n84
Scotch-Irish Society of America, 102
Scott, Michael, 83
Shake Hands with the Devil (Anderson), 50–51
Shamrock. *See* Irish, as code; St. Patrick's Day
Shamrock Handicap, The (Ford), 174–75
Shamus O'Brien (Boggs), 174, 266n89
Shand, A. T., 146
Shannon (Ireland, airport), 83, 148, 150, 188, 204, 210, 216
Shannon (Ireland, river), 81, 195, 199; Ardnacrusha, 197
Sheahan, Dennis B. (D. B.), 55, *80*
Sheehan, Winfield, 178–79, 185, 268n116, 269n145
Sheldon, James H., 114
Sheridan, Martin, 10, 71–72, 223n24
Simons, Evelyn (Marie Irish), 168, 170–71, 264n64
Sinn Féin, 22, 28
Smiddy, Timothy, 110, 250n122
Smiling Irish Eyes (Seiter), 179–80, *181*, 268n124
Smith, Alfred E., 158
Smith, Josephine Patricia, *80*; *Rambles in Erin*, 80
Sperry, Muriel, 20, 36
Stage Irish(man), 4, 67–68, 72, 78. *See also* Irish, as code
Steele, John, 25
Story of the Irish Nation, The (Hackett), 23
St. Patrick, 155, 157, 165–66
St. Patrick's Day, 36, 215; as American holiday, 5, 167, 212; Catholic Dramatic Guild and, 172; costumes, *3*, 153, 157, 169, 222n11, 265n71; de Valera broadcast for (1943), 35; *The Ed Sullivan Show* special for (1959), 85–86; food, 171, 212, 265n82; games, 170–72; greeting cards, 162, 187, 263n43; as holiday

in Ireland, 154, 187–88, 261n3; holiday paraphernalia, 157–58, 163–65, 263n48; novelties, 161–64, 169, 174, 213, 263n48, 264n52; parties, 168–72; plays, 164–68, 195, 264n62; postcards, 72, 159–62, *161*, 191, 192, *194*, 213, 262n35; recipes, 171; shamrocks, 158–59, 163, 165, 188; "wearing of the green," 157, 166, 169
St. Patrick's Day (Dublin): festival, 6; parade, *3*
St. Patrick's Day (New York City): dress code for, 72; parade, 3, 153–54, 163, 202
St. Patrick's Society of the City of Brooklyn, 55
Student's History of Ireland, The (Gwynn), 44
Sullivan, Ed, 85–86
Sweeney, Patrick M., 138
Synge, John Millington, 201, 264n62; *The Playboy of the Western World*, 69–74, 213, 239nn86–87, 239n92, 240n95

television, 212, 215; CBS, 49–50, 209; *The Ed Sullivan Show*, 85–86, 211
Temple, Patrick J., 111
Tin Pan Alley, 17, 65, 82, 88, 159–60, 162, 192–93. *See also specific titles*
Tipperary Hurler, The (Keating), 76–77
Touhey, Patrick J. (Patsy), 64–65, 67–69, 190; "Shaskeen Reel," 69
trademarks, 139, *141–42*, 144, 256n56; on Belleek, 132–35, 255n54; for Guinness, 146; Irish Trade Mark, 132, 134–37, 257n71; for Jameson, 147; for Notre Dame, 144–45; for used cars, 139–44. *See also* Ireland, exports
Trevor, John B., 92, 99–100, 103, 106, 110–11, 249n102
Troy, Dermot (Irish Festival Singers), 84–85
Truman, Harry S., 112, 153–54, 158, 185, 202
Tumulty, Joseph P., 60
Tynan, Brandon, 61, 69, 266n89. *See also* Emmet, Robert

UICA. *See* United Irish Counties Association
Ulster, 34, 102, 195; stereotypes and, 42, 104; U.S. soldiers in, *37*. *See also* Giant's Causeway; Great Britain; Scotch Irish
Ulster Unionist Party, 40
United Artists, 50–51
United Distillers of Ireland, 150–52
United Irish Counties Association (UICA), *14*, 116; Anti-Partition Committee of, 39; Feis, 77–79, *80*, 85, 213
United Irish League of America, 30
United Irishmen, 54, 56, 235n14
United Kingdom, 20, 90, 110, 132, 146, 155; dominions of, 40, 110. *See also* England; Great Britain
United States (U.S.), 9, 224n32; acculturation, 6, 16; census, 90–92, 96–97, 111, 246n54, 247n64, 247n66; civil rights and, 113, 122; Civil War battlefield flags, 19, 63; colonial history, 87, *93*, 96–99, 102–3; economy of, 56; ethnic origins and history wars, 88, *93*, 96, 104–5, 114, 117; opportunity and, 10–11, 117, 186; Production Code Administration, 184–85; Prohibition, 147–48, 163–64, 213; Protestants, 57, 71, 87, 116, 118, 156, 174; soldiers in Northern Ireland, *37*; Tariff Acts, 159
United States, Espionage and Sedition Acts (1917–18), 100
United States, European Recovery Program, 48. *See also* Marshall Plan
United States, Federal Trade Commission, 137–38
United States, immigration, American Consular Service, 89, 111; Ellis Island, 88, 90, 244n8, 245n26; Immigration Act of 1907, 89; Passport Act of 1918, 89
United States, immigration restriction, 5, 11, 87–90, 92–93, *93*; Emergency Quota Act (1921), 87, 90–91, 245n24; Immigration and Nationality Act (1965),

United States, immigration restriction (*cont.*) 115–18; Irish American opposition, *93*, 94–96, 115–18; Irish quota, 90–92, 111, 113, 115–18; Johnson-Reed Immigration Act (1924, national origins), 90–91, 94, 96, 106, 110, 111, 113, 119, 245n26; McCarran-Walter Act, 112–14. See also *Century of Population Growth, A*

United States, State Department, 33, 36, 38–39, 110, 113, 115, 198

United States, Treaty of Friendship, Commerce, and Navigation with Ireland, 50

Wagner, Robert, *205*
Walker, Harrison Howell, 203
Walsh, Maurice, 144
Walshe, Joseph Patrick (J. P.), 30
Warner Brothers, 175–76, 179–80, 183
Washington, George, 83–84, 107
Waterford Glass (crystal), 150, 188, 260n134
"Wearing of the Green" (Boucicault), 17–18, 65, *109*, 156–57, 160, 168, *173*, 250n116, 261n16
Weaver, John, 59
Wellman, Walter R. ("Smiling Irishman"), 143
whiskey, Irish, 145–46, 150, 163–64, 187, 216; advertising and, 147–48, 152; competition with Scotch, 147–48, 152; imitations of, 147–48; Irish coffee and, 148–49, *149*; perceptions about, 150–51; United Distillers, 150. *See also* Bushmills; Jameson, John J.

Why Did They Sell Killarney? (Dillon), 192
Wilson, Woodrow, 22, 60–61, 247n69
Wingate, James, 176
World's Fair (Chicago, 1893), 123, 124–26, 131, 262n24; Lady Aberdeen's Irish Village, 125–26; Mrs. Hart's Irish Village, 124–25
World's Fair (Chicago, 1933–34), 81
World's Fair (St. Louis, 1904), 62–63, 74, 123, 127–29, 190, 192, 254n23; Belleek in, 131–32; drama at, 64–67; McKinley cottage at, 62; music and, 64–65, 237nn48–49. *See also* Irish Village (St. Louis, 1904)
World's Fair (New York, 1939–40), 18, 83–84, 202, 213; Blarney Stone, 84; Giant's Causeway, 84; Ireland Day, 84; Irish Day, 84; Irish Village, 84; *Race of the Gael*, 104; Shamrock Building, 83, 243n145
World's Fair (New York, 1964–65), 145; Pavilion of Ireland, 149–50

Yeats, William Butler, 67, 71–72, 206; American tours, 46
Young, Victor (Vic), 208

ABOUT THE AUTHOR

Marion R. Casey is a clinical professor of Irish Studies and affiliated faculty in the Department of History at New York University. She founded the Archives of Irish America in NYU's Bobst Library Special Collections, co-founded the initiative that became the Ireland House Oral History Collection, has contributed to many public history projects including exhibits and documentary films, and has published essays on a wide range of subjects. With J. J. Lee, she co-edited *Making the Irish American: History and Heritage of the Irish in the United States* (2016).

www.ingramcontent.com/pod-product-compliance
Lightning Source LLC
Chambersburg PA
CBHW030636150426
42811CB00077B/2165/J